An Introduction to the Nonprofit Sector

A Practical Approach for the 21st Century

4th Edition

Gary M. Grobman

Harrisburg, Pennsylvania

An Introduction to the Nonprofit Sector
A Practical Approach for the 21st Century
4th Edition

Copyright © 2015 by Gary M. Grobman
Published by White Hat Communications.
Copies may be ordered from:

White Hat Communications
PO Box 5390
Harrisburg, PA 17110-0390
(717) 238-3787
(717) 238-2090 (fax)
Web Site: http://www.whitehatcommunications.com

All rights reserved. No portion of this book may be reproduced in any form, or by any means, mechanical or electronic, or by any information storage and retrieval system or other method, for any use, without the written permission of Gary M. Grobman.

Some of the material in Chapter 5 on boards and Chapter 10 of this publication are written by Michael Sand, and is reprinted with permission. The vision statement of the Young Adult Library Services Association, a division of the American Library Association, which appears in Chapter 6 is reproduced with permission. The author gratefully acknowledges the contributions Mr. Sand made to the material that comprises Chapter 8. The material in Chapter 7 is based on *Ethics in Nonprofit Organizations: Theory and Practice* by Gary M. Grobman. Some of the material in Chapter 16 is co-written by Gary Grobman, Gerald Gorelick, and Frederick Richmond, and is used with permission of the authors. Some of the material in Chapter 15 is based on the book *Fundraising Online: Using the Internet to Raise Serious Money for Your Nonprofit Organization*, written by Gary Grobman and Gary Grant, and is reprinted with permission. Some of the material in this chapter is based on the book *The Nonprofit Organization's Guide to E-Commerce* by Gary Grobman (White Hat Communications, 2001). The ARNOVA financial statements that appear in Appendix 9 are reprinted with permission.

DISCLAIMER: This publication is intended to provide general information and should not be construed as legal advice or legal opinions concerning any specific facts or circumstances. Consult an experienced attorney if advice is required concerning any specific situation or legal matter. Neither the author nor the publisher make any warranties, expressed or implied, with respect to the information in this publication. The author and publisher shall not be liable for any incidental or consequential damages in connection with, or arising out of, the use of this book.

Contact the author in care of White Hat Communications, or by e-mail at:
gary.grobman@paonline.com

Front cover photos ©1999 PhotoDisc, Inc. with the exception of the photograph of the Greater Harrisburg Concert Band. Greater Harrisburg Concert Band photograph is © 2003 Dave Getz, and is printed with the permission of the Greater Harrisburg Concert Band and Mr. Getz.

Printed in the United States of America.

ISBN: 978-1-929109-44-9

Library of Congress Cataloging-in-Publication Data

Grobman, Gary M.
  An introduction to the nonprofit sector : a practical approach for the 21st century / by Gary M. Grobman. -- 4th Edition.
      pages cm
  Includes bibliographical references and index.
  ISBN 978-1-929109-44-9
  1. Nonprofit organizations--Management. 2. Nonprofit organizations. I. Title.
  HD62.6.G7616 2015
  658'.048--dc23
                              2014032702

Table of Contents

Introduction 5

Chapter 1. Defining and Describing the Nonprofit Sector 13

Chapter 2. History of the Nonprofit Sector 35

Chapter 3. Theory of the Nonprofit Sector 55

Chapter 4. Legal and Regulatory Issues 67

Chapter 5. Bylaws and Governance 95

Chapter 6. Mission and Vision Statements 117

Chapter 7. Ethics 125

Chapter 8. Fundraising 151

Chapter 9. Marketing 163

Chapter 10. Grant Management 179

Chapter 11. Financial Management 191

Chapter 12. Personnel 215

Chapter 13. Communications and Public Relations 247

Chapter 14. Lobbying 259

Chapter 15. The Internet for Nonprofits 271

Chapter 16. Strategic Planning and Change Management 293

Chapter 17. Quality Issues 321

Chapter 18. Liability, Risk Management, and Insurance 327

Chapter 19. Forming and Running a Coalition 337

Chapter 20. The Future of the Nonprofit Sector 345

Chapter 21. The Spirit of the Nonprofit Sector 379

Appendix 1. Case 1: Jane's Dilemma—Hiring the
   Development Director 389

Appendix 2. Case 2: I Choose to Live Foundation—
   One Man's Vision to Form a New Charity 395

Appendix 3. Case 3: Museum and Historical Association
   State Budget Cuts 401

Appendix 4. Case 4: The One Wo(Man) Band Running
   the Kenmore Midget Baseball League 409

Appendix 5. Case 5: Cutting the Budget of the
   Harristown Family Service 417

Appendix 6. Case 6: Public Relations Dilemma at
   the Harristown Hospital and Health System 425

Appendix 7. Case 7: Reporting Financial
   Misconduct at Uncommon Agenda 433

Appendix 8. Case 8: The Disruptive Board Member
   of the Harristown Vet Center 441

Appendix 9. ARNOVA Financial Statements 448

Appendix 10. Nonprofit Ethics Scenarios 452

Index 463

About the Author 469

Introduction

Americans of all ages, all stations in life, and all types of disposition are forever forming associations. There are not only commercial and industrial associations in which all take part, but others of a thousand different types—religious, moral, serious, futile, very general and very limited, immensely large and very minute. Americans combine to give fetes, found seminaries, build churches, distribute books, and send missionaries to the antipodes. Hospitals, prisons and schools take shape in that way. Finally, if they want to proclaim a truth or propagate some feeling by the encouragement of a great example, they form an association. In every case, at the head of any new undertaking, where in France you would find the government or in England some territorial magnate, in the United States you are sure to find an association.

—Alexis de Tocqueville
Democracy In America
1835

Little has changed about the American propensity to form benevolent associations in the 180 years since de Tocqueville wrote the above words.

In our highly competitive, individualistic society, the nonprofit sector provides a way to express our humanitarian values, to preserve our cultural heritage, to promote various causes, to educate, and to enlighten. It is often through coming together in nonprofit organizations that our citizens exercise their constitutional rights to petition their government, free speech, assembly, and freedom of religion.

Nonprofits play a unique role as an intermediary between the citizens and their government. They maintain and transmit values to a degree that government has been unable to do.

Maybe most important of all, nonprofits formulate much of the moral agenda for society. One only has to think of the response to the September 11, 2001 terrorist attacks, the 2005 Katrina and Rita natural disasters, the 2010 BP oil spill in the Gulf of Mexico, the environmental movement, rape crisis and domestic violence centers, public subsidies of arts and humanities, public awareness of AIDS and support of AIDS programs, and countless other issues that people coming together in voluntary organizations were able to put on the nation's agenda.

Historically, the primary distinguishing characteristic of the nonprofit sector is that it is mission- and value-driven. Nonprofit organizations exist to accomplish some social good, however that may be defined. A set of values and assumptions underlies this view of the voluntary sector, including altruism, benevolence, cooperation, community, and diversity. The privileges granted to the sector and public expectations are grounded in this belief.

Nonprofits in the United States sometimes take the form of soup kitchens such as Our Daily Bread in Harrisburg, Pennsylvania, which operate on a shoestring budget and charge their clients virtually nothing for their services. They also take the form of enterprises such as hospitals, with budgets in the hundreds of millions of dollars, which often act in ways very much like their for-profit counterparts, seeking to maximize revenue and capture market share.

In January 2000, a Dauphin County (PA) Common Pleas Court judge ruled against the tax exemption eligibility for Hershey Medical Center (HMC), affiliated with Penn State University. One of his objections was that the facility paid salaries to some individuals on staff in excess of a half-million dollars annually. Like almost all hospitals, HMC enters into sophisticated business arrangements. In 1997, the hospital merged with Geisinger, a for-profit health system. The merger collapsed after two years, chiefly as a result of conflicting organizational missions and cultures between the two parent organizations, compounded by financial and operational difficulties. In June 2014, HMC announced a planned merger with a nonprofit hospital system, PinnacleHealth, governed by a new board with equal representation from the two organizations, with the expectation that its new partner will be a much better fit.

In contrast to the soup kitchen, the financial aspects of decision-making are of paramount importance to HMC's decision-making strategy. Yet, as one wag pointed out on the tangible benefits of a nonprofit being selected as a "Point of Light" by the White House, even a "point of light" has to pay the electric bill.

Neither Hershey Medical Center nor Our Daily Bread, about ten miles away from each other, is atypical of the nonprofit sector. Although they may appear to be as different as night and day, they also share many things in common. Both depend on government grants, donations from foundations, businesses, and individuals to keep them operating in the black and to supplement fees for service. Both provide free services to those who are unable to pay for them. Both depend on volunteers. Both are governed by a board of directors whose members do not share in any surplus revenues that may be generated, and that consists of unpaid volunteers from the community.

These are some of the aspects that differentiate nonprofit organizations from their government and private sector counterparts that also provide inpatient health care and food services. Nonprofit organizations, especially those qualified under section 501(c)(3) of the Internal Revenue Code, occupy a special and unique place in American society. Their uniqueness has many attributes.

Introduction

All such organizations are supported by the nation's taxpayers. They are exempt from federal and state income taxes. Contributors, for the most part, can deduct their contributions from their federal income tax (and from their state income tax in most states). They are eligible to have their postage subsidized by the federal government. Many are exempt from state and local sales and property taxes.

Some people, including those who formulate tax and regulatory policies that apply to charities, have a vision of charitable organizations that resembles those of the 19th century. In that vision, the workers are all volunteers. Recipients of services are too poor to provide for themselves. Funding comes from wherever it can be found. An example of what this looked like is described on the Web site of Yale University's School of Medicine:

> *A 19th century hospital was predominantly a charity institution, although from the beginning, some patients paid for their stay. It was intended for the worthy poor, for sailors, and for other strangers in town. People of means, such as the donors who were members of the General Hospital Society of Connecticut, would receive medical care in their homes, and not in a hospital. The hospital as yet offered no advantages over home care. Physicians served in the hospital without salary on a rotating basis as attending physicians. They did so as a form of charity and civic duty, but hospital service also provided valuable experience, professional recognition, and the possibility of training students in the wards.*
>
> from *Connecticut and New Haven's First General Hospital: Hospitals in the Nineteenth-Century;* Harvey Cushing/John May Whitney Medical Library; Yale University School of Medicine; *http://doc.med.yale.edu/library/news/exhibits/hospitals/*

Benjamin Franklin convinced the Pennsylvania Legislature to participate in chartering the nation's first hospital, Pennsylvania Hospital. He received a commitment to match 2,000 pounds donated by private individuals with a like amount appropriated by the state government. Founded in 1751, the institution was created "to care for the sick poor of the Province and for the reception and care of lunaticks" (see: *In the Beginning: The Story of the Creation of the Nation's First Hospital; http://www.uphs.upenn.edu/paharc/features/creation.html*; University of Pennsylvania Health System).

The modern charitable institution, however, may bear little resemblance to the typical charity of the 19th century. Burgeoning demands for services, increased government regulation, keen competition for funds, the advance of technology, demographic changes, and the public's changing perception of our institutions have all worked to increase the complexity of decision-making to those in leadership positions with nonprofit organizations. Pennsylvania Hospital, started with perhaps a handful of employees, has evolved into the University of Pennsylvania Health System, with a 2010 workforce of 17,900, making it one of the largest private employers in the entire state *(http://www.linkedin.com/companies/university-of-pennsylvania-health-system)*. Other nonprofits, such as educational institutions and other integrated health care systems, are on the roster of the state's largest employers. In fact, one such institution, The University of Pennsylvania, is the largest nongovernmental employer in Pennsylvania other than Wal-Mart (source: *http://www.portal.state.pa.us/portal/server.pt?open=514&objID=1222062&mode=2)*.

Virtually every American is touched in some way by the services of this country's nonprofit organizations. Organizations such as institutions of religious worship, civic groups, hospitals, day care centers, libraries, colleges, symphonies, art museums, the Red Cross, Salvation Army, and the American Cancer Society work in partnership with government and the public to improve our lives and those of our neighbors.

The nonprofit sector's participation in the American economy is impressive. According to Independent Sector, the voluntary sector contributed 5.6% of our national economy ($836.9 billion in output) and employed 13.7 million workers in 2010. Employees of nonprofit organizations account for 9.2% of wages paid in the U.S. in 2010, and the nonprofit sector paid $587 billion in wages and benefits to its employees. (source: *http://independentsector.org/economic_role*). In 2011, 589,505 nonprofit organizations reported to the IRS that they collectively controlled property, cash, and investments with a value of about $4.63 trillion (source: *http://www.urban.org/publications/412923.html)*. This figure does not including wealth controlled by churches or small nonprofits that are not required to file Form 990 annual tax returns.

Most Americans recognize the value of nonprofit organizations in society. Of 142.35 million individual tax returns filed nationally for tax year 2011 by individuals and couples, almost 37.8 million claimed a tax deduction for charitable giving, totaling $174.5 billion in deductions, according to the IRS (source: *http://www.irs.gov/uac/SOI-Tax-Stats---Individual-Statistical-Tables-by-Filing-Status#_grp2;* --see Table 2.2). Many more billions of dollars were donated by persons who do not itemize, or who do not bother to declare the value of their charity on their tax returns. The business community also donates billions of dollars each year to charitable institutions. More than half of individual taxpayers who take a deduction also make non-cash contributions, valued at $58.7 billion for tax year 2007 (source: *http://www.irs.gov/pub/irs-soi/10sprbulindcont07.pdf)*.

According to the June 2014 annual report of *Giving USA*, published by the American Association of Fund-Raising Counsel Trust for Philanthropy, total charitable giving by individuals, corporations, and foundations in 2013 increased over the previous year to an estimated $335.17 billion, $240.60 billion of this from private citizens, 83% of whom itemized these gifts on their income tax returns (source: *http://www.forbes.com/sites/tomwatson/2014/06/17/annual-philanthropy-numbers-on-the-rise-u-s-giving-nears-pre-recession-levels/*). This represented a 2.7% increase in giving over the previous year in current dollars, a reflection of an improving economy. Additionally, billions of hours annually are volunteered to nonprofits. The Urban Institute estimates that about 64.5 million Americans, or 26.5 percent of the adult population, averaged 193 hours of volunteer service during 2012 worth an estimated $259.6 billion, based on an estimate that each hour is worth $22.55 for 2013 (Source: *http://independentsector.org/volunteer_time*). As those who volunteer can attest, the value to society, such as the relief of human suffering, far exceeds the dollar value.

Purpose of this Textbook

The purpose of this textbook is to provide students with a sense of what the nonprofit sector is all about—why it developed, how it developed, and what role it plays in society. I anticipate that many users of this textbook will go on to careers in the nonprofit sector. Thus, this textbook also provides practical advice on running a modern nonprofit organization and guidance to practitioners.

This text cannot purport to answer every conceivable question, but it does attempt to provide sources for answers to many of the questions posed by students, as well as nonprofit board members and staff. It also provides references to primary source material, much of it available on the Internet, on important state and federal laws and regulations, where to find some of the most useful government forms, and sound advice about many nonprofit management issues.

Who Can Use This Book

This textbook will be useful for—

- Undergraduate and graduate students in introductory courses on nonprofit management

- Graduate students in more advanced courses such as strategic planning, institutional leadership, ethics, fundraising, and theory of the nonprofit sector

- Practitioners participating in continuing education to improve their management skills.

Every effort has been made to make this textbook as useful and free from errors as possible. It is the intent of the author to seek corrections as well as suggestions for improving this publication, and to incorporate these contributions in future editions.

What's New in the Fourth Edition

There is one completely new chapter—*Marketing* (Chapter 9). The marketing chapter expands upon the information about e-commerce that appeared in previous editions of this book with a discussion of many offline aspects of nonprofit marketing. The ethics chapter (Chapter 8) has been expanded substantially. There is additional material in Chapter 5 relating to the structure and duties of boards. There is a new section in Chapter 11 on investment policy. There is a new appendix with fictional ethics scenarios of some typical, and some not so typical, situations involving ethical decision-making. And new to the 4th edition are four cases, illustrating government relations, budgeting, board management, and whistleblowing.

Acknowledgments

This textbook is based on the 6th edition of *The Nonprofit Handbook: Everything You Need to Know to Start and Run Your Nonprofit Organization,* published in 2011, which itself was based on *The Pennsylvania Nonprofit Handbook,* first published in 1992. The author gratefully acknowledges the contributions of scores of individuals and organizations to the first edition of *The Pennsylvania Nonprofit Handbook*. Among them are Michael A. Sand, Kathleen Steigler, and Linda Grobman, all of whom edited various editions of the *Handbook;* Mr. Sand, who wrote much of the chapter on governance as well as the chapter on grant management, which appeared for the first time in the fourth edition; Bob Mills, Esq., who completely rewrote and expanded the sections on volunteer and staff liability that appeared in the first edition; the Nonprofit Advocacy Network, which published and distributed the first and second editions; and the Hospital and Health System Association of Pennsylvania, which subsidized the printing of the first edition.

Thanks are also due to those who reviewed and edited specific chapters of the current and previous editions of the *Pennsylvania Nonprofit Handbook,* including Patricia Mogan, Standards for Excellence Officer for the Pennsylvania Association of Nonprofit Organizations; Richard Utley, past Director of the Pennsylvania Department of State's Bureau of Charitable Organizations; Karl Emerson, another former director of the Bureau; Terry Roth, Esq.; W. Barney Carter; George Bell, Esq.; Bill Knoll, Classification Reform Instructor for the U.S. Postal Service; Otto Hofmann, Esq.; Phil McKain; Jim Fritz, Esq.; Bob Mills, Esq.; Frederick Richmond; Steve Zneimer; Jim Redmond; Elizabeth Hrenda-Roberts; Ron Lench; Christine Finnegan; Joan Benso; Dick Shelly; John Briscoe; and Ken Wickham. The Pennsylvania Department of State; the Pennsylvania Department of Revenue; Independent Sector; the Internal Revenue Service's Statistics of Income office in Washington, DC; and

Introduction

the Internal Revenue Service Public Affairs Office in Philadelphia cooperated in researching previous editions of those publications.

I am also appreciative of the contributions to this publication made by Gerald Kaufman, a nonprofit consultant from Philadelphia, who wrote much of the ethics chapter of *The Nonprofit Handbook* (Sixth Edition), which served as the template for the expanded chapter in this textbook. Some of the material in the chapter on change management was adapted from material on outcome-based management that I wrote with Frederick Richmond, and from material on large group intervention that I wrote with Gerald Gorelick. Melanie Herman of the Nonprofit Management Risk Center revised much of the material in Chapter 18 that relates to organization liability.

Thanks to my wife, Linda Grobman, who proofread and edited this textbook and the book upon which this textbook is based, *The Nonprofit Handbook*. Barbara Trainin Blank was the principal editor of the first edition of this textbook, and I am grateful for her work, as well as that of my sister, Judith Grobman, who proofread the second edition, and John Hope, who contributed to the proofreading of the 3rd edition. Among those who proofed all or parts of the 4th edition were Ivy Schneider, Barbara Trainin Blank, and Linda Grobman.

I am also grateful for the many suggestions and contributions made to this textbook by my colleagues who are members of the teaching section of the Association for Research on Nonprofit Organizations and Voluntary Action (ARNOVA). Among those making contributions to the first edition of this textbook were Norman Dolch of Louisiana State University–Shreveport (now at the University of North Texas); Martha Dede of California State University–Long Beach; Janet Greenlee of the University of Dayton, Elizabethann O'Sullivan of North Carolina State University; C. Bayne of Concordia University (Montreal, Quebec); Paul Govekar of P&M Associates; Marios Katsioloudes of St. Joseph's University (Philadelphia); Judith Miller of Ohio University; John McNutt of the University of South Carolina (now at the University of Delaware); Michael Biseli, Director of the Center for Nonprofit and Social Enterprise Management at Seattle University; Patricia Hardy, President of The Tunnelwood Group; and Steven W. Ross. Dr. Ross's practical and theoretical knowledge of the nonprofit sector and his meticulous editing skills were an important resource in making the first edition the best it could be. He deserves a special tip of the hat from me for his efforts.

Contributors of comments and suggestions for the second edition of this textbook included Wes Lindahl of Northpark University, Putnam Barber of Seattle University, Antonin Wagner of the New School, Theresa Ricke-Kiely of the University of South Carolina—Upstate (now at the University of Notre Dame), and Diane Vinokur-Kaplan of the University of Michigan. Dr. Vinokur-Kaplan's suggestions and corrections to the financial management chapter were particularly extensive and valuable.

The fourth edition benefited from comments provided by Annette V Godissart; John McNutt; Martin Berg; Barbara Metelsky; Alonzo Villarrell, Jr.; William Suhs Cleveland; Eric Korn; Stan Sheppard; Maghann Rother, and Ivy Schneider.

And finally, I express my gratitude to my students at Bay Path College, Marylhurst University, Indiana University of Pennsylvania, and Gratz College who provided valuable feedback about the first three editions, and permitted me a greater understanding of what concepts needed to be clarified or fine-tuned.

G.M.G.
September 2014

Chapter 1
Defining and Describing the Nonprofit Sector

> **Synopsis:** The nonprofit sector is a significant part of our national economy and social fabric. There are significant differences between nonprofit and for-profit organizations, although both are forms of businesses. Nonprofits are mission-driven rather than profit- or power-driven, despite the fact that revenues come more from fees and dues than from contributions from private sources. The assets of U.S. nonprofit organizations exceed $4 trillion.

Nonprofit organizations take many forms and have been collectively referred to in many ways, including "nonprofits," "not-for-profits" (Brinckerhoff, 1994), "non-governmental organizations," (Najam, 1999), voluntary sector (Smith, 1972, Van Til, 1988), the "Third Sector" (Gidron, Kramer, and Salamon, 1992), the "philanthropic sector" (Hansmann, 1989) the "voluntary agencies" (Kramer, 1987), the "independent sector" (Independent Sector, 2001), the "social sector" (Drucker Institute, 2007), and "the charitable sector" (Office of Foreign Assets and Control, 2010). To that list, economist Burton Weisbrod adds "collective" and "nonmarket" organizations (Weisbrod, 1975, in Rose-Ackerman, 1996).

Nonprofit organizations are included in the construct "mediating structures," defined as those institutions that stand between the individual and government, including families, neighborhoods, institutions of worship, and voluntary associations, and which are the value-generating and value-maintaining society structures (Berger and Neuhaus, 1977).

In recent years, the term "civil society" has been used to describe this broader, social infrastructure of organizations and associations, although there appears to be no clear agreement on what the term encompasses. The term "hollow state" (Milward, et al., 1993) has been applied to organizations that perform the duties of government through contracts, including the nonprofit sector.

From hospitals, day care centers, cemeteries, and museums to youth organizations, community centers, schools, and religious institutions, nonprofit organizations have a pervasive influence on everyday life.

Certainly, this influence is apparent in the United States. According to the IRS, there were 1.442 million organizations with 501(c) tax-exempt status in FY2013 (IRS, 2014). Just over 1,052 million of these held 501(c)(3) status.

Because of the sector's diversity, some writers suggest that there is reason to question whether nonprofits constitute a distinctive sector at all, although these writers acknowledge that this uncertainty is just as applicable to the business sector (Gidron, Kramer, and Salamon, 1992).

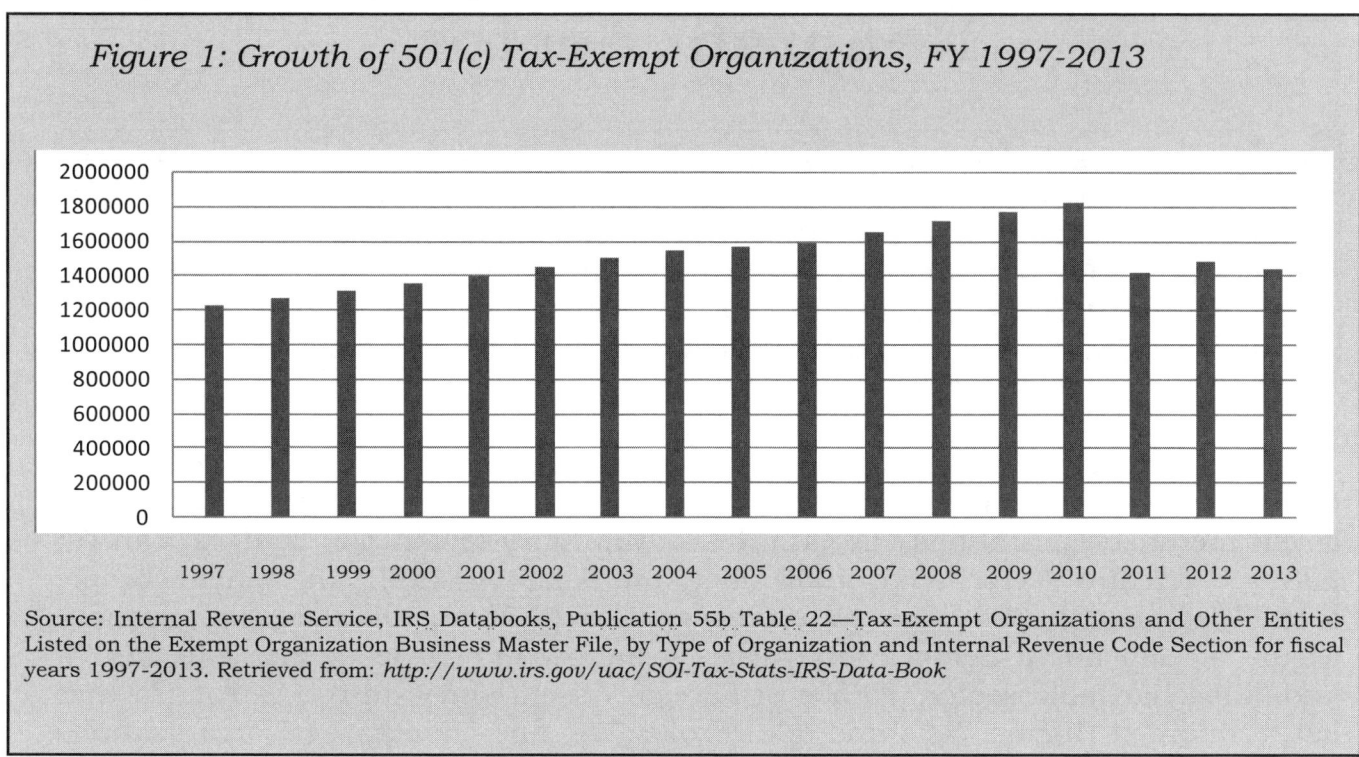

Figure 1: Growth of 501(c) Tax-Exempt Organizations, FY 1997-2013

Source: Internal Revenue Service, IRS Databooks, Publication 55b Table 22—Tax-Exempt Organizations and Other Entities Listed on the Exempt Organization Business Master File, by Type of Organization and Internal Revenue Code Section for fiscal years 1997-2013. Retrieved from: *http://www.irs.gov/uac/SOI-Tax-Stats-IRS-Data-Book*

Definition of Nonprofit Organizations

What distinguishes nonprofit organizations from their for-profit counterparts is that nonprofits have no outside equity interests. That is, they are not privately owned, but rather are controlled by a self-perpetuating board of directors with constraints on their activities, as provided in their articles of incorporation (or corporate charter document). Although the United States Congress has chartered more than 150 nonprofits under Title 36 (IRS, 2010), including the American Red Cross and the U.S. Olympic Committee, most are either incorporated or structured in other ways under state law (Hopkins, 1992).

Being a nonprofit does not preclude the organization from making a profit (often called "net revenue"), but these profits must be used to further the purpose of the organization rather than being distributed. It is this "private inurement doctrine" that is the essential difference between nonprofit organizations and their for-profit counterparts (Hopkins, 1992).

There are other distinctions between nonprofits and for-profits. Among them are the principal purpose (i.e., accomplishing a particular mission, compared with making money), governance structure (members of the community with diverse backgrounds compared to businesspersons), level of public accountability (substantial for nonprofits compared to minimal for for-profits), and destination of net revenue (required to further the purposes of a nonprofit organization rather than go into the pockets of the owners). Charities benefit from donations made to them by businesses and individuals who support their missions and purposes. The nonprofit sector also relies on the generous support of the tens of millions of American adults who volunteer on behalf of nonprofits.

An academic definition is provided by Salamon and Anheier (1996). According to this definition, nonprofit organizations have five things in common:

1. They are formally constituted.
2. They are organized separately from government.
3. They are non-profit-seeking.
4. They are self-governing.
5. They are voluntary to some significant degree.

In a subsequent book published in 1999, Salamon adds "of public benefit" to this list (Salamon, 2001, in Ott, 2001). Although this is certainly true of charities, many nonprofits are formed to serve the interests of a broad class of membership, and are "of mutual benefit" rather than being "of public benefit."

I offer the following four distinctions between nonprofits and for-profits:

1. They are privately governed, but the benefits of what the organization produces accrue no more to the organization's governors than to other members of society or the organization's beneficiaries.

2. The principal purpose of the organization is to promote a collective goal that is perceived to increase the benefit to the collective (defined as a constituency) much greater in number than the organization's board, such as a group with a common interest, a neighborhood, community, city, state, nation, or globe, rather than to generate profits.

3. The organization makes "business" decisions designed to increase the benefits to that constituency rather than to maximize profits, and it is not viewed as making a "bad" business decision if it implements a strategy that advances the interests of its constituency while resulting in

financial loss. As Ott (2001, p. 1) points out, "Revenues are resources, not the end purpose."

4. Because of these first three factors, people feel that their contributions to the organization, in time and money, will benefit that constituency rather than any private interest, and are thus willing to volunteer their time and donate their money to the organization.

Despite these differences, nonprofits have much in common with commercial businesses.

Tax-exempt nonprofit corporations can, and do, operate in all other particulars like any other sort of business. They have bank accounts; own productive assets of all kinds; receive income from sales and other forms of activity, including donations and grants if they are successful at finding that sort of support; make and hold passive investments; employ staff; enter into contracts of all sorts; etc. (McNamara, 2000).

Nonprofits and for-profits share many aspects in common. Both need capital to launch their operations; both need cash flow to pay their bills in a timely manner; and both need revenues to pay for staff, supplies, utilities, rent, equipment, printing, and other goods and services. Charities typically generate revenue beyond that which is donated by the public, the business community, or foundations. For example, they sell services. It is typical that 70% or more of the revenue from a charity that provides social services comes from user fees. Although many agencies charge on a sliding scale based on income, it is not unusual for them to charge a market rate to those who can afford to pay and use the surplus so generated to cross-subsidize those who cannot afford to pay the full costs of services.

Models of Nonprofit Organizations

There is no monolithic model of the direction a nonprofit organization's activities may take to alleviate a societal problem. Advocates for the nonprofit sector are fond of relating the following illustration:

A person taking a stroll along a riverbank sees children floating down the river, all of them in obvious distress: one strategy the person can use to alleviate this distress is to jump in and rescue them one at a time. Another strategy is to trace their path upstream and see what is causing the children to fall into the river and fix that. A third strategy is to leave the scene and mobilize others to help pull children out of the water. And a fourth strategy is to raise funds to support organizations that will perform one or all of these strategies.

Each strategy, translated to the establishment of an organization, has its place in nonprofit organization purposes and activities.

For example, during the spring and summer of 2001, the nation's attention focused on the case of a missing Washington intern, Chandra Levy. Government at all levels participated in the search for the missing woman. Voluntary sector organizations were created as a result of this case, including a foundation established by the parents of the missing woman. An organization using the first model described above might create a database of missing persons, and provide support and counseling to the families of victims. An organization using the second model might fund research to find out the core reasons that people become missing and what preventive steps might work to mitigate this. An organization using the third model might create an advocacy organization to increase public awareness about the degree to which finding missing persons is high or low on the law enforcement agenda, and increase the issue's visibility so as to encourage the devotion of more resources to finding missing children. An organization using the fourth model would provide grants to law enforcement agencies, advocacy organizations, or direct service providers that follow one of the other three models.

Classification of Nonprofit Organizations

Salamon (1999) divides the nonprofit sector into two broad categories: those that primarily serve the public and those that primarily serve the organization's members.

Public-Serving Organizations

A subclass of public-serving nonprofit organizations provides direct service, such as day care services, hospitals, nursing homes, mental health services, shelter to the homeless, and arts and music organizations. About 40% of known nonprofits fit in this category, and they account for about 80% of nonprofit organization employment.

A second subclass consists of those organizations whose principal mission is to mobilize others to engage in activities that promote the public good. To do this, the organizations will be involved in substantial direct lobbying of legislative bodies to promote the passage or defeat of legislation, and/or engage in substantial grass-roots lobbying and public education efforts to change public attitudes. They include political action organizations that are primarily concerned with influencing the political process. These organizations may apply for federal tax-exempt status under Section 501(c)(4) of the Internal Revenue Code.

By law, nonprofits that are 501(c)(3) organizations may engage in lobbying efforts provided this activity is not "substantial," but they are prohibited from participating in partisan political activity in support of, or opposition to, any candidate for public office. Organizations exempt under Section 501(c)(4) of the Internal Revenue Code, on the other hand, may (and do) engage in substantial lobbying activities—often this is their sole purpose—but their donors are not eligible for tax deductions on donations to these organizations.

A third subclass of public-serving nonprofit organizations consists of educational and research organizations, such as the Brookings Institution, the Urban Institute, and the Heritage Foundation. These organizations are eligible for federal tax exemption under Section 501(c)(3) of the Internal Revenue Code.

A fourth subclass of public-serving organizations is comprised of "funding intermediaries," or "umbrella" fundraising organizations—those whose principal mission is to channel financial support to other nonprofit organizations" (Salamon, in Ott, 2001). The role of these intermediaries is to "help generate...private funding, to manage it once it is accumulated, and to make it available for use by other organizations in the sector" (Salamon, in Ott, 2001, p. 26). Included in the roster of funding intermediaries are foundations and federated funders, such as the United Way and Jewish federations.

Of the 81,777 foundations in the United States in 2011, 90% were independent foundations. The total amount of assets of all foundations was $662.335 billion as of 2011. The remaining 10% of the foundations are corporate foundations, community foundations, and operating foundations. The IRS classifies operating foundations as private foundations, but they function as both grantmakers and operators of charitable programs, particularly research, social welfare, or other charitable programs (Foundation Center, 2014).

Figure 2: Number and Type of Foundations, 2007 and 2011

Year	2007	2011
Total #	75,187	81,777
Independent	67,034	73,764
Corporate	2,498	2,689
Community	717	750
Operating	4,938	4,574

Source: *Foundation Growth and Giving Estimates: Current Outlook*, 2010 Edition, Foundation Center, p. 9 and Foundation Stats: *http://data.foundationcenter.org/#/fc1000/subject:all/all/top:foundations/list/2011* (2014)

In 2011, the 2,689 corporate foundations controlled 3% of foundation assets—$22.195 billion—and accounted for 11% of all foundation grants. The 750 community foundations controlled 9% of total foundation assets—$57.937 billion—and over 9% of all foundation grants (Foundation Center, 2014).

A second group of funding intermediaries consists of organizations such as United Ways. These organizations typically solicit contributions from corporations and individuals with the promise to allocate the bulk of these donations to member charities, all of which are required to be accountable to the intermediary through financial reports and community-based planning.

Member-Serving Organizations

Some member-serving organizations are business leagues, granted federal tax-exempt status under Section 501(c)(6) of the Internal Revenue Code. The most common form of business league is the trade association, "a nonprofit, cooperative, voluntarily-joined, organization of business competitors designed to assist members and its industry in dealing with mutual business problems" (Hopkins, 1992, p. 582). The IRS defines a business league as "an association of persons having some common business interest, the purpose of which is to promote that common interest and not to engage in a regular business of a kind ordinarily carried on for profit. Trade associations and professional associations are considered business leagues" (Internal Revenue Service, 2003). Examples of business leagues include Chambers of Commerce, boards of trade, real estate boards, and other organizations formed to promote business interests and are "devoted to the improvement of business conditions of one or more lines of business as distinguished from the performance of particular services for individual persons" (Internal Revenue Service, 2003). The number of organizations exempt under Section 501(c)(6) of the Internal Revenue Code during FY 2013 was 90,908 (Internal Revenue Service, 2014).

Other types of member-serving organizations include social and recreational clubs (exempt under Section 501(c)(7)), labor and agricultural organizations (exempt under Section 501(c)(5)), benevolent life insurance associations (exempt under Section 501(c)(12)), and political organizations—both political action committees and political parties.

Differences Between Private Foundations and Public Charities

Public charities and private foundations are both granted tax-exempt status under Section 501(c)(3) of the Internal Revenue Code. Section 509(a), however, differentiates organizations that receive their income from a broad range of public sources from those organizations that receive their income principally from one, or a limited number of sources plus investment income (Kramer and Sykes, 2001). Private foundations pay a federal tax on net investment income, must meet a minimum annual threshold for making distributions of their assets to charities, and are flatly prohibited from lobbying. To be considered a public charity rather than a private foundation, an organization must pass a public support test enforced by the IRS. There are two such tests, one of which the organization must pass to be

An Introduction to the Nonprofit Sector

Figure 3: Source of Charitable Organization (by %) Revenue by Asset Size (FY 2001)

	<$100K	$100K-$500K	$500K-$1M	$1-10 M	$10M-$50M	>50M
Contributions	55	53	45	44	29	15
Program Service	32	35	46	50	65	70
Investment Income	<1	1	1	2	2	3
Other	13	11	8	5	4	2

Source: Internal Revenue Service: *Figure C, Charities and Other Tax-Exempt Organizations, 2001* by Paul Arnsberger. Retrieved from *http://www.irs.gov/pub/irs-soi/01eochin.pdf*

considered a public charity. The test is based on financial data for a four-year period. If one test is passed, the organization will qualify as a public charity for the following two years. The full requirements are described in IRS Publication 557, *Tax Exempt Status for Your Organization.*

Nonprofits that do not fit neatly into the public-serving or member-serving category are the 375,000 religious congregations, about 80% of which do not register with the IRS or file a 990 federal annual tax return because there is no requirement to do so (Ott, 2001, p. 35, notes). As Salamon (1999) points out, although these congregations exist primarily to serve their members, their tax treatment is as if they primarily serve the public. In fact, nonprofit organizations are not required by law to file for exempt status with the Internal Revenue Service provided they have a recognized creed or form of worship, are "sacerdotal" in character, carry on regular religious services, and operate for other than private gain (Salamon, 1999).

Figure 4: Categories of Charitable Organizations (2010 Tax Year)

	# of Tax Returns	Revenue (in $ millions)
Arts, Culture, & Humanities	26,053	30,018
Education	47,916	309,485
Environment, Animals	12,312	14,683
Health	34,463	909,890
Human Services	103,577	219,030
International/Foreign Affairs	5,390	23,689
Mutual Membership/Benefit	747	2,906
Public/Societal Benefit	23,720	73,045
Religious Related	15,296	10,266

Source: Internal Revenue Service: Statistics of Income Bulletin, Winter 2014, Nonprofit Organizations 2010, Figure D, p. 74. by Paul Arnsberger.

Figure 5: Top 10 Foundations, 2011	Total Giving
Bill & Melinda Gates Foundation	$4,394,055,135
Walton Family Foundation	$482,676,504
Ford Foundation	$425,300,890
Susan Thompson Buffet Foundation	$347,779,418
Robert Wood Johnson Foundation	$333,116,656
W. K. Kellogg Foundation	$303,040,612
Foundation to Promote Open Society	$247,795,395
David and Lucile Packard Foundation	$247,401,241
Andrew W. Mellon Foundation	$230,624,301
Silicon Valley Community Foundation	$211,712,014

Source: Foundation Stats, Foundation Center. Retrieved from: http://data.foundationcenter.org/#/fc1000/subject:all/all/)

Henry Hansmann (1987) typologized nonprofits into four types, depending on their primary source of income (from either sales or donations) and their governing structure (a board consisting of members who do, or do not, directly benefit from the organization's services any more than anyone else in the community). The four types are: *donative and mutual, donative and entrepreneurial, commercial and mutual,* and *commercial and entrepreneurial.*

Organizations that generate most of their income from sales of goods and services are "commercial" nonprofits. Those that generate most of their revenue from donations are "donative" nonprofits. Those whose members directly benefit from the services provided by the organization are "mutual" nonprofits, and those organizations whose members benefit no more from the organization than others in the community are "entrepreneurial" nonprofits. Examples are:

- **Donative and Mutual:** National Audubon Society, political clubs
- **Donative and Entrepreneurial:** CARE, March of Dimes, art museums
- **Commercial and Mutual:** American Automobile Association, Consumers Union, country clubs
- **Commercial and Entrepreneurial:** National Geographic Society, Educational Testing Service, hospitals and nursing homes (Handsmann, 1987).

Michael O'Neill has proposed differentiating the nonprofit sector into nine subsectors: religious, private education and research, health care, arts and culture, social services, advocacy and legal services, international assistance, foundations and corporate funders, and mutual benefit organizations (in Ott, 2001, p. 5). These functional categories are not necessarily mutually exclusive (e.g., a health care organization provides social services, and an international assistance organization might provide services related to one or more of the other eight categories), but this provides a useful framework for distinguishing a "field of interest."

How Organizations Are Funded

Nonprofit organizations are funded through a combination of grants and donations, sales and fees for service, and investment income. According to a study by the Urban Institute, nonprofit organization revenue for 2006 was comprised of 69.7% from sales and service fees, 25.9% from grants and donations, and 4.5% from investment income. Disregarding hospitals and institutions of higher education that typically are much more dependent on fees for goods and services, public charities that filed 990s with the IRS reported receiving 40.3% of their income from grants and donations; 53.6% from service fees and sales; 2.3% from investment income; and 3.9% from other sources such as dues, special events, and rental income (Wing, Pollak & Blackwood, 2008). Similar data collected by the IRS provides additional evidence about the importance of the sale of goods and services by exempt organizations. The IRS reports that for Tax Year 2010, total revenue reported by charities reached $1.6 trillion, $1.1 trillion (72%) of which was revenue in program service fees (Internal Revenue Service, Winter 2014). This contrasts to just $344.9 billion (21.6%) in donations and grants. See Chapter 8 for a discussion on practical organizational fundraising strategies and Chapter 9 for marketing strategies.

Legal Definition of Tax-Exempt Charitable Organizations

Nonprofit status is conferred by individual states through incorporation procedures. It is federal law, however, which authorizes federal tax exempt status for nonprofit organizations that meet certain criteria. Such status has influence in many states on whether an organization will qualify for state and local sales, income, and property tax exemptions.

Section 501(c) of the Internal Revenue Code grants tax-exempt status to 25 categories of nonprofit organizations, including charities, business and trade associations, fraternal organizations, cemeteries, and credit unions (see Chapter 4). With limited exceptions, only one category, nonprofits exempt under Section (c)(3), provides that donations made by the public to such organizations are tax-deductible. These organizations are forbidden from engaging in substantial lobbying or propaganda activities, or engaging in political activities that advance the cause of any candidate for public office (Internal Revenue Service, 2001).

Size and Growth of the Voluntary Nonprofit Sector

The growth of the sector registered with the Internal Revenue Service in recent years has been significant. Between 1989 and 1994, the population in the United States increased by 1.1%, while the number of reporting public charities increased by 6.3% (Stevenson, Pollack, and Lampton, 1997). This increase substantially continued until 2012 when the IRS purged 275,000 organizations for failing to file timely tax returns (Chiu, 2011).

As pointed out by Lester Salamon, "under American law organizations are not required to incorporate, or even to seek formal recognition by the tax authorities, in order to function as tax-exempt nonprofit organizations. This organizational fluidity is, in fact, one of the prized features of this sector, enabling groups of people to meet together to pursue common purposes without having to seek official approval or even acknowledgment" (Salamon, 2001, p. 23). Yet federal tax-exempt status is highly prized, and only 501(c)(3) organizations, those that operate "exclusively for religious, charitable, scientific, literary, or educational purposes," are eligible to receive tax deductible donations from individuals and corporations. A standard justification for this policy is that "the organizations are serving purposes that are public in character and that government might otherwise have to support through tax revenues" (Salamon, 1999, p. 24).

According to the Internal Revenue Service, there were 1.442 million nonprofit organizations with 501(c) status in FY 2013 (Internal Revenue Service, 2014). This compares to 87,000 units of federal, state, and local government (California University at Berkeley, 2003) and 27.8 million private, for-profit business firms in 2007 (U.S. Census Bureau, n.d.). The estimate does not include religious organizations, which are not required to register.

The sector accounts for 8.3% of all wages and salaries, and accounted for 5.6% of the gross domestic product in 2011, according to the Urban Institute (Pettijohn, 2013). Employment in the sector is more racially diverse than the other sectors and provides more employment for women. In 1994, 68% of employees were women and 15% were African-American, compared to 44% women and 10% African–American for the other sectors (Hodgkinson and Weitzman, 1996). A more recent estimate suggests that not much progress is being made to increase the diversity of the sector, with nonprofit employees being comprised of approximately 82 percent white, ten percent African American, five percent Hispanic/Latino, and four percent other. Employees of color make up about 14 percent of leadership or upper management roles, but less than six percent of specialized positions (Hayes, 2012).

Between 1977 and 1994, the nonprofit sector expanded at a faster rate than the rest of the economy, with a 3.7% growth rate (which includes the assigned value of volunteer time) compared with 2.1% for the for-profit sector and 2.3% for the government sector. During this period, the annual increase in total employment in the nonprofit sector was 3.3% compared to 1.9% for for-profits and 1.4% for government (Hodgkinson and Weitzman, 1996). Hodgekinson and Weitzman attribute much of this growth to federal policies that funded Medicaid and Medicare, education grants, housing, job training, and other social welfare programs. By 1994, there were 1.03 million nonprofit entities (4.2% of all entities), generating 6.5% of national income, employing 9.7 million full- and part-time workers, and an additional 5.5 million full-time equivalent employee volunteers.

In 2011, the portion of the nonprofit sector that excludes organizations serving businesses accounted for $836.9 billion of a total economy of $14.958 trillion (5.6%) (Pettijohn, 2013, Trading Economics, 2014). This amount compares to 5.05% in 2006, 4.7% in 1996, 3.82% in 1986, 3.28% in 1976, 2.53% in 1966, 1.78% in 1956, 1.26% in 1946, and 1.55% in 1936 (Wing, Pollak & Blackwood, 2008).

Nonprofit Taxonomies

There are several classification systems that provide a taxonomy of nonprofit organizations. The National Taxonomy of Exempt Entities (NTEE) is used by the Internal Revenue Service as part of its Master List of Exempt Organizations. There are approximately 645 different subcategories, with major categories including arts, culture, and humanities; education; environment and animals; health, human service; international and foreign affairs; and others (Wing, Pollak & Blackwood, 2008). An updated version of the NTEE-CC, which reduced the number of original subcategories of the NTEE to approximately 400, is available at: *http://nccs.urban.org/classification/NTEE.cfm*

A broader classification system—the North American Industry Classification System (NAICS)—is used by the Census Bureau and for purposes of compliance with the North American Free Trade Agreement (NAFTA). This system includes 1,065 categories of organizations. Nonprofit organizations are included in the Standard Industrial Codes (SIC) taxonomy first published in the 1930s by the Central Statistical Board of the United States. Major SIC classifications include "health services," "educational services," "social services," and "museums, botanical & zoological gardens," each with subcategories. The NAICS replaced SICs in 1999. It is reviewed every five years, and was last updated in 2012.

Section 501(c) of the Internal Revenue Code provides a taxonomy of various categories of nonprofit organizations that are eligible for tax-exempt status (see Chapter 4).

Assets of the Sector

One early estimate of $600 billion in total sector assets appears in the literature (Bakal, 1979). Gaul and Borowski estimated that nonprofit organizations control property, cash, and investments valued at $850 billion, a figure that they consider "conservative" (Gaul and Borowski, 1993, p. 3) because it does not take into account wealth controlled by churches or small nonprofits that are not required to file federal Form 990 tax returns. They estimate that the "true figure probably exceeds $1 trillion" (p. 3). These estimates of real estate value are considered flawed for two reasons. First, nonprofit property is typically not subject to regular appraisal. Second, it is difficult to appraise property of tax-exempt institutions under standards that apply to residential or business property, because the value of a property is based on the profit it can generate (Simon, 1987).

Government estimates of sector assets are considerably higher. The Internal Revenue Service, using data from annual tax returns, reported that assets of the sector increased from $899 billion in 1975 to $1.9 trillion in 1995 (Meckstroth and Arnsberger, 1998). This more than tripling of assets during the period contrasts with a 74% increase in gross domestic product during the same period. Assets of organizations reporting to the IRS increased from $1.57 trillion in 2001 to $2.83 trillion in 2011, and the estimate of sector total assets was $4.63 trillion in 2011 (Pettijohn, 2013).

Boundaries of the Sector

As pointed out by Ott (2001), many nonprofit organizations that started out as voluntary associations have evolved into organizations that resemble large business organizations. Examples are Blue Cross/Blue Shield, credit unions, and the American Association for Retired Persons (AARP). Many large nonprofit hospitals, financial services companies, and mutual benefit companies also fit into this hybrid category of what he calls "corporatized nonprofits" (Ott, 2001, p. 5).

Added to this list are nonprofits that depend so heavily on government contracts that they have become almost indistinguishable from the government agencies that fund them. Some governmental instrumentalities form nonprofit organizations to avoid the managerial constraints they would have if a program or function were to be directly carried out by government, and to attract private funding.

Figure 6: Size of the Nonprofit Sector, 2001-2011

	2001	2006	2011
# of All Organizations Filing Returns	461,470	560,495	589,505
Total Revenue	$1.21 trillion	$1.77 trillion	$2.10 trillion
Total Expenses	$1.11 trillion	$1.59 trillion	$1.99 trillion
Assets	$2.70 trillion	$3.85 trillion	$4.63 trillion
# of Reporting 501(c)(3) Public Charities	263,142	326,388	335,037
Total Revenue	$876 billion	$1.29 trillion	$1.59 trillion
Total Expenses	$812 billion	$1.17 trillion	$1.50 trillion
Assets	$1.57 trillion	$2.27 trillion	$2.83 trillion

Source: Table 1. Size and Financial Scope of the Nonprofit Sector, 2001-2011 The Nonprofit Sector in Brief: Public Charities, Giving, and Volunteering, 2013, Urban Institute Press.

Ott considers these organizations to be nonprofit organizations because they satisfy the legal definitions of this type of organization. Including them in the sector for this reason is not "uplifting," and if they are indeed part of the sector, they are on its outer fringes.

Differences Between the Sectors

The following are nine of the more salient differences between the sectors described in the literature, both academic and other:

1. *Distribution of output differences.* The nonprofit can provide for individual choice that could not otherwise be provided by the private sector. The private sector has incentives to provide a uniform service in order to stay economically competitive (Ferris and Graddy, 1989). In general, nonprofits provide their output to the most needy, while for-profits provide their output to those who pay the most. Burton Weisbrod points out one interesting manifestation of this. Nonprofit organizations often have waiting lists for the services they provide. Weisbrod notes that profit-maximizing firms have little incentive to keep a waiting list, because if there is an excess of demand for their services, they will increase their price (although there may be a waiting list to deal with uncertainties of unpredictable demand). Since the nonprofit is mission-driven and its goals are not to maximize profit, but rather to distribute its services to the most needy (under financial constraints that often result in the nonprofit engaging in cross-subsidization), waiting lists are appropriate (Weisbrod, 1988).

2. *Dissemination of information differences.* Studies by Weisbrod (1988) of facilities for long-term nursing care, long-term psychiatric care, and long-term care for the mentally handicapped showed that nonprofits were more willing than their for-profit counterparts to share information. Weisbrod attributes this willingness to the fact that nonprofit organizations do not gain an advantage by covering up information or otherwise taking advantage of the consumer.

3. *Willingness of people to volunteer.* People do not generally volunteer for for-profit organizations. Volunteering for government organizations, such as by student interns, or to "adopt a highway" for cleanup, is not uncommon, but it is not visible to the extent to which American adults volunteer in nonprofit organizations. Volunteering for nonprofit organizations is ingrained in our culture.

4. *Governance by a diverse volunteer board of community members.* Typical nonprofit organizations have volunteer, diverse board members, who make collective decisions and have a fiduciary responsibility for the affairs of the organization. This contrasts to boards of for-profit corporations, who frequently receive lucrative fees, are relatively homogeneous, and often receive direct benefit from the decisions they make (through the ownership of stock in the organization, for example).

5. *Mission-driven rather than profit-driven (or by a quest for political power or votes).* The voluntary sector has traditionally had a distinct role compared to the public and private sectors, such as pioneering service delivery, promoting volunteerism, and advocacy (Kramer, 1981). Because "mission" is the driving force for nonprofits, rather than profits, nonprofits are more likely to respond to the heterogeneity of public demand, rather than simply providing a one-size-fits-all product. An example would be the programming of a public radio station compared to a top 40 station that lives or dies on ratings.

At least in theory, decisions regarding what services to provide and to whom to provide them are based not on profit-maximization considerations, but rather whether doing so is consistent with the mission of the organization, given financial constraints. The incentive to maximize profits is at least reduced, if not eliminated, because any profits cannot by law inure to the benefit of the organization's board or trustees. The compensation of its employees must be reasonable and not based on the amount of net revenue. This constraint is enforced by the 1996 *Taxpayer Bill of Rights 2* law, final regulations of which were published by the Internal Revenue Service in the *Federal Register* in January 2001 (see Chapter 4).

Some nonprofits also seek to maximize profits. They create health care conglomerates, for-profit subsidiaries, partnerships, and mergers, although by law, the profit may not inure to the benefit of private persons. It is fashionable, consistent with New Public Management, for units of government to seek to "make a profit" by entrepreneurship, finding creative ways to generate revenue to respond to the burgeoning recession-induced deficits of the late 1980s and early 1990s (Osborne and Gaebler, 1992). However, a case can be made that people (including employees, volunteers, and donors) are attracted to a nonprofit more because of the values it seeks to instill in society rather than its thirst for either power or profits (Van Hook, 1998).

6. *Accountability to the public, not stockholders.* Because nonprofits do not have stockholders who seek a return on their investment, the boards of directors of nonprofits do not have accountability to private seekers of profit. Rather, these organizations are authorized to exist by the state for limited purposes and, in order to qualify for their tax exemptions and other benefits, must not have a private profit motive.

Unlike most for-profit businesses, nonprofits must register, and file public reports with various agencies of the federal and state government about their finances. Many states authorize their state attorney general to intervene in the affairs of the organization if there are allegations that decisions made by the board are not in the public interest. For example, decisions by a board to convert a nonprofit hospital to a for-profit hospital are typically subjected to state review.

Specialized tax rules and accounting practices apply to tax-exempt nonprofit corporations. Larger organizations are required to disclose many details to the general public and to state regulators and watchdog agencies. They are required to file an annual tax return, Form 990, showing any salaries paid to officers or directors and to the five highest-paid employees (McNamara, 2000). Even the smallest tax-exempt organizations must file an informational form with the IRS at least every three years or automatically lose their tax exemption.

Organizations that raise at least $25,000 in donations from the public in Pennsylvania (most other states have similar reporting and registration requirements) must register and file reports with the Pennsylvania Department of State's Bureau of Charitable Organizations. The Attorney General has the power to review asset transfers of nonprofit organizations, and to make recommendations to a court about any questionable transfer. These may include a transaction not at arm's length, when fair market value is not obtained, or when one of the board members of an organization receives some financial benefit from the transaction.

7. *An ethical framework and a set of values geared to the benefit of society and the collective rather than to any single individual.* Lohmann

(1992) writes that the nonprofit sector serves as the "commons" in which people voluntarily form communities with shared visions and values.

An ethical framework is primary to the nonprofit, compared to being only secondary within the government or business milieu.

> *The ethical frame can be shifted by the exigencies of organizational life in the government or private sectors. Government and business utilize ethical frames only as secondary mechanisms by which to measure performance. The rightness or wrongness of an act may be modified by whether it makes a profit for the firm or supports a government's appropriate need to control. However, for a non-profit organization the ethical frame is primary. Thus the very existence of a non-profit organization depends on its moral standing, its integrity, and its virtue (van Hook, 1998, p. 798).*

8. *Depends on donations for some of its revenue, and may be directly subsidized by government grants and indirectly subsidized by tax laws that encourage the public to make these donations.*

As Professor Hansmann points out, donors to a public radio station, symphony, or theater company can be reasonably assured that the donations will be used to enhance the service provided by the nonprofit organization. If the donations were made to a profit-making institution, there would be no reasonable expectation that the donations would go to improving the product rather than simply being added to profits. An overwhelming majority of donors of these organizations also attend performances. Donations, therefore, provide a form of voluntary differential pricing based on ability to pay (Hansmann, 1996, p. 231-232).

9. *Depends for its existence on people behaving in ways not necessarily to increase their personal benefit but rather to increase the benefit to society.* This is the case, whether it be at the level of a neighborhood, community, city, state, country, species, or any one of thousands of subcategories such as an ethnic group, those who appreciate a particular form of music, those who wish to cure a particular disease, or those who want to save a particular animal from extinction. This is in contrast to government, which can invoke coercive power of law and imprison those who do not submit to it, or business, which depends on using the market for voluntary compliance with quid pro quo transactions.

As pointed out by Douglas (1987, in Ott, 2001, p. 206), "The problem arises when the benefits from a transaction cannot be confined to those who have contributed to the exchange and there is nothing to stop non-contributors from taking a free ride on the backs of the contributors."

It is this "free rider" problem that is of intense interest to economists and others who study nonprofits. When WITF, the local public radio station in Harrisburg, Pennsylvania, asks listeners for their annual membership contributions, the listeners probably assume that the station will continue broadcasting even if they choose not to contribute. The listener who pays membership dues will benefit from the station to approximately the same degree as his or her neighbor who may also listen to the station but chooses not to become a member.

Discussion Questions

1. Is the nonprofit sector really a distinctive sector?

2. Do you agree with the theory that typical nonprofit organizations make programming decisions based on "mission" more than the "bottom line"? Is this generally true of nonprofit organizations in your own community?

3. Referring to the riverbank story on page 16, what are some of the differences among nonprofit organizations with respect to structure, fundraising methods, staffing, advocacy, and public relations, based on each of the methods chosen to address a social problem?

4. Discuss your own participation (making donations, volunteering, being a member, and so on) in national and local nonprofit organizations. Does it follow a pattern with respect to any of the four types of organizations described on page 21 (e.g., donative and mutual) that have benefited from your participation? If so, what type of appeal do you think would be effective in convincing you to participate in a different type of organization?

5. Do you think nonprofit organization executives and/or board members make decisions based more on the interests of their communities, their organizations, or their own personal self-interest? How do you compare this with executives and/or legislators in government and executives and/or board members in the private sector?

6. What would the nonprofit sector look like if the federal government required all of these organizations' work to be performed by volunteers in order to qualify for government subsidies and tax benefits?

Activities

1. Research how the nonprofit sector is developing in Eastern Europe since the breakup of the Former Soviet Union and Warsaw Pact.

2. Visit Web sites that provide the full text or summaries of new final and proposed regulations and laws that affect the nonprofit sector, and summarize the issues that are on the current public policy agenda.

3. Research your university's public records that are filed with respect to accountability, such as its 990 annual tax returns and its reports to state charitable solicitation regulatory authorities. Discuss what information is disclosed, and what can remain private. Note: Obviously, public universities will have different accountability requirements than private schools.

4. Research state laws affecting nonprofit organizations in the state where your university is located, and compare them to the laws of neighboring states.

Online Resources to Explore

Independent Sector
http://www.independentsector.org

National Center for Charitable Statistics
http://nccsdataweb.urban.org/

Nonprofit Genie
htttp://genie.org

Council on Foundations
http://www.cof.org/index.cfm

The National Council of Nonprofits
http://www.councilofnonprofits.org/

References

Bakal, C. (1979). *Charity U.S.A.* New York: Times Books.

Berger, P. L., & Neuhaus, R. J. (1977). *To empower people: The role of mediating structures in public policy.* Washington, DC: American Enterprise Institute.

Brinckerhoff, P. C. (1994). *Mission-based management: Leading your not-for-profit into the 21st century.* New York: Wiley and Sons.

California University at Berkeley. (2003). *Public affairs report.* 43(2), Winter 2002-2003.

Chiu, L. (June 2011). 275,000 groups lose tax exemptions after failing to file paperwork with IRS. *Chronicle of Philanthropy,* June 8, 2011. Retrieved from *http://philanthropy.com/article/275000-Nonprofits-Lose-Tax/127854/*

Douglas, J. (1987). Political theories of nonprofit organizations. In J. S. Ott (Ed.). *The nature of the nonprofit sector.* Boulder, CO: Westview Press.

Drucker Institute. (2007). New York conference spotlights a social sector enjoying tremendous growth and new opportunities. November 1, 2007. Retrieved from *http://www.druckerinstitute.com/link/new-york-conference-spotlights-a-social-sector-enjoying-tremendous-growth-and-new-opportunities/*

Ferris, J. M., & Graddy, E. (1989). Fading distinctions among the nonprofit, government and for-profit sectors. In V. Hodgkinson, R. W. Lymen & Associates (Eds.). *The future of the nonprofit sector* (pp. 129-139). San Francisco: Jossey-Bass.

Foundation Center. (2014). *Foundation growth and giving estimates: Current outlook.* Foundation Center, p. 9 and Foundation Stats. Retrieved from *http://data.foundationcenter.org/#/fc1000/subject:all/all/top:foundations/list/2011*

Gaul, G., & Borowski, N. (1993). *Free ride: The tax-exempt economy.* Kansas City, MO: Andrews and McMeel.

Gidron, B., Kramer, R. M., & Salamon, L. M. (Eds.). (1992). *Government and the third sector.* San Francisco: Jossey-Bass.

Hansmann, H. (1987). Economic theories of nonprofit organizations. In W. W. Powell (Ed.). *The nonprofit sector: A research handbook* (pp. 28-42). New Haven, CT: Yale University Press.

Hansmann, H. (1989). The two nonprofit sectors: Fee for service versus donative organizations. In V. A. Hodgkinson, R. W. Lyman & Associates (Eds.), *The future of the nonprofit sector* (pp. 91-102). San Francisco: Jossey-Bass.

Hansmann, H. (1996). *The ownership of enterprise.* Cambridge, MA: Harvard University Press.

Hayes, J. (November 2012). Is the nonprofit sector doing enough for diversity? *Diversity Journal.* November 9, 2012. Retrieved from *http://www.diversityjournal.com/9897-is-the-nonprofit-sector-doing-enough-for-diversity/*

Hodgkinson, V. et al. (Eds.). *Nonprofit almanac (1996-97): Dimensions of the independent sector.* San Francisco: Jossey-Bass.

Hopkins, B. R. (1992). *The law of tax-exempt organizations* (6th Ed.). New York: John Wiley and Sons.

Independent Sector. (2001). *The new nonprofit almanac in brief: Facts and figures on the independent sector 2001.* Washington, DC: Author.

Internal Revenue Service. (2001). *Tax-exempt status for your organization (Publication 557).* Washington, DC: U.S. Treasury Department.

Internal Revenue Service. (2003). *Tax exempt/Employee plans statistics—exempt organizations.*

Internal Revenue Service. (2009). IRS Data Book 2008. Retrieved from *http://www.irs.gov/pub/irs-soi/08databkrevised.pdf*

Internal Revenue Service. (2010). IRS Databook 2009. Retrieved from *http://www.irs.gov/pub/irs-soi/09databk.pdf*

Internal Revenue Service. (2014). IRS Databook 2013. Retrieved from *http://www.irs.gov/uac/SOI-Tax-Stats-IRS-Data-Book*

IRS. (2003, 2004, 2005). Publication 55b Table 22—*Tax-Exempt Organizations and Other Entities Listed on the Exempt Organization Business Master File, by Type of Organization and Internal Revenue Code Section, Fiscal Years 2002-2005.* Washington, DC: Author.

Kramer, D., & Sykes, V. (2001). *The guide for nonprofit organizations.* Dresher, PA: Nonprofit Issues.

Kramer, R. M. (1981). *Voluntary agencies in the welfare state.* Berkeley, CA: University of California Press.

Kramer, R. M. (1987). Voluntary agencies and the personal social services. In W. W. Powell (Ed.). *The nonprofit sector: A research handbook* (pp. 240-257). New Haven, CT: Yale University Press.

Lawrence, S. & Mukai, R. (2010). *Foundation growth and giving estimates: Current outlook.* New York: The Foundation Center.

Lohmann, R. (1992). The theory of the commons. In J. S. Ott (Ed.). *The nature of the nonprofit sector* (pp. 89-95). Boulder, CO: Westview Press.

McNamara, C. (2000). *Two basic types of U.S. business organizations: For-profit and nonprofit.* Retrieved from *http://www.managementhelp.org/org_thry/types.htm#anchor1387675*

Meckstroth, A. & Arnsberger, P. (1998). *A 20-Year Review of the Nonprofit Sector, 1975-1995.* Washington, DC: Internal Revenue Service.

Milward, H. B.; Provan, K. G.; & Else, B. (1993). The nongovernmental provision of public services to the mentally ill: What does the hollow state look like? In B. Bozeman (Ed.). *Research on public management* (pp. 309-322). San Francisco: Jossey-Bass.

Najam, A. (1999). Review of the book *Non-governments: NGOs and the political development of the third world. Nonprofit and Voluntary Sector Quarterly, 3,* 364-367.

Office of Foreign Assets and Control. (2010). Risk matrix for the charitable sector. Retrieved from *http://docsfiles.com/pdf_risk_matrix_for_the_charitable_sector.html*

Osborne, D. & Gaebler, T. (1992). *Reinventing government: How the entrepreneurial spirit is transforming the public sector.* Reading, MA: Addison-Wesley.

Ott, J. S. (Ed.) (2001). *The nature of the nonprofit sector.* Boulder, CO: Westview Press.

Pettijohn, S. (2013). *The nonprofit sector in brief.* Washington, DC: The Urban Institute Press. Retrieved from *http://www.urban.org/publications/412923.html*

Rose-Ackerman, S. (Ed.). *The economics of nonprofit institutions* (pp. 21-44). New York: Oxford University Press.

Salamon, L. (1999). *America's nonprofit sector: A primer* (2nd Ed.). Washington, DC: The Foundation Center.

Salamon, L., & Anheier, H. K. (1996). *The emerging nonprofit sector.* New York: Manchester University Press.

Simon, J. G. (1987). *The tax treatment of nonprofit organizations: A review of federal and state policies.* In W. W. Powell (Ed.). *The nonprofit sector: A research handbook* (pp. 67-98). New Haven, CT: Yale University.

Smith, D. H. (Ed.). (1972). *Voluntary action research: 1972.* Lexington, MA: Lexington Books.

Trading Economics. (2014). United States GDP. Retrieved from *http://www.tradingeconomics.com/united-states/gdp*

U.S. Census Bureau. (n.d.). Statistics about business size (including Small Business) from the U.S. Census Bureau. Retrieved from *http://www.census.gov/econ/smallbus.html*

Van Hook, P. J. (1998). Ethics in non-profit organizations. In *The international encyclopedia of public policy and administration.* Boulder, CO: Westview.

Van Til, J. (1988). *Mapping the third sector: Voluntarism in a changing social economy.* New York: The Foundation Center.

Weisbrod, B. A. (1975). Toward a theory of the voluntary nonprofit sector in a three-sector economy. In S. Rose-Ackerman (Ed.). *The economics of nonprofit institutions* (pp. 21-44). New York: Oxford University Press.

Weisbrod, B. A. (1988). *The nonprofit economy.* Cambridge, MA: Harvard University Press.

Wing, K., Pollak, T., & Blackwood, A. (2008). *The nonprofit almanac.* Washington, DC: The Urban Institute Press.

Wing, K., Pollak, T., & Blackwood, A. (2010). *The nonprofit sector in brief.* Washington, DC: The Urban Institute Press. Retrieved from *http://www.urban.org/publications/412085.html*

Chapter 2
History of the Nonprofit Sector

> **Synopsis:** Religious tradition sustained the nonprofit sector in the United States. The growth of secular organizations is a relatively recent phenomenon. Modern nonprofit law has its roots in England. Government policies have encouraged the nonprofit sector to flourish. Organizations advocating for the nonprofit sector have been established in recent decades.

Introduction

Voluntary "associations" first formed about 10,000 years ago, during the Neolithic Period. Villages developed complex linkages that were not totally integrated into the local political and economic system (Anderson, 1973).

"For pragmatic reasons, primitive societies were the first to develop and exhibit the concept of charity or philanthropy" (Bakal, 1979). In these early societies, the welfare and preservation of individuals and families required the community to share in the tasks of food gathering, hunting, and providing shelter (Block, 2001, in Ott, p. 98).

Religious associations were among the first voluntary associations of civilization and were "often of a secret nature, playing important roles in conserving traditions, building bonds and alliances across family and tribal structures" (Scott, 1998 in Ott, 2001, p. 40).

The values inherent in the work of nonprofit organizations are deeply ingrained in American culture, having evolved out of a religious tradition of serving community needs. Their roots go back to the Torah, New Testament, Koran, and other holy books written thousands of years ago.

The religious tradition motivating the formation of nonprofit organizations continues to this day as perhaps the most potent factor (James, 1987). That motivation occurs not only proactively as a way to proselytize, but also as a defensive reaction to enforce and maintain traditional values, such as providing an alternative to public schools when secular ideology is inconsistent with that of the religious ideology of a particular constituency (James, 1987).

A concept of philanthropy existed in ancient Egypt as far back as 2,300 B.C.E. (Block, 2001) with Egyptian aristocrats being buried with records of their gifts to the poor and needy. During the reign of Ramses III, as much as 15% of the cultivatable land was tax-exempt. Religious leaders were granted exemption for their temples, slaves, and other personal property (Columbo and Hall, 1995).

In contrast, the ancient Greek philanthropy consisted more of charitable giving designed to make the community stronger, such as gifts of theaters and stadiums, rather than targeted to help the poor (Block, 2001). The Code of Hammurabi (1780 B.C.E.), who ruled Babylonia from 1795-1755 B.C.E., instructed his subjects to protect their community's vulnerable and serves as an example of one of the first secular references to charity (Horne, 2001, Block, in Ott, 2001, p. 98; Harper, 1904 in Ott, 2001, p. 98).

> *That the strong might not injure the weak, in order to protect the widows and orphans, I have in Babylon the city where Anu and Bel raise high their head, in E-Sagil, the Temple, whose foundations stand firm as heaven and earth, in order to declare justice in the land, to settle all disputes, and heal all injuries, set up these my precious words, written upon my memorial stone, before the image of me, as king of righteousness* (Hammurabi, in King, 1910).

The Rosetta Stone, famous for helping archeologists find the keys to translating Egyptian hieroglyphics, was carved by a group of priests in Egypt in 196 B.C.E. to document all of the good works of the King Ptolemy, including providing revenues for the operation of temples and providing tax benefits to the priests (Dull, 2004).

In the 14th century, William Langland wrote a poem, *The Vision of Piers Plowman*, which listed the type of activities that would be supported by a wealthy businessman in order to save his soul:

> *...and therewith repair hospitals*
> *help sick people*
> *mend bad roads*
> *build up bridges that had been broken down*
> *help maidens to marry or to make them nuns*
> *find food for prisoners and poor people*
> *put scholars to school or some other crafts*
> *help religious orders, and*
> *ameliorate rents or taxes* (in Wellford and Gallagher, 1988, p. 117)

The activities we associate with nonprofit organizations, such as health care, religion, the arts, and social welfare activities, were organized and administered by non-secular bodies. It was only after the Reformation that civil law, rather than canon law, prevailed (Douglas, 1987, in Ott, p. 205).

Modern Roots of American Charitable Law and Organizations

The laws granting tax exemptions in the United States, which are similar to the charitable activities described in the poem by Langland, have their roots in laws passed by the British Parliament starting in 1601. The first of these laws, *The Statute of Charitable Uses,* was accepted by Queen Elizabeth I just before the end of her reign. It was intended to create a new relationship between the secular and non-secular institutions of Elizabethan England.

These laws had a long shelf life, maintaining their effect long after the American Revolution (Hammack, 2001). The statute, among other provisions, set out a list of legitimate objects of charity, and established a procedure for accountability for charitable fraud. It authorized an investigation by a bishop of the Church of England concerning allegations against charitable boards, even if the allegations were against church-based charities of religious dissenters, such as Quakers, Baptists, or Presbyterians (Hammack, 2001).

The Elizabethan Poor Laws of 1597 and 1601 required churches to care for the poor, and made local communities responsible for their care in the event charitable gifts were not able to do so—although the gifts were, for the most part, sufficient to forestall any government intervention (Wellford and Gallagher, 1988).

As in England, the tradition in the colonies was for government to establish religion. One notable exception was Pennsylvania, established by William Penn, a Quaker with a personal aversion to government-sponsored religion.

The earliest "charitable" organizations in the New World were Harvard College, established in 1636, and locally based hospital societies (Scott, 1998). With its tax exemption under attack, Harvard president Charles Elliot convinced the Massachusetts General Assembly that the general public benefited by the organization. It responded by expanding the range of institutions eligible for exempt status, and other states adopted this model (Scott, 1998).

Benjamin Franklin created a voluntary association to defend Pennsylvania. Soon thereafter, he created voluntary associations for the Free Library Company, the Philadelphia Hospital, and the University of Pennsylvania, all of which were independent of government, although some government funds subsidized these efforts (Hammack, 2001). *The Autobiography of Ben Franklin* provides a practical example of Weisbrod's public goods theory (see Chapter 3) that many activities of government first began as activities of voluntary associations, which then became acceptable to "the median voter." An example:

> *Our city, tho' laid out with a beautiful regularity, the streets large, strait, and crossing each other at right angles, had the disgrace of suffering*

those streets to remain long unpav'd, and in wet weather, the wheels of heavy carriages plough'd them into a quagmire, so that it was difficult to cross them; and in dry weather the dust was offensive...After some inquiry, I found a poor, industrious man, who was willing to undertake keeping the pavement clean, by sweeping it twice a week, carrying off the dirt from before all the neighbors' doors for the sum of sixpence per month, to be paid by each house...I then wrote and printed a paper setting forth the advantage to the neighborhood that might be obtain'd by this small expense...I sent one of these papers to each house, and in a day or two went round to see who would subscribe an agreement to pay these sixpenses; it was unanimously signed...and this rais'd a general desire to have all the streets paved, and made people more willing to submit to a tax for that purpose (Franklin, 1964, p. 202-203).

Despite the efforts of Franklin, who was a pioneer in establishing nonprofit organizations, there were few corporations in the colonies before 1780. This emanated from hostility toward corruption of the Stuart monarchy and the Church of England (Hall, 1987). Although there were a few colonial associations, the Church of England was established with a "near-monopoly of legal authority" (Hammack, 2001, p. 157) in Georgia, the Carolinas, Virginia, Maryland, New Jersey and New York. The Church provided educational, social, and religious services, and churches not associated with the Church of England, such as those founded by the Puritans, provided similar services.

Following the American Revolution, the established governments in the former colonies, now states, adopted a new doctrine of not funding religious institutions. Private organizations were created to provide services funded through donations and purchases of service rather than through direct and indirect grants from government (Hammack, 2001).

In Europe, social welfare for the needy was originally provided for by the nobility, then by cities and local provincial bodies. Later, this authority was assumed by centralized national governments. In contrast, it is often illustrated by the writings of Alexis de Tocqueville (1835/1956), who compared the United States of the early 19th century to his French homeland, voluntary associations sprung up in the New World to meet community needs that were routinely addressed by national governments in Western Europe (Ott, 2001, p. 91).

In a landmark case decided by the United States Supreme Court, Daniel Webster argued on behalf of Dartmouth College that nonprofit organization trustees, on behalf of their institutions, had property rights (Hammack, 2001). The State of New Hampshire wanted to alter the charter of the institution against the will of its trustees. The opinion by Chief Justice Marshall set an important legal precedent that protected nonprofit corporations from arbitrary government interference.

By the 1830s, foreign visitors were describing voluntary organizations supported by private contributions as the prototypical American contribution to the democratic idea (Hall, 1992).

It was not until 1844 that nonprofit organizations had a firm legal footing under federal law, as a result of the case decided by the U.S. Supreme Court involving the will of Philadelphia philanthropist Stephen Girard, which enforced the charitable trust he established with $7 million for a school for orphans (Hall, 1987).

During the civil war, the federal government outsourced medical care services for soldiers to religious-based nonprofits. Other services, such as vice law enforcement and Native American education, also were provided by these nonprofits (Hammack, 2001).

In 1894, the Congress enacted the first federal income tax, and provided an exemption for "corporations, companies or associations organized and conducted solely for charitable, religious or educational purposes" without any substantive debate on this exemption (Colombo and Hall, 1995, p. 15). This exemption was extended with every subsequent income tax law (Colombo and Hall, 1995). See Chapter 4 for more on the history of the federal tax-exemption for charities.

The number of nonprofit organizations grew dramatically between the end of the Civil War and 1920 as corporate America and private wealth, along with religious congregations, financed the growth of universities, libraries, hospitals, professional organizations, and private clubs (Hall, 1987). Some of this effort was fueled by the views of business leaders who were against using government to solve societal problems (Hall, 1987).

Many wealthy industrialists established foundations that were granted tax advantages, and that funded operating charities. The early part of the 20th century was called "The Golden Age of Philanthropy" (Scott, 1998) as industrialists, such as Andrew Carnegie and John D. Rockefeller, donated millions of dollars to create libraries and fund universities.

Supplementing the philanthropy of affluent individuals was the flourishing of the settlement house movement. Modeled after the Toynbee House settlement in England, social activists such as Jane Addams, founder of the social work profession, created institutions in poor neighborhoods to help the poor improve their social conditions by offering social and educational services, such as day care, playgrounds, counseling, places to meet, and advocacy (Block, 1990, in Ott, 2001).

A second philanthropic movement, also secularly based, called the Charity Organization Society, took a rational approach to providing charity, seeking and ruling on applications for charitable assistance from service providers and coordinating services through planning. These organizations predated federated fundraising campaigns such as Jewish Federations and United Ways.

The earliest estimate of charitable giving, for 1922, amounted to .6% of Gross National Product (Hammack, 2001). Indications are that charitable giving, through churches and other private charities, was "measurable, if meager" (Hammack, 2001, p. 161) between 1900 and 1930—increasing to about 1% of GNP in 1930, a fraction of giving estimated for all later years. This percentage doubled during the next 30 years, and has stabilized at about 2% (Hammack, 2001). Traditional values of limited government, church-state separation, and low taxes encouraged growth of the private nonprofit sector, which increased to 2.5-3% of the total labor force by 1960 (Hammack, 2001).

Gidron, Kramer, and Salamon write that the relationship between government and the voluntary sector has been a zero-sum game in that the growth of the welfare state in the half-century since the Depression occurred at the expense of the voluntary sector. This observation conjured up the statement they attribute to President Reagan in 1981 that "We have let government take away those things that were once ours to do voluntarily" (in Gidron, Kramer and Salamon, 1992, p. 5). In direct contradiction, Hall (1987) writes that "Overall, the growth of the welfare state after 1936 appears to have stimulated rather than discouraged the growth of the nonprofit sector, but the direction of its growth changed markedly (Hall, 1987, p. 17). According to Hall (1994), more than 90% of existing nonprofits were founded since World War II (in Scott, 1998).

Lester Salamon validates Hall's perspective when he writes that the Great Depression of the 1930s laid the foundation for the welfare system that exists today in the United States (Salamon, 1999). Salamon writes that local governments and private charitable groups maintained the responsibility for responding to poverty and other social needs that emanated from urbanization and industrialization. The federal role took center stage only after President Franklin Roosevelt responded to need that far outstripped the ability of local governments and private organizations.

Despite landmark federal legislation that provided programs for old age pensions, unemployment insurance, and income maintenance, coverage under these programs was "patchy" (Salamon, 1999, p. 59). Cash assistance payments were held artificially low so as not to compete with salaries paid for agricultural and household jobs.

Hammack (2001) writes that several government policies contributed to the growth of the nonprofit sector in the early to mid 20th century. First, some government decision makers, notably Herbert Hoover, gave preference to business associations to coordinate economic and social activity. This was accomplished by permitting professional associations and private standard-setting bodies (such as the Educational Testing Service) to "regulate" rather than relying on government agencies. Nonprofit sector growth was limited in the 1930s, because the devastated American economy made it difficult for the public to pay for services provided by the sector (Hammack, 2001). One intent of the New Deal was to beef up the voluntary sector through government initiatives, but the U.S. Supreme Court rejected Roosevelt's approach (Hammack, 2001).

It was not until the 1960s when increasing poverty and urban riots spurred a quantum increase in government social welfare spending. Rather than replacing nonprofit organizations as providers of services, the expanded government role in social welfare "promoted, rather than displaced" the nonprofit sector (Salamon, 1999, p. 62). The primary reason was the federal government chose to fund these services using local governments and private organizations, including the nonprofit sector, rather than delivering the services itself.

Despite federal policies encouraging the growth of the sector during this period, state restrictions reined in some of the potential growth. Hammack (2001) points out that many African-Americans were simply denied their rights to form associations prior to the passage of civil rights laws, and dissident groups also were denied legal status. In some states, judges had the right to approve nonprofit charters, and could, and did, arbitrarily deny applications based on sexism, racism, or xenophobia.

A 1982 economic analysis by Lester Salamon and Alan Abramson made it clear that the large increase in the nonprofit sector after 1940 "was in large part funded by government, which depended on private-sector organizations to implement its policies" (Hall, 1992, p. 18). The nonprofit sector, particularly private foundations, was put under increased political scrutiny in the years leading up to the United States' entry into World War II (Hall, 1992). Some political leaders who were committed to keeping the United States on the sidelines perceived a threat from some private foundations and other tax-exempt organizations that were supportive of American intervention.

After the war, the anti-Communist hysteria, fueled by the demagoguery of Sen. Joseph McCarthy, targeted foundations and other exempt organizations to determine if they were using their resources for the purposes for which they were established. The implication was that instead, they were diverting these resources for subversion. In 1952, the 82nd Congress approved H. Res. 561 to launch this investigation. The final report of the Select Committee to Investigate Tax-Exempt Foundations and Comparable Organizations was benign to the sector, but did recommend better public reporting by these organizations.

A follow-up investigation in 1954 raised the issue that unchecked power by unregulated foundations could become a threat to democratic values (Hall, 1992, in Ott, 2001).

These and subsequent political challenges to foundations and other tax-exempt organizations culminated in the sector launching an effort to organize and respond to the Congress. The Council on Foundations was established in 1949 (initially under another name), as well as the Foundation Library Center. As the Congress focused on legislation that would affect nonprofits, the nonprofit sector needed to be able to defend itself with professional and technical responses. As Hall writes, "Quite clearly, quoting Tocqueville to Congress would no longer serve as an effective defense. Future efforts would have to rely on technical language of law and economics that had come to frame the creation of tax policy by the late 1960s" (Hall, 1992).

During the 1970s, scholarly research on the nonprofit sector increased substantially, as public awareness of the sector increased. The Commission on Private Philanthropy and Public Needs, chaired by insurance industry executive John Filer, provided a stimulus for research of the sector (Powell, 1987). This effort was commissioned by John D. Rockefeller in 1973 to respond to a perception that the Nixon Administration was hostile to nonprofits. Some of this alleged hostility was attributed to the fact that President Nixon and his allies felt that staff at nonprofit institutions, such as think tanks and universities, were outspoken critics of the President's Vietnam War policies (Ott, 2001). This seven-volume report detailed the importance of the sector as employers, as a provider of important social services, and as a force in the political life of the nation (Hall, 1987).

Filer summarized the commission's findings in four broad observations:

1. "The voluntary sector is a large and vital part of American society, more important today than ever...

2. "Giving in America involves an immense amount of time and money, is the fundamental underpinning of the voluntary sector, encompasses a wide diversity of relationships between donor, donations, and donee, and is not keeping pace.

3. "Decreasing levels of private giving, increasing costs of non-profit activity and broadening expectations for health, education and welfare services as basic entitlements of citizenship have led to the government's becoming a principal provider of programs and revenues in many areas once dominated by private philanthropy...

4. "Our society has long encouraged 'charitable' nonprofit activity by excluding it from certain tax obligations. But the principal tax encouragement of giving to nonprofit organizations—the charitable deduction in personal income taxes—has been both challenged in some quarters in recent years on grounds of equity and eroded by expansion of the standard deduction" (Van Til, 1988, p. 23).

The report recommended retaining the charitable deduction; expanding it to permit those who take the standard deduction to also deduct charitable contributions; allowing those with incomes under $15,000 to deduct twice their charitable contributions and those with incomes of $15,000-$30,000 to deduct 150% of their contributions; and setting a goal that corporations should give 2% of their pretax net income to charity. The report further recommended requiring all larger charities other than churches to prepare and make available detailed annual reports on their finances, programs, and priorities; requiring all tax-exempt organizations to maintain "arms-length" business relationships with for-profits; delegating to the state governments the duty to regulate intrastate charitable solicitation and establishing a federal system to regulate interstate charitable solicitation; permitting nonprofits other than charities to have the same right to lobby as business organizations; and establishing a permanent national commission on the nonprofit sector (Filer, 1975).

Most importantly, the work gave substance to what, up to then, had been only an idea: that charitable tax-exempt organizations composed a coherent and cohesive 'sector' of American political, economic, and social life. This unified conception of nonprofits as part of a 'third,' 'independent,' or 'nonprofit' —or, as the commission preferred to call it, 'voluntary'—sector lay the groundwork for establishing organizations that could give its common interests unified expression (Hall, 1992).

There has been little literature addressing nonprofit institutions as a distinct sector; most of the literature has examined particular fields, such as education, health care, and social welfare (Hall, 1987). Although the Filer Commission sought to show the nonprofit sector as having some autonomy, the government funding cuts of the Reagan era demonstrated the interdependence of the voluntary sector (Hall, 1987).

Much of the current literature on nonprofit organizations is generated by members of the Association for Research on Nonprofit Organizations and Voluntary Action (ARNOVA), an international, interdisciplinary network of scholars and nonprofit leaders formed in 1971 (initially as the Association of Nonprofit Scholars) to foster the creation, application, and dissemination of research relating to the nonprofit sector on voluntary action. There are around 1,500 members of ARNOVA, and hundreds of academic papers were presented at the organization's 2013 conference in Hartford, CT.

In 1976, Yale University initiated an interdisciplinary research program based at the Institution for Social and Policy Studies to study the role, character, organization, and impact of the nonprofit sector (Powell, 1987).

The Carter Administration resisted a recommendation of the Filer Commission to create a quasi-governmental agency in the Treasury Department to formulate public policy that would apply to the nonprofit sector. The reason for this resistance was, ostensibly, to keep public policy on the sector from being too highly influenced by the political process.

Almost simultaneously with the election of Ronald Reagan, the nonprofit sector established a major national trade association, Independent Sector, to represent its divergent political interests. Independent Sector was formed in 1980 with a formal mission statement: "To promote, strengthen, and advance the nonprofit and philanthropic community to foster private initiative for the public good" (Independent Sector, 2002). Today, it serves as the chief nexus for advocacy on behalf of the sector, and represents about 600 national organizations, foundations, and corporate philanthropy programs, collectively representing tens of thousands of charitable groups in every state across the nation (Independent Sector, 2014).

As pointed out previously (see page 41), there is a direct link between government spending for social welfare and revenues received by nonprofit organizations as a result of public policy favoring limited government. By the end of the 1970s, increasing federal deficits spurred selective cuts in domestic spending, translating into braking a decade and a half of accelerated federal social welfare spending (Salamon, 1999).

In 1980, federal government support of nonprofit organizations reached $40.4 billion. State and local governments also made sizable contributions to nonprofit organization revenues (Salamon, 1999).

The election of President Reagan launched "a much more basic assault" (Salamon, 1999, p. 64) on this spending. Putting aside health and pension expenditures, federal social welfare spending declined by 17% (adjusted for inflation), and state and local government social welfare spending declined by 10% during 1977-1982. The Reagan Administration justified some of the reductions on the basis that nonprofit organizations would have more opportunities to meet human needs and that private donations could fill any gaps left by government retrenchment.

Research studies summarized by Salamon (1999) indicate that the nonprofit sector did undergo a rapid expansion during the 1977-1996 period, but that this expansion was not fueled by increases in charitable donations. Rather, the increase in revenues by social service organizations came from commercial income, such as from fees, investment income, and sales of products. Despite the changing character of nonprofits during this period, the sector expanded at a rate much faster than the nation's economy. The Gross Domestic Product (GDP) of the United States increased by 62% from 1977-1996. In comparison, total nonprofit sector revenues increased by 96%.

> *Increasing American affluence is certainly one key explanation of the nonprofit expansion. An increasingly wealthy American population buys more nonprofit services than ever; revenues from fees and charges now account for about half of all nonprofit income* (Hammack, 2001).

Hammack points out that increasing affluence resulted in the purchase of more services. Since these organizations provided services rather than goods generally, the fact that the share of services comprising GDP increased from just over 8% in 1950 to nearly 20% in 1990 translated to more business for the sector. When compounded by the increase in services purchased by government, the result was a tripling of the nonprofit share of the U.S. economy between 1945 and 1990.

In 1992, the administration of President George Herbert Walker Bush participated in a bipartisan effort to create the National Civilian Community Corps "as a demonstration program to explore the possibility of using post-Cold War resources to help solve problems here at home" (Washington Commission for National and Community Service, 2012).

On September 21, 1993, President Clinton signed into law the *National and Community Service Trust Act*. This legislation created the Corporation for National Service, which administers the AmeriCorps and several other programs. These programs promote service-learning and national service.

Beginning with the Clinton Administration, serious proposals came from the White House to expand the ability of religious-based social service organizations to receive federal funding. A so-called "Charitable Choice" provision was included in Section 104 of the 1996 welfare reform legislation, *Personal Responsibility and Work Opportunity Act of 1996*. The section permitted faith-based organizations to be eligible to receive government funds for social services, and prohibited states from placing constraints on these organizations with respect to the display of religious arts, icons, scripture or other symbols as a condition for receiving a federal contract (Lindner, 2003).

The proposed *Charitable Choice Act of 1999* provided that faith-based organizations accepting government funds would not be required to change their religious character, systems of internal governance, or requirements that employees follow religious teachings. President Clinton's antipoverty proposals, dubbed the New Markets/Renewal Communities Agreement, also included charitable choice provisions. He proposed opening a percentage of program funding to competitive bidding for faith-based organizations (Wilson, 2001).

Nine days after his swearing in, President George W. Bush signed an executive order creating the Centers for Faith-Based and Community Initiatives in the Departments of Health and Human Services, Housing and Urban Development, Labor,

Justice, and Education. The President signed two other executive orders related to this initiative. The first created the White House Office of Faith-Based and Community Initiatives. The order authorized the head of this office to report directly to the President. The purpose of the second executive order was to clear bureaucratic barriers "that make private groups hesitate to work with government" (White House, 2001). In his official remarks launching the proposal, the President said:

> *It is one of the great goals of my administration to invigorate the spirit of involvement and citizenship. We will encourage faith-based and community programs without changing their mission. We will help all in their work to change hearts while keeping a commitment to pluralism* (White House, 2001).

In his 2002 State of the Union address, months after the September 11 terrorist attacks, President Bush called on each American to dedicate at least 4,000 hours of service during his or her lifetime to community service. He launched the USA Freedom Corps, charged with building "a culture of service, responsibility, and citizenship" (White House, 2002).

In April 2003, the Senate passed some proposals of President Bush's Faith-Based Initiative as part of the *Charity Aid, Recovery, and Empowerment* (CARE) *Act* (White House, 2003), but did not approve two key elements supported by the President—to allow the government to directly fund the social service programs of houses of worship and allow these institutions to conduct taxpayer-funded social service programs in locations inundated with religious icons, texts, and sacred scriptures. The intent of the legislation was to promote, chiefly through tax incentives, a healthy increase in charitable giving to both secular and nonsecular institutions.

In June and July 2004, the Senate Finance Committee, chaired by Sen. Charles Grassley (R-IA), held hearings beginning a national debate on the role of the federal government in regulating and monitoring philanthropy, and to curb abuses in the sector. Senate committee staff prepared more than 200 potential reforms (Wolverton, 2004). Among the committee chairman's targets of criticism during the following two years included the entire hospital industry, the American Red Cross, and American University. In January 2007, Democrats recaptured majority control of the Senate (with the help of one elected as an Independent), and the chairmanship of the Senate Finance Committee switched from Sen. Grassley to Sen. Max Baucus (D-MT). Sen. Baucus publicly stated that under his leadership, reform of the nonprofit sector would not be a high priority (Perry, 2007).

Scandals continue to plague the nonprofit sector. One of the most visible in recent years involved the advocacy organization ACORN, particularly because of its ties to Democratic candidates. One aspect of this scandal that was particularly troublesome was that once the embezzlement of hundreds of thousands of dollars was uncovered, ACORN officials covered it up for eight years (Mowbray, 2008). In my home state of Pennsylvania, a powerful state senator was indicted in February 2007 on 139 federal counts stemming from alleged abuses involving charities he founded. He served 55 months in prison (Loeb, 2013). Perhaps the most visible national scandal involving charities was the largest Ponzi scheme in history in which Bernie Madoff, according to the court-appointed trustee with the job of finding any hidden assets and distributing them to their rightful owners, bilked hundreds of charities of approximately $20 billion (Smith, 2009). Madoff pleaded guilty and is serving a 150-year sentence in federal prison, little consolation to the hundreds of charities that were crippled as a result of investing their endowments.

In October 2004, the Congress enacted legislation authorizing the National Institute of Standards and Technology (NIST) to expand the Malcolm Baldrige National Quality Award Program to include nonprofit and government organizations. The program solicited applications from nonprofit organizations in 2006 for a pilot program, and two of the five award winners in 2007 went to nonprofit organizations (Baldrige National Quality Program, 2007). A 2013 award winner, California's Sutter Davis Hospital, is a nonprofit organization, but won the award in the health care category.

In 2006, the National Council of Nonprofit Associations (NCNA) began organizing The Nonprofit Congress for the purpose of bringing together nonprofit leaders to "forge a common identity based on shared values, to develop a unified vision and message, and exercise a collective voice." Approximately 500 nonprofit delegates gathered in Washington, D.C. in October 2006 to create a policy platform for the sector and strategize for outreach and united action (Nonprofit Congress, 2006). A subsequent conference was held in Washington, DC in 2008. The 2009 Nonprofit Congress scheduled for New Orleans, Louisiana was abruptly cancelled, attributed to a weak economy and projected poor attendance. NCNA indicated it was abandoning this initiative.

On February 17, 2009, President Barack Obama signed into law the American Recovery and Reinvestment Act (ARRA) of 2009, P.L. 111-5. Included in the $787 billion law with the goal of jumpstarting a declining economy was a grant program for capacity building for existing nonprofit organizations, and organizations that fund them, such as state and local governments. The Strengthening Communities Fund, administered by the Department of Health and Human Services (HHS), is comprised of two programs, both of which are intended to boost the capacity of community and faith-based organizations to engage in activities such as job training and retention and access to state and federal benefits. All grants are one-time, two-year awards. The first program, the State, Local, and Tribal Government Capacity Building Program, provides funds for government entities, which then in turn work with community-based organizations. The second, the Nonprofit Capacity Building Program funds intermediary agencies, which also work with community organizations to enhance their economic recovery activities. On September 30, 2009, HHS announced its grant recipients under the program, awarding $46 million to 84 recipients (U.S. Department of Health and Human Services, 2009). It is not clear if funding for this program will be reauthorized.

In 2010, the IRS informed hundreds of thousands of small nonprofit organizations that they were in danger of losing their federal tax exemptions because they had not complied with their legal obligation to file the 990-N e-postcard. This filing for tax-exempt organizations with gross income of $25,000 or less annually was authorized by the *Pension Protection Act of 2006*. The Act requires organizations to lose their exemptions automatically if they fail to file for three consecutive years. With perhaps as many as 320,000 organizations missing the May 17 filing deadline, the IRS offered a one-time extension in filing, providing organizations that missed the deadline the opportunity to comply by October 15, 2010. According to the IRS, 275,000 organizations had their exemptions automatically revoked in 2011 and posted their names on a Web site with a searchable database at: *http://apps.irs.gov/app/eos/mainSearch.do?mainSearchChoice=revoked&dispatchMethod=selectSearch*

As a result of a 2010 Supreme Court decision *(Citizens United v. FCC)* striking down political spending limits on corporations, applications to the IRS for 501(c)(4) status, the tax exemption reserved for social welfare organizations, doubled. 501(c)(4) organizations are not required to disclose the names of their donors, which many organizations forming for the purpose of funding political campaigns find attractive. Although 501(c)(4) organizations may engage in partisan political activities, organizations whose primary purpose is this activity are not permitted to qualify for 501(c)(4) status. Later that same year, the IRS began screening applications from organizations applying for 501(c)(4) status based solely on the name of the organization. The ostensible justification provided for doing so was that organizations with particular words in their name, such as "Tea Party" or "Patriots," were likely to have been formed principally to engage in political activities, and thus should not eligible for this status (Condon, 2014).

Congressional critics of the IRS charged that the agency was targeting conservative nonprofit groups for political reasons, not responding at all to many applications for months (and in some cases, three years), and requesting unnecessary information from applications. Defenders of the IRS responded that there was no evidence of White House involvement or political motivation, that the IRS also took similar actions against organizations with names suggesting support for liberal causes, and that the IRS was simply taking a shortcut to delay or deny exempt status to organizations that were most likely not to qualify. The issue became quite controversial, being the subject of at least four congressional committee investigations, one by the Justice Department, and one by the Inspector General of the Treasury Department. The Inspector General concluded that the IRS—

1) allowed inappropriate criteria to be developed and stay in place for more than 18 months, 2) resulted in substantial delays in processing certain applications, and 3) allowed unnecessary information requests to be issued (Treasury Inspector General, 2013).

This scandal was front-page news for months during 2013 through 2014, and resulted in the resignation, forced retirement, firing, or reassignment of several top IRS employees. Among them was Lois Lerner, director of the Tax Exempt and Government Entities Division at the IRS, who took the Fifth Amendment during two appearances before Congressional committees investigating the scandal. Ms. Lerner announced her retirement in September 2013, after being on paid leave for more than three months (Ohlemacher, 2014, Martasko, 2014, Condon, 2014).

In November 2013, the IRS proposed new rules to clarify what activities are permissible with respect to qualifying for 501(c)(4) tax-exempt status. These rules generated more than 150,000 comments, the most responses to an IRS proposed rule in history (Internal Revenue Service, 2014).

Discussion Questions

1. Why was President Richard M. Nixon perceived as hostile to the nonprofit sector? Do any of these reasons seem to influence political leaders today? Do you think that the current Administration in Washington is supportive or hostile to the nonprofit sector?

2. Why does Harvard University, with billions of dollars in assets in its endowment fund, deserve to be exempt from property taxes, and have donors to its endowment fund qualify for a deduction on their personal income taxes?

3. Why did so many of the so-called "robber barons" donate generously to establish nonprofit institutions, rather than simply keep the money for themselves and their families?

4. Do you think that the growth of federal spending for the welfare state in the mid-20th century stimulated or hindered the growth of the nonprofit sector in the United States?

5. Do any of the recommendations of the Filer Commission have relevance today?

Activities

1. Research advocacy efforts, both pro and con, on the Bush Administration's Faith-Based Initiatives, and which members of your state's Congressional delegation are supporting and opposing it.

2. Visit the Web sites of nonprofit advocacy organizations such as Independent Sector, the National Council of Nonprofit Associations, your state's nonprofit association, and others, and research which public policy issues are on the agenda that they perceive to be worthy of active advocacy.

3. Research the Congressional debates on the various Istook Amendments, which were intended to place limitations on advocacy efforts by nonprofit organizations. What are the major arguments that were made in favor of, and in opposition to, these amendments?

4. Research the history of organizations established to serve the political and social needs of particular minority communities—particularly with respect to any resistance among those who viewed their establishment as a threat to the political status quo.

Online Resources to Explore

An Abbreviated History of the Philanthropic Tradition in the United States
http://www.elkhartccf.org/about/early-philanthropy

Yale University School of Medicine Medical Library: New Haven's Hospitals
http://doc.med.yale.edu/library/news/exhibits/hospitals/

IUPUI Philanthropy Studies Historical Collections
http://www.ulib.iupui.edu/special/collections/philanthropy

US History.Org's Virtual Tour of Historic Philadelphia
http://www.ushistory.org/tour/pennsylvania-hospital.htm

References

Anderson, R. (1973). Voluntary associations in history: From paleolithic to present times. In D. H. Smith (Ed.). *Voluntary action research: 1973* (pp. 9-28). Lexington, MA: Lexington Books.

Bakal, C. (1979). *Charity U.S.A.* New York: Times Books.

Baldrige National Quality Program. (2007). *Update: December 2007.* Author. Retrieved from *http://www.baldrige.nist.gov/PDF_files/Update.12_07.pdf*

Block, S. R. (1990). A history of the discipline. In J. Ott (Ed.). *The nature of the nonprofit sector* (pp. 152-156). Boulder, CO: Westview Press.

Columbo, J. D., & Hall, M. A. (1995). *The charitable tax exemption.* Boulder, CO: Westview Press.

Condon, S. (2014). The IRS targeting scandal: 4 things to know. June 28, 2014. Retrieved from *http://www.cbsnews.com/news/the-irs-targeting-scandal-4-things-to-know*

Douglas, J. (1987). Political theories of nonprofit organizations. In J. S. Ott (Ed.). *The Nature of the Nonprofit Sector.* Boulder, CO: Westview Press.

Dull, D. (2004). *Text of the rosetta stone.* Retrieved from *http://www.daviddull.com/firstsite/rosetta.html*

Filer, J. H. (1975). The Filer commission report—Giving in America: Toward a stronger voluntary sector. In J. S. Ott (Ed.). *The nature of the nonprofit sector.* Boulder, CO: Westview Press.

Franklin, B. (1964). *The autobiography of Benjamin Franklin.* New Haven, CT: Yale University Press.

Gidron, B., Kramer, R. M., & Salamon, L. (Eds.). (1992). *Government and the third sector.* San Francisco: Jossey-Bass.

Hall, P. D. (1987). A historical overview of the private nonprofit sector. In W. Powell (Ed.). *The nonprofit sector: A research handbook.* New Haven, CT: Yale University Press.

Hall, P. D. (1992). Inventing the nonprofit sector: 1950-1990. In J. S. Ott (Ed.). T*he Nature of the Nonprofit Sector.* Boulder, CO: Westview Press.

Hammack, D. C. (2001). Introduction: Growth, transformation, and quiet revolution in the nonprofit sector over two centuries. *Nonprofit and Voluntary Sector Quarterly, 2,* 157-173.

Horne, C. F. (2001). The code of Hammurabi: Introduction. Retrieved from *http://www.fordham.edu/halsall/ancient/hamcode.html*

Independent Sector. (2002). About us: Independent Sector's mission, vision, and statement of values. Retrieved from *http://www.independentsector.org/mission_and_values*

Independent Sector. (2014). *About us.* Retrieved from *http://www.independentsector.org/about*

Internal Revenue Service. (2014). IRS update on the proposed new regulation on 501(c)(4) organizations, May 22, 2014. Retrieved from *http://www.irs.gov/uac/Newsroom/IRS-Update-on-the-Proposed-New-Regulation-on-501%28c%29%284%29-Organizations*

James, E. (1987). The nonprofit sector in comparative perspective. In W. Powell (Ed.). *The nonprofit sector: A research handbook* (pp. 397-415). New Haven, CT: Yale University Press.

King, L. W. (1910). Hammurabi's Laws. Retrieved from *http://www.mythome.org/hammurabicoedicil.html*

Lindner, E. W. (2001). Considering charitable choice. In *The yearbook of American and Canadian churches.* Retrieved from *http://www.ncccusa.org/news/01news10a.html*

Loeb, P. (2013). Former Pa. Sen. Vince Fumo to be released from prison next week. Retrieved from *http://philadelphia.cbslocal.com/2013/08/02/former-senator-fumo-to-be-released-from-prison-next-week/*

Martosko, D. (July 2014). Lois Lerner, embattled official at the heart of IRS tea party scandal, retires with full pension likely worth more than $50,000 as an internal review called for her firing. *Mail Online,* July 11, 2014. Retrieved from *http://www.dailymail.co.uk/news/article-2430174/Lois-Lerner-embattled-official-heart-IRS-tea-party-scandal-retire-pension-likely-50-000-year-Congress-seeks-answers.html*

Mowbray, Rebecca. (2008). ACORN'S first hearing cancelled. *The Times-Picayune.* October 3, 2008. Retrieved from *http://www.nola.com/timespic/stories/index.ssf?/base/money-1/1223011241131460.xml*

Nonprofit Congress. (2006). *Nonprofit Congress: Many missions, one voice.* Retrieved from *http://www2.guidestar.org/rxa/news/articles/2006/nonprofit-congress-many-missions-one-voice.aspx?articleId=742*

Ohlemacher, S. (2014). Lois Lerner pleads the fifth at IRS hearing. Retrieved from *http://www.huffingtonpost.com/2014/03/05/lois-lerner-pleads-the-fifth_n_4903783.html*

Ott, J. S. (2001). *The nature of the nonprofit sector.* Boulder, CO: Westview Press.

Perry, S. (2007). No Senate effort to curb charity abuses expected. *Chronicle of Philanthropy.* August 23, 2007. Retrieved from *http://philanthropy.com/premium/articles/v19/i21/21004401.htm*

Powell, W. (Ed.) (1987). *The nonprofit sector: A research handbook.* New Haven, CT: Yale University Press.

Salamon, L. (1999). *America's nonprofit sector: A primer.* (Second Ed.). Washington, DC: The Foundation Center.

Scott, J. T. (1998). Voluntary sector. In J. S. Ott (Ed.). *The nature of the nonprofit sector.* Boulder, CO: Westview Press.

Smith, A. (2009). *Madoff's victims: One year later.* CNN Money.com. Retrieved from *http://money.cnn.com/2009/12/10/news/companies/madoff_ponzi_victims/index.htm*

The White House. (2001, January 29). Remarks by the president in announcement of the faith-based initiative. Retrieved from *http://georgewbush-whitehouse.archives.gov/news/releases/20010129-5.html*

The White House. (2002). USA Freedom Corps: Strengthening service to meet community needs. Retrieved from *http://georgewbush-whitehouse.archives.gov/infocus/bushrecord/factsheets/needs.html*

The White House. (2003). President commends senate passage of faith-based legislation. Retrieved from *http://georgewbush-whitehouse.archives.gov/news/releases/2003/04/20030409-2.html*

Tocqueville, A. de. (1835/1956). *Democracy in America* (R.D. Heffner, Ed.). New York: Penguin Books.

Treasury Inspector General. (2013). Inappropriate criteria were used to identify tax-exempt applications for review. May 14, 2013. Retrieved from *http://www.treasury.gov/tigta/auditreports/2013reports/201310053fr.pdf*

U.S. Department of Health and Human Services. (2009). *HHS awards $46 million in recovery act funds to create jobs and spur economic improvement.* Press release of 9/30/2009, HHS. Retrieved from *http://www.acf.hhs.gov/press/hhs-awards-46-million-in-recovery-act-funds-to-create-jobs-and-spur-economic*

Van Til, J. (1988). *Mapping the third sector: Volunteerism in a changing social economy.* New York: The Foundation Center.

Washington Commission for National and Community Service. (2012). *A brief history of national and community service.* Retrieved from *http://www.ofm.wa.gov/servewa/about/history.asp*

Wellford, W. H., & Gallagher, J. (1988). *Unfair competition? The challenge to charitable tax exemption.* Washington, DC: The National Assembly of Voluntary Health and Social Welfare Organizations.

Wilson, S. (2001). *Election year proposals affecting charities: A prelude to future legislation?* Retrieved from *http://www.urban.org/publications/310255.html*

Wolverton, B. (2004). Rethinking charity rules. *Chronicle of Philanthropy*, 16(19), July 22, 2004, p. 31. Retrieved from *http://philanthropy.com/article/Rethinking-Charity-Rules/62353/*

Chapter 3
Theory of the Nonprofit Sector

> **Synopsis:** Economic models of nonprofit organization formation and behavior dominate current thinking. These models have serious flaws and drawbacks. Among the leading theories explaining the existence of nonprofits are government failure, market failure, contract failure, and externality theory. Pluralistic theory and the Theory of the Commons are alternatives to these economic theories.

Theories relating to nonprofit organizations have tended to focus on two phenomena—how they are created and how they behave once they are created. They can be further differentiated by whether they are economic, i.e., based on economic self-interest, or noneconomic theories.

One economic model explains the existence of the sector as a response to the failure of government. The Weisbrod Model (see below under "Public Goods Theory") falls in this category. A competing economic theory explains the existence of the sector as a response to information differences between the buyer and seller (referred to in the literature as information asymmetries) and transaction costs in the for-profit sector. Henry Hansmann's theories fit into this category.

Another economic model theorizes that individual entrepreneurs take advantage of the special treatment afforded to nonprofit organizations (such as tax treatment, the halo effect, cheaper postage rates, and perceived lack of direct competition) as a way to further their individual goals and agendas. The research by Dennis Young and Estelle James looks at the personal characteristics of nonprofit executives and attempts to draw some distinctions between their motivations and those of executives who work in other sectors. Among noneconomic theories are those that relate to pluralism, mediating structures, and the "Theory of the Commons."

Some of the leading organizational theories relating to the formation of nonprofit organizations are presented in this chapter.

Economic Theories

1. Public Goods Theory

This economic theory, proposed by Burton Weisbrod, suggests that nonprofit organizations are formed because of "government failure." Government fails to provide enough public goods because of the structure of the democratic process that is tied to the needs of the median voter. This process leaves many voters dissatisfied with the output of government and/or the level of taxation. They address this dissatisfaction in four ways:

- *migration* ("vote with your feet")—This strategy has a high transaction cost (i.e., moving costs, finding employment in another locality, and finding a new house), but people do leave a jurisdiction because of high taxes or the lack of adequate services (such as a substandard school system).

- *formation of a lower level of government*—Voters may take action to break away from a jurisdiction and form their own municipal government, or address the lack of services provided by a state government by convincing a local government to provide them (such as may be the case with a park or library).

- *seek private market alternatives*—An example is hiring private security guards to patrol a housing development if public police protection is considered inadequate, or to install fences, better locks, and alarms. In many cases, Weisbrod points out that there are private alternatives to collective goods (also called public goods, defined as goods that are provided by government and which cannot be practically excluded from one citizen without withholding them from all citizens), even though these may be economically inefficient to produce.

- *create voluntary organizations to provide collective goods*—Weisbrod theorizes that public demand for a collective good will first be fulfilled by a voluntary agency, until the demand increases to the extent that the service is demanded by the median voter, at which point the government will consider providing it. He points to the fact that services provided by voluntary organizations in 16th century England included schools, hospitals, fire-fighting apparatus, parks, bridges, dikes, libraries, care of prisoners in jails, and charity to the poor (Weisbrod, 1975, in Rose-Ackerman, 1986).

This process can be facilitated when subgroups, such as those of a particular religion or culture, desire goods that the government is unwilling or unable to provide.

The Weisbrod theory of government failure predicts that the nonprofit sector will be most active where citizen populations are most diverse, and that nonprofit organizations are important for satisfying the service needs of political minorities (Douglas, 1987).

2. Market Failure Theory

Nonprofit organizations may form as a result of market failure. Burton Weisbrod and Henry Hansmann are among those who wrote extensively on market failure explanations of nonprofit organization formation. Market failure occurs when the private market demand for a good or service is too low to encourage private firms to provide it—because they would fail to make a profit (or the opportunity cost for investing in the provision of a high-demand good or service would be higher). If the good or service is provided by a nonprofit, that organization can have access to private donations and be exempt from taxes that a for-profit would have to pay.

Thus, a nonprofit organization might form to pay for a meals-on-wheels service, leveraging government grants, private donations, and minimal fees from homebound elderly who use the service. Such a service would not otherwise be economically efficient for a for-profit provider to offer.

3. Market Failure And High Transaction Costs

The United States has adopted a European pattern of responding to the private market's failure to provide for collective goods by first regulating the private sector, and then taking over the function when that does not work. However, there are problems that arise that involve both market failure and the government being unwilling or unable to take over the function. Rather than being an intermediate step between private regulation and government takeover, nonprofit intervention is a generic alternative (Wellford and Gallagher, 1988, p. 11).

According to this model, government is too bureaucratic, takes too long to solve a problem, and lacks the ability to respond to local problems. Government's transaction costs are too high compared with the nonprofit sector—such as the time it takes to build a political consensus, enact authorizing legislation, provide appropriations and develop regulations, issue and distribute checks, provide for fiscal accountability of the program, evaluate the program, and so on.

Furthermore, according to this model, government could not politically afford to move too quickly, because it would run the risk of compelling citizens to pay taxes for services of which they do not approve. Thus, nonprofit organizations can effectively fill this void. Wellford and Gallagher have written extensively about this theory.

4. Externality Theory

One way of looking at the formation and role of some nonprofit organizations is to view them in the context of externalities. This term is used by economists to describe the costs and benefits of a market transaction that accrue to those who are not direct parties to the transaction. For example, a battery maker charges a price for its batteries, which is approximately the same regardless of the consumer's geographical location. However, the people who live near the battery plant experience both positive and negative externalities from the plant.

Negative externalities might include the increased healthcare costs of breathing in pollutants emitted from the plant, decreased property values as a result of the pollution, loss of recreational opportunities because fish in the streams have high levels of mercury, higher stress levels from noise made by the plant, and higher commuting times during rush hour as hundreds of workers drive to and from the plant. Positive externalities might include lower costs of searching for employment, financial support for local community organizations, leadership of community organizations provided by executives who have relocated to work at the plant, and better schools as a result of property tax payments made by the plant's owners, and increased advocacy for schools from those who work at the plant.

Many nonprofit organizations are formed for the purpose of addressing externality issues, both positive and negative. For example, a nonprofit organization might be formed by residents in a community who object to a proposal to build a Wal-Mart or a McDonald's in their neighborhood. The fear is that while the benefits of having a Wal-Mart will mean profits to that company, externalities—such as putting "Main Street" businesses out of business, creating traffic tie-ups, and contributing to suburban sprawl—will have negative consequences.

Other nonprofit organizations are formed to promote positive externalities. For example, organizations that form to provide recreational activities to at-risk youth, such as midnight basketball, have as one objective the improvement of the quality of life for these youngsters. But an equally compelling objective is to keep youngsters off the streets during high-crime hours. In this case, all businesses and homeowners in the area benefit from the program.

5. Contract Failure Theory

This theory of Henry Hansmann suggests that in cases in which consumers are unable to adequately evaluate the quality or quantity of a service, a nonprofit organization is more likely to be chosen to provide the service. The reason is that the consumer is likely to feel that the nonprofit will not have an incentive to shortchange the customer, because excess revenues will not be distributed to the organization's "owners." In contrast, the for-profit firm has both the incentive and the opportunity to exploit the customer.

In some respects, this theory has its origins in principal-agent theory, which is based upon information imbalances between two parties. The theory is used to explain how to get the employee or contractor (agent) to act in the best interests of the principal—the employer—when the employee or contractor has an informational advantage over the principal and different interests from the principal. Principal-agent theory assumes that parties providing services—the agents—will shirk their responsibilities unless policed, such as by tightly drafted contracts, supervision, or quality control by those purchasing the services—the principals.

Researchers who studied nonprofit and for-profit day care centers found that parents had more trust in nonprofit day care centers. These parents felt that nonprofit centers did not have the incentives to take advantage of them despite the fact that they lacked sufficient information to judge the quality of the centers.

Dennis Young writes of three cases of information asymmetry. The first occurs when the good or service is too complex or technical for the consumer to judge, such as is the case with health care or higher education. The second occurs when the consumer as an individual is not competent to evaluate the good or service, such as might be the case with seeking care in an assisted living arrangement. The third case occurs when the purchaser of the service is not the ultimate consumer, or is not in close contact with the place where the service or goods will be provided—such as when a person seeks to obtain long-term care for an elderly parent located in a distant city, or when a donor seeks to provide disaster relief funds in response to a flood in another part of the country.

As Young points out (in Rose-Ackerman, 1981), there are alternatives to using nonprofit organizations to provide services when there are information dissymmetries, such as government regulation, professional standards for practitioners, accreditation bodies, or using third-party experts—such as insurance claims adjusters, or doctors who work for the health insurer—to reduce the information dissymmetry.

Young suggests that nonprofits are trustworthy not so much because the profits do not accrue to the benefit of the individuals, but rather because leaders of nonprofit organizations are intrinsically different from those of profit-making organizations. They are much more motivated to act in the public interest than feathering their own nests or seeking power.

Another factor that explains why the behavior of nonprofits is more trustworthy than those of for-profits, or at least, is perceived as such by consumers, is that their governing structure is more pluralistic and has more direct influence by those who have an interest in the organization behaving honorably, such as donors, consumers of the services, and community leaders. The existence of this so-called "halo effect" of nonprofits has been verified by empirical research (see page 68).

Colombo and Hall (1995) suggest that charities deserve tax exemptions because of market failure and government failure. Market failure results from the fact that capitalism meets individual needs well, but is not as well-suited to meet collective needs. This is because of "free riders"—those who make no effort to donate money or volunteer time for public goods. Government failure occurs because of the inefficiencies of the political process in allocating goods and services to those who need it.

The nonprofit producer, like its for-profit counterpart, has the capacity to raise prices and cut quality in such cases without much fear of customer reprisal; however, it lacks the incentive to do so because those in charge are barred from taking home any resulting profits (Hansmann, 1980). However, this perspective has been challenged by Bennett and DiLorenzo (1989). They write:

> *A fatal flaw in the "contract failure" rationale ...is the assumption that CNE (commercial nonprofit enterprise) managers cannot benefit from the organization's profits and so will devote all of the organization's resources to improvements in service quality....Managers, board members and others involved with CNE operations can and do personally benefit from the profits. In fact, since competitive pressures are weaker in the nonprofit sector, a strong case can be made that CNE managers are even more prone than private sector managers to use their organization's resources for personal benefit rather than improving service quality* (Bennett and DiLorenzo, 1989, p. 63).

Bennett and DiLorenzo acknowledge that there are generally four rationales for the granting of subsidies to nonprofit organizations—*thin markets* (the demand for goods is too small for private enterprise to make a profit), *public goods* (the goods provided will not be provided by private firms), *contract failure* (consumers cannot judge a product's quality before purchasing it, such as in health care), and the *promotion of equity* (such as serving vulnerable populations)—although they suggest that none of these situations occurs to any great extent.

6. Subsidy Theory

This theory posits that initiation of nonprofits in some fields is encouraged because of the government subsidies that are available to them, such as direct government funding for services, the tax exemption, lower postage rates, the ability to issue tax-exempt bonds, and favorable personnel regulations.

7. Consumer Control Theory

This theory explains why social clubs and cooperatives form nonprofit organizations rather than for-profits. Incorporating as a nonprofit helps patrons maintain control of an organization. Otherwise, the owners of a firm could maintain monopolistic control of a service.

Non-Economic Theories

1. Pluralistic Theory

A theory related to Weisbrod's government failure theories, also attributable to a form of "government failure" (albeit less related to economics), applies even to the case in which government does have the political support to begin providing a collective good. Private, nonprofit organizations may still be called upon to deliver a service when the public perceives that governmental provision of these services would be less politically expensive (even if government could deliver the services with higher economic efficiency). This occurs, as Lester Salamon points out, "because of the cumbersomeness, unresponsiveness, and bureaucratization that often accompanies governmental action" or because of cultural resistance to expanding government.

One example might be the fierce opposition to President Obama's initial plans to increase the federal role for financing health care, with opponents of the plan exploiting the public's skepticism about government expansion while concurrently holding views favorable about Social Security and Medicare. Nonprofit organizations have a history of both being entrepreneurial and responsive to many societal interests when government has, for one reason or another, not been responsive. The social value of freedom and pluralism is highly valued in American society, and the political system is designed to encourage the formation of organizations that can meet a variety of interests. Atkinson (1997) terms this feature of the nonprofit sector a "meta-benefit" that serves as an additional justification for government subsidization beyond the direct benefits provided to the collective.

Lester Salamon's view is that nonprofit organizations are perceived as encouraging individual action for the public good in the same way that business corporations encourage individual action for private gain. Unlike the cookie-cutter approach of government, this theory takes the view that the independence of nonprofit organizations from government fosters values of freedom and pluralism.

> *Even if it were the case that government was far more efficient than the nonprofit sector in responding to citizen needs, Americans would still insist on a vibrant nonprofit sector as a guarantor of their liberties and a mechanism to ensure a degree of pluralism* (Salamon, in Ott, 2001, p. 165).

2. Mediating Structures

Peter Berger and Richard John Newhaus (1977), in *To Empower People: The Role of Mediating Structures in Public Policy,* defined the term "mediating structures" to include those organizations that come between the individual and megastructures, such as large capitalist conglomerates, labor unions, and government. These mediating structures, such as families, neighborhoods, religious institutions, and voluntary associations, help shape cultural values in a positive way, and thus should be encouraged by government public policy.

Through mediating structures, people are drawn to seeking the well-being of others. This contrasts with many other popular theories that emphasize self-interest. "Meaning and purpose is found in individual private life, while public life is impersonal, unsatisfying, and ultimately seems illegitimate. Mediating structures are a means of overcoming this" (Pennings, 2003).

3. Theory of the Commons

Roger Lohmann (1992) defines the "commons" as "an economic, political, and social space outside the market, households, and state in which associative communities create and reproduce social worlds"—defined as "the images, meanings and sense of reality shared by autonomous, self-defining collectivities of voluntarily associating individuals." In the commons, transactions are governed by a basic norm of fairness rather than by a quid pro quo norm of the marketplace or equity in democratic governments (in Ott, p. 172).

Those in the commons share a common language, common training/education, and a common culture that transcends the marketplace dominated by maximizing individual utility.

In contrast to virtually all other nonprofit theories, Lohmann limits his Theory of the Commons to exclude those nonprofit organizations, formal or not, that are engaged in "unproductive or volunteer labor." This is regardless of whether they are incorporated, have employees, or are included in national data about the voluntary sector. The term "unproductive labor" can be traced to Adam Smith's *Wealth of Nations,* first published in 1776, which was meant to refer to labor that did not add value to "the subject upon which (it) is bestowed."

The common goods produced in the "commons" include religious worship, contemplation, scientific inquiry, helping and charity, artistic expression, play, and many other desirable projects of voluntary-action groups (Lohmann, 1992). The goods produced in the commons are distinguishable from both private goods and public goods in that they are produced for purposes that benefit individuals or groups other than the producer. Lohmann bases his theory on nine initial premises and assumptions:

1. *Social Action.* These organizations engage in social action to which the participant attaches some subjective meaning, ignoring or rejecting a profit orientation in favor of doing something for the good of others.

2. *Affluence.* The participants in these organizations are not primarily concerned with their own self-interest. As a result, it is assumed that the participants are "affluent," Lohmann's term to describe those who do not face any immediate threats to their own safety, security, health, or well-being and thus have the luxury of choosing to engage in behavior that is not self-serving.

3. *Authenticity.* This is an enforced norm in the sector; that is, those who are perceived to be acting in their own self-interest rather than having altruistic motivations are sanctioned by their peers (by, perhaps, being expelled from the organization) or by the state (such as by enforcement of charity fraud laws).

4. *Continuity.* The organizations in the sector engage in rituals and ceremonies, have norms and folkways, and conduct other activities that link the past, the present, and the future.

5. *Rationality.* These organizations make rational decisions—setting goals and objectives and obtaining the resources necessary to meet those goals.

6. *Near–universality.* Most, if not all, human cultures engage in collective action in which individuals voluntarily associate to pursue common objectives outside of markets, households, and government.

7. *Autonomy.* Participants in these organizations exercise both individual and group self-control and create their own autonomous social worlds.

8. *Intrinsic valuation.* The proper way to evaluate these organizations is on the basis of their values, rather than on conventional measures such as, among others, efficiency or effectiveness.

9. *Clarity.* The theory must be stated in language that participants in the sector can understand.

Are Nonprofits Altruistic or Self-Maximizing?

The academic literature is split with respect to the motivations for forming nonprofit organizations and the ways they and those who form them behave. Dennis Young writes:

> *In particular, the rationales for nonprofits offered by Weisbrod (1979), Douglas (1979), and others have a selfless, public-spirited quality to them. Nonprofits are seen as providers of semi-public goods, or as agents of trust for consumers whose abilities to discern quality differences are*

> *impaired. Yet those who have developed explicit models of behavior of nonprofit organizations set quite a different tone. Scholars such as James (1978), Pauly and Redisch (1973), Niskanen (1971), Feigenbaum (1979), Tullock (1966), and Rose-Ackerman (1979) have basically assumed revenue enhancing or other self-seeking objectives on the part of management of various types of nonprofit organizations—universities, hospitals, and charities among them* (Young, in White, 1981, p. 135).

Young suggests that these two competing views of nonprofits may not be inconsistent. The nonprofit may very well have been established for altruistic reasons, but once in operation and the beneficiary of grants, tax advantages, and a monopoly over the delivery of some collective good, some participants "severely test the imposed constraints and manipulate them toward selfish ends" (Young, 1981, p. 136).

Discussion Questions

1. Do you think there is any evidence to support the theory that legislators vote in favor of new programs that benefit "one more than the median voter"? What do you think is the threshold for a legislator voting in support of a new program, and what might be some of the other influences that affect a legislator's vote?

2. Based on what you know to be the requirements for establishing a nonprofit organization in your state and qualifying for federal tax-exempt status, do you believe it should be easier or more difficult for entrepreneurs to establish a new nonprofit, tax-exempt organization?

3. What social problems can you identify either locally, statewide, or nationally, that might benefit from the establishment of a new nonprofit organization, and why would government not be likely to address these problems directly?

4. Compile a list of representative types of nonprofit organizations operating in your community. Which theory or theories best explain why these organizations were formed? Explain.

5. Make a list of collective goods being provided by nonprofit organizations and discuss why anyone is willing to pay anything for a collective good?

Activities

1. Compile a list of nonprofit organizations in your community, and make a list of externalities, if any, that these organizations address. Do these organizations also create externalities that might not have existed otherwise?

2. Select a nonprofit organization with which you have some affiliation, either as a client, volunteer, donor, or member, and discuss how that organization meets, or does not meet, each of the criteria listed in the Theory of the Commons.

3. Put together a survey instrument that seeks to answer the basic question of whether students in your school trust nonprofit organizations more or less than government organizations or for-profit businesses with respect to delivering human services, such as mental health services, day care, nursing home care, or hospital care. With permission and assistance from your professor, administer the survey to a representative sample of those in your school, department, or program.

4. Make a list of collective goods. Then, debate whether these goods are more appropriately delivered by the public sector, nonprofit sector, or both.

Online Resources to Explore

University of Otago, School of Business: Economic Theories of the Voluntary Sector: A Survey of Government Failure and Market Failure Approaches
http://www.business.otago.ac.nz/econ/research/discussionpapers/DP0208.pdf

Institute of Agricultural Development in Central and Eastern Europe: Explaining Nonprofit Organisation: The Social Value Approach
http://www.emes.net/fileadmin/emes/PDF_files/ISTR_EMES_Paris/PS_5/PS5_S3/PS5_S3a_ISTR-EMES_Valentinov.pdf

National Center on Nonprofit Enterprise
http://www.nationalcne.org/

The Paideia Project: Short Circuits and Market Failure: Theories of the Civic Sector
http://www.bu.edu/wcp/Papers/Soci/SociZuid.htm

References

Atkinson, R. (1997). Nonprofit symposium: Theories of the federal income tax exemption for charities: Thesis, antithesis, and synthesis. *Stetson Law Review.* 27 Stetson L. Rev. 395. Fall, 1997. 395-431.

Bennett, J., & DiLorenzo, T. (1989). *Unfair competition: The profits of nonprofits.* Lanham, MD: Hamilton Press.

Berger, P., & Neuhaus, R. (1977). *To empower people: The role of mediating structures in public policy.* Washington, DC: American Enterprise Institute for Public Policy Research.

Colombo, J. D., & Hall, M. A. (1995). *The charitable tax exemption.* Boulder, CO: Westview Press.

Douglas, J. (1987). Political theories of nonprofit organizations. In J. S. Ott (Ed.). *The nature of the nonprofit sector* (pp. 179-189). Boulder, CO: Westview Press.

Hansmann, H. (1980). The role of nonprofit enterprise. *Yale Law Journal* (53): pp. 880.

Lohmann, R. (1992). The theory of the commons. In J. S. Ott (Ed.). *The nature of the nonprofit sector* (pp. 89-95). Boulder, CO: Westview Press.

Ott, J. S. (Ed.). (2001). *The nature of the nonprofit sector,* Boulder, CO: Westview Press.

Pennings, R. (2003). *Kuyper's sphere sovereignty and modern economic institutions.* Retrieved from http://www.cardus.ca/comment/article/192/

Weisbrod, B. A. (1975). Toward a theory of the voluntary nonprofit sector in a three-sector economy. In S. Rose-Ackerman (Ed.). *The economics of nonprofit institutions* (pp. 21-44). New York: Oxford University Press.

Wellford, W. H., & Gallagher, J. (1988). *Unfair competition? The challenge to charitable tax exemption.* Washington, DC: The National Assembly of Voluntary Health and Social Welfare Organizations.

White, M. (1981). *Nonprofit firms in a three-sector economy.* Washington, DC: The Urban Institute.

Young, D. R. (1981). Entrepreneurship and the behavior of nonprofit organizations. In S. Rose-Ackerman (Ed.). *The economics of nonprofit institutions: Studies in structure and policy* (pp. 161-184). New York: Oxford University Press.

Chapter 4
Legal and Regulatory Issues

> **Synopsis:** Nonprofit organizations are typically established by incorporating them, which includes filing Articles of Incorporation and supporting documents with a state authority. It is desirable to quickly achieve federal tax-exempt status for those organizations that are eligible. Most states regulate charitable solicitation.

Introduction to Incorporation

There is no legal requirement that organizations incorporate in order to successfully fulfill their missions of serving the public. However, incorporation provides many distinct advantages, so most organizations will want to accomplish this quickly. Incorporation also has some disadvantages.

Advantages of Incorporation

1. Limited Liability. Of all the reasons to seek corporate status, this is perhaps the most compelling. Under most state laws, the officers, directors, employees, and members of a corporation, except under very limited and unusual circumstances, are not personally liable for lawsuit judgments and debts relating to the organization. Thus, the personal assets of the organization's executive director or board members are not at risk in the event there is a successful suit against the corporation, or in the event the organization goes out of business while owing money to creditors. Assets of an organization may be minuscule, although the individuals running it may have substantial assets. Corporate status protects those personal assets. Many people will not even consider participating in the leadership of an organization unless their personal assets are shielded by incorporation.

2. Tax Advantages. Income accruing to an individual running an organization is subject to federal, state, and local taxes at the individual rate, which can be substantially more than the corporate rate. In the case of nonprofit incorporation, an organization can be exempt from many taxes, depending upon its type.

For organizations that are charitable, educational, religious, literary, or scientific, 501(c)(3) tax-exempt status is particularly attractive. Many types of charitable institutions, such as colleges and hospitals, which have substantial property holdings, would be taxed beyond their ability to operate if they were denied tax exemptions. Many funding sources, such as government, foundations, and the public, will not make grants or contributions to an organization that is not federally tax exempt under Section 501(c)(3) of the Internal Revenue Code, since this status provides a tax-exemption to the contributor and assures that there is at least some minimal level of accountability on behalf of the organization.

3. Structure, Accountability, Perpetuity, and Legally Recognized Authority. When people and organizations interact with a bona fide corporation, they have confidence that there is some order and authority behind the decision-making of that entity. A reasonable expectation exists that the corporation will continue to honor agreements even if the principal actor for the organization dies, resigns, or otherwise disassociates himself or herself from the organization. They know that there is a legal document governing decision-making (as detailed in the bylaws), succession of officers, clear purposes (as detailed in the Articles of Incorporation), a system for paying bills, accounting for income and expenses, and a forum for the sharing of ideas on policy and direction from the corporation's board members. So long as the necessary papers are filed, the organization will continue in perpetuity regardless of changes in leadership. This gives such organizations an aura of immortality, which is seen as an advantage in planning beyond the likely tenure of an individual board chairperson or executive director.

4. Ancillary Benefits. Nonprofit incorporation can provide lower postage rates; access to media (through free public service announcements); volunteers, who would be more hesitant volunteering for a comparable for-profit entity; and the so-called "halo effect," in which the public is more willing to do business with a nonprofit because of a real or perceived view that such an organization is founded and operated in the public interest. Charities are often eligible for free or discounted goods and services, such as computer equipment and software.

5. Strength of Collegial Decision-Making. Decision-making in an autocracy is clearly easier and more efficient than in an organization run as a democracy. Yet, there is a value in making decisions by building a consensus among a majority of members of a diverse, volunteer, community-based board. Members of a board often bring different experience and talents and provide information that would otherwise not be available in making decisions. Issues are often raised that, if overlooked, could possibly result in disastrous consequences for the organization.

Disadvantages of Incorporation

1. Loss of Centralized Control. Many organizations are formed and run by a charismatic leader with a vision of how to accomplish a particular task or mission. Decision-making is enhanced without the distractions of the scores of issues that relate not to the actual mission of the organization but to maintaining the organization itself. The very act of forming a nonprofit corporation can be draining—preparing and filing Articles of Incorporation; negotiating bylaws; finding quality colleagues to serve on a board of directors; hiring qualified staff, if necessary; and dealing with the myriad of issues that emanate from hiring staff, preparing budgets, raising money, and preparing minutes of board meetings. Even finding a convenient time and place where the board can meet to ensure that a quorum is present can pose a troublesome and potentially overwhelming problem at times.

Incorporation is a legal framework that trades off the advantages addressed earlier in this section with some serious disadvantages. Decisions can no longer be made in a vacuum by one person without oversight or accountability, but are legally under the purview of a board of directors. Decisions have to withstand scrutiny of *all* persons on the board, some of whom may be hostile or have personal axes to grind. By definition, boards of directors are committees, and committees often make decisions that are compromises in order to mollify members with divergent viewpoints and competing interests.

For those used to making quick decisions "on the fly" and who revel in not having those decisions subject to second-guessing, modification, or otherwise being meddled with, incorporation can be a personally shackling experience and can dilute one's control over the organization.

2. Paperwork, Paperwork, Paperwork. Even in the smallest nonprofit corporation, the paperwork load related to corporate status can at times be overwhelming. There are deadlines for virtually every filing. Keeping ahead of the paperwork wave requires discipline, commitment, and a sense of humor. Forms get misfiled or lost in the bureaucracy or in the mail.

Failure to handle this paperwork can result in criminal penalties, in some cases. There are penalties for missed filings (e.g., failure to file a timely 990 federal tax return results in a $20/day penalty, up to a maximum of $10,000, or 5% of the organization's gross revenues, whichever is smaller—and $100/day up to $50,000 for organizations with annual gross receipts exceeding $1 million). Even the smallest tax-exempt organization can lose its exemption if it does not electronically file a 990-N e-postcard at least once every three years. As soon as the first employee is hired, the paperwork wave accompanying that addition is substantial.

In the first year, the filings can be intimidating, time-consuming, and frustrating. A new corporation must develop a bookkeeping system that is understandable by the accountant who will perform the audit and prepare the financial reports, pass resolutions, file forms to open up corporate savings and checking accounts, order checks, file tax returns, and pay taxes.

There are many different federal, state, and local taxes, each of which requires its own filing at varying times of the year. A new corporation must also reconcile savings and checking accounts, prepare board meeting announcements and minutes, devise a system to pay bills, and establish a process for the reimbursement of expenses. Other tasks the corporation must accomplish are filing forms to protect its corporate name, preparing an annual report, adopting a personnel policy, purchasing office equipment, renting an office, preparing budgets, writing fundraising letters, and finding and retaining board members.

Few of these tasks have a direct impact on the actual work of the organization, but typically they will consume more time during the initial year after incorporation than does the work related to the actual mission of the organization.

The only consolation is that after a few years, one becomes familiar with the required filings. Then they become routine and just a minor nuisance.

3. Expenses in Money and Time. Significant resources are required to establish a corporation and run it efficiently. No law prohibits running a corporation from one's home with volunteer staff. Legally, the only monetary requirement is to pay a fee to file Articles of Incorporation. Yet, doing so often sets off a chain of events that dramatically increases the organization's complexity. Opening up corporate bank accounts, doing expense reports, filing tax returns, and doing the paperwork described above are difficult to accomplish solely with volunteer labor. Raising the funds necessary to hire a person to do all of this work—in addition to coordinating the actual work of the organization—adds to this burden, and requires even more filing and paperwork.

Many of these tasks would be required even in the absence of a decision to incorporate. One can avoid much of the "wasted" time and energy by keeping "small," but that places a substantial limit on what one can accomplish.

Although incorporation is a legal procedure, it does not require the services of a lawyer. However, lawyers with training and experience in state nonprofit law can be useful in reviewing, if not preparing, Articles of Incorporation and bylaws that are consistent with both statutory requirements and the purposes of the organization. State libraries, law school libraries, and many public and private libraries have a set of books that have all of the state laws codified by topics that typically include "corporations." These laws provide for minimal levels of accountability, decision-making procedures, and ethical constraints that apply to corporations in general and nonprofit corporations in particular.

Role of Incorporators

Incorporators are those legally responsible for forming the corporation. It is common for one person to serve as an organization's incorporator and do most, if not all, of the work involved. Several persons may sign the Articles of Incorporation form as formal incorporators. Some states require more than one incorporator.

Incorporators frequently play a more active role than just being a name on the Articles of Incorporation filing. If they act to promote the interests of the new corporation (e.g., raise funds, recruit personnel, negotiate leases, or purchase property for the organization), their legal status is augmented by the responsibility of serving in a fiduciary capacity. This legal status confers on them the duty to take actions in the best interest of the corporation rather than their own personal interest, and to disclose any conflicts of interest that may occur in their business dealings on behalf of the corporation.

By law, the incorporators make agreements on behalf of the corporation while it is in the process of legal formation. However, these agreements have no legal effect until they are approved by the corporation's board of directors, which assumes authority once the corporation legally exists. As a result, the incorporators involved in these agreements must make it clear to the other party that the agreement is not binding until the corporation exists as a legal entity and its board ratifies the agreement.

Once the Articles of Incorporation are filed and the state government agency with jurisdiction over incorporation (usually the Department of State) approves them, incorporators have no formal status, with one exception. They are invited to be present at the organizational meeting required by law, at which the board of directors is chosen.

It is a common practice that the incorporators include members who will be serving on the first board of directors. Thus, care should be taken as to the qualifications of incorporators, since they may continue their association with the corporation as directors.

The form of Articles of Incorporation varies by state, but most require contact information, the corporate name, purposes, duration, whether the corporation will have members, a statement that excess revenue will not inure to the benefit of board members, and how assets will be distributed upon dissolution.

Choosing a Corporate Name

One of the most important and basic decisions in forming a corporation is choosing a corporate name. This name will be the organization's corporate identity, and the image created by it provides the first impression held by those outside the corporation. "Short" and "descriptive" are two desirable characteristics in a corporate name. Many nonprofit organizations choose a name that gives the connotation of helping, or otherwise doing charitable activities in the public interest, rather than implying a for-profit motive.

If the organization plans to apply for 501(c)(3) status, it should avoid names that would be suitable for organizations whose activities are clearly not eligible for this status. The organization may wish to consider suitable acronyms comprising the first letter of each word of its name, but cute or frivolous acronyms often give an unprofessional impression. It is useful to check the U.S. Patent and Trademark Office's database and type the name as a keyword in Internet search engines to determine if anyone is already using the prospective name.

For obvious legal reasons, the name must be unique in the state of incorporation, although it is usually legal to adopt a name similar to another existing corporation after receiving permission from that corporation and filing the necessary forms to do so. Typical state laws permit the name to be in any language, but require that it be expressed in English letters or characters.

Choosing Corporate Purposes

It is generally advisable to state broad corporate purposes in a manner that permits the corporation to grow and change direction without requiring its Articles of Incorporation to be amended. However, the purposes should be specific enough to permit the corporation to be eligible for 501(c)(3) status, if this is expected.

The Internal Revenue Service provides guidance on drafting a purpose statement that will facilitate a successful 501(c)(3) eligibility determination. Two examples illustrate clauses that will satisfy the IRS:

1. *Charitable and educational purposes within the meaning of IRC 501(c)(3).*
2. *To grant scholarships for deserving junior college students residing in Gotham City.*

"To operate a hospital" is an example of a purpose that is insufficient to the IRS. The explanation provided by the IRS is that the purpose is ambiguous, since a hospital may be exempt or not exempt, depending upon how it is operated.

The IRS provides language that nonprofit organizations may use if they choose a broad corporate purpose consistent with the first example:

This corporation is organized exclusively for one or more purposes as specified in Section 501(c)(3) of the Internal Revenue Code or the corresponding section of any future federal tax code, including, for such purposes, the making of distributions to organizations that qualify as exempt organizations under Section 501(c)(3) of the Internal Revenue Code, or the corresponding section of any future tax code.

A second consideration when devising the purpose statement to facilitate exemption is to provide that the organization benefits an indefinite class of individuals, not specific persons. For example, if the purpose of the organization is intended to be establishing a scholarship fund for members of a specific family orphaned by the September 11th World Trade Center disaster, the purpose should be "to grant scholarships to deserving American students orphaned by terrorist attacks" rather than "to grant scholarships to the children of John A. Smith."

Choosing to Have Members or No Members

"Membership" in the legal sense has a different meaning than those in an organization who pay dues. In the context of incorporation, having members refers to providing broad governance authority beyond an organization's board of directors. In general, it is desirable for most nonprofit corporations to have no members. This will assure that all power and authority will be maintained by the board of directors, and it will prevent the difficult legal problems of expelling an individual member should that occasion arise. It is also expensive and time-consuming to conduct elections, change bylaws, and make major organizational decisions when all members have the legal right to participate. Outsiders, including those who would pay dues in exchange for participating in organizational programs and activities, can still participate in the activities of the nonprofit corporation without being legal members who are entitled to vote on the affairs of the corporation.

As with almost every issue, there are exceptions to this. Many organizations will find it desirable for each participant in the organization's programs and activities to have an equal voice in the internal governance of the organization. Many individuals bristle at the fact that a nonprofit organization's governance is often controlled by a self-selected group of individuals that at times are perceived by members to be elitist, paternalistic, or secretive about the organization's affairs. Some feel that having legal members is more egalitarian and democratic.

Additional Provisions

Many corporations that wish to qualify for 501(c)(3) status add one or more provisions to facilitate tax-exemption approval. One such provision is a statement forbidding the corporation from engaging in partisan political activity on behalf of a candidate or substantially engaging in lobbying. The language for this provision can be adopted from 501(c)(3) itself:

> *No substantial part of the Corporation's activities shall consist of carrying on propaganda, or otherwise attempting to influence legislation (except in accordance with Section 501(h) of the Internal Revenue Code). The*

> *Corporation shall not participate in any political campaign on behalf of or in opposition to any candidate for public office.*

Another provision required for Section 501(c)(3) eligibility relates to corporate dissolution:

> *Upon the dissolution of the organization, assets shall be distributed for one or more exempt purposes within the meaning of Section 501(c)(3) of the Internal Revenue Code, or corresponding section of any future federal tax code, or shall be distributed to the federal government, or to a state or local government, for a public purpose.*

Once the Articles of Incorporation are filed and approved, all actions taken on behalf of the Corporation should clearly indicate that they are actions for the corporation and not on behalf of individuals. Otherwise, such individuals may be personally liable for fulfilling the terms of contracts and other agreements, such as paying rent, staff salaries, telephone installation costs, and so on. One way to indicate that persons are acting on behalf of the corporation is to explicitly sign legal contracts and other documents as follows:

(corporate name)
By (individual's signature)
(individual's corporate title)

Figure 7: Number of 501(c)(3)s and Number of Total 501(c)s on the IRS Master List—FY 1997-2013

Fiscal Year	501(c)(3)s	Total 501(c)s
FY 1997	692,524	1,230,294
FY 1998	733,790	1,271,742
FY 1999	773,934	1,312,647
FY 2000	819,008	1,354,395
FY 2001	865,096	1,399,558
FY 2002	909,574	1,444,905
FY 2003	964,418	1,501,772
FY 2004	1,010,365	1,540,554
FY 2005	1,045,979	1,570,023
FY 2006	1,064,191	1,585,479
FY 2007	1,128,367	1,648,306
FY 2008	1,186,915	1,710,567
FY 2009	1,238,201	1,772,229
FY 2010	1,280,739	1,821,824
FY 2011	1,080,130	1,494,882
FY 2012	1,081,891	1,484,818
FY 2013	1,052,495	1,442,197

Source: IRS Databooks, FY 2002-20013. Retrieved from *http://www.irs.gov/taxstats/charitablestats/article/0,,id=97176,00.html*

Figure 8: IRS Action on Applications for 501C(3) Status, FY 1998-2013

Fiscal Year	# of Applications	Approved	Denied	Other
FY 1998	68,796	51,329	382	17,085
FY 1999	65,058	52,773	447	11,838
FY 2000	74,534	61,005	456	13,073
FY 2001	74,361	59,909	629	13,823
FY 2002	79,379	64,188	531	4,660
FY 2003	83,843	66,580	1,094	16,169
FY 2004	80,601	64,545	1,027	15,079
FY 2005	77,539	63,402	765	13,372
FY 2006	83,350	66,262	1,283	15,805
FY 2007	85,771	68,378	1,607	15,886
FY 2008	79,236	54,969	1,221	23,046
FY 2009	70,623	42,484	472	27,667
FY 2010	59,945	48,934	500	10,511
FY 2011	55,319	49,677	205	5,437
FY 2012	51,748	45,029	123	6,596
FY 2013	45,289	37,946	79	7,264

Source: IRS Databooks, 1998-2013. Table 21, Table 24, Table 25: Tax-Exempt Organization and Other Entity Applications or Disposals, by Type of Organization and Internal Revenue Code Section.

Section 501(c)(3) Tax-Exempt Status

After filing the Articles of Incorporation, achieving 501(c)(3) status should be the principal objective for virtually all nonprofits organized and operated for religious, charitable, scientific, literary, or educational purposes, testing for public safety, fostering national or international amateur sports competitions, and preventing cruelty to children or animals.

The federal regulation implementing Section 501(c)(3) tax-exempt status states (Reg. §1.501(c)(3)-1(d)):

> *(d) Exempt purposes. (1) In general.*
> *(i) An organization may be exempt as an organization described in section 501(c)(3) if it is organized and operated exclusively for one or more of the following purposes:*
> *(a) Religious,*
> *(b) Charitable,*
> *(c) Scientific,*
> *(d) Testing for Public Safety,*
> *(e) Literary,*
> *(f) Educational, or*
> *(g) Prevention of cruelty to children or animals.*

> *(ii) An organization is not organized or operated exclusively for one or more of the purposes specified in subdivision (i) of this subparagraph unless it serves a public rather than a private interest. Thus, to meet the requirement of this subdivision, it is necessary for an organization to establish that it is not organized or operated for the benefit of private interests such as designated individuals, the creator or his family, shareholders of the organization, or persons controlled, directly or indirectly, by such private interests...*

Federal 501(c)(3) tax-exempt status confers five major benefits to the organization:

1. The nonprofit will be exempt from federal income taxes other than unrelated business income taxes (UBIT).

2. Persons contributing to the nonprofit can take a deduction on their own income taxes for their contributions.

3. Many major donors (such as United Ways and certain foundations) will not make contributions to organizations that do not have 501(c)(3) status.

4. The designation of 501(c)(3) status indicates a minimal level of accountability, policed by the Internal Revenue Service, which is a useful governmental stamp of approval of the charitable activities of the organization.

5. In some states, qualifying 501(c)(3) organizations may elect to self-insure for purposes of complying with unemployment compensation laws.

There are four major disadvantages:

1. A 501(c)(3) may not engage in partisan political activity on behalf of political candidates.

2. Such organizations may not substantially engage in lobbying or propaganda.

3. Such organizations have a higher level of accountability, and are required, as must all 501(c) exempt organizations, to make copies of their 990 tax returns available in their offices upon request.

4. There is a substantial application fee, and this fee is not refunded if tax-exempt status is denied.

Although not always the case, most incorporators of nonprofits have some altruistic motive for incorporating. The motives of the incorporators cannot be for personal gain. As one might expect, the motives are usually of an "eleemosynary" nature, i.e., related to charity.

Many nonprofit corporations are formed because a person or group of persons is frustrated with the lack of government action to solve a societal problem that, in that person's view, should be solved by government. Congress historically has recognized that government cannot do everything for everybody, even when the cause is just. Instead, Congress provides an opportunity for citizens to form organizations to do the activities themselves. They are rewarded by having certain privileges and subsidies, such as the tax-exemption, provided that the activity falls within a statutorily enumerated list of activities.

Section 501(c) of the Internal Revenue Code lists more than 20 classes of activities that can qualify a nonprofit corporation for tax-exempt status. A list of these classes is provided on pages 79-80. Only one of these classes, 501(c)(3), permits a tax deduction for contributions made to organizations in that class, and requires that such organizations not engage in substantial lobbying or propaganda activities, or in political activities that advance the cause of candidates.

501(c)(3) status is not granted pro forma. Because of this, 501(c)(3) status is prized, and it is viewed by many in the public as a stamp of approval by the federal government. The fact is that 501(c)(3) status does not necessarily imply government's endorsement of the organization's activities. In FY 2013, the Internal Revenue Service granted 37,946 (c)(3) applications, denied 79, and took "other" action on 7,264 (Internal Revenue Service, 2014), many of which were eventually approved after additional information was provided.

Successful application is facilitated by having certain provisions in the organization's governing documents. These provisions are discussed on pages 73-74.

How To Apply for 501(c)(3) Status

To apply, an organization needs the following forms and booklets from the Internal Revenue Service:

- Form 8718—*User Fee for Exempt Organization Determination Letter Request* (for organizations that have had annual gross receipts averaging not more than $10,000 during its preceding four years, or new organizations that anticipate averaging not more than $10,000 during its first four years). This form may be downloaded at: *http://www.irs.gov/pub/irs-pdf/f8718.pdf*

- Form SS-4—*Application for Employer Identification Number*
  This form may be downloaded at: *http://www.irs.gov/pub/irs-pdf/fss4.pdf*
- Form 5768—*Election by an Eligible Organization to Make Expenditures to Influence Legislation*
  This form may be downloaded at: *http://www.irs.gov/pub/irs-pdf/f5768.pdf*
- Package 1023—*Forms and instruction booklets for applying for 501(c)(3) tax-exempt status*
  This form may be downloaded at: *http://www.irs.gov/pub/irs-pdf/f1023.pdf*
- Publication 557—*Tax-Exempt Status for Your Organization*
  This form may be downloaded at: *http://www.irs.gov/pub/irs-pdf/p557.pdf*

The above forms and booklets also may be obtained at any local IRS office.

According to page 24 of the IRS's instruction book accompanying Form 1023, it takes an average of nine hours and 39 minutes to complete the basic form and several more hours to complete supplemental schedules. It also takes an additional five hours to learn about the law and how to complete the forms. It is advisable to be as careful as possible in completing the forms, since the wrong phrase can result in denial.

Some organizations are exempt from having to file the 1023. Among them are:

1. Those that will have gross receipts of less than $5,000 annually.

2. Bona fide religious institutions.

3. Certain groups affiliated with a parent organization that already has tax-exempt status and will send a letter extending its exemption to them.

4. Organizations eligible to file Form 8718 (see above).

The Internal Revenue Service expects that an application for 501(c)(3) status will be filed within 15 months after the end of the month in which the Articles of Incorporation are filed. If the organization files on time and the application is approved, 501(c)(3) status will be retroactive to the date of the Articles of Incorporation. There is a form to file if the 15-month deadline is not met. For more information about this option, see IRS Publication 557.

Fees

There is a $850 application fee to file Form 1023, *Application for Recognition of Exemption*. New organizations expecting gross receipts of not more than $10,000 for each of the first four years, or existing organizations that have not had gross receipts in that amount in each of the last four years, can qualify for a reduced fee of $400 and file Form 8718, *User Fee for Exempt Organization Request*. The fee must be paid by check, but a corporate check is not required. If you choose to file the form online using the IRS Cyber Assistant Web-based software program when it becomes available, the fee is $200 for online applications, regardless of organization size. First conceived in 2002, the IRS has expressed difficulty rolling out a final version, despite almost annual announcements that it would be imminently available (501c(3)book.org, 2012).

Tax-Exempt Status Other than 501(c)(3)

The Internal Revenue Code provides more than 20 other categories of tax-exempt status besides 501(c)(3). Those who wish to file for tax-exempt status under section 501(c) for other than 501(c)(3) need to request Package 1024 from the IRS. Note: You can download this package, and all other common IRS forms and instruction booklets at: *http://www.irs.gov*

Among the other categories are:

>
> 501(c)(4)—civic leagues, social welfare organizations
> 501(c)(5)—labor, agricultural, or horticultural organizations
> 501(c)(6)—business leagues, chambers of commerce, trade associations
> 501(c)(7)—social clubs
> 501(c)(8)—fraternal beneficiary societies
> 501(c)(9)—voluntary employee beneficiary associations
> 501(c)(10)—domestic fraternal societies and orders that do not provide life, sick, or health benefits
> 501(c)(11)—teacher retirement fund associations
> 501(c)(12)—benevolent life insurance associations and other mutual businesses
> 501(c)(13)—cemeteries and crematoria
> 501(c)(14)—credit unions
> 501(c)(15)—mutual insurance companies
> 501(c)(16)—farmers' co-ops
> 501(c)(17)—unemployment compensation benefit trusts
> 501(c)(20)—prepaid group legal services organizations
> 501(c)(25)—title holding corporations or trusts.

With limited exceptions, these organizations have the same federal tax benefits as a 501(c)(3). One major difference is that with few exceptions, contributors cannot deduct the amount of their donation from their personal income tax payments. For many of these organizations, there is no limitation against lobbying activities, and most are permitted to engage in partisan political activity (although there may be a substantial federal excise tax associated with political expenditures).

A Short History of Tax-Exempt Status

In ancient times, government, whether secular or non-secular, recognized that certain activities assisted the role of government and were deserving of tax exemptions. A passage in the Bible (Ezra 7:24) provides that "it shall not be lawful to impose toll, tribute, or customs" upon certain priests and their staff. Several thousand years ago, some of the best land in the Nile Valley was set aside tax-free by the Egyptian pharaoh for the priests of Osiris.

Modern tax-exemption law has its roots in England, with the passage of the Statute of Charitable Uses in 1601. Current U.S. tax-exemption law draws its roots from an 1891 court case in Britain *(Commissioners of Income Tax v. Pemsel)* that provided a judicial definition of charity strikingly similar to the American legal standard (Wellford and Gallagher, 1988).

The modern federal tax-exemption can be traced to 1863, when the income of religious organizations was exempted from a corporate tax enacted to finance the Civil War. The Wilson-Gorman Tariff Act of 1894, the first general U.S. corporate income tax, imposed a 2% flat tax and statutorily exempted charitable income. Section 32 of this Act extended this exemption to charitable, religious, educational, fraternal, and some savings and loan institutions. It was eventually declared unconstitutional and subsequently repealed. It did, however, serve as the precedent for exempting organizations that were for "charitable, religious, or educational purposes." The Revenue Act of 1913, passed after the 16th Amendment was ratified, included identical language (Arnsberger, et al., 2008). The Revenue Act of 1917 included a tax deduction for contributions made to charitable organizations (Arnsberger, et al. 2008).

A 1924 Supreme Court case, *Trinidad v. Sagrada*, ruled that for purposes of tax-exempt status, the destination of the funds, rather than the source, was the key determinant. This case involved a religious order that sold food, wine, and other goods to support its school, mission, church, and other operations. Thus, tax-exempt organizations were permitted to run profit-making enterprises provided that the net profits were funneled to tax-exempt purposes. This policy was revised by Congressional enactment of an "unrelated business income tax" (UBIT) in 1950. The rationale for this was that charities were seen as competing unfairly with for-profit enterprises, the most celebrated case of which was New York University's ownership of a macaroni factory.

From 1909 to the present, many other categories of tax-exempt status were added by federal statute, including labor, horticultural and agriculture organizations (1909), business leagues, chambers of commerce, scientific organizations, and mutual cemetery companies (1913), public utilities, social clubs, land banks, title holding companies, and farming associations (1916), societies for the prevention of cruelty to animals (1918), foundations and community chests (1921), and homeowner associations, fishing associations, and organizations that promote national and international sporting competitions (1976).

The Tax Reform Act of 1969 established an explicit category for private foundations, defined them as either operating or nonoperating foundations, provided for an excise tax on their investment income, and required minimum distributions to be made annually by nonoperating foundations (Arnsberger, et al. 2008).

Charitable Solicitation Registration

All but 11 states in the United States—Delaware, Idaho, Indiana, Iowa, Montana, Nebraska, Nevada, South Dakota, Texas, Vermont, and Wyoming—regulate charitable fundraising (The Unified Registration Multistate Filer Project, 2014). State laws requiring charities to register and to provide information about fundraising activities to the government is not a recent development—for example, the Pennsylvania General Assembly enacted a law to regulate fundraising back in 1919.

Many states during the 1980s and 1990s enacted tough laws regulating charitable solicitation. This trend was motivated by abuses in virtually every state in which unscrupulous organizations posed as charities. Engaging in deceptive practices, these organizations generated contributions from the public that were intended for charitable purposes. Some of these organizations took names similar to those of reputable charities and diverted most, if not all, of the proceeds of their solicitation to line the pockets of private individuals. Other abuses involved professional fundraising organizations that solicited business from bona fide charities, offering to raise funds in exchange for an unreasonably large percentage of the contributions received. Even if the charity received a minuscule percentage of what was raised and the charity benefited—it was at the expense of an unwary public.

Abuses such as these continue to this day. State laws have made it tougher for deceptive practices to occur, and have given law enforcement officials new authority to take action to enjoin illegal or deceptive fundraising activities. On May 5, 2003, the U.S. Supreme Court unanimously decided a case *(Illinois Ex Rel. Madigan v. Telemarketing Associations, Inc.)* that validated the authority of Illinois state regulators to regulate the fraudulent practices of telemarketers who attempt to raise charitable funds. The case involved a telemarketer in Illinois who diverted 85% of the funds raised to his own pockets rather than for charitable purposes.

Perhaps as importantly, these state laws have provided the public (and the media) with easy access, often a toll-free telephone call or mouse click on a Web site away, to information about charities, their leadership, and how much of the money contributed is actually being funneled to the charity and used for charitable purposes.

From the perspective of most bona fide charities, these laws are a positive development—despite the prospect of costly and burdensome reporting requirements. The public, generous with charitable giving, was becoming more cynical with each fundraising scandal. As one mainstream charitable association (United Way of Pennsylvania) explained in its newsletter on why it testified in support of the 1990 Pennsylvania charitable solicitation law:

> *United Ways and hundreds of other legitimate charities, which are "squeaky clean," are adversely affected and risk loss of public credibility and confidence as a result of a small but growing number of "charitable" fundraising efforts which raise money solely or primarily for personal gain under the guise of charity.*

Although most of these laws are weak in prescribing a minimum threshold on the percentage of donations required to be actually put to use for charitable purposes (rather than paying the expenses of professional fundraisers), the public policy philosophy is more along the lines of "a little sunlight is the best antiseptic."

One can find similar patterns, although each state that regulates charitable solicitation has its own law, regulations, and forms for registration, registration renewal, and expense/fundraising reporting. Many states also require registration and reporting for professional solicitors and fundraising counsels, and they require those who make their living in this manner to post a bond with the state.

For charities that raise funds in more than one state (on the Internet or by direct mail, for example), complying with the requirements of each state can be problematic, expensive, and time-consuming. For several years, national and regional charities legitimately have complained about the impracticality of keeping up with the legal requirements for solicitation law compliance. An innovative project, the Unified Registration Statement, has addressed this concern.

The Unified Registration Statement

The National Association of Attorneys General and the National Association of State Charities Officials have developed the Unified Registration Statement (URS). The purpose of the URS is to provide a standardized reporting form that charities can use when they are required to submit information to many different states with respect to charitable solicitation activities. This document can be downloaded from the Internet at: *http://www.multistatefiling.org*

Although each state regulating charitable solicitation maintains the practice of providing its own individual registration form, 36 states and the District of Columbia will accept the URS for registration purposes—all but three of the states (Colorado, Florida, and Oklahoma) that require registration. Fourteen of the 37 jurisdictions that accept the URS (Arkansas, California, District of Columbia, Georgia, Maine, Minnesota, Mississippi, North Carolina, North Dakota, Tennessee, Utah, Washington, West Virginia, and Wisconsin) also require a supplemental filing. These supplemental forms are not extensive and are available on the Internet as an appendix to the URS forms (see: *http://www.multistatefiling.org/#no_states*).

Charities may print out the form, in the format of a PDF file, directly from the Internet (or save it for printing out later), fill in the information, and file it with each participating state. Instructions are provided at the Web site for printing or saving the file. A version of the form in HTML can be reviewed on the Web site, but this version is not acceptable for printing out and submitting to state regulatory offices.

The URS is continually updated and improved in response to comments provided by participating charities and state regulators. As this book went to press, the latest version of the form was 4.02, which was made public in March 2014. The following Web site provides details about the latest version:

http://www.multistatefiling.org/#version

As of July 2014, the District of Columbia and the following states accept the URS for registration: Alabama, Alaska, Arizona, Arkansas, California, Connecticut, Georgia, Hawaii, Illinois, Kansas, Kentucky, Louisiana, Maine, Maryland, Massachusetts, Michigan, Minnesota, Mississippi, Missouri, New Hampshire, New Jersey, New Mexico, New York, North Carolina, North Dakota, Ohio, Oregon, Pennsylvania, Rhode Island, South Carolina, Tennessee, Utah, Virginia, Washington, West Virginia, and Wisconsin.

Each state has individual exemptions and exclusions from registration requirements based on, for example, the type of organization or the amount of fundraising conducted annually. Also, each state requires different supporting documents to accompany the URS and charges an individual registration fee. Charities may still submit the state's individual registration form, but most charities soliciting in several states that accept the URS find it much more convenient to submit the standardized form.

The general Unified Registration Statement, version 4.02, consists of three pages of questions. It requests:

- general information about the charity
- whether there was a previous legal name used
- information about misconduct by the organization's officers, directors, employees, or fundraisers
- a list of states where the charity is registered and the dates and type of solicitation conducted
- information about the organization's federal tax status
- methods of solicitation
- information about the purposes and programs of the organization for which funds are being solicited
- the names, titles, addresses, and telephone numbers of officers, directors, trustees, and principal salaried executives
- information that describes relationships (such as financial interest or relationship by blood, marriage, or adoption) between organizational leaders and professional fundraising organizations, suppliers, or vendors
- information about felonies or misdemeanors committed by the organization's leaders
- the names of those who are responsible for custody and/or distribution of funds, fundraising, financial records, and those authorized to sign checks
- banks where funds are deposited, along with the account numbers and bank telephone numbers
- the name and address of the accountant/auditor
- the name and address of the person authorized to receive service of process
- whether the organization receives financial support from other nonprofit organizations, shares revenue with other nonprofits, whether anyone owns an interest of 10% or greater in the organization, and whether the organization owns a 10% or greater interest in any other organization (and explanations for all of these)
- whether the organization uses volunteers or professionals to solicit directly to the public
- a list of professional fundraisers, solicitors, fundraising counsels, or commercial co-venturers accompanied by information about their services, compensation arrangements, contract dates, dates of the campaign, and whether these persons/organizations have custody or control of donations
- the amount paid to these persons during the previous year.

It also requests financial information about the charity, including:

- contributions in the previous year, program service expenses, fundraising expenses in the previous year, management and general expenses
- fundraising costs as a percentage of funds raised
- fundraising costs plus management and general costs as a percentage of funds raised.
- program services as a percentage of total expenses.

Note that the URS can be used only for registration and registration renewal, but not for the annual financial reporting required by almost all states that regulate charitable solicitation. A standardized reporting form for annual financial reporting is being developed.

State Regulation of Fundraising on the Internet

The use of the Internet for fundraising has raised legal questions that previously were not relevant. For example, is a charity in Pennsylvania that is not registered in Utah violating the Utah solicitation law if it puts a general solicitation on its Web site and receives contributions from someone in Utah? This area of law is not clear, and it will likely take several years, if not decades, for a body of case law and statutory law to provide guidance to charities wrestling with these questions.

Beginning in the late 1990s, the National Association of Attorneys General (NAAG) and the National Association of State Charity Officials (NASCO) began meeting to reach a consensus national policy on how states should appropriately regulate charitable solicitation conducted over the Internet. The public dialogue on this issue began in Charleston, S.C. at the October 1999 NAAG/NASCO annual conference. In September of 2000, NASCO released a draft proposal of model state guidelines and posted it on the Internet. The final version was approved by the NASCO Board in March 2001, and can be found at: *http://www.nasconet.org/wp-content/uploads/2011/05/Charleston-Principles-Final.pdf*

Charities that shied away from putting solicitation information on their Web sites for fear of attracting out-of-state enforcement proceedings can breathe a bit easier and feel comfortable reposting this information. Charities that took the time and effort (and considerable expense) to register in all of the 39 states requiring registration may reconsider if the extent to which they solicit falls within the thresholds of these principles. And charities that target their Internet solicitations to out-of-state residents, either via their Web pages or e-mail, should be put on notice that these direct and indirect solicitations will, rightfully so, be treated the same as charitable solicitations conducted by conventional media.

The *Charleston Principles* consist of a preamble and four broad principles, each with subprinciples. Here is a synopsis:

The *preamble* lays out the general purpose of the document, recognizing that although most charities provide valuable services, fraud and misuse of contributions are significant problems, and oversight by state regulators is a reasonable function of government.

Principle 1 underscores that using the Internet for fundraising is legitimate and should not be discouraged. However, since state laws vary and technology is still developing, the application of these principles by individual states may change and, in any case, is not binding upon any state.

Principle II provides that states should be enforcing the law against charities that use the Internet to mislead or defraud those in any state, regardless of which state the charity calls home.

Principle III is divided into two parts—principles applicable to charities soliciting contributions in the state where they are based, and those that apply to solicitations and donations in a foreign state. A charity that uses the Internet to conduct solicitations in its home state is required to register in that state, as it would be with conventional solicitations.

It is the wording of the second part of this principle that *could* have been drafted in a manner problematic to charities but, perhaps, strikes the right balance between over-regulation and no regulation. It provides that—

> *An entity that is not domiciled within a state must register in accordance with the law of that state if: Its non-Internet activities alone would be sufficient to require registration; The entity solicits contributions through an interactive Web site; and (e)ither the entity: (s)pecifically targets persons physically located in the state for solicitation, or {r)eceives contributions from the state on a repeated and ongoing basis or a substantial basis through its Web site; or (t)he entity solicits contributions through a site that is not interactive, but either specifically invites further offline activity to complete a contribution, or establishes other contacts with that state, such as sending e-mail messages or other communications that promote the Web site, and (t)he entity satisfies Principle III.B.1.b. (2)*

(Note: III.B. 1.b.{2} relates to specifically targeting persons in another state or receiving contributions from the state on a repeated and ongoing or substantial basis through a Web site.)

Principle III also defines terms used above. "Interactive" refers to sites that have the capacity to accept donations by obtaining funds directly from a contributor, such as via credit card or electronic funds transfer. The principles do not provide specific guidelines on what thresholds of donations trigger regulation; states are encouraged to set thresholds for what is meant by "repeated and ongoing or substantial."

Another section of this principle responds to the issue of charity portals that solicit funds from the public, often providing a list of every charity that is on the Internal Revenue Service's Master List. The principle proposed on this issue is that if state law technically requires such a charity to register as a result of receiving donations from that portal, the state should exercise "prosecutorial discretion" and not enforce that law. Also, companies that pledge to devote a portion of the sale of a product or service to a charity or for a charitable purpose, often referred to as "cause marketing," should not be exempt from state registration requirements.

Finally, those who merely provide administration, support, or technical services to charities, such as processing Web donations, should not be required to register, provided they do not actually solicit donations. However, the principle includes a statement that "Compensation for services based on the amount of funds raised may be a strong indication that entity is doing more than simply providing technical services."

Principle IV addresses general issues relating to easing the administrative burden of multi-state filing for those charities required to do so consistent with these principles. It encourages charities to post their Unified Registration Statements, completed federal tax exemption applications, and their last three 990s online.

Taxpayer Bill of Rights 2—Intermediate Sanctions

The *Taxpayer Bill of Rights 2* was signed into law by President Clinton on July 30, 1996. The principal purpose of this law is to punish individuals affiliated with charities and social welfare organizations who are participating in financial abuses, and to provide the government with a sanction other than simply revoking the charity's exemption status. The law also includes expanded public disclosure requirements for annual federal tax returns.

Previous law required charities to make their 990 tax returns available for public inspection, but did not require that copies be provided. The law was changed to require that if a person requests a copy of the 990 in person, it must be immediately provided for a reasonable fee for copying. If the request is made in writing, it must be provided for a reasonable copying and postage fee within 30 days. Organizations that make these documents "widely available," such as posting them on the Internet, are exempt, although they still must make the document available for public inspection. The law expands the disclosure that must be made on the 990, adding information about excess expenditures to influence legislation, any political expenditures, any disqualified lobbying expenditures, and amounts of "excess benefit" transactions.

The law raises the fine for failure to file a timely 990 from $10 per day to $20 per day, with a maximum of $10,000. Higher fines apply to organizations with gross receipts over $1 million.

Both state and federal law have prohibitions against "private inurement"— permitting a charity's income to benefit a private shareholder or individual. Legislation at the federal level was enacted to define what constitutes a prevalent form of private inurement and to refine the definition of a private shareholder. It aims to respond to alleged financial abuses by some organizations perceived as providing unreasonable compensation to organization "insiders."

To curb financial abuses, the law authorizes the IRS to impose an excise tax, 25% in most cases, on certain improper financial transactions by 501(c)(3) and 501(c)(4) organizations. The tax applies on transactions that benefit a "disqualified person," defined as people in positions to exercise substantial influence over the organization, their family members, or other organizations controlled by those persons.

Disqualified persons include voting members of the board, the president or chair, the CEO, the chief operating officer, the chief financial officer, and the treasurer, among potential other officers and staff. The benefit to the disqualified person must exceed the value that the organization receives in order to be subject to the tax. To avoid problems, tax experts are advising organizations to treat every benefit to a director or staff person as compensation, and reflect these benefits in W-2s, 1099s, and their budget documents. Seemingly innocent benefits, such as paying for the travel and lodging expenses for a spouse attending a board retreat or a health club membership for an executive director, may trigger questions about excess benefit. Luxury travel could be considered an excess benefit.

Compensation is considered reasonable if it is in an amount that would ordinarily be paid for similar services by similar organizations in similar circumstances. The term "compensation" is defined broadly, and includes severance payments, insurance, and deferred compensation.

Most of the provisions relating to intermediate sanctions apply retroactively to September 14, 1995, the date the legislation was first introduced. Steep additional excise tax penalties, up to 200% of the excess benefit plus the initial 25% excise tax, apply for excess benefit transactions that are not corrected in a reasonable amount of time. An excise tax may also be applied to an organization's managers (a term that is meant to include an officer, director, trustee) who approve the excess benefit transaction in an amount of 10% of the excess benefit, up to $10,000 maximum per transaction.

Although these excise taxes apply to individuals and not to the organizations themselves, there is nothing in this law that prohibits organizations from paying the tax or purchasing insurance to cover an individual's liability for the tax penalty. However, if the organization does purchase this insurance, the premium must be considered compensation to the individual. This insurance could become the basis for an excess benefit if total compensation to the individual, including this insurance, exceeds the fair market value that the person provides to the organization in exchange for the total compensation that person receives from the organization. It makes sense to consult an attorney who is knowledgeable about the *Taxpayer Bill of Rights 2* if there are any unresolved issues that would make an organization's directors and staff vulnerable to an IRS audit.

The Internal Revenue Service published draft regulations on this section of the Revenue Code in the *Federal Register* on August 4, 1998. Final regulations were published in the *Federal Register* on January 23, 2002.

The final regulations provide more examples of situations that might be faced by charities. One change in the final regulations is that they permit organizations to rely not only on the advice of their attorneys (as was a feature of the draft regulations), but also on the advice of other outside consultants, such as their accountants.

Legal Responsibilities of Board Members

Being a board member of a nonprofit organization is not an honorary position. Laws in every state hold board members accountable for violating accepted standards of conduct and decision-making. Although each state regulates board member behavior differently, there are some common themes in what constitutes illegal conduct. Generally, boards may make bad decisions with impunity. They are required, however, to have made those decisions believing at the time that they were in the best interests of the organization rather than themselves, and consistent with the organization's mission.

Among the legal duties of board members are—

- *Duty of Care.* They must take reasonable care when making decisions for the organization.
- *Duty of Loyalty.* They must act in the best interest of the organization.
- *Duty of Obedience.* They must act in accordance with the organization's mission.
- *Avoid Conflicts of Interest.* They must not participate in decision-making in

which they have a personal interest that may constitute a conflict of interest (Source: Non-Profit Board Responsibilities by Estela Kennen, http://denverfoundation.wordpress.com/related-articles/overview-of-nonprofit-board-governance/).

Then Pennsylvania Attorney General Tom Corbett, in a booklet *Handbook for Charitable Organizations*, explains the "duty of care" standard he has enforced as—

When performing their duties, board members, senior management and members of committees must use the degree of care, skill, caution and diligence that a prudent person would use in handling corporate affairs. Decision-makers are required to make reasonable inquiries when analyzing contracts, investments, business dealings, and other matters. An individual who is acting in conformance with this standard will:

- *attend and participate in board meetings on a regular basis;*
- *attend and participate in committee meetings when the individual is a member of the committee;*
- *diligently read, review, and inquire about material that affects the corporation;*
- *keep abreast of the affairs and finances of the corporation; and*
- *use independent judgment when analyzing matters that affect the corporation....*

Board members, trustees and senior management have a fiduciary responsibility when handling finances and investments. That simply means, they must exercise the degree of care, caution and diligence that prudent persons would exercise in handling their own personal investments and finances. Individuals who have or claim to have special knowledge or skills in the area of investment will be held to a higher standard. Fiduciaries who carelessly or negligently invest funds may be personally liable for any losses sustained.

He explains "duty of loyalty" to be—

Board members and senior management must always perform their duties in good faith with the best interests of the organization in mind. This means that they must not seek to derive private gain from business transactions that involve the nonprofit corporation or advance their own interests at the expense of the corporation. Acts of self-dealing constitute a breach of fiduciary duty which may result in personal liability to the nonprofit organization. Board members, trustees, and senior management should avoid conflicts of interest and even the appearance of impropriety. Individuals who take advantage of corporate opportunities to make profits for themselves at the expense of the corporation may be liable for the profits they received at the organization's expense.

With respect to avoiding conflicts of interest, he writes that—

It is particularly important for board members to disclose the following facts:

- *whether they have a potential conflict of interest with respect to any transaction, business decision or other matter in which the organization is involved;*
- *whether they have a financial, business or personal interest in an entity with which the nonprofit organization is or will be doing business;*
- *whether individuals related to them have a financial, business or personal interest in an entity with which the nonprofit organization is or will be doing business; or*
- *whether they serve as a director, member or employee of either a competitor of the corporation or a corporation with which the nonprofit organization is or will be doing business.*

The board should proceed with caution when any of the above facts are present because there may be a conflict of interest. An individual who has a potential conflict with respect to a particular transaction should disclose it to fellow managers and board members and abstain from participating in the negotiations and decisions surrounding that transaction. To avoid the appearance of impropriety, the individual who has the conflict of interest should not be present in the room during any discussions that relate to the transaction. (See: http://www.attorneygeneral.gov/uploadedFiles/Consumers/nonprofitbooklet.pdf)

Discussion Questions

1. Eleven states do not regulate charitable solicitations. What might be some of the factors that influence a state to regulate or not regulate charitable solicitations? What might be some of the factors that influence whether the charitable community in a state might favor or oppose such regulation?

2. Why did the Congress prohibit tax-exempt charities from engaging in partisan political activity? Are there any reasons to think that this prohibition is unwise in every case? Why did the Congress prohibit "substantial lobbying" rather than all lobbying?

3. How should Internet solicitations be regulated (i.e., by the federal government, by the state government, or both)? What types of solicitations should be proscribed?

4. To what extent do you think state regulation of charitable solicitations has reduced fraudulent solicitation?

5. How much of a charity's internal operations (such as salary information, budgets, and board membership) should be public information?

Activities

1. Research how many corporations are registered in your state, how many of these are nonprofit corporations, and the total number of each type that have registered within each of the previous two years.

2. Research the number of nonprofit corporations that had penalties imposed upon them in your state for fraudulent charitable activities, the penalty they were assessed, and the process by which they were penalized. If your state does not regulate solicitation, research the number of nonprofit corporations that were involuntarily dissolved by state regulatory authorities and the reason(s) for such action.

3. Obtain all of the forms required by your state to incorporate a nonprofit organization and to register for charitable solicitation. Fill them out, using a fictitious organization name and purpose.

4. Using public records from your state's corporation bureau and the Internal Revenue Service's Master List of Exempt Organizations, determine what percentage of new nonprofits that incorporate successfully obtain their federal tax-exempt status within their first three years of existence.

Tips for Practitioners

1. Review federal and state nonprofit laws and decide whether your organization is willing to be subjected to the limitations and accountability required by these laws.

2. Avoid incorporating if it is essential to maintain complete control of the organization, and if it is possible to keep the scale of operations small.

3. Contact someone who runs a nonprofit corporation of similar size and type envisioned for your organization. Ask questions about paperwork requirements, office equipment, rental space, and the benefits and pitfalls of running such a corporation.

4. Have a lawyer review, if not draft, the Articles of Incorporation.

5. Include in the Articles of Incorporation additional provisions to enhance the prospects for achieving the appropriate federal tax status (e.g., 501(c)(3)) if such status is desirable.

6. If you know that your organization is not in compliance with charitable solicitation regulations, consider "turning yourself in" rather than being "caught red-handed."

7. To protect tax-exempt status, serve clients who cannot afford to pay the full costs of services, and make services accessible to some clients who cannot afford to pay at all.

8. Periodically review the organization's bylaws and tax-exempt status purposes and update these documents to reflect changing conditions.

Online Resources to Explore

Nonprofit Coordinating Committee of New York: How to Read the IRS Form 990 & Find Out What it Means
http://www.npccny.org/Form_990/990.htm

Internal Revenue Service: Tax Information for Charities and Other Nonprofits
http://www.irs.gov/charities/index.html

National Association of State Charity Officials
http://www.nasconet.org

Tax and Accounting Sites Directory
http://www.taxsites.com/state.html

Federal Register
http://www.archives.gov/federal-register/index.html

References and for Further Reading

501c3book.org. (2012). *Should you wait for the cyber 1023?* Retrieved from *501c3book.org/Cyber_1023.html*

Anonymous. (2005). Everything you never wanted to know about your nonprofit corporation (by The Unknown Attorney Ms. Cellaneous). Jamul, CA: Bellissima Publishing.

Arnsberger, P., Ludlum, M., Riley, R., & Stanton, M. (2008). A history of the tax-exempt sector: An SOI perspective. Internal Revenue Service, Statistics of Income Bulletin, Winter 2008.

Fishman, J. & Schwarz, S. (2010). *Taxation of nonprofit organizations, cases and materials* (3rd Ed.) (University Casebook Series). Eagan, MN: Foundation Press.

Hansmann, H. (1981). *The rationale for exempting nonprofit organizations from corporate income taxation.* New Haven, CT: Institute for Social Policy Studies.

Hopkins, B. (2005). *Nonprofit law made easy.* New York: Wiley & Sons.

Hopkins, B. (2011). *The law of nonprofit organizations* (10th Ed.). New York: Wiley & Sons.

Hopkins, B. (2013). *Starting and managing a nonprofit organization: A legal guide.*(6th Ed.). New York: Wiley & Sons.

Hutton, S. (2013). *Nonprofit kit for dummies.* (4th Ed.). New York: For Dummies (Wiley & Sons).

IRS. (2014). IRS Databook 2013. Retrieved from *http://www.irs.gov/uac/SOI-Tax-Stats-Tax-Exempt-Organizations-and-Nonexempt-Charitable-Trusts-IRS-Data-Book-Table-25*

Kirschten, B. L. (2014). *Nonprofit corporate forms handbook* (2014 Ed.). New York: Clark Boardman Co.

Pakroo, P. (2013). *Starting & building a nonprofit: A practical guide.* (5th Ed.). Berkeley, CA: Nolo Press.

Picarda, H. (2014). *The law relating to charities.* London: Bloomsbury Professional

The Unified Registration Statement MultiState Filer Project. (2014). *The unified registration statement.* Retrieved from *http://www.multistatefiling.org*

Wellford, W. H., & Gallagher, J. (1988). *Unfair competition? The challenge to charitable tax exemption.* Washington, DC: The National Assembly of Voluntary Health and Social Welfare Organizations.

Chapter 5
Bylaws and Governance

> **Synopsis:** Bylaws provide general policy guidelines for nonprofit corporations. There are statutory provisions that go into effect automatically in the absence of comparable bylaw provisions. It is a critically important function for nonprofit organizations to find and retain qualified, experienced board members and officers. Board meetings generally have a routine order of business and provide the forum for governing a nonprofit organization.

Bylaws

Every corporation must have a set of bylaws that provides for its internal management and regulation. Perhaps the best advice on formulating organizational bylaws can be found in the publication Robert's Rules of Order Newly Revised, 10th Edition, published in November 2000 by Perseus Books ($37.50). The 802-page book contains an invaluable wealth of knowledge not only on parliamentary procedure but also on organizational leadership. This book provides guidance on drafting certain bylaw provisions, and includes a sample set of bylaws. An abridged, inexpensive paperback parliamentary guide, Robert's Rules in Brief (Second Edition), published in 2011, is available (Da Capo Press 208 pages, $7.50).

Each state has individual requirements for the content of bylaws for nonprofit corporations, although these requirements tend to be similar. Beyond legal requirements, corporate bylaws are a necessary and important document, and great thought and care should be exercised as to what will be included in them.

Typical bylaws include provisions governing the following internal procedures and policies of the nonprofit corporation:

- The purposes of the corporation, consistent with any federal tax law limitation or state laws governing lobbying or other activity
- Limitations of liability of directors, consistent with state law
- Types of officers
- Terms, powers, and succession of officers
- Location of principal office
- Whether the corporation will have members, or whether all powers will be vested in a board of directors
- How directors will be selected and how vacancies will be filled
- How many directors there will be

- Length of terms of board of directors, limits on consecutive terms, and if and how such terms will overlap with other board members
- Terms under which a member of the board of directors can be disqualified
- Conditions under which the annual meeting and other regularly scheduled board meetings are held
- How unscheduled meetings of the board may be called
- Terms under which notice of board meetings must occur
- What constitutes a quorum for the transaction of business
- How many directors are required to approve an action
- Whether actions of the board may be ratified through the mail or by conference call, or require directors to be present at a meeting
- Power of the chairperson (or president) to appoint committees, and to provide for rules, powers, and procedures of such committees
- Whether alternates may be empowered to represent directors, and who selects them
- Who is responsible for preparing board meeting minutes
- Who is responsible for keeping and reviewing the corporate books, and dispersing corporate funds
- How amendments may be made to the bylaws
- Terms and conditions regarding compensation, if any, paid to directors
- What committees are authorized, and what powers and duties they have
- The terms under which the corporation will be dissolved
- Which, if any, parliamentary procedure will be used at board meetings.

Legal Requirements of Bylaws

Each state has laws providing for some minimum standards with respect to nonprofit corporation bylaws.

Most of these laws provide rules on many of the above bylaw options in the absence of explicit directions in the nonprofit corporation's bylaws. Thus, it is important to place provisions in the bylaws that will be intended to supersede these statutory legal guidelines, if the directors feel that the guidance provided in law is not acceptable to the corporation.

Among the bylaws provisions that deserve the highest consideration and thought are the following, with some comments about the issues they raise:

Quorum Requirements

A quorum is the minimum number of members or directors required to be present for a meeting to be held for the legal transaction of business. The purpose of a quorum requirement is to assure that actions are taken by a representative number of duly authorized participants rather than by an elite few. Standard advice, in the absence of relying on any statutory requirement, is to set the quorum at the minimum number of people who will be expected to attend a meeting, taking into account emergencies, adverse weather conditions, or conflicts with competing meetings. If the bylaws permit it, board members may participate in meetings and be counted as part of a quorum if they are in communication by speaker phone or by conference call.

Because actions cannot be taken legally at board meetings without a quorum present, it is best to begin with a conservatively low quorum requirement. Then change the bylaws to increase that number as appropriate. Otherwise, it is possible that the corporation will never have a quorum for its meetings, even if the sole purpose of the meeting is to change the bylaws to decrease the number of directors constituting a quorum.

Voting Rights

Boards need to vote to formally demonstrate that they have taken actions. Many organizations can be effectively run by consensus rather than by formal voting, but even the most congenial and tolerant boards will eventually face issues that will divide them. In the absence of a provision in the bylaws, action may be taken at a board meeting with the approval of a majority of directors who are present at the meeting. Nothing prohibits a two-thirds vote from being required to ensure that actions are closer to representing a consensus. A two-thirds vote may be suggested for changing bylaws, or for changing membership dues requirements. Generally, a majority vote is sufficient for most routine board decisions, and avoids the inability to take positions and actions that can occur as a result of a two-thirds voting requirement.

Selection of Officers

Many organizations are attracted to the democratic notion of offices being opened to all. With such a policy, any director can run for an office, ballots are prepared, and the winner is selected by the majority (or plurality) of voters from the board of directors or the membership at large. Other organizations feel that democracy puts at risk an orderly succession and threatens the existing power structure. Orderly succession can be accomplished by providing for a nominating committee, appointed by the chairperson, which selects a slate of officers. This slate is then perfunctorily approved by the full board. Both systems have their advantages and disadvantages.

Some organizations utilize a third alternative that combines the two. The nominations committee recommends a slate of candidates, but the procedures permit other candidates to run as well.

Executive Committees

Board meetings may occur at regular intervals, but issues arise in the interim that demand immediate attention. In such cases, it is valuable to have a mandated procedure for taking legally legitimate actions in the absence of board meetings. The mechanism to accomplish this is the executive committee, provided for in the corporate bylaws. Although the executive committee typically is comprised of the corporation's officers, many state laws authorize executive committees comprised of one or more directors appointed by the board. Typically, by law, the executive committee has all of the power and authority of the full board with the following exceptions:

- The executive committee cannot fill vacancies on the board.
- The executive committee cannot adopt, amend, or repeal bylaws.
- The executive committee cannot have powers inconsistent with the resolution passed by the board establishing it.

Governance

The term "governance" refers to the exercise of authority over an organization that relates to providing direction and control for the purpose of ensuring that it stays true to its mission and achieves its purposes. Governance in a nonprofit organization is entrusted to the board of directors (also often referred to as "board of trustees"). Governance responsibilities include hiring, evaluating, and disciplining the chief staff officer, who may be called the executive director, president, or chief executive officer. Governance is comprised of the structures, responsibilities, and processes that the organization uses to support its mission. It is the process of setting and safeguarding the strategic direction for the organization, and includes four principal components:

1. *accountability*—requires that these decision-makers are legally liable for the actions they take, and apply sanctions against those who violate the organization's rules.

2. *transparency*—provides for stakeholder access to reliable information about the organization's operations, including financial information.

3. *predictability*—assures that the organization is in compliance with all laws and regulations, and that the policies of the organization are fairly and uniformly enforced.

4. *participation*—assures that in making decisions, the board members receive wide input with respect to planning, decision processes, and evaluation. (Gill, 2005).

Governance differs from management in that the latter consists of the processes used to *carry out* the strategic leadership of those governing the organization, including the supervision of those who do the work of the organization, such as staff and volunteers. Management is typically reserved for paid staff, although it is, of course, not unusual for a nonprofit organization to have no staff, with all management responsibilities divided up among board members.

Governance and management functions occasionally overlap in organizations, and each one develops its own culture with respect to what responsibilities are those of the board and what is handled by staff. Ideally, there should be a delineation between management and governance functions.

Most nonprofit organizations, particularly those that will seek tax-exempt status from the state and federal government, will formalize their organizational structure by filing corporate papers with the state's corporation bureau. Having a board as a governance structure is a requirement for all corporations. The board is the legally constituted "owner" of a nonprofit organization, and each board member has a fiduciary responsibility to act in the interest of the organization rather than his or her own individual interests (see chapter 4).

Typologies of Boards

As one might expect, nonprofit boards differ substantially with respect to the number of members, the diversity of their composition, the degree to which they get involved in the day-to-day operations of the organization, the committee structures they may have, and the amount of authority they delegate to the executive director. Scholarly attempts to categorize boards into general types have been made, and this section conveys two attempts to classify boards based on general characteristics.

The first, offered by Mel Gill (2005), proposes nine general types:

1. *Operational*—Board members and other volunteers do all of the work of the organization. Organizations with this model are typically newly founded and do not have any staff.

2. *Collective*—Board and staff work together to do the work of the organization, and staff have a strong role in typical governance issues.

3. *Management*—Board members are the primary managers of the work of the organization, but there may be a staff coordinator. The staff report to individual board member managers, who may be committee chairs who are responsible for various organization activities, such as personnel, finances, and service delivery.

4. *Constituent Representational*—Board members are comprised of various stakeholder constituencies, and tend to represent the interests of the organizations who elected them to the nonprofit board.

5. *Traditional*—Oversight of management staff is achieved through functional committees, and staff manage and report to these committees. At times, these committees may be involved in management activities.

6. *Results-Based*—The board sets direction of the organization, and the executive director is charged with achieving the goals set by the board. The executive director is often a non-voting member of the board, has a major role in setting this direction, but is evaluated by the board periodically.

7. *Policy Governance*—Often referred to as the "Carver Model," the board sets general goals and policies, provides some general limitations (particularly relating to ethics), and then gets out of the way and lets the executive director have the freedom to choose the means to achieve those goals. One aspect that distinguishes this model from others is that the board uses ad hoc task forces to assist management rather than permanent committees.

8. *Fundraising*—These boards typically serve primarily to raise money to support the work of the organization.

9. *Advisory*—This type of board is comprised of high profile (and perhaps wealthy) members of the community who rubber-stamp whatever the executive director suggests, and typically have little, if any, role in what is traditionally considered to be governance.

Gill suggests that these board types fall along a continuum. Organizations of the first type (operational) are at one extreme of this continuum, and are small, not complex, and have board members with a high degree of involvement in management activities. At the other extreme of the continuum are those in the ninth type (advisory) where the organizations tend to be quite large, complex, and have board members with minimal day-to-day involvement in management operations. The other types are in the middle, in approximate order along this continuum.

A second typology, offered by Chait, Ryan, and Taylor, et al. (2005), has three types of boards. It is based on the role that the board members play in dealing with the organization's future.

The three types of governance are:

Type I: Fiduciary—These boards have as their principal focus the stewardship of resources. Its committees are often structured along the lines of their focus, such as fundraising, budgeting, auditing, investments, and program review.

Type II: Strategic—These boards create a strategic partnership with management to plan for the future. They look at the organization's strengths and weaknesses, how the outside environment is changing, and consider modifying the direction of the organization to respond. Type II boards focus more on "big thinking questions" such as "what is the future of the organization when there are likely changes in demographics or service needs?" rather than how much money should be allocated next year for staff conferences, and whether the amount spent this year for that line-item was appropriate—typical Type I questions.

Type III: Generative—These boards spend more time dreaming about the organization's future, thinking "outside of the box" to develop new ways to think about the organization's problems, how to deal with them in new ways (often through brainstorming sessions), and raising existential questions. They may consider problems that do not even exist yet, and where the organization fits into the big picture of accomplishing the core mission for which it was established.

The authors suggest that boards should be engaging in all three types of modes for peak performance, but that most boards tend to engage in one mode more than the others.

Forming a Board of Directors

One important requirement of a nonprofit organization is the formation of a board of directors. The board has the responsibility to set policy for the organization consistent with all applicable federal, state, and local laws and to see that the policies are implemented.

The size of the board should depend on the needs of the organization. If the board's role is strictly policy-making and the policies are implemented by a qualified staff, a small board might be appropriate. However, if extensive board time is required for fundraising or implementing programs, then a larger board is in order.

The number of board members is established in the bylaws. One effective technique is to set a minimum and maximum number of board members and to allow the board to determine its own size within these parameters. Then the board can start small and add members as the need arises.

The term of board members must be included in the bylaws. Board members should have fixed terms of office. One common practice is for all board members to have three-year terms, with one-third of the members having their terms expire each year. In this way, board continuity is assured. Some boards allow their members to serve unlimited terms; other boards wish to limit the number to ensure new members with fresh ideas.

The election process should also be spelled out in the bylaws.

Many organizations have a nominating or governance committee that is responsible for recommending new board members to the full board. Additional candidates for board membership can be nominated either in advance or from the floor during the election.

The titles, duties, length of term, and process for the election of officers should be spelled out in the bylaws.

Organizational Officers

The elected officers of most organizations are similar:

Chairperson, Chair, or President
Convenes and leads the meetings of the organization. Appoints committee chairs. Either signs checks or delegates this duty to another individual.

Vice-Chair or Vice-President
Assumes the duties of the president or chair in his or her absence, or upon his or her death or resignation. In many organizations, is given specific responsibilities either in the bylaws or by vote. In some organizations, automatically becomes the next president. Some organizations have more than one; some may have a President-elect.

Secretary
Either takes minutes at the board meeting or approves the minutes if taken by another individual. Responsible for all official correspondence.

Treasurer
Responsible for finances of the organization. Usually makes financial reports to the board and signs checks. The actual responsibilities will depend upon whether the organization has staff who manage fiscal duties.

In some organizations, the officers are elected by the full membership. In others, the board of directors elects its own officers.

Recruiting Good Board Members

Many organizations are finding it more difficult than ever to attract excellent board members. This is due to many factors, such as the large increase in the number of nonprofit boards, the increasing demands of being in the work force, and the fact that upwardly mobile professionals often relocate.

In order to ensure excellence, many nominating committees meet several times during the year rather than just once, to search for potential board members. One effective technique is to strive for a diverse board, and to list the types of characteristics desired. Some might be:

- *Expertise*: Some board members should have personnel management, fiscal, fundraising, or legal expertise.

- *Ages*: It is helpful to have older people represented, as well as youth and individuals in between.

- *Races and Religions:* All major races and religions in the community should be represented on a diverse board.

- *Backgrounds:* It would be helpful if some board members had corporate backgrounds, some were government leaders, and others served on boards of other nonprofit groups.

- *Users of the service:* Many boards include representatives of the client population being served.

A short version oft repeated is that nominations committees should seek those who fulfill at least one, and ideally more than one, of the following three W's: wealth, wisdom, and work, but not an over-reliance on any single attribute.

The nominating committee or board development committee can search throughout the year for individuals with these characteristics, who are then asked if they want to be considered for board membership.

Each board should have a list of board member responsibilities. These might include attending board meetings on a regular basis, serving on at least one standing committee, and participating in fundraising. The list of duties should be provided to each prospective board member, and no board member should be elected who will not agree to meet these responsibilities.

Keeping Good Board Members

One technique for keeping good board members is to require all new board members to participate in an orientation program before they attend their first board meeting.

The first step in the process is to review materials that all board members should have received prior to the program. These include—

- Articles of Incorporation
- Bylaws
- Funding applications
- Personnel, fiscal, and other board policies
- Annual reports
- Names, addresses, phone numbers, and biographical sketches of other board members and key staff members
- List of committees and committee duties
- Minutes of the last several board meetings
- Audits, budgets, and recent financial statements.

The second step is to hold a meeting with the board chair and the executive director. This provides an opportunity to ask questions about the materials received, visit the staff offices and programs, get an update of current issues, and review board member responsibilities. Other steps to encourage productivity of board members include—

- Give board members specific projects. A board member who serves as the chair of a committee or who has specific fundraising responsibilities is more likely to stay active.
- Keep board meetings interesting.
- Thank board members for their work.
- Have social events periodically, in addition to formal board meetings.

One other technique is to remove unproductive board members quickly and replace them with new and productive ones.

Other ways to increase board productivity include—

- Having a policy in the bylaws that missing a specified number of board meetings without a reason will result in automatic dismissal.
- Re-electing only board members who have been meeting their responsibilities.

- Calling board members who have not been active to ask them if there are any problems. In some cases, the chairperson should ask for their resignation if they do not agree to meet board responsibilities.

Board Responsibilities

There are three functions of the board that are of paramount importance.

Perhaps the most important function of the board of directors is to define and safeguard the organization's mission and values. The board is expected to disapprove any proposed program or change of direction proposed by management, unless it formally votes to approve such a change. The board also should periodically review the programs and operations of the organization to assure they are consistent with the mission, and are effectively meeting the needs for which they were established.

The second most important is to hire (and then periodically evaluate, and if necessary, discipline or remove) the executive director, the chief paid staff person of the organization (who also may be referred to as the CEO, President, or CEO and President), if it has one. The board then makes assignments to that individual and monitors his or her's performance. It is appropriate for the board or its Personnel Committee to do a formal performance appraisal of the CEO at least annually. The board approves salary scales and job descriptions for the other staff members, who are hired by the executive director. The board approves the personnel policies for the organization.

And third, the board should be responsible for setting policy with respect to the ethical values of the organization (for example, approving an ethics code), not delegating this important function to management.

Among other typical functions of the board of directors include—

Finance
The board approves budgets for the organization. No funds are expended unless the funds are included in a budget approved by the board. The board approves spending reports, which are submitted on a regular basis.

Fundraising
The board approves plans for special events and fundraising, and board members are expected to participate in these special events.

Planning
Board members approve short- and long-range plans for the organization. They then monitor the effectiveness of the organization's programs to see if they have met the goals outlined in the plans.

Board Development
The board selects new board members and adopts procedures to see that excellent board members are selected and continue to serve.

Public Relations
Board members are aware of all of the organization's activities and encourage participation in appropriate activities by the community.

Advising
Board members advise the executive director on policy implementation as requested.

How Boards Function Effectively

Boards set policies through a majority vote of their members at board meetings, unless the bylaws provide otherwise. For boards with staff, one effective method of policy-making is to ask the staff to draft proposed policies. These policies are then sent to a board committee for review.

The chair of each committee should be a board member appointed by the board president. Members of committees are frequently selected by the committee chair and may include non-board members.

All committees are advisory, except that the bylaws may permit the executive committee to act on behalf of the board between board meetings. Once a committee approves a proposed policy, it is submitted to the board for approval. The board may delegate authority to committees to implement some decisions.

Board members who want a policy to be adopted begin the discussion by making a motion that it be approved. If another board member seconds the motion, discussion can begin; if not, the motion fails.

Once a motion is seconded, the chairperson opens the floor for discussion. Members are recognized by the chairperson before they may speak, and they can discuss only the motion on the floor. When the discussion has ended, the chairperson announces that a vote will be taken.

The easiest way to vote is by a show of hands. The secretary can then record the vote. If more than a majority approves a policy, it becomes the board's policy (unless the bylaws provide otherwise). It is the responsibility of the executive director to implement that policy.

The executive director receives instructions from the board at a board meeting. It is improper for individual board members to give assignments to any staff member without prior board authorization.

Holding High-Quality Board Meetings

One key factor in getting and keeping excellent board members is the quality of the board meetings. If board meetings are unproductive, board members tend to be unproductive.

An important technique for improving board meetings is to do as much planning *before the board meeting* as possible.

This might include:

- Sending a notice of the date, time, and location of the meeting to the members several weeks before the meeting. Even if the board meets the same day of each month at the same place and time, a reminder notice is important.

- Giving the board members the telephone number and e-mail address of the individual (usually the chairperson) to contact if they cannot attend the meeting. This way, the chairperson can get input on important items from individuals who cannot attend the meeting. Moreover, if a quorum will not be present, the meeting can be canceled in advance.

- Notifying members of important items to be discussed at the meeting. For major items, information or issue papers might be included in the meeting notice packet.

- Including as many written items as possible with the meeting notice rather than distributing them at the meeting. These may include the minutes of the previous meeting and the treasurer's report, for example. Members then have an opportunity to read items before the meeting, and members who do not attend the meeting are kept informed more effectively.

- Developing a preliminary agenda before the meeting. Committee chairs who will be asked to report at the meeting should be notified. Background reports should be developed for important issues.

The board meetings should start on time. Once the members know that every board meeting starts on time, it is much more likely that they will be prompt. Each board meeting should start with the distribution of a written agenda. The agenda should be as detailed as possible, listing each separate item on which to be voted.

Once the secretary announces that a quorum is present, the chairperson asks all those present if there are any additional items for the agenda. Thus, there will be no surprises, and the chairperson can run the meeting more effectively. The chairperson has the option of referring new items to committees or postponing items until future meetings.

A typical order of business at a board meeting is as follows:

- *Approval of the Minutes of the Previous Meeting.* A formal vote is needed to approve the minutes. Minutes should be distributed to all members and should not be read aloud at the meeting.

- *Chairperson's Report.* The chairperson should state before each item whether it is informational only or requires board action. The chairperson should remind the members that only policy-making recommendations require board action.

- *Executive Director's Report.* This report should be in writing. If it is lengthy, it should be distributed before the meeting. The executive director should then highlight important aspects of the written report and take questions.

- *Committee Reports.* Committee reports should be in writing unless they are very brief. After giving the report, the committee chair should make specific motions when board action is required. Only policy items require board action; no board action is required when the committee chair is simply providing information.

- *Unfinished Business.* The only items belonging in this section are ones raised at previous board meetings. The chairperson should remind the members when the item was raised originally and why it was postponed.

- *New Business.* Major items of business are discussed as part of the chairperson's report, executive director's report, or committee reports. At the beginning of the meeting, members are asked if they have additional agenda items, and the chairperson has the option of placing some of these items under New Business.

- *Good and Welfare.* Many organizations provide an opportunity for members and guests to make short announcements, raise issues to be discussed at future meetings, or comment on items of interest.

- *Adjournment.* No formal action is needed. The chairperson announces the date, time, and place of the next meeting, reminds the members of steps to be taken before the meeting, such as committee meetings, and adjourns the board meeting.

After the board meeting, the minutes are sent to board members for their review. The minutes must include a list of attendees and the motions made and votes taken. Additional information may be included at the discretion of the board. Many organizations include only the minimum required, and the minutes do not include individual comments made at the meeting. Although the minutes need not be taken by the board secretary, they should be distributed over the signature of the board secretary.

Relationship Between Board and Staff Members

The board of directors sets policy for the organization. Several examples of the types of policies set by the board are provided above. The only way policy can be set is by a majority vote of the board at a board meeting (unless the bylaws provide otherwise).

The executive director of the organization attends all board meetings, and is responsible for implementing the policies set by the board. The executive director hires other staff members (whose salary ranges and job descriptions often, but not always, have been approved by the board) to assist in implementing these policies.

When an item arises at a board meeting, the chairperson rules whether the item is a policy matter. If so, a vote of the board is required in order for action to be taken. If the item is not a policy matter, no board vote is taken. The purpose of the discussion is to provide guidance to the executive director on non-policy matters.

Certain types of communications between board members and staff members are not appropriate. For example, individual board members may not give assignments to staff members. Assignments are given to the executive director by vote of the board at a board meeting. The executive director is responsible for assigning tasks to other staff members.

Staff members should not complain to individual board members about programs, assignments, or policies. Complaints should be made according to specific procedures established by the board.

When a board member volunteers to help out in the office, that person must be treated as a staff person and no longer wears the "board hat." The executive director remains the person to make assignments to that person.

Parliamentary Procedure

Board meetings of nonprofit organizations may be formally or informally conducted, but its decisions made consistent with law and its bylaws are legally binding and may be enforced by a court. At times, decision-making can be a contentious exercise. Without an acceptance of basic rules for conducting meetings by those who attend, a meeting could become highly dysfunctional, with meaningful decision-making becoming impossible. Members may all decide to speak at once, may disagree on whether a decision has been really been made, may refuse to accept decisions made by the chair, or otherwise become frustrated when they do not feel that their participation has been treated respectfully and have been given a fair opportunity to voice their opinions and advocate for their positions.

Over the centuries, a set of standardized, basic rules for conducting meetings fairly has been developed. The standard used by many nonprofit organization boards is based on Roberts Rules of Order, first published in 1874. Henry M. Roberts, a West Point graduate, based his manual on a 15-page set of parliamentary rules he developed to help him, his wife, and others who served on the boards of various nonprofit organizations (source: Darwin Patnode, History of Parliamentary Procedure; *http://eagle.orgfree.com/parliamentary.society.of.toronto_40rogers.com/ Presentations/History_of_Parliamentary_Procedure.htm).* Roberts was influenced by the writings on the topic by Thomas Jefferson (Jefferson's Manual, which still serves as the rules of debate for the U.S. House of Representatives) and others that governed the debates of the Senate. These rules are based on rules of the English Parliament, from which the term "parliamentary procedure" derives its name.

Several other parliamentary procedure manuals are in use, among them the *Standard Code of Parliamentary Procedure* by Alice Sturgess (1950), George Demeter's *Demeter's Manual of Parliamentary Law and Procedure* (1969), and *Modern Parliamentary Procedure* by Ray E. Keesey (1974).

In nonprofit organizations, in which participants volunteer their time, it makes some sense to follow parliamentary procedure a bit more loosely compared to legislative bodies, keeping an eye on the objective of keeping meetings civil and assuring that decisions made by the board truly reflect either a consensus of members, or at least a majority. The more participants there are at a meeting, the more likely that increased formality will be productive.

There are five clear advantages to conducting meetings using parliamentary procedure, including—

1. There are procedures to ending debate, which in some cases could otherwise drag on interminably
2. Everyone with something to say has the opportunity to be heard
3. Debate on any issue remains on topic, and new topics are considered only after there is closure on the previous topic, or there is agreement to postpone closure
4. There is a procedure to reconsider decisions that may have been made in haste and without complete information
5. There are rules to deal with destructive, personal confrontations

Typically, board meetings are conducted by the President (or Chair) of the board. It helps when that individual has a basic understanding of parliamentary procedure, although some organizations will hire a Certified Professional Parliamentarian with specific knowledge of parliamentary procedure to advise the chair (see: *http://www.jimslaughter.com/handouts.cfm* for lots of free resources about conducting a meeting using parliamentary procedure).

Many organizations will indicate in their bylaws that meetings shall use a particular form of parliamentary procedure, such as—

The rules contained in the current edition of Robert's Rules of Order Newly Revised *shall govern the organization in all cases to which they are applicable and in which they are not inconsistent with these bylaws and any special rules of order the Society may adopt.*

For an explanation of Robert's Rules and details about how it works in practice, see the Robert's Rules Web site at: *http://www.robertsrules.com/*

Discussion Questions

1. What do you think are the difficulties that arise when an organization has too many or too few board members? What types of organizations should have larger/fewer board members than other types of organizations?

2. What strategies might you suggest for an organization that has a board member who is always disruptive or oppositional?

3. What should be the role of an executive director in choosing board members?

4. What should the response be of a board member who feels that a board decision is unethical, but is receiving no support from other board members to thwart that decision?

5. Should a board member be expected or required to make financial contributions to an organization?

6. Is it ever appropriate for a board member to have business relationships with his or her organization? If so, what safeguards should be in place?

Activities

1. Seek permission to attend, as a class or as an individual, a board meeting of your school or other community nonprofit organization.

2. Invite the Chair of the board of directors of a local nonprofit organization to speak to the class about the tensions of board/staff relations and the responsibilities of serving as a volunteer Chair.

3. Invite the executive director of a local nonprofit organization to discuss his or her perspective about the issues noted in Activity #2.

4. Research the John Carver model of board governance and compare and contrast it to a more typical board governance model.

5. Hold a mock board meeting of a nonprofit organization after assigning roles of officers and staff to members of the class and creating an agenda of required action and decision-making.

6. Draft mock bylaws for an organization that will advocate on behalf of work-study students at your university.

Tips for Practitioners

1. Review state law with respect to corporate bylaws. Identify which provisions are required, which provisions apply only in the absence of a different provision in the bylaws, and which act to pre-empt the statutory guideline.

2. Give careful consideration to the more important bylaw provisions, such as—

    - Quorum requirements
    - Succession of officers
    - Powers of the executive committee
    - Voting by the board of directors

3. Have an attorney review the bylaws to ensure that they are in compliance with state law, and ensure that the organization's desires with respect to internal decision-making will be consistent with efficient operating procedures.

4. Schedule an organizational meeting to approve the bylaws, and distribute a draft of proposed bylaws before this meeting.

5. After a final version of the bylaws is approved, provide a final copy of the bylaws to all members of the board of directors.

6. If leaning toward incorporation, identify potential incorporators/board members who are—

    - Accessible, and not spread too thin among many other competing organizations
    - Potential contributors to the organization
    - Experienced fundraisers
    - Knowledgeable about the issues of concern to the organization
    - Respected and well-known in the community
    - Experienced in legal, accounting, and nonprofit management issues.

7. Develop a list of typical decision areas that are likely to arise in the course of routine corporate operations and reach a board consensus on whether the decisions should be made by—

    - The executive director alone
    - The executive director, in consultation with the board
    - The executive director, in consultation with the board chairperson
    - The board alone
    - The chairperson alone
    - A committee of the board.

    Review, revise, and update this list annually.

8. Consider adopting a policy on the responsibilities and privileges of board members, and include a conflict-of-interest policy. A sample IRS-recommended conflict of interest policy may be found on the Web at:

    http://www.irs.gov/pub/irs-pdf/i1023.pdf

Online Resources to Explore

Carter McNamara's Overview of Roles and Responsibilities of Corporate Board of Directors
  http://www.managementhelp.org/boards/brdrspon.htm

Institute on Governance (Canada)
http://iog.ca/

PolicyGovernance.com: The Policy Governance Model
http://www.carvergovernance.com/model.htm

Alliance for Nonprofit Management
http://www.allianceonline.org/

BoardSource
http://www.boardsource.org

BoardnetUSA
http://www.boardnetusa.org/public/home.asp

For Further Reading

Bates, D. (1983, Winter). *How to be a better board member: Guidelines for trustees.* Voluntary Action Leadership.

Board Source. (2012). *The nonprofit board answer book: A practical guide for board members and chief executives.* (3rd Ed.) Washington, DC: Author.

Board Source. (2010). *The handbook of nonprofit governance (Essential texts for nonprofit and public leadership and management).* San Francisco: Jossey-Bass.

Carver, J., & Carver, M. M. (1996a). *CarverGuide, Basic principles of policy governance.* San Francisco: Jossey-Bass.

Carver, J., & Carver, M. M. (1996b). *CarverGuide, Your roles and responsibilities as a boardmember.* San Francisco: Jossey Bass.

Chait, R., Ryan, W., and Taylor, B. (2005). *Governance as Leadership.* Hoboken, NJ: Wiley.

Conrad, W. R. Jr. (2003). *New effective voluntary board Of directors: What it does and how it works.* Chicago, IL: Swallow Press.

Gill, M. (2005). *Governing for results: A director's guide to good governance.* Victoria, BC: Trafford.

Gottlieb, H. (2008). *Board recruitment and orientation: A step-by-step common sense guide.* Tucson, AZ: Renaissance Press.

Grace, S. (2013). *The ultimate board member's book, newly revised edition: A 1-hour guide to understanding and fulfilling your role and responsibilities.* Medfield, MA: Emerson and Church.

Howe, F. (1995). *Welcome to the board: Your guide to effective participation.* San Francisco: Jossey Bass.

Ingram, R. (2009). *Ten basic responsibilities of nonprofit boards* (2nd Ed.). Washington, DC: Board Source.

Mancuso, A. (2011). *Nonprofit meetings, minutes & records: How to run your nonprofit corporation so you don't run into trouble.* Berkeley, CA: Nolo.

O'Connell, B. (1993). *The board member's book: Making a difference in voluntary organizations.* (2nd Ed.). New York: The Foundation Center.

O'Connell, B. (1988a). *Finding, developing and rewarding good board members.* Nonprofit Management Series (#2). Washington, DC: Independent Sector.

O'Connell, B. (1988b). *The role of the board and board members.* Nonprofit Management Series (#1). Washington, DC: Independent Sector.

Tesdahl, D. B. (2005). *The nonprofit board's guide to bylaws: Creating a framework for effective governance.* Washington, DC: Board Source.

Chapter 6
Mission and Vision Statements

> **Synopsis:** Mission and vision statements provide a foundation for your organization's future and help keep it focused on the purposes for which it was created. The mission statement includes the core organizational purpose. The vision statement describes the ideal future of the organization. Both are useful in maintaining the stability of organizations.

Every nonprofit organization should have a mission statement and a vision statement. Many nonprofit executives are confused about the difference between the two, and this is not surprising, since organizational consultants disagree among themselves about what they should contain.

The Mission Statement

The mission statement should be a succinct description of the basic purpose of the organization, including the nature of the work to be carried out, the reason the organization exists, and the clients and constituencies it is designed to serve. It may also include some principles and values that are to guide the organization, although these can be enumerated in a separate values/principles statement.

The mission statement serves two main purposes.

First, it is a basic document guiding decision-making for the organization. The mission statement can effectively place a constraint on decision-making that is inconsistent with the organization's core purpose, and thus provide a mechanism for organizational stability. Any decision made by an organization that would result in activities that contradict the mission statement should either not be implemented, or should require a major soul-searching by the organization's board of directors.

A second purpose is to provide the organization's board and staff with a useful short description of the organization. This permits all who work with the organization to be on the same page with respect to its core purpose. The mission statement serves an important public relations function by explaining to important stakeholders, such as funders, government regulators, and clients, what the organization is about.

Many mission statements contain two parts, although the first part is sufficient. The first part is often referred to as the "umbrella," a short overview of the purpose of the organization. For example, the Pennsylvania Jewish Coalition's mission is "to monitor legislative and regulatory developments in Harrisburg that affect Pennsylvania's organized Jewish community."

A second part of the mission statement, which many consider to be optional, provides more detail. One way to do this is to add the following after the umbrella: "In support of this mission, we..." followed by general, bullet-pointed objectives relating to who we are, who we serve, what benefits we provide to those we serve, and how we provide this benefit. For example, objectives that might be included are increasing public awareness about the organization's goals and objectives; meeting the needs of clients; providing quality services; and maintaining relationships with officials from the government, the media, the advocacy community, and the public.

The Vision Statement

The vision statement is related to, but clearly different from, the mission statement. Its purpose is to convey the ideal future of the organization—what it hopes to become in the eyes of its board, staff, and stakeholders. One purpose of the vision statement is to inspire those in the organization to achieve goals. Another is to help frame decisions made by the organization in the context of achieving these goals.

Among the issues that might be appropriate in a vision statement include the organization's place in society, its intended growth, its use of new technology, quality improvement, its reputation in the community, and how the public perceives the organization's effectiveness and efficiency. It also could include how it will serve as a good organizational citizen in the community, a measurement of the degree to which it hopes to contribute to solving (or mitigating) particular social problems, and whether and to what degree the problem is solved as a result of the organization's actions.

One of the best guides on the preparation of mission statements and vision statements is a 1996 book, *A Guide to Strategic Thinking: Building Your Planning Foundation* by George Morrisey (Jossey-Bass).

Examples of Mission and Vision Statements

The following are examples of mission and vision statements:

Mission Statement of the Pennsylvania Association of Nonprofit Organizations (reprinted with permission):

PANO is the statewide membership organization serving and advancing the charitable nonprofit sector through leadership, advocacy, education and services in order to improve the quality of life in Pennsylvania.

Mission Statement of the Iowa Nonprofit Resource Center (reprinted with permission):

The Iowa Nonprofit Resource Center is a University of Iowa interdisciplinary collaboration to make more accessible educational and service programs focused on strengthening the operational capacity of Iowa nonprofit organizations. The Center provides information and training resources to charitable, nonprofit organizations and interested persons throughout Iowa.

Our mission is to build the capacity and develop the effectiveness of community-based organizations and to enhance the overall effectiveness of local organizations in building communities. Moreover, by involving students the Center can introduce them to the nonprofit sector and develop their sense of community service.

Mission Statement of The NonProfit Alliance (reprinted with permission):

The NonProfit Alliance is dedicated to serving, supporting and strengthening the nonprofit community of Calhoun County, Michigan

Vision Statement of California State University, Monterey Bay (CSUMB) (reprinted with permission):

California State University, Monterey Bay (CSUMB) is envisioned as a comprehensive state university which values service through high quality education. The campus will be distinctive in serving the diverse people of California, especially the working class and historically undereducated and low-income populations. It will feature an enriched living and learning environment and year-round operation. The identity of the university will be framed by substantive commitment to multilingual, multicultural, gender-equitable learning. The university will be a collaborative, intellectual community distinguished by partnerships with existing institutions both public and private, cooperative agreements which enable students, faculty, and staff to cross institutional boundaries for innovative instruction, broadly defined scholarly and creative activity, and coordinated community service.

The university will invest in preparation for the future through integrated and experimental use of technologies as resources to people, catalysts for learning, and providers of increased access and enriched quality learning. The curriculum of CSUMB will be student and society centered and of sufficient breadth and depth to meet statewide and regional needs, specifically those involving both inner-city and isolated rural populations, and needs relevant to communities in the immediate Tri-County region (Monterey, Santa Cruz, and San Benito). The programs of instruction will strive for distinction, building on regional assets in developing specialty clusters in such areas as: the sciences (marine, atmo-

spheric, and environmental); visual and performing arts and related humanities; languages, cultures, and international studies; education; business; studies of human behavior, information, and communication, within broad curricular areas; and professional study.

The university will develop a culture of innovation in its overall conceptual design and organization, and will utilize new and varied pedagogical and instructional approaches including distance learning. Institutional programs will value and cultivate creative and productive talents of students, faculty, and staff, and seek ways to contribute to the economy of the state, the well-being of our communities, and the quality of life and development of its students, faculty, and service areas.

The education programs at CSUMB will:

- *Integrate the sciences, the arts and humanities, liberal studies, and professional training;*
- *Integrate modern learning technology and pedagogy to create liberal education adequate for the contemporary world;*
- *Integrate work and learning, service and reflection;*
- *Recognize the importance of global interdependence;*
- *Invest in languages and cross-cultural competence;*
- *Emphasize those topics most central to the local area's economy and ecology, and California's long-term needs;*
- *Offer a multicultural, gender-equitable, intergenerational, and accessible residential learning environment.*

The university will provide a new model of organizing, managing, and financing higher education:

- *The university will be integrated with other institutions, essentially collaborative in its orientation, and active in seeking partnerships across institutional boundaries. It will develop and implement various arrangements for sharing courses, curriculum, faculty, students, and facilities with other institutions.*
- *The organizational structure of the university will reflect a belief in the importance of each administrative staff and faculty member, working to integrate the university community across "staff" and "faculty" lines.*
- *The financial aid system will emphasize a fundamental commitment to equity and access.*
- *The budget and financial systems, including student fees, will provide for efficient and effective operation of the university.*
- *University governance will be exercised with a substantial amount of*

autonomy and independence within a very broad CSU systemwide policy context.
- *Accountability will emphasize careful evaluation and assessment of results and outcomes.*

Our vision of the goals of California State University, Monterey Bay includes: a model pluralistic academic community where all learn and teach one another in an atmosphere of mutual respect and pursuit of excellence; a faculty and staff motivated to excel in their respective fields as well as to contribute to the broadly defined university environment. Our graduates will have an understanding of interdependence and global competence, distinctive technical and educational skills, the experience and abilities to contribute to California's high quality work force, the critical thinking abilities to be productive citizens, and the social responsibility and skills to be community builders. CSUMB will dynamically link the past, present, and future by responding to historical and changing conditions, experimenting with strategies which increase access, improve quality, and lower costs through education in a distinctive CSU environment. University students and personnel will attempt analytically and creatively to meet critical state and regional needs, and to provide California with responsible and creative leadership for the global 21st century.

Vision Statement of the Young Adult Library Services Association, a division of the American Library Association (reprinted with permission).

In every library in the nation, quality library service to young adults is provided by a staff that understands and respects the unique informational, educational and recreational needs of teenagers. Equal access to information, services and materials is recognized as a right not a privilege. Young adults are actively involved in the library decision-making process. The library staff collaborates and cooperates with other youth-serving agencies to provide a holistic, community-wide network of activities and services that support healthy development.

To ensure that this vision becomes a reality, the Young Adult Library Services Association (YALSA), a division of the American Library Association (ALA):

- *advocates extensive and developmentally appropriate library and information services for young adults, ages 12-18;*
- *promotes reading and supports the literacy movement;*
- *advocates the use of information and communications technologies to provide effective library service;*
- *supports equality of access to the full range of library materials and services, including existing and emerging information and communication technologies, for young adults;*

- *provides education and professional development to enable its members to serve as effective advocates for young people;*
- *fosters collaboration and partnerships among its individual members with library and information services that meet the unique needs and interests of young adults;*
- *encourages research and is in the vanguard of new thinking concerning the provision of library and information services to youth.*

Discussion Questions

1. Do you think that in practice, a mission statement can ever be truly effective in constraining the expansion of activities of a nonprofit organization?

2. Should a vision statement be put together by staff, the board, a consultant, or some combination? How do you think the outcome would be predictably different in each of these cases?

3. When do you think it is appropriate for an organization to change its mission statement, and when might it need a "change management strategy" (see Chapter 16) to get back to performing its core mission rather than changing it?

Activities

1. Create a collection of nonprofit organizational mission and vision statements found on the Web. Make a table to analyze these statements using fields such as type of statement, length, and types of issues considered in the statement.

2. Create a mission statement and vision statement for each of four mock nonprofits that differ in the way they focus on a public policy issue consistent with the four types of organizations described on page 21.

3. Take existing mission and vision statements of an organization with which you are affiliated, such as your school, and rewrite it so that it more clearly reflects the principles and purposes of the statements in this chapter.

Tips for Practitioners

1. Keep your mission statement focused on a narrow, specific purpose, to an extent that your organization will not be seen as potentially duplicative of other organizations in your area. In other words, carve out your own organizational niche, highlighting a unique service or serving a unique population of clients.

2. Do not try to put too much into your mission statement; a single sentence is usually sufficient.

3. Consider the mission and vision statements of similar organizations. You can find many examples on the Internet.

4. Periodically revisit your mission and vision statements and determine if they might be constraining your organization from adapting to new environmental conditions.

Online Resources to Explore

The Grantsmanship Center: How to Write a Mission Statement
http://unix4.com/h/how-to-write-a-mission-statement---the-grantsmanship-center-w7157.html

Leader to Leader Institute
http://www.leadertoleader.org/
Note: This site is under construction, although material can be found at: http://www.leader101.com/?tag=leader-to-leader-institute

MissionStatements.com
http://www.missionstatements.com/nonprofit_mission_statements.html

For Further Reading

Arams, L. (2013). *How to create memorable, practical mission, value, vision and business philosophy statements for non-profits.*(Kindle Edition). Seattle, WA: Amazon Digital Services.

Briggs, B. (2007). *Mission expert: Creating effective mission and vision statements.* Deerfield, IL: Kinetic Wisdom.

Edward Lowe Foundation. (2001). Developing a mission statement. Retrieved from *http://www.edwardlowe.org/index.elf?page=sserc&storyid=0018&function=story*

Talbot, T. (2003). *Make your mission statement work.* (2nd Ed.). Oxford, UK: How to Books.

Taylor, R. (2014). *The mission statement: A framework for developing an effective organizational mission statement in 100 words or less.* (Kindle Edition). Seattle, WA: Amazon Digital Services.

Chapter 7
Ethics

> **Synopsis:** Nonprofit organizations have a special obligation, both legally and morally, to uphold the highest standards of ethical practice, to be accountable to their boards and to the public, to avoid conflicts of interest, and to treat their employees with dignity.

Introduction

In January 2013, the New York Chapter of the NAACP and Hispanic Federation publicly opposed a City of New York law that banned over-sized sugary drinks. The source of this opposition raised some eyebrows, as the intent of the law is to help reduce the incidence of obesity and diabetes, which public health officials report disproportionately affect minority communities. One might have expected that both organizations would be by the side of Mayor Michael Bloomberg, who had spearheaded the crusade against these health-damaging products.

In response to questions about why these organizations filed court motions to oppose the March 2013 implementation of the law, reporters were sent a joint statement from the NAACP, Hispanic Federation, and the American Beverage Association—the trade association that represents the soft drink industry, which is the target of the law. As one might have guessed, the association's members are some of the largest financial supporters of both of these nonprofit organizations, as documented by the media (Pilkington, 2013).

Did the NAACP and Hispanic Federation join the American Beverage Association as a quid pro quo for donations they received? If so, this is likely not illegal in New York, or perhaps any other state, but most "reasonable" people would consider this to be unethical behavior by these two organizations. Other "reasonable" people might disagree.

Ethics is a branch of philosophy that refers to "well-based standards of right and wrong that prescribe what humans ought to do, usually in terms of duties, principles, specific virtues, or benefits to society" (Johnson, 2005, p.10). The origin of the word, *ethicos,* is Greek for habit, or customs relating to morals (Guttman, 2006). Ethical issues come up all of the time in nonprofit organizations, and board and staff may spend hours deciding the "right" approach to take and passionately argue compelling, but opposite, positions.

The purpose of this chapter is to explore in some detail what it means to take the "right," or ethical, approach. Included in the appendix to this book are cases and scenarios that illustrate are some common, and some not so common, situations that have ethical implications for nonprofits. For some of these situations, there may be no obvious right answer. And in some situations, each apparent option may have drawbacks that may violate competing principles—creating ethical dilemmas. Even the most ethical people will have differing opinions on how one should deal with any particular issue. Some of this disagreement may occur because they take differing approaches to ethics.

Nonprofit Ethics in the News

Nonprofit ethics cases can regularly be found in newspaper headlines. In 2012, there was a major scandal involving Penn State University and a loosely affiliated charity, the Second Mile. This charity was founded by Penn State football assistant coach Jerry Sandusky, now serving a long prison term for his conviction on child sex-abuse charges. This scandal evolved into one of the top general news stories of the year (USA Today, 2012) resulting in the Second Mile charity having to liquidate and forcing the firing of a university's president and its revered football coach. It severely tarnished the reputation of a highly respected institution. William Aramony of United Way, John Bennett, Jr. of The New Era Foundation, and Bernie Madoff of Bernard L. Madoff Investment Securities, might be charter members of any Nonprofit Hall of Shame. It would be naïve to think that such a mythical shrine would have any difficulty finding new members to induct each year.

Some recent national news stories involved nonprofit organizations in ethical lapses that were more complex than these topics.

In November 2012, the Lance Armstrong Foundation severed its ties with its organization's founder and chief spokesperson, Lance Armstrong, and changed its name to the Livestrong Foundation. Armstrong was forced out as Chairman of the board of directors a month prior to that change of name. In mid-January 2013, Armstrong publicly admitted his involvement in the much-publicized bike doping scandal and lying about it under oath. Expecting a strong decline to its fundraising attributable to the scandal, despite its courageous action to sever all ties with its founder, the charity reduced its spending budget by more than 10% (MacLaggan, 2013).

In June 2013, CNN reported on a major investigation into how funds raised by some major charities were being diverted for purposes other than the organization's mission (Hundley, K. and Taggart, K., 2013). In July 2014, the state of New York announced a $25 million settlement with one of these charities, the Disabled Veterans National Foundation and its affiliated for-profit fundraiser, Quadriga Art, to pay a $25 million fine. The settlement is believed to be the largest ever for fundraising deceptive practices. The charity also agreed to replace all of its founding board members (*Philanthropy News Digest*, 2014).

Also that month, one of the most respected charities, Susan G. Komen for the Cure, formerly known as the Susan G. Komen Breast Cancer Foundation, decided to scale back one major fundraiser, a 3-day, 60-mile walk in seven major cities, because of a 37% decline in participation. Much of this decline was attributed to charges that the organization, founded in 1982, bowed to political pressure from pro-life advocates from within and outside the organization and withdrew its funding for Planned Parenthood in January 2012. After enduring a strident backlash for this, the organization restored its funding after four days of heated controversy. But not until several organization officials, including the CEO, were ousted from leadership positions.

During 2012-2013, there was one other salient story of questionable ethics involving a nonprofit organization, or as some might characterize Penn State University, a government-nonprofit hybrid.

Graham Spanier, president of Penn State University during the Jerry Sandusky child sex-abuse scandal, was fired by the board of directors back in 2012. At the time of his firing, he was earning a reported $700,000 annually, not including benefits. He was charged with several crimes, including endangering the welfare of children, perjury, and obstruction of justice. At a preliminary hearing in July 2013, a judge cleared the way for a trial on these charges.

Spanier's alleged inaction against the since convicted perpetrator not only caused pain and suffering to scores of victims, but ruined the reputation of the university, not to mention requiring payments of tens of millions of dollars in fines and likely multi-million dollar settlement payments to victims. Yet, newspapers reported that he was provided with a golden parachute worth more than $3 million (PennLive Editorial Board, 2012).

Perhaps if some of these nonprofit leaders had been required to take an ethics course or training of some kind, we would be reading more positive stories in the newspapers about the nonprofit sector.

Approaches to Ethics

Various approaches to ethics exist. A typology was provided by Dr. Leslie Leip at her presentation at the 2000 Annual Meeting of the American Society for Public Administration (Leip, 2000). Although noting that these are not completely inclusive of approaches and that there are subapproaches within them, her list included, among others:

- Utilitarian approach (the most good for the most people)
- Virtue approach (a focus on personal character)

- Divine approach (What "God" commands)
- Ethics of care approach (from the feminist literature)
- Ethical egoism approach (based on "what's good for me")
- Communitarianism approach (based on "what's good for the community")
- Pluralism (a combination of the above, depending on the situation).

Each of these approaches has a distinct frame of reference, although there are common origins to many of them.

Among the more general approaches found in the ethics literature are:

Teleological Approach

In shorthand, this approach has been labeled "the ends justify the means" (Fox, 1994). The overarching principle is that decision-making should be governed by creating the most good and the least evil. What matters most are the results that come about once the decision is made, not whether any high moral principles are served. The utilitarian approach is an offshoot of teleological ethics (see below).

Deontological Approach

This approach suggests that there are higher-order principles that are immutable because either "God said so" or because of the equivalent in a secular context. People following this approach will tell the truth even when considerable serious consequences to the individual or society would result by doing so. When a husband answers "I don't like it" to his spouse's question of "Do you like this dress?", he is not being incredibly stupid and self-destructive, but rather he is following a deontological approach to ethics.

Utilitarian approach

A derivative of the teleological approach, it involves measuring and calculating the relative benefits to all members of a society of each act or behavior and then choosing the act or behavior that creates the greatest good for the aggregate (Pops, 1994). Utilitarianism is not a simple concept; it is differentiated among three types of utilitarianism: act utilitarianism, general utilitarianism, and rule utilitarianism.

Act utilitarianism considers the single action of the individual as the level of analysis, and judges what the consequences to society would be if only that individual performed that single act only once. *General utilitarianism* expands that concept to judge what the effect on society would be in the aggregate if everyone acted the same way in that particular case. *Rule utilitarianism* suggests an ethical rule that would likely have the most benefit to society if everyone followed it, even though any single, individual application of the rule might have some negative utility occasionally. What binds all three of these types together is the notion that the consequences of following this philosophy are most important, and that, in the aggregate, the act is ethical if society would be better off.

This approach has several shortcomings, according to critics. First, the definition of "society" can change. It is not clear whether the greatest good refers to one's community, one's state, one's nation, one's species, or one's biosphere. Second, it is not always easy to measure and make calculations on what is the benefit. Third, this approach can trample basic values that many utilitarianists might still value, such as justice, fairness, and social equity. For example, it may be consistent with utilitarian values to put an innocent man to death if doing so would result in deterring the murder of hundreds of others, a concept that would be anathema to an adherent of liberal ethics (see page 131).

Classic, market-based economic theories such as transaction cost theory first articulated by Ronald Coase but now associated with Oliver Williamson (Pessali and Fernandez, 1999) and public choice theory (Buchanan and Tullock, 1965), have found their way into the public administration realm. These have their roots in utilitarianism. Many of the principles of New Public Management are also consistent with a utilitarian approach to administration in that they stress efficiency and "most bang for the buck," rather than being sensitive to individual justice and democratic citizenship values (Grobman, 2011). Proponents of public choice theory contend that it is the job of government to do the measurement and calculations and then make public policy decisions based on this calculation. "Efficiency is clearly the preeminent normative force in this baseline view" (Harmon and Mayer, 1986, p. 114). This is a direct utilitarian approach.

The utilitarian approach is the dominant form of ethical framework in the American political system, and is consistent with the values of American culture (Fox, 1994), as indicated in this quote:

> *Americans live in a society that reveres and rewards performance. The pragmatic nature of America stresses outcomes (ends) over process (means) even to the point that they define ethics in terms of performance and institutionalize it in their laws (Smith and Carroll, 1984). This performance ethic, which lies at the heart of American culture, reflects the American obsession with growth, wealth creation, and achievement at both the individual, group, and organizational levels* (Lynch and Lynch, 2000).

Virtue ethics

This approach was first advanced in the public administration context by George Frederickson and David Hart. Much of the academic literature during the previous decade focused on *resolving* ethical dilemmas. Virtue ethics shifts the focus toward the personal character of the decision-maker, suggesting that there is a distinct character trait, which they call "benevolence," defined as "the extensive and non-instrumental love of others" (Cooper, 1994, p. 547).

This theme was picked up by Edmund L. Pincoffs in his 1986 book, *Quandaries and Virtues*. The basic idea of this approach is that if a public administrator has the "right" character, he or she will not require a written code of ethics or a set of principles that describe the appropriate behavior.

In *The Spirit of Public Administration* (Frederickson, 1997), this concept is extended to citizens of a democratic society. Under this theory, democracy requires virtuous citizens so that the government will reflect their values.

The genesis of this perspective is found in a special issue of *Public Administration Review* (March 1984), edited by Frederickson and R. C. Chandler. In *The Virtuous Citizen, the Honorable Bureaucrat and Public Administration*, D. K. Hart (1984) wrote that there are four aspects to the "virtuous citizen." First, the citizen must have a historical perspective and understand the Declaration of Independence, the Constitution, the Federalist Papers, and the general theory and philosophy that undergirds our Republic. The virtuous citizen must have a civic life and make judgments about public policy. Second, the virtuous citizen must accept the underlying values of the American regime, the so called "natural rights" that a majority cannot deny the minority. Third, the individual citizen takes moral responsibility. That means standing up to injustice, discrimination, violation of rights, and violation of privacy. Fourth, the virtuous citizen advances his or her ideas through civility, with a tolerance for ideas of others.

In *The Six Pillars of Character,* a publication of the Josephson Institute (Josephson Institute, 2002), some of these virtues are described. Among them are *trustworthiness* (honesty, integrity, promise-keeping, loyalty), *respect* (autonomy, privacy, dignity, courtesy, tolerance, acceptance), *responsibility* (accountability, pursuit of excellence), *caring* (compassion, consideration, giving, sharing, kindness, loving), *justice and fairness* (procedural fairness, impartiality, consistency, equity, equality, due process), and *civic virtue and citizenship* (law abiding, community service, protection of the environment).

One major difference that distinguishes virtue ethics from other approaches is that it suggests that government does much more than serve as the marketplace for reaching a majority consensus in collective decision-making while reducing the transaction costs of doing so.

In the nonprofit world, virtue ethics is often what brings people to the table in the first place to do the work that government should be doing but is not. Modern writers in the nonprofit management field, such as Drucker (1990), Covey (1997), and Wheatley (1994), have recognized that the personal traits of the nonprofit leader with respect to ethical culture create the climate that bonds the organizational members to a common purpose.

According to Van Hook, (1998), the primary role of a nonprofit executive is to set an ethical tone for the organization in its internal and external relationships.

John Carver, whose book *Boards That Make a Difference* proposes a model of governance in nonprofit organizations that is becoming increasingly attractive (despite being controversial), suggests that the board give the executive director a virtual free hand in achieving its desired outcomes. However, the one area in which the board is permitted to micromanage the executive director under the Carver model is in the area of ethics, in which constraints are explicitly put down in writing and are inviolate (Carver, 1990).

Of course, what is "virtuous" to one nonprofit executive can be unethical to another. Being loyal to the organization is virtuous, and so is whistleblowing, defined as "the disclosure by organization members (former or current) of illegal, immoral, or illegitimate practices under the control of their employers, to persons or organizations that may be able to effect action" (Near and Miceli, 1985, p. 4, in Barnett, 1992).

Liberal Ethics

This approach is based on the view that the rights of individuals override the needs of groups and societies. For example, there is currently a public policy debate in state governments concerning whether some innocent inmates on death row are being executed. To those who adhere to the liberal ethical framework, executing a single innocent person out of the hundreds executed who are guilty invalidates the death penalty as an appropriate sanction. A traditional teleological approach would argue that it is virtually impossible to eliminate the execution of one innocent person out of hundreds. Society is best served in the aggregate, they would assert, by having hundreds of those guilty of first-degree murder executed because of its deterrent effect—even if one innocent person happens to fall through the cracks and is executed. The liberal ethics approach emphasizes individual autonomy and a right to privacy. The "don't ask-don't tell" approach derives from a liberal ethics perspective.

Ethics in Organizations

Although writing on the broad topic of ethical behavior is generally attributed to Plato and Aristotle, the first writing on business ethics per se is traced to Cicero, who wrote *On Duties* (McNamara, 2000). Cicero is considered "one of the great authorities on the necessity of virtue for the good of society" (Hart, 1994).

Once thought to have little relevance to the bottom line in organizations, some of the more recent management strategies, such as Total Quality Management (TQM) and diversity training, are seen as giving ethical training practical relevance (McNamara, 2000).

Madsen and Shafritz (1990, in McNamara, 2000) divide ethical problems of organizations into two principal types. "Managerial mischief" consists of behavior that reasonable people would recognize as "wrong," such as illegal, unethical, or questionable practices that perhaps can be distinguished from the other type by the lengths to which the perpetrator of the behavior will go in order not to be caught. The other type, "moral mazes," encompasses issues such as potential conflicts of interest, wrongful uses of resources, mismanagement of contracts, and other behaviors with which managers deal on a daily basis.

A description of highly ethical organizations is provided by Pastin (1986):

1. They are at ease interacting with diverse internal and external stakeholder groups. The ground rules of these firms make the good of these stakeholder groups part of the organizations' own good.

2. They are obsessed with fairness. Their ground rules emphasize that the other persons' interests count as much as their own.

3. Responsibility is individual rather than collective, with individuals assuming personal responsibility for the actions of these organizations. The organizations' ground rules mandate that individuals are responsible to themselves.

4. They see their activities in terms of purpose—a way of operating that members of these organizations highly value. Purpose ties the organizations to their environments (in McNamara, 2000).

Doug Wallace (in McNamara, 2000) asserts that a high integrity organization has the following six characteristics:

1. A clear vision and picture of integrity exist throughout the organization.

2. Over time, the vision is owned and embodied by top management.

3. The reward system is aligned with the vision of integrity.

4. Policies and practices of the organization are aligned with the vision; there are no mixed messages.

5. It is understood that every significant management decision has ethical value dimensions.

6. Everyone is expected to work through conflicting-stakeholder value perspectives (McNamara, 2000).

Codes of Ethics

A code of ethics is a systematic effort to define acceptable conduct (Plant, 1994). Ethical behavior in the workplace is enforced through the use of codes of ethics, codes of conduct, ethicists, ethics committees, policies and procedures relating to ethical dilemmas, and ethics training (McNamara, 2000).

Codes of ethics may be general or specific, aspirational or idealistic, coercive or legalistic, and apply to members of a profession, an organization, or an association representing a class of organizations (Plant, 1994). Codes of ethics may be a simple list of ten golden rules (Plant, 1994) or a lengthy, codified system of procedures and ideals such as the one adopted by the National Association of Social Workers (National Association of Social Workers, 1999). It may have the force of law (such as a statutory ethics code for public officials), be a collection of principles that are not law but are morally binding, or simply provide a system of symbolic principles for meaningful communication (Plant, 1994).

Codes of Ethics for public officials are fundamentally different from codes for nonprofit organizations (Plant, 1994), and codes for nonprofit organizations differ equally from those for government officials or private business persons. Yet they share many elements.

In recent years, there has been a trend toward turning nonprofit management into a recognized profession, with credentialing becoming available for fundraising executives, association managers, and nonprofit organization managers. Organizations such as the Association of Fundraising Professionals (AFP), the American Society of Association Executives (ASAE), and the National Council of Nonprofit Associations—and the state and local chapters of these organizations—have sought to professionalize their memberships.

Unlike government (which has the taxing power) and for-profit business (which generates revenue through market transactions), charities generate much of their revenue through nonmarket mechanisms such as seeking donations—in the form of contributions from the public and grants from foundations and government. This form of revenue generation offers a ripe area for fraudulent practices, and many of the ethics-related principles that differentiate nonprofit organizations from their government and private sector counterparts focus on this area.

Until 2003, there were two major ethical codes focusing on fundraising standards for charitable organizations. The first, which was developed during the late 1980s and went into effect in 1992 (NCIB, 2000), is the National Charities Information Bureau's (NCIB) Standards in Philanthropy. Almost all of these ethical standards would have been meaningless in anything other than a nonprofit context. The standards were not enforceable by law, but served as a guide to both donors and those who run the charities. The standards were grouped into nine areas:

1. Board Governance
2. Purpose
3. Programs
4. Information
5. Financial Support and Related Activities
6. Use of Funds
7. Annual Reporting
8. Accountability
9. Budget

Another code, the Council of Better Business Bureau's Standards for Charitable Solicitations were first published in 1974.

In 2001, NCIB merged with the Foundation of the Better Business Bureau and its Philanthropic Advisory Service (PAS). The new organization, the Better Business Bureau's Wise Giving Alliance, developed an updated code, published in March 2003. In 2007, the BBB rebranded its charity resources with a "Start With Trust" campaign. Charities that meet its standards are now referred to as "BBB accredited charities" (Better Business Bureau, 2010). The 20 standards that comprise this influential ethics code can be found at: *http://www.bbb.org/us/charity*

Among the most controversial aspects of this code is the provision that calls on charities to allocate at least 65% of their donations for program expenses, spending no more than 35% of related contributions on fundraising. This is a higher standard than either the NCIB (60%) or the BBB's Philanthropic Advisory Service (50%) had enforced prior to the merger.

In December 2009, the Wise Giving Alliance announced that it was temporarily loosening its standards because of the severe recession. For the fiscal years ending in June 2008-2010, organizations still qualified for the Wise Giving Alliance stamp of approval if the organization spent at least 55% of donations on program expenses and no more than 45% on fundraising (Hall, 2009). As of 2014, the standard is back to a minimum of 65% for program expenses and a maximum of 35% for fundraising expenses (Better Business Bureau, n.d.)

Other standards in this code provide for regular assessment of the CEO's performance, establishment of a conflict-of-interest policy, the completion of a written assessment of the charity's performance at least every two years, and standards protecting donor privacy. The new standard frowns upon accumulating unrestricted net assets available for use that exceed either three times the amount of the past year's expenses or three times the current budget, whichever is higher.

The national professional association of fundraisers also has an ethics code. The Statement of Ethical Principles of the Association of Fundraising Professionals (AFP) was adopted in 1991 when that organization was known as the National Society of Fund Raising Executives (NSFRE). AFP "exists to foster the development and growth of fund-raising professionals and the profession, to promote high ethical standards in the fund-raising profession and to preserve and enhance philanthropy and volunteerism" (NSFRE, 1991). This code was amended in 2007 and expanded to 25 principles.

AFP's ethics code consists of a set of general ethical principles, introduced by a preamble that recognizes the stewardship of fundraisers and the rights of donors to have their funds used for the intent they expect.

Many of these principles are deontological, and would be appropriate for any type of organization, such as to "foster cultural diversity and pluralistic values, and treat all people with dignity and respect" and "value the privacy, freedom of choice and interests of all those affected by their actions." Some of the principles are appropriate for public organizations, such as having an obligation to "safeguard the public trust," and others are parochial to the profession, such as to "put philanthropic mission above personal gain," and "affirm, through personal giving, a commitment to philanthropy and its role in society."

One year after the adoption of the AFP principles, the organization adopted its "Standards of Professional Practice" and incorporated them into its ethics code. Its 25 principles are mostly in the form of "members shall" and "members shall not."

A statement within the Code notes that violations "may subject the member to disciplinary sanctions, including expulsion, as provided by the (AFP's) Ethics Enforcement Procedures."

Some of these standards are perfunctory, such as "members shall comply with all applicable local, state, provincial, federal, civil and criminal laws." Others are general and broad, with implications that are not easily subject to interpretation, such as "Members shall not exploit any relationship with a donor, prospect, volunteer or employee to the benefit of the member or the member's organization." Among issues raised by the standards are conflicts of interest, truthfulness, privacy, and financial accountability.

Another issue raised in the principles that is of current interest in a number of professions is the standard that "Members shall not accept compensation that is based on the percentage of charitable contributions...."

Some states have expressly prohibited lobbyists from signing contingency fee contracts in which they are paid only when they are successful in getting a bill or amendment passed by the legislature. The theory is that such contracts encourage lobbyists to engage in efforts that go beyond the boundaries of acceptable behavior. On the other hand, contingency fees are routine for attorneys in civil cases. It is also not unusual for professional fundraisers to be paid a percentage of the amount they raise. Many in the field find that this practice promotes unethical solicitations (e.g., presentations that exaggerate facts, minimize disclosure, and other behavior to intimidate and harass potential donors), and it is interesting that a major professional organization such as the AFP has taken an unequivocal position in opposition to compensation based on the amount a fundraiser raises. This is an example of a teleological approach to ethics, in that there is nothing inherently unethical about basing compensation on "performance."

A 2001 White Paper published by the Association of Fundraising Professionals (AFP) with an excellent discussion about this issue can be found at: *http://www.afpnet.org/Ethics/EthicsArticleDetail.cfm?itemnumber=734*

In February 2004, Independent Sector adopted a *Statement of Values and Code of Ethics for Nonprofit and Philanthropic Organizations*, and recommended that it serve as a model. The statement identifies a set of values to which nonprofits may subscribe, including commitment to the public good, accountability to the public, and commitment beyond the law. It also outlines broad ethical principles in the following areas: personal and professional integrity, mission, governance, legal compliance, responsible stewardship, openness and disclosure, program evaluation, inclusiveness and diversity, and fundraising. The full text can be accessed at: *http://www.independentsector.org/code_of_ethics*

Standards for Excellence

In 1998, the Maryland Association of Nonprofit Organizations initiated a program whereby charities can receive certification that they meet basic ethical and accountability standards. As a result of two major grants, the program has been expanded beyond Maryland to include five other states. The performance standards required for an organization to be certified by the program are grouped in six areas:

1. Mission, Strategy and Evaluation
2. Leadership: Board, Staff, and Volunteers
3. Legal Compliance and Ethics
4. Finance and Operations
5. Resource Development
6. Public Awareness, Engagement, and Advocacy

Participating charities may demonstrate that they carry out the standards by participating in a peer review process. They submit an application, document their compliance with the standards, and pay a fee. If the peer-review panel affirms that the organization meets the standards, the organization receives a Seal of Excellence, with the expectation that having the Seal will provide the organization with increased credibility with donors and grantmakers. The full set of standards can be found at: *http://www.marylandnonprofits.org/html/standards/04_02.asp*

Among the standards are:

1. On average, over a five (5) year period, a nonprofit should realize revenue from fundraising and other development activities that are at least three times the amount spent on conducting them. Organizations whose fundraising ratio is less than 3:1 should demonstrate that they are making steady progress toward achieving this goal, or should be able to justify why a 3:1 ratio is not appropriate for their organization.

2. Fundraising personnel, including both employees and independent consultants, should not be compensated based on a percentage of the amount raised or other commission formula.

3. Nonprofits should have a written conflict of interest policy. The policy should be applicable to board members and staff, and volunteers who have significant independent decision making authority regarding the resources of the organization. The policy should identify the types of conduct or transactions that raise conflict of interest concerns, should set forth procedures for disclosure of actual or potential conflicts, and should provide for review of individual transactions by the uninvolved members of the board of directors.

Ethical Issues in Nonprofit Management

Among the general categories of ethical conflicts that are endemic to the nonprofit sector are accountability, conflict of interest, and disclosure (Kaufman and Grobman, 2011). Specific issues of interest are relationships between board members and the staff; board members and the organization (such as business relationships); self-dealing; charitable solicitation disclosure; the degree to which donations finance fundraising costs rather than programs; the accumulation of surpluses; outside remuneration of staff; the appropriateness of salaries, benefits, and perquisites; and merit pay (Kaufman and Grobman, 2011). For example, pay based on income received rather than mission accomplished is considered unethical. Staff of charities are under more of an obligation not to exploit their position on staff for personal gain (such as charging a fee for outside speaking engagements on their own time) than their for-profit counterparts. Unlike their for-profit or government counterparts, charities generally are under an ethical, if not legal, obligation not to accumulate large surpluses (Kaufman and Grobman, 2011). Salaries, benefits, and perquisites must be "reasonable," and prior to the promulgation by the IRS of temporary regulations on January 10, 2001 relating to this and other "excess benefit" transactions, the legal requirements applying to these issues were in a gray area (Grobman, 2011).

A different set of ethical issues exists around disclosures to foundation and corporate funders. For instance, what is the obligation to disclose changed circumstances after a proposal is submitted and before it is acted upon, such as when key staff have announced plans to leave? If the organization knows that the changed circumstance might affect the decision, is it unethical not to disclose it?

Ethical Dilemmas

There are circumstances that leaders in nonprofit organizations can identify in which there is a clear choice about how to behave. We know it is clearly unethical (and illegal) to embezzle funds that belong to our organizations. We know it is unethical (and usually illegal) to lie to or otherwise deceive potential donors to manipulate them to give. And we know it is unethical (and illegal) to make false statements on our 990 tax returns to make our organizations' performance appear better than it really is. These are just a few examples of situations in which there is little doubt about the choices we can make between doing the right thing and the wrong thing.

Yet, there are often circumstances in which there is some ambiguity about what one's behavior should be, even if the individual has an absolute commitment to behaving ethically. This can occur when there are two or more important ethical principles in conflict, and behaving in a manner that honors one principle may bring about conflict with honoring a different ethical principle that may be equally important.

For example, a co-worker may come to you to discuss a problem, and ask you to swear beforehand that you will keep what he says in total confidence, and you agree. And then that coworker shares information that you feel ethically compelled to share with your board chair, or even law enforcement authorities, to avoid potential harm to the organization or to individuals. In this example, one principle, "preserving confidentiality," might conflict with another, the "duty to report." You have to make a choice not between doing the right thing and doing the wrong thing—as would be the case in deciding whether or not to divert organization resources to one's personal benefit. Rather, you must make a choice between doing the right thing or doing another right thing when one cannot reasonably do both.

Regardless of which choice one makes, there is at least one ethical principle that would be violated.

This is what is known as an ethical dilemma—a situation in which there is a conflict between honoring two moral principles, and one cannot act in a way that satisfies one of them without not satisfying the other.

Acting with loyalty and in the best interests of one's organization is considered ethical. So is being a whistle-blower when that organization is acting unethically itself. It is considered ethical to act in the best interest of your stakeholders (duty of care), and also ethical to let them make decisions for themselves (self-determination). How should you act when they have made a choice, and you strongly feel that this choice is not in their own interests? These are common examples of two ethical principles colliding.

Some of the cases and scenarios in this book highlight examples of nonprofit organization leaders facing a choice between being ethical and unethical. Other cases include examples of ethical dilemmas. In these, nonprofit leaders with the best intentions of acting ethically find themselves in situations that are difficult to deal with, because of conflicts among two or more lofty ethical principles that come into conflict.

Resolving Ethical Dilemmas

There are many standard models that ethicists have developed to make decisions about one's behavior when facing an ethical dilemma. One popular model is called RESPECT, developed by Yeo and Moorhouse in 1996 (in Guttman, 2006), and is an acrostic for:

- Recognize the moral dimensions of the problem.
- Enumerate the guiding and evaluative principles.
- Specify the stakeholders and their guiding principles.
- Plot various action alternatives.
- Evaluate alternatives in light of principles and stakeholders.
- Consult and involve stakeholders as appropriate.
- Tell stakeholders the reason for the decision.

A model I like just a bit better is attributed to Frederic Reamer (2006), modified slightly for the purpose of this discussion. It is comprised of the following steps:

- Identify the ethical issues that are controversial.
- Identify those who will be affected by the decision.
- Identify the potential courses of action, and the pros and cons of doing each.
- Analyze how each stakeholder might be affected, and how the decision is or is not consistent with one's values, one's organization, and one's profession.
- Consult others who are not affected about the dilemma for some input and advice.
- Make the decision, and document it.
- Follow up and evaluate the result of the decision.

It might not be unusual for a party adversely affected by a decision made by a nonprofit organization leader to contest it in some way. By following a standard model, it is more likely that the decision can be justified. This is certainly welcome if one finds himself or herself on the witness stand in a criminal or civil trial having to defend a decision one has made in response to a situation in which any course of action could be questioned on legal or ethical grounds.

Practical Ethics Issues to Consider in Nonprofit Organizations

The following are some ethics issues that are appropriate for nonprofit boards and staff to consider:

1. Accountability

Accountability often is overlooked in discussions about ethics. Because of the unique status of 501(c)(3) organizations, they have a special obligation to the public to be accountable for the results of their activities that justify their tax exemptions and other privileges. Organizations should continually challenge themselves by asking if the outcomes produced are worth the public investment.

Nonprofit boards of directors have a special obligation to govern with integrity. Governing with integrity means that the organization recognizes that it is accountable to the public, to the people it serves, and to its funders. Accountability includes the concept that nonprofit organizations exist only to produce worthwhile results in furtherance of their missions.

In addition, accountability encompasses a core system of values and beliefs regarding the treatment of staff, clients, colleagues, and community. Yet, organizational survival needs too often undercut core values. Although everyone in the organization is responsible, it is the board's ultimate responsibility to ensure that its values are not compromised, and that the activities are conducted within acceptable limits.

Staff will sometimes pursue grants and contracts, or engage in direct solicitation campaigns, for the primary purpose of growing. This subtle issue of accountability is seldom discussed. Boards sometimes ask whether the executive director "grew the organization" as the primary criterion for measuring success. Boards have an obligation to ascertain that all activities support the organization's mission.

2. Conflict of Interest

A potential conflict of interest occurs any time organizational resources are directed to the private interests of a person or persons who have an influence over the decision to use those resources. Examples might include the leasing of property owned by a relative of the executive director or a board member, the board awarding itself a salary, the organization hiring a board member to provide legal representation, or the executive director hiring a relative or a board member's relative.

A conflict also can occur when the person (or persons) making a decision expects something in exchange from the person in whose favor the decision is made. One example is the case in which an executive director retains a direct mail firm, and the executive director's spouse is hired by that direct mail firm shortly thereafter.

With regard to board members, the cleanest approach is to adopt a policy that does not allow any board member to profit from the organization. It is the duty of every board member to exercise independent judgment solely on behalf of the organization. For example, suppose a board member who owns a public relations business successfully argues that the nonprofit needs a public relations campaign and then is hired to conduct the campaign. The board member's self-interest in arguing for the campaign will always be subject to question.

Suppose, in the above example, the board member offers to do the campaign at cost, and that is the lowest bid. It may be that even "at cost," the board member's firm benefits, because the campaign will pay part of the salary of some staff members or cover other overhead. It may be perfectly appropriate to accept the board member's offer, even though it is a conflict of interest. However, it is absolutely essential that the board have a procedure in place to deal with these types of issues.

Some organizations permit financial arrangements with board members, provided that the member does not vote on the decision. Given the good fellowship and personal relationships that often exist within nonprofit boards, such a rule can be more for show and without substance.

A similar conflict can occur in the awarding of contracts to certain individuals who do not serve on the board. There may be personal reasons for one or more members of the board or the executive director to award contracts to particular persons, such as enhancing their personal or professional relationships with that person.

There are instances in which it is appropriate to have a contract with an insider, such as when a board member offers to sell equipment to the organization at cost, or agrees to sell other goods or services well below market value. Here, too, the organization should assure itself that these same goods or services are not available as donations.

It is essential for the board to confront and grapple with these issues and adopt a written policy to govern potential conflicts of interest, in order to avoid the trap of self-dealing or its appearances. Many potential abuses are not only unethical, but also illegal as a result of the Taxpayer Bill of Rights 2, enacted in July 1996 (Public Law 104–168, 110 Stat. 1452).

3. Disclosures

There is much disagreement within the nonprofit sector regarding how much disclosure is required to those who donate to charitable nonprofits. The first obligation of every organization is to obey the laws and regulations governing disclosure. Nonprofits have a legal and ethical obligation to report fundraising costs accurately on their IRS Form 990, to obey the requirement regarding what portion of the cost of attending a fundraising event is deductible, and to comply with state charitable registration laws and regulations.

Nonprofits face a more difficult ethical issue when deciding how much disclosure to make that is not required by law, particularly if the organization believes that some people may not contribute if those disclosures are made. One controversial example of this is Kiva *(http://kiva.org)*, which many feel does excellent work in facilitating micro-loans to deserving entrepreneurs. But, among other criticisms, the organization has been criticized for making it appear that potential investors choose to whom to make loans, when in most cases, the entrepreneur any investor chooses to make a micro-loan to has already received a loan, and the investor's funds are channeled to others. (See: *http://www.nytimes.com/2009/11/09/business/global/09kiva.html?_r=0)*

In the for-profit corporate world, the Securities and Exchange Commission demands full, written disclosure of pertinent information, no matter how negative, when companies are offering stock to the public. There is no comparable agency that regulates charitable solicitations by nonprofits. Nonprofits must be very careful to disclose voluntarily all relevant information and to avoid the kind of hyperbole that misrepresents the organization.

Another difficult issue is whether fundraising costs should be disclosed at the point of solicitation. The costs of telemarketing campaigns or of maintaining development offices are sometimes 80%, or even more, of every dollar collected. Some argue that people would not give if these costs were disclosed. Others argue that if the soliciting organization cannot justify these costs to the public (and in many cases, they are not justifiable), then the organization is not deserving of support.

4. Accumulation of Surplus

If the funds of a charitable nonprofit are to be used for charitable purposes, what is a reasonable amount of surplus to accumulate? The Wise Giving Alliance has suggested a ceiling of three times the current year's expenses or the next year's budget, whichever is greater.

Organizations should consider the circumstances under which it is appropriate to disclose to prospective donors the amount expected to be used to accumulate a surplus. Clearly, if a major purpose of the solicitation is to build a surplus, that should be disclosed.

5. Outside Remuneration

Executive directors and other staff often are offered honoraria or consulting fees for speeches, teaching, providing technical assistance, or other work. The ethical issue is whether the staff person should turn the fees over to the nonprofit employer or be able to retain them. Potential conflicts can be avoided if the policy is based on the principle that all reasonably related outside income belongs to the organization. For example, an executive director's honorarium for speaking to a national conference as a representative of the organization or an expert in his or her field would revert to the employer, but his or her fee for playing in a rock band on weekends could be individual income.

The argument for this policy is that the line between the employer's and the employee's personal time is not so easy to draw. An argument against this principle is that employees' usage of their spare time should be of no concern to the employer. Is it ethical for an employee to exploit the knowledge and experience gained on the job for personal gain? Are we buying only time from our employees, or do we expect that we are getting the undivided professional attention of that person?

If the board or executive director is silent on this issue, the assumption is that earning outside income is a private matter. It makes sense to have a clear policy on outside income before an employee is hired.

6. Salaries, Benefits, and Perquisites

Determining an appropriate salary structure is perhaps the most difficult ethical issue in the nonprofit sector. Ethical considerations arise at both the high and low ends of the salary spectrum.

If an organization is funded by grants from foundations and corporations or by government contracts, the funders can and do provide some restraint on excessive salaries. However, if the nonprofit is funded primarily by individual donations or fees for service, such constraints (other than, perhaps, those relating to the intermediate sanctions regulations of the Internal Revenue Service) are absent.

Boards fall into an ethical trap if they reward executive directors based on the amount of income received, rather than on how well they have accomplished the organization's mission. A board can consider many criteria when setting the salary of the executive director. These include the size and complexity of the organization, what others in similar organizations are earning, and whether the salary is justifiable to the public. Some nonprofits include proportionality in their salary structures by limiting the highest paid to a factor of the lowest paid (e.g., the highest can be no more than three times the lowest).

As a result of enactment of the *Taxpayers Bill of Rights 2,* there are now legal as well as ethical restrictions on paying excessive compensation. Ethical management of employees requires that each person be treated with dignity and respect, paid a salary that can provide a decent standard of living, and given a basic level of benefits, including health insurance coverage. A potential critical conflict arises when a charitable organization working to spread its social values treats its staff in a way that conflicts with its organizational values.

7. Personal Relationships

Nonprofit organization executives and board members must not engage in sexual harassment, or behavior that makes an employee feel uncomfortable at best or threatened and intimidated, at worst. Employees should be treated fairly, which among other things, means that no favoritism should be permitted with respect to work assignments. Discrimination should not be permitted, even if it does not meet the threshold required for legal violations.

Nepotism—the hiring of family members—should be prohibited. Nonprofit executives and board members should seek to keep personal friendships from influencing professional judgment. Managers should not make it difficult for employees to maintain an appropriate work-family balance. Privacy and confidentiality of workers should be respected. A diverse workforce means that cultural differences among staff should be respected to the maximum extent possible.

Conclusion

There are many other ethical issues that nonprofit organizations may encounter, such as the personal use of office supplies and equipment; time off for volunteering for other nonprofit organizations; personal use of frequent flier mileage; the extent of staff and board diversity; and the use of private discriminatory clubs for fundraisers, board meetings, or other events. The list is endless. Many of these issues are raised in the nonprofit ethics scenarios that appear in Appendix 10.

It is important that nonprofit organizations make a conscientious effort to engage in discussions about ethics and values on a regular basis, recognizing that the charitable nonprofit sector has a special obligation to uphold the very highest standards. Boards of directors of charitable nonprofits have a pivotal role in this regard. Boards cannot play a more important role than ensuring that nonprofits are accountable, and that they operate as mission- and value-driven organizations.

Many who choose to work in the nonprofit sector do so because the stated values of the sector and their personal values are in harmony. It is crucial that such people be vigilant against the erosion of those very principles that initially attracted them to the work.

Only in this way can the public be assured that the charitable nonprofit sector remains worthy of its privileges and continues to occupy its special and unique place in our society.

Discussion Questions

1. Should the nonprofit sector be held to a higher ethical standard than its for-profit counterpart? Why or why not? What about compared with the government sector?

2. Discuss the advantages and disadvantages of having a formal organizational ethics code.

3. If a nonprofit executive writes a book about the public policy issues related to his or her work, as the leader of an organization, should the royalties go to the author or to the organization?

4. Discuss how nonprofit executives who share a virtue ethics approach might have widely divergent responses to dealing with some typical ethical dilemmas. Compare this with those who share a utilitarian approach.

5. The term "charity jacking" has been defined by Beth Kanter as "imitating a successful fundraising campaign theme or idea that has become popular and instead of encouraging donations to the original charity, redirecting donations to another cause" (Kanter, 2014). Discuss the conditions when charity jacking might be acceptable or when it might be unethical.

Activities

1. Compare and contrast the three fundraising ethics codes of Independent Sector *(http://www.independentsector.org/code_of_ethics)*, the Wise Giving Alliance *(http://www.bbb.org/us/Charity-Standards/)*, and the Standards for Excellence *(http://www.marylandnonprofits.org/html/standards/04_02.asp)*. Consider who developed them, to whom they apply, how strict the standards are, and what they cover. Create a table to compare provisions relating to common topics covered by these codes.

2. Download a sample of nonprofit organization ethics codes that you find on the Internet. Make a list of ethics codes provisions that tend to be featured in these codes.

3. Devise an ethics dilemma or ethical challenge that might be faced by a non-profit executive, and make a table showing actions that the executive might take to address the dilemma consistent with the various ethics approaches described in this chapter and the models to resolve them described on pages 139-140.

4. Visit the Web sites of the Josephson Institute of Ethics, Independent Sector, the United Way of America, and the Society for Nonprofit Organizations, and review ethics-related articles that are posted on these sites.

5. Create a Code of Ethics for a new nonprofit organization that might be established to serve as a state association for therapists who deal with child abuse.

Tips for Practitioners

1. Challenge yourself and your organization to hold yourself up to the highest ethical standards, avoiding even gray areas of conflicts of interest and appearances of conflicts of interest.

2. When in doubt about how to deal with any situation, ask yourself, "How would I feel if my family and friends read about this on the front page of the daily newspaper?"

3. Obtain salary surveys published by state associations that represent nonprofit organizations, and determine whether anyone in your organization has an unreasonable salary.

4. Demand that all business relationships with the organization be at "arm's length," and obtain at least three bids on any work that costs at least $1,000,

even if a board member claims that he or she will provide the product/service at cost.

5. Consider adopting a formal conflict-of-interest policy. See a model policy developed by the Internal Revenue Service included in its 1023 Form (see: *http://www.irs.gov/instructions/i1023/ar03.html*), or find an annotated version at: *http://www.cof.org/files/Documents/Building%20Strong%20Ethical%20Foundations/Conflicts_of_Interest_IRS_Sample_Policy.pdf*

6. Support efforts to improve disclosure and accountability of the voluntary sector. Cooperate with expanded enforcement of laws governing this sector, so that the few nonprofits that are abusing the law do not stain the reputation of the entire sector.

Online Resources to Explore

Nonprofit Ethics Education Pages
http://www.socialworker.com/nonprofit/ethics

Independent Sector: Accountability Overview
http://www.independentsector.org/accountability

Carter McNamara's Business Ethics: Managing Ethics in the Workplace and Social Responsibility
http://www.managementhelp.org/ethics/ethics.htm

BBB's "Start With Trust" Nonprofit Ethics Pages
http://www.bbb.org/us/charity/

Standards for Excellence
http://www.marylandnonprofits.org/html/standards/index.asp

Josephson Institute of Ethics
http://josephsoninstitute.org/

References

Barnett, T. (1992). A preliminary investigation of the relationship between selected organizational characteristics and external whistleblowing by employee. *Journal of American Business Ethics.* 1 1(12): p. 949-959.

Better Business Bureau. (2010). *Where is Give.org?* Retrieved from *http://www.bbb.org/us/Give-org*

Better Business Bureau. (n.d.). *Standards for charity.* Retrieved from *http://www.bbb.org/us/standards-for-charity-accountability/*

Buchanan, J., & Tullock, G. (1965). *The calculus of consent: Logical foundations of constitutional democracy.* Ann Arbor, MI: University of Michigan Press.

Carver, J. (1990). *Boards that make a difference.* San Francisco, CA: Jossey-Bass.

Cooper, T. L. (1994). The emergence of administrative ethics. In T. Cooper (Ed.). *Handbook of administrative ethics.* New York: Marcel Dekker.

Covey, S. R. (1997). *The 7 habits of highly effective people.* Provo, UT: Franklin Covey Co.

Drucker, P. F. (1990). *Managing the non-profit organization: Practices & principles.* New York: HarperCollins.

Fox, C. J. (1994). The use of philosophy in administrative ethics. In T. Cooper (Ed.). *Handbook of administrative ethics.* New York: Marcel Dekker.

Frederickson, G. (1997). *The spirit of public administration.* San Francisco, CA: Josey-Bass.

Grobman, G. (2011). *The nonprofit handbook* (6th Edition). Harrisburg, PA: White Hat Communications.

Guttman, D. (2006). *Ethics in social work: A context of caring.* New York: Haworth.

Hall, H. (2009). Recession prompts watchdog agency to loosen fund-raising standards. *Chronicle of Philanthropy.* Retrieved from *http://philanthropy.com/article/Recession-Prompts-Watchdog/63201/*

Harmon, M. M., & Mayer, R. T. (1986). *Organization theory for public administration.* Burke, VA: Chatalaine Press.

Hart, D. K. (1994). Administration and the ethics of virtue. In T. Cooper (Ed.). *Handbook of Administrative Ethics* (2nd Ed.) (pp. 107-123). New York: Marcel Dekker.

Hundley, K. And Taggart, K. (2013). Above the law: America's worst charities. CNN. Retrieved from *http://www.cnn.com/2013/06/13/us/worst-charities*

Johnson, C. (2005). *Meeting the Ethical Challenges of Leadership.* Thousand Oaks, CA: Sage.

Josephson Institute. (2002). *The six pillars of character.* Retrieved from *http://josephsoninstitute.org/MED/MED-2sixpillars.html*

Kanter, B. (August 2014). Has the ice bucket challenge spawned charity jacking? Beth's Blog. August 28, 2014. Retrieved at: *http://www.bethkanter.org/icebucket-challenge3/*

Kaufman, G., & Grobman, G. (2011). Nonprofit organization ethics. In G. Grobman, *The nonprofit handbook.* (6th Ed.). Harrisburg, PA: White Hat Communications.

Leip, L. (2000, April). Developing ethical decision-making frameworks: A means for 20/20 vision in the 21st century. Presentation made at the annual meeting of the American Society for Public Administration, San Diego, CA.

Lynch, T. D., & Lynch, C. E. (2000, April). Virtue ethics: A public policy recommendation. Paper presented at the annual meeting of the American Society for Public Administration, San Diego, CA.

MacLaggan, C. (2013). "We expect Lance to be completely truthful: Livestrong." *Reuters*, January 16, 2013. Retrieved from *http://www.reuters.com/article/2013/01/16/us-cycling-armstrong-livestrong-idUSBRE90F0ZP20130116*

McNamara, C. (2000). *Complete guide to ethics management.* Retrieved from *http://www.managementhelp.org/ethics/ethxgde.htm*

National Association of Social Workers. (1999). Code of ethics. Retrieved from *http://www.naswdc.org/pubs/code/default.asp.*

National Society of Fundraising Executives. (1991). NSFRE code of ethical principles and standards of professional practice. Retrieved from *http://www.afpnet.org/ethics/guidelines_code_standards*

NCIB. (2000). NCIB's standards in philanthropy. Retrieved from *http://www.bbb.org/us/charity/*

Pastin, M. (1986). *The hard problems of management: Gaining the ethics edge.* San Francisco: Jossey-Bass.

PennLive Editorial Board. (2012). Editorials: Graham Spanier's golden parachute illustrates out-of-control college executive pay. December 9, 2012. Retrieved from *http://www.pennlive.com/opinion/2012/12/graham_spanier_golden_parachute.html*

Pessali, H. F., & Fernandez, R. G. (1999). Institutional economics at the micro level? What transaction costs theory could learn from original institutionalism (in the spirit of building bridges). *Journal of Economic Issues, 2,* 265.

Philanthropy News Digest. (July 2014). New York State Wins $25 Million Settlement in Veterans Charity Fraud. July 2, 2014. *Philanthropy News Digest.* Retrieved from *http://philanthropynewsdigest.org/news/new-york-state-wins-25-million-settlement-in-veterans-charity-fraud*

Pilkington, E. (2013). NAACP joins fight against Bloomberg's New York soda ban. *The Guardian.* January 23, 2013. Retrieved from *http://www.theguardian.com/lifeandstyle/2013/jan/23/naacp-fights-bloomberg-new-york-soda-ban*

Plant, J. (1994). Codes of ethics. In T. Cooper (Ed.). In *Handbook of administrative ethics* (pp. 221-242). New York: Marcel Dekker.

Pops, G. (1994). A teleological approach to administrative ethics. In *Handbook of Administrative Ethics* (2nd Ed.), T. Cooper (Ed.). New York: Marcel Dekker.

Reamer, F. (2006). *Social work values and ethics.* (3rd Ed.). New York: Columbia University Press.

USA Today. (2012). Poll ranks top 10 news stories of 2012. December 20, 2012. Retrieved from *http://www.usatoday.com/story/news/2012/12/20/year-top-news/1783303/*

Van Hook, P. J. (1998). Ethics in non-profit organizations. In *The international encyclopedia of public policy and administration.* Boulder, CO: Westview.

Wheatley, M. J. (1994). *Leadership and the new science: learning about organization from an orderly universe.* San Francisco: Berrett-Koehler Publishers.

Chapter 8
Fundraising

> **Synopsis:** One aspect of nonprofit organizations that differentiates them from their government and for-profit counterparts is the need, in most cases, to raise funds from the public to support their activities. The basic rule of fundraising is to ask—ask the right people at the right time in the right way. There are many conventional and creative ways to raise funds for a nonprofit organization.

ASK.

The rest of what is needed to know about fundraising—the amount to ask, whom to ask, when to ask—are technical details that will be expanded upon in this chapter. However, the simple task of asking for funds for an organization is the major point of this chapter, since it is rare, though not unheard of, that funds are sent to an organization unsolicited.

There are enormous differences in the recommended fundraising techniques if one is trying to raise $10 million for a new hospital wing compared to $1,000 to finance the costs of filing Articles of Incorporation, 501(c)(3) application, and a roll of first-class stamps. There also are many similarities.

First, the organization must start with a reasonable budget plan (see Chapter 11). How much is needed to finance the organization's first-year activities? Will it have paid staff? Staff salaries, benefits, and payroll taxes generally are the largest line-items in any budget. The next decision that determines the order of magnitude in an organization's budget is whether the organization will have an office, which requires rent, telephone, furniture, equipment, and supplies.

A good practice is to prepare three budgets:

1. A "low-end" budget, which assumes a minimum level to get the organization off the ground. The organization would cease to function if revenue did not cover expenses in this budget.

2. A "middle-end" budget, which is as realistic as possible and considers the likely availability of funds for the year, and

3. A "high-end" budget, which is optimistic enough to assume the organization can pay for almost anything it seeks to do.

In asking for money, one should tailor the "pitch" to the demographics of the contributors. It helps to understand the motivation of the contributors, as well. People give money for a reason. It may be they share the organization's motivation for starting up. It may be they feel guilty because otherwise they would not be doing anything to address a problem. It may be they desire power in the organization that they can get only by contributing. They also may be looking for ways to get a tax deduction, align themselves with a popular cause, or they seek immortality (such as by contributing an endowed chair or building wing with their name on it). They may be contributing to an organization because they want a particular organizational leader to be their friend or to contribute to their own favorite cause. Or perhaps none of these—they are simply participating in a 5K fundraiser or "ice bucket challenge" for fun without even thinking about the sponsoring charity.

The most successful fundraising is done by requesting contributions from people who have money to give away, who both know and respect the organization (or someone on its board or staff), and who are given reasons for contributing that are sensitive to their private motivations. Many organizations select some board or advisory committee members based on their ability to tap funds from their friends and associates. Many of their friends will write a check to virtually any cause solely because that influential board member picked up the telephone and asked them to do so.

The donations of board members are often an important source of revenues for new organizations. Many organizations will identify members of the community to serve on their boards because of their willingness and ability to make substantial financial contributions, rather than having governance expertise.

Board members are usually—but not always—delighted to donate when asked, recognizing that the organization, to be successful, does need some start-up funding, and it would make them look foolish if the organization is stillborn as a result of lack of seed money. It is not unusual for external funding sources to consider the extent to which board members make contributions. Therefore, the participation percentage of board member contributions may be as important, or more so, as the dollar amount raised from them.

IRS Substantiation Rules

Most states require organizations to register before they raise funds for charitable purposes (see Chapter 4). However, states are not the only source of government regulation of charities. The federal *Omnibus Budget Reconciliation Act* (OBRA), enacted in 1993, imposed new requirements on charities and donors with respect to substantiation of donations made beginning with the 1994 tax year. The law requires charities to provide a contemporaneous written acknowledgment of contributions of

$250 or more; the donor may not take a charitable tax deduction without having such a written acknowledgment.

The practical effect is that charities are sending these statements routinely to their donors as a part of a "thank you" letter. The written acknowledgment must include the amount of cash paid or a description of property transferred by the donor, a statement of whether the donor received goods or services in exchange for the donation, and a good-faith estimate of the value of such goods and services, if any.

Additional requirements of this law apply in cases when charities provide goods or services in exchange for the donation. If the donation is in excess of $75, the charity must provide a written a statement to the donor that the deductibility of the donation is limited to the excess of the amount donated over and above the value of the goods and services provided, and an estimate of the value of these goods and services provided by the charity. For example, if a 501(c)(3) organization holds a fundraising dinner and estimates that the costs for catering and entertainment are $45 per person and the charge is $100 per ticket, federal law requires disclosure to ticket holders that they can deduct a contribution of $55 per ticket purchased. IRS Publication 1771 provides examples of fact situations that require this disclosure.

Final regulations issued in December 1996 by the IRS provide some guidance to charities on several issues. First, charities may ignore benefits provided to members that can be used "frequently," such as gift shop discounts, free or discounted parking, or free or discounted admission to the organization's facilities or events. Second, there are safe harbors (examples that an organization can follow and avoid violating the law) for benefits of minimal value. One safe harbor permits a donor to deduct the entire value of the contribution if the benefit received has a value less than 2% of the contribution or $96, whichever is less. For example, a $1,000 contributor may receive a T-shirt and mug as a thank you gift without tax penalty to the donor, provided these gifts have a value of under $20.

A second safe harbor applies in the case of small contributions when the benefit received is relatively small. This applies to contributions of at least $51.00 when the value of the benefit provided to the contributor is less than $10.20.

The dollar thresholds mentioned above were for calendar year 2013. Each year, the IRS adjusts these numbers (referred to as the "de minimis threshold amounts") for inflation. Current thresholds can be obtained by downloading Publication 1771 from the IRS Web site *(http://www.irs.gov/pub/irs-pdf/p1771.pdf)* or by calling 877-829-5500.

The regulations require charities to provide written substantiation of a donation to volunteers who wish to claim as a deduction the cost of unreimbursed expenses of $250 or more. They also require that institutions such as colleges that raise money by offering their alumni the right to purchase hard-to-get athletic tickets must consider 20% of the payment for the tickets as the fair market value for the right to purchase the tickets. This amount may not be deducted on the alumni's tax returns as charitable contributions.

Many gray areas remain with respect to substantiation issues, and advocates for the charitable community continue to complain that the IRS has not been totally clear in providing guidance on the regulations implementing substantiation requirements.

Sources of Funding

Among potential sources for funding are:

1. Umbrella Fundraising Groups (e.g. United Ways, Jewish Federations, Catholic Charities, Women's Way, and similar organizations)

In addition to providing an important source of funding, membership in a federated fundraising organization provides added visibility and community endorsement. This is especially important for agencies that lack name recognition.

Although membership in a federated fundraising organization carries no ironclad guarantee that funding levels will be sustained or increased (especially in a recessionary and highly competitive fundraising environment), member organizations fulfilling needs that are a priority to the funding agency can count on relatively stable funding.

Although members sometimes chafe at accountability, program, and fundraising requirements imposed by umbrella organizations, few would trade their federated funding for total independence.

2. Foundations

Major foundations usually require written proposals, many of which can be time-consuming to prepare. There is also a time lag between when the application is submitted—and perhaps, a response to questions from the foundation on issues that were not adequately covered by the application—and when the "check is in the mail."

Many smaller foundations are managed by the philanthropists themselves who establish the foundations for tax purposes. The benefactor may write a check as soon as the request for funds is received.

Most foundation proposals can be prepared by someone without special training or education. The trick is to research the kinds of organizations and activities of interest to the foundation and tailor the grant application to that information. It is also vitally important to tailor it to the application guidelines of the foundation, since many proposals are rejected on technical grounds even before they are judged on their substance.

Many local libraries have sections devoted to foundation fundraising, including research materials with the names, addresses, and type of funding provided by each foundation.

According to *The Art of Fund Raising* by Irving R. Warner, foundations are responsible for just five percent of philanthropy. However, the individual gift may be quite substantial, and the awarding of a major gift by a name foundation can have benefits beyond the financial reward. It can serve as a catalyst for other grants and give the beneficiary organization increased credibility.

3. Direct Mail

The key to direct mail fundraising is a mailing list of people who are likely to consider making a contribution. Professional services sell mailing lists categorized by various interests and demographics. Organizations may wish to send a few newsletters to such a list, and then follow up with a direct mail appeal.

If an organization is a membership organization, its members should be among the first to receive an appeal for voluntary contributions. After all, they have already indicated their interest in the organization's activities and are most likely to know what the organization is doing and how its funds are being spent.

Others to include on solicitation lists are—

- Persons who benefit from the service provided by the organization and families of such persons, provided this is appropriate
- Individuals who are in attendance at speaking engagements
- Persons who make contributions to similar organizations.

Successful fundraising letters often appeal to some basic instinct that will make the reader have an irresistible urge to run to his or her checkbook and write a check to the organization. Appeals that honestly portray the needs of the organization and the importance of the services it provides are a basic component of direct mail letters. Among the most popular are those that appeal to:

- *Guilt.* They make people feel guilty that they are not participating in solving some urgent problem.

- *Affiliation.* They appeal to the need to belong to an organization that is doing something worthwhile.

- *Self-interest.* They find some way to show that by helping the organization, donors' own lives will be improved in some way.

- *Ego.* They make prospective donors feel they are wonderful people only if they make a contribution.

- *Idealism.* They appeal to the idea that the world or community will be a better place for everyone, and only a chosen few selfless people will help this cause.

- *Religious obligation to give to charity.* Religious organizations have relied on this for years, but many secular organizations find this line of appeal equally effective for certain target audiences.

4. Businesses

Many organizations receive operating funds and in-kind contributions of services, equipment, and supplies from businesses in their communities. These businesses include—

- Employers of board members

- Suppliers of goods and services to the organization

- Businesses that make contributions to other nonprofit organizations in the community

- Businesses that sell goods and services to board members, organizational members, or clients

- Major employers in the community.

Rather than visiting a business "cold," organizations sometimes find it effective to involve representatives of businesses in the organization's program before asking them for funds. Among ways they do this are:

- They have business representation on the board.

- They establish a "business advisory committee" consisting of local businesspeople.

- They invite business representatives to an "open house" to see the organization in action.

- They place business representatives on the organization's mailing list, and send them the newsletter and newspaper clippings about the organization's accomplishments.

- They invite business representatives to speak to the organization's board or membership about their products and services.

Many business corporations have established foundations that are specifically staffed to consider funding applications from charities.

5. Telephone Solicitation

Similar to direct mail, telephone solicitation is effective if done with the right list of names and correct telephone numbers. A college making calls to its alumni using student volunteers will certainly have a much better response than if it makes calls at random. Similarly, an organization is well served if it can tailor calls to those with a likely interest in its purpose.

6. Government Grants

During the 1980s, federal government grants to nonprofits, particularly for social services, plummeted. Yet, there are millions of dollars in federal and state grants available to nonprofits that still go begging for takers. The trick is to identify the source of funds and determine eligibility.

The *Catalog of Federal Domestic Assistance* is available in many libraries. It can also be found on the Internet, in searchable format, at *http://www.gsa.gov/portal/content/101097*. This document provides a summary of available federal grants and the qualifications and conditions for applying.

Government grants usually are accompanied by lots of paperwork and operational requirements, some of which may be inconsistent with the manner in which an organization intends to operate. Some analysts view a 1991 U.S. Supreme Court decision (*Rust v. Sullivan*) as clearing the way for the federal government to impose even greater restrictions on how government funds may be spent. If you are applying for government grants, learn about any additional requirements in order to be in compliance with law.

7. Revenue Generation Other Than Voluntary Contributions

The following are examples of strategies used by nonprofits to increase income:

- Newsletter subscriptions
- Newsletter and Web site advertising
- Annual fundraising dinner
- Reception for a famous person or someone well known in the field of expertise of the organization/testimonial dinner
- Sale of publications
- Fees for services to clients
- Sale or rental of mailing lists (make sure the buyer will use the list in a manner consistent with the organization's goals and not resell it to others)
- Small games of chance (provided they comply with state regulatory laws)
- Wills and bequests
- Social events (e.g., bus trips to sports events)
- Newspaper advertising to request contributions
- In-kind donations
- Card calling (using board and organizational members to do peer one-on-one solicitation)
- Fees from workshops and conferences
- Sale of exhibit space at workshops and conferences
- Special fundraising events such as bake sales, flea markets, and running races
- Auctions of donated items (including those from celebrities) conducted over the Internet or at a live event
- Participating in crowdsourcing Web sites to finance specific programs, such as Kickstarter *(http://www.kickstarter.com)* and Indiegogo *(http://www.indiegogo.com)*
- Use of online personal fundraising pages to generate donations from friends of stakeholders
- Events similar to the ALS's "ice bucket challenge" (see page 271).

Hiring a Consultant

There are hundreds of honest, hard-working, professional fundraising consultants who will, for a fee, provide an organization with fundraising advice or even handle all of its fundraising. There also are hundreds who are not reputable.

Most states regulate this industry, and there are opportunities to obtain information about consultants before making a hiring commitment. State associations of nonprofit organizations may be helpful in identifying candidates. Since most states require consultants to register, the public may look at these records (some states post reports online) or contact organizations that have hired them to see if they are pleased with the services being provided.

Discussion Questions

1. Discuss whether you feel that the general public is becoming more cynical or weary with respect to the motivations behind fundraising appeals. If "yes," what steps can the leadership of the sector take to reverse it?

2. How might the motivations, culture, expectations, methods, and vision of professional fundraisers differ from those of their client organizations? What are some of the questions that would be appropriate to ask a professional fundraiser to determine if he or she would be a good match with a charity?

3. Are there fundraising techniques in which you would not engage, even if empirical research demonstrated that such techniques were effective in raising money?

4. Should donors have full access to information about how their funds will be used? When should this information be withheld or restricted?

5. Why do fundraisers often find it more difficult to find donors to pay for operating expenses, compared with project or capital expenses, such as building a new building or wing?

6. How has social media been used successfully by nonprofit organizations to increase the reach of their fundraising efforts?

7. Discuss how the ALS Association's experience of the "ice bucket challenge" in 2014 has influenced how charities strategize about fundraising.

Activities

1. Compile a collection of direct mail fundraising letters you receive. What do these letters have in common? What are some of the appeals being made to you to convince you to donate (see the typology of appeals on pages 155-156).

2. Research what it would cost in out-of-pocket expenses to produce and mail a 5-page fundraising letter that includes a sheet of personalized address labels for the recipient. Consider costs such as printing, postage, labor, and purchasing a mailing list. For purposes of this activity, assume the mailing is for 100,000 people. Then calculate what the break-even point of donations

needs to be to raise $100,000 from the mailing, assuming an average response rate of a half-percent, or the response rate you would need given an average donation of $20.

3. Research the growth of fundraising conducted over the Internet. Compare and contrast the techniques and skills needed to fundraise over the Internet with other fundraising techniques.

Tips for Practitioners

1. Review other organizations' solicitation materials and identify those presentations that can serve as an effective model for solicitation.

2. Keep a file of newspaper clippings about benefactors in the community and others who would have a potential interest in the work of the organization. A few well-placed and well-timed telephone calls can be effective in reaching these influential people.

3. Involve everyone in the organization in the fundraising effort. It is not prudent to isolate fundraising from the programs the organization funds.

4. Always thank each donor, regardless of the amount received. A $5 check from an individual may have required as much personal sacrifice as a $1,000 check from a wealthier contributor.

5. Make sure your organization complies with all state regulations that apply to charitable solicitation, such as disclosing if a telephone solicitation is being made by professional fundraisers, and including required disclaimer statements on written materials.

Online Resources to Explore

Association of Fundraising Professionals
http://www.afpnet.org/

Idealist.org Nonprofit FAQ (Development and Fundraising)
http://www.idealist.org/if/i/en/faqcat/100-7

PayPal Giving Fund (formerly known as MissionFish)
https://www.paypalgivingfund.org/index.html

Fundraising.com
http://www.fundraising.com/

Carter McNamara's Nonprofit Fundraising and Grantwriting
 http://www.managementhelp.org/fndrsng/np_raise/np_raise.htm

For Further Reading

Barksdale, B., & Garecht, J. (2002). *25 fundraising secrets.* Collierville, TN: Fundcraft Publishing.

Cannon, C. (2011). *An executive's guide to fundraising operations: Principles, tools & trends.* New York: Wiley.

Dannelley, P. (1986). *Fundraising and public relations.* Norman, OK: University of Oklahoma Press.

Davis, M. (2013). *The fundraising rules.* (Self-Published): CreateSpace.

Eisenstein, A. (2013). *50 asks in 50 weeks: A guide to better fundraising for your small development shop.* Sioux Falls, SD: CharityChannel Press.

Grobman, G. & Grant, G. (2006). *Fundraising online: Using the internet to raise serious money for your nonprofit organization.* Harrisburg, PA: White Hat Communications.

McCrea, J., Walker, J., & Weber, K. (2013). *The generosity network: New transformational tools for successful fund-raising.* Carlsbad, CA: Deepak Chopra.

Mutz, J.& Murray, K. (2010). *Fundraising for dummies.* New York: Wiley and Sons.

Seltzer, M. (2002). *Securing your organization's future: A complete guide to fundraising strategies.* (Revised Ed.). New York: The Foundation Center.

Stallings, B., & McMillion, D. (1999). *How to produce fabulous fundraising events: Reap remarkable returns with minimal effort.* Pleasanton, CA: Building Better Skills.

Warwick, M. (2013). *How to write successful fundraising appeals.* San Francisco: Jossey-Bass.

Chapter 9
Marketing

> **Synopsis:** Marketing is an appropriate, if not essential, activity of nonprofit organizations that need to sell goods and services, and to develop a mix of desirable goods and services to support their missions. Nonprofits market by shaping an attractive message, and delivering that message through a variety of methods, including print and electronic advertising, social media, special events, and direct mail. A formal marketing plan can be effective in implementing a strategy to increase an organization's marketing success.

Definition of Marketing

Marketing is defined as "the activity...and processes for creating, communicating, delivering, and exchanging offerings that have value for customers, clients, partners, and society at large" (American Marketing Association, 2013). It includes that function of the organization that can keep in touch with the organization's consumers, read their needs, develop 'products' that meet these needs, and build a program of communications to express the organization's purposes" (Kotler and Levy, 1969).

A more narrow definition of nonprofit marketing can be: activities of a nonprofit organization, including developing and improving its services, that are designed to result in a transaction between two entities (for our purposes, the organization and either another organization or an individual) to exchange money for goods or services provided by that nonprofit organization. Funds derived from this transaction may be used for any legal purpose consistent with the organization's mission, including paying overhead or expanding the availability of its goods and services to those who may not be able to pay the full cost.

Nonprofit marketing also includes those activities in which money is not exchanged, but the activities are designed to increase the accessibility of the organization's services. For example, when a museum that offers free admission designates funds for advertising for the purpose of increasing its reach into the community, it is also engaging in marketing. Even those who accept an offer of free admission will likely avail themselves of the museum's cafeteria and perhaps its gift shop, contributing to the organization's net revenue, putting aside any benefits a free admission policy might have on contributions. Nonprofits also engage in marketing when they seek volunteers using traditional marketing techniques.

There are two major components to marketing—developing the message that needs to be communicated, and delivering that message to the target through some medium. Both of these components are crucial to the success of any marketing campaign. Organizations that take marketing seriously engage in research prior to the campaign to collect data on what message should be communicated, and which is the most effective way to have that message delivered. Advances in technology, particularly the Web, social media, e-mail, blogging, and texting, have enhanced the opportunities for nonprofit organizations to connect with their stakeholders in ways that these stakeholders find are the most comfortable.

Introduction to Nonprofit Marketing

It was not that long ago that few, if any, nonprofit organizations thought it was appropriate to engage in the traditional marketing campaigns that were considered essential by for-profit business organizations. Many nonprofit leaders felt that engaging in these activities was not consistent with the spirit of being a nonprofit. Mission was paramount, and keeping a vigilant eye on the "bottom line" was a secondary, yet necessary, annoyance. Times have changed. Today's modern nonprofit CEOs often brandish an MBA and are quite comfortable using terms such as "return on investment," "market share," "branding," "profit center," and "SWOT analysis"—terms one never used to hear from those who led nonprofit organizations.

An active marketing program is now not only acceptable for nonprofit organizations, but one is virtually required to keep pace in the turbulent business environment of the sector—particularly among the mega-nonprofits such as institutions of higher learning and hospitals. Some of these organizations have annual budgets in the billions of dollars and market their services with the same aggressiveness as their for-profit competitors.

A strong case can be made that a nonprofit organization is obligated to do what it can to sustain itself, particularly during times when it is threatened by declining donations and government support during economic downturns. A strong marketing program helps an organization acquire the revenues it needs to grow and provide more free and subsidized services than it might otherwise have the capacity to provide.

This book maintains the perspective throughout that nonprofit organizations have many things in common with their for-profit counterparts. One of these is that neither type of organization can take for granted that simply offering services will generate enough "business" to provide financial stability for the purpose (in the case of a for-profit) to generate profit or (in the case of a nonprofit) to generate net revenue to expand services and make up for possible deficits. Both types of organizations typically engage in activities to offer a mix of goods and services for which there is sufficient consumer demand to justify offering them. They communicate with these consumers about the availability of these goods and services. They communicate information about themselves that builds trust with potential customers. And they promote the value of their particular services compared to any competition they might have. These activities are the essence of marketing.

If you recall our discussion of the diversity of the nonprofit sector in the introduction to this book, there is no monolithic model for financing the operations of nonprofit organizations. It is not unusual for a nonprofit organization to obtain its revenues through three major sources of income—a mix of grants, private contributions, and fees for goods and services. To a lesser extent, investment income provides an additional source of revenue. The proportion of these three major sources of income varies by subsector, according to statistics compiled by the Urban Institute in its report, The Nonprofit Almanac. This report documents that the sale of goods and services provided 72.4% of the sector's revenue in 2010 (Roeger, Blackwood, & Pettijohn, 2013).

One conclusion that can be drawn from these data is just as meaningful today as it was decades ago—the modern charity depends substantially more on the sale of goods and services for its revenue than one might expect. In fact, of the 310,000 plus charitable organizations included in the survey database of the National Center for Charitable Statistics, through a review of 990 and 990EZ tax returns, only about a fifth of their income came from donations in the form of private contributions and government grants.

There is no way to interpret this other than to marvel at how important the sale of goods and services is to the financial health of nonprofit organizations. Fundraising is important, of course, and certainly fundraising for some organizations underwrites virtually all of their operating expenses. But to an increasing extent, this situation is unusual. Imagine how long a typical nonprofit hospital, university, nursing home, family service agency, or day care center could survive financially if it had to depend totally on donations to meet payroll and provide for other expenses.

Nonprofit organizations receive more than $335 billion annually in donations (Hrywna, 2014), and nonprofit organizations engage in increasingly sophisticated strategies to augment their donations. The same is true with marketing, and even more important with revenues from the sale of goods and services approaching a trillion dollars annually. It is common sense that a dollar in revenue that comes from the sale of goods and services has the same value in paying a staff member's salary as a dollar raised in contributions. Putting aside the effects of the economy, the amount of donations made to charities tends to be quite stable over long periods of time. However, organizations that fail to engage in effective marketing strategies to respond to competition, respond to consumer needs, and trumpet their positive attributes may find that their total revenues shrink despite increases in donations.

Differences Between Nonprofit Marketing and Fundraising

Marketing shares much in common with fundraising. One aspect that differentiates the two is that fundraising implies a relationship whereby a donor makes a gratuitous contribution to the organization without an expectation of anything substantially tangible received in return, and does not benefit directly from the donation any more than someone who does not make a donation. Marketing, on the other hand, implies a transaction in which the organization seeks to convince an individual or organization to make a voluntary exchange of money for goods and services provided by the organization, and the organization can use these funds without any strings attached. The lines between fundraising and marketing are certainly not as black and white as this, but I see this as an important distinction.

There are certainly many techniques in Chapter 8 on fundraising that apply to marketing goods and services. Similarly, there are techniques described in this chapter that are equally relevant to a fundraising campaign.

What Nonprofits Market

The following is a typology of what nonprofit organizations market (Grau, 2014), with each followed by real-life examples from my recent experience:

- services and programs—A day care center seeks to find enough children of appropriate ages for which to provide services by placing an advertisement in a local ethnic newspaper.

- goods—My alma mater's gift shop tries to sell me t-shirts and football tickets, and tries to sell my son, a newly minted graduate, an expensive frame for his diploma.

- experiences—A symphony orchestra arranges for its assistant conductor to have a pre-concert lecture providing background about the featured composers and artists.

- concepts—A state-wide conservative think tank prepares and runs a television spot in markets in my state to advocate for state legislation that would prohibit teacher unions from using union dues to finance partisan political activities, thus improving the organization's name recognition (Commonwealth Foundation, 2014).

- group benefits—A leading organization for senior citizens (in this case, the AARP) markets benefits such as discounts at movie theaters and inexpensive car insurance to its membership.

To the above list, one of my ARNOVA colleagues, Martin Berg, who teaches nonprofit marketing at the University of Illinois-Chicago, adds: "Personal satisfaction—In the wake of a devastating hurricane, thousands send money to the Red Cross for no other reason than that they feel a responsibility for their fellow humans. The only "product" they receive in return is the donor's own satisfaction—the warm glow of knowing they could help someone else."

We all have seen firsthand similar marketing efforts by nonprofit organizations, many of which are designed to contribute to net revenues (which, in the for-profit context, would be referred to as "profit"). A Jewish Community Center holds an open house, offering the public free access, so prospective members can check out the fitness center facilities. A local hospital has a booth set up at a 5K race to offer free blood pressure screenings and body fat analysis for the purpose of funneling new patients to its outpatient clinics, and provides free pens at the booth with the name of the hospital prominently printed on them. These marketing efforts by "charities" no longer seem as strange as they might have in years past.

How Nonprofits Market

A few decades ago, nonprofit organizations had a limited menu of options to deliver their message to the public. There were a limited number of TV and radio stations on which to advertise. The print media were also limited. Many of today's options of choice for message delivery, such as YouTube, blogs, podcasts, electronic newsletters, Facebook, Twitter, e-mail, texting, and the World Wide Web, did not even exist then.

Among the more conventional methods to communicate a marketing effort are (Grau, 2014)—

- *Paid media.* Traditional media used by nonprofits to communicate their messages include both paid and free placements on radio and television outlets, newspapers and magazines, and other outlets such as highway billboards and transit vehicle advertising. Traditional advertising has the advantage of being subject to some targeting of the market the organization wishes to reach. In most cases (magazines and billboards being salient exceptions), traditional advertising can be prepared quickly and reach a wide audience in a short time. Many broadcasters will even offer to help an organization prepare a public service announcement without charge.

- *Commercial media.* This refers to communications prepared by the organization that are sent to media outlets with the hope (but not the requirement, as would be the case with paid media), that the message will be communicated. Included in this are press releases, Op-Ed articles, and blog and podcast interviews in which the organization makes an effort to convince others with market reach to provide some "air" time.

- *Owned media.* This refers to media owned by the organization such as in-house magazines, newspapers, newsletters, messages on its buildings and vehicles, its Web site, and other media for which the organization can control (such as its Facebook page, blogs, discussion boards, and podcasts).

- *Direct Marketing.* Perhaps of most use by nonprofit organizations to hawk their goods and services is direct marketing. This approach includes contacting individuals directly, typically through the mail, by telephone, by e-mail, and door-to-door. The major benefit of this strategy is that unlike television and radio ads, a mailing can be targeted to those who purchased goods and services from the organization in the past. The communication can be customized to appeal to a particular segment of one's market. The obvious disadvantage is that direct marketing can be costly compared to mass broadcasting. One strategy organizations engage in to facilitate these efforts is to methodically collect names, addresses, telephone numbers, and e-mail addresses of as many individuals as possible who come in contact with the organization, and to note the nature of that contact. This database becomes invaluable for both marketing and fundraising efforts.

- *Event Marketing.* Nonprofit organizations often sponsor events, such as golf tournaments, 5K road races, casino nights, and other events that are designed as fundraisers, but can have marketing benefits, as well. In an article in *The Chronicle of Philanthropy* (May 10, 2007), the author criticized organizers of 5K races for charity that often spent more money on directing the race than was raised. There was a backlash that illustrated the fact that conducting these and other special events had substantially more benefits to the organization than simply raising funds for the cause (Panapento, 2007). Among these benefits is giving visibility to both the organization and the mission it supports.

- *Social media.* Any credible marketing plan by nonprofit organizations these days must have a social media component, with Twitter and Facebook accounts on center-stage. In the past, organizations could be comfortable with making a sizeable investment in encouraging potential donors and clients to "like" their Facebook page, and be assured that all of these "likers" would be able to view any and all posts made, with the potential that these viewers would share the posts with their "friends." This is no longer the case, and organizations who engage in this strategy are finding that they may need to allocate funds in their budget to purchase advertising to assure that more of their likers are able to see these posts in their newsfeeds. Beyond this, purchasing advertising on social media sites is generally low cost, and technology has improved the capacity of any message to be targeted to any particular demographic the organization seeks to reach with its message.

The advantage of making social media the centerpiece of any nonprofit marketing campaign is the apparently high cost-benefit of this marketing strategy, as well as its speed. A good communication to a relatively small group of supporters has the ability to "go viral," as recipients of a Facebook post or a tweet have the ability to share (in the case of Facebook) or retweet (in the case of Twitter) to relay the communication to those who otherwise have no relationship with the organization. Facebook and Twitter accounts are free, and a single individual with social networking savvy can create an effective organizational marketing campaign at little or no out-of-pocket cost. Social networking marketing can be coordinated with YouTube videos, organizational Web site content, and traditional marketing efforts.

In their book, *The Dragonfly Effect,* Aaker and Smith suggest a framework for effective marketing by nonprofit organizations with respect to social media. This framework has value in the context of general nonprofit marketing, as well. The authors suggest a 4-component framework, beginning with engagement, defined as "truly making people feel emotionally connected to helping you achieve your goals." This connectedness is achieved through "storytelling, authenticity, and establishing a personal connection" (McKinsey Quarterly, 2011). Ethical organizations must be careful to assure that what they promise in their marketing campaigns are consistent with what they deliver, or risk harm to their reputations.

Branding

The term "branding" refers to an organization's total image, and includes all of the factors that distinguish it from its competition. Among these factors are its reputation, its logo, its taglines (such as the United Way's "Thanks to you, it's working"), its particular print fonts (Coca Cola has one of the most recognized examples), particular colors (the ubiquitous pink that shows up in breast cancer marketing and fundraising efforts), and tchotchkes (such as the Livestrong yellow wrist band). Branding connects the organization to its customers, clients, and the public, in powerful ways. When I participate in the American Cancer Society's "Relay for Life," I feel comfortable my donation will be used to advance the cause of fighting cancer rather than lining the pockets of some for-profit fundraiser. Its logo (view it at: *http://www.brandsoftheworld.com/logo/american-cancer-society*) is one of the most recognized in the nonprofit world, and its brand image is high in the rankings of the most valuable in the world, based on public perception of the organization, media coverage, and the percentage of revenue from direct public support.

The concept of the value of branding is not simply an academic exercise; some try to calculate how much the value of an organization's brand directly or indirectly contributes to the amount of revenue it nets and can be measured in the billions of dollars. (See: *http://www.marketingcharts.com/wp/traditional/top-100-nonprofit-brands-ymca-salvation-army-rank-high-9591/*).

An intriguing 2009 study/article by Cone and Intangible Business concluded that the YMCA had the most valuable brand, worth almost $6.4 billion (Intangible Business, 2009). Interesting enough, the organization rebranded itself as the "Y" beginning in 2010 (YMCA, 2014). The Salvation Army and the United Way trailed with $4.7 billion and $4.5 billion respectively. One conclusion that can be drawn from this type of analysis is that everything an organization does affects the value of its brand. For example, a new charity's brand value can skyrocket if it can convince a popular celebrity to actively endorse it. And at the other end of the spectrum, a charity's brand value can plummet when it is involved in a scandal, as was evident by the scandal of the United Way in the late '90s, and the more recent scandal involving the charity started by Lance Armstrong, the Lance Armstrong Foundation.

The case involving the Lance Armstrong Foundation, at one time the fastest growing U.S. charity and one of the most respected, will be studied for years. No one suggests that the Foundation itself was involved in any unethical activity. But its founder's eventual admission of unethical conduct unrelated to the activities of the charity resulted in clear damage to the charity's brand. The board of the organization took steps to at first distance itself from its iconic founder, and then completely severed its relationship with Mr. Armstrong, even changing its name to the Livestrong Foundation in November 2012 (Maclaggan, 2012). It may take decades (as was the case with the United Way of America scandal involving its national CEO, William Aramony) to regain its stature as one of the most respected charities in America.

Donors clearly prefer to buy goods and services from an organization with a trusted brand. Doing so eliminates much of the uncertainty that any net revenue will be used for good. It also is useful in creating a strong bond between a donor or consumer and the organization.

Rebranding

The Lance Armstrong Foundation rebranded itself as a result of scandal. The March of Dimes is also a classic example of rebranding—as a result of success. This nonprofit organization had an almost universally recognizable and positive brand, and it launched a successful campaign to rebrand itself in the 1950s. A survey had indicated that 83% of the U.S. could identify the March of Dimes, which for decades had a stellar reputation in helping find a cure for the dreaded polio virus. With success in finding a cure for polio through the application of effective vaccines, the organization changed course to focus on preventing birth defects. There was a longer lead time, as the public's perception of the organization lagged with respect to its new mission. The organization launched a marketing campaign, mostly through advertising targeted to those who were the most likely donors. This campaign was tested in one particular community to collect data on which appeal was the most effective (Mindak & Bybee, 1971).

Demographics

When considering the startup of a new program or expanding an existing one to offer goods and services, it is important to consider how demographics will affect success or failure. The term "demographics" refers to the characteristics of a particular group of people that might be served by the organization. Demographic factors typically considered in marketing include income, gender, age, religion, political affiliation, and ethnic origin. An organization's goods and services are likely to have much more appeal to one particular demographic group compared to another. With limited resources, marketers will be wise to target their communications to those most likely to purchase them, i.e., engaging in market segmentation.

Market Research

Market research includes activities designed to collect and analyze data that will enable the organization to make good decisions with respect to how to market its goods and services. Among the questions that are often the focus of this research are those affecting the four "p's" related to marketing, also referred to as the "marketing mix" (Mathews, 2006, Manktelow & Carlson, n.d.):

- product (what goods and services to offer)
- price (how much to charge)
- promotion (how to shape the communication with potential buyers)
- place (what media to use to communicate).

Grau (2014) suggests that market research provides information about what is going on with respect to the organization's sales (descriptive research), why it is going on (explanatory research), and what is likely to occur if the organization pursues one particular marketing strategy compared to another (predictive research).

Many of the techniques used in market research are the same ones organizations use to improve their fundraising. Among them are focus groups, surveys, interviews, and analysis of the organization's web and social media pages. Organizations need to know basic information, such as which demographic groups are more likely to use their services, and why, so that their marketing communications can be targeted to appeal to these groups. Conversely, it is helpful to know why certain demographic groups who might benefit from them are not using the organization's services. A special effort can be made to change marketing materials and the method of delivery of those communications. Many smaller organizations do not have much capacity to conduct formal market research. But if they begin a new program or service without a good sense of whether there is sufficient demand for it, the resulting loss of net revenue could threaten the viability of all other programs conducted by the organization.

Even organizations that have too few resources to pay a marketing research firm or to launch a traditional research effort can benefit from low-cost technology strategies. Focus groups can be conducted online using Google+ Hangouts. Survey instruments can be prepared, disseminated, and analyzed using free or inexpensive Web-based services such as Survey Monkey *(http://www.surveymonkey.com)*. Interviews can be conducted using the chat feature of a social networking site or applications that can be added inexpensively to the organization's Web site. Feedback can be obtained using information gleaned from in-house discussion boards. There is certainly benefit to hiring professionals who are trained to find valid answers to research questions and collect and analyze data, avoiding threats to validity that might not be understood by those who are not trained to do this. For many organizations, this is unrealistic. Collecting and analyzing data, even through convenience surveys and the collection of anecdotal comments about the organization's goods and services, is an essential part of any marketing program. "Listening to your customers" gives you a heads-up when something is not going right. Many of your stakeholders will not be shy in complaining, or making helpful suggestions, to improve their transactions.

Among other considerations for marketing are having an effective media relations program (see Chapter 13), engaging in cause-related marketing (see page 363-364), and using special events to communicate the availability of the organization's goods and services to its target markets (see page 168).

Marketing Plan

A marketing plan can consist of a couple of pages of material or be as involved as a comprehensive strategic plan. It does not need to be costly. A basic marketing plan needs to set goals and objectives, a list of what needs to be done to accomplish those objectives, a time frame, a budget, who will be doing the work, and how the plan will be evaluated. You can find basic nonprofit marketing templates on the Web that can provide a more comprehensive framework for advancing your organization's marketing program. One of these (Pava, n.d.) can be found at:

http://www.civicactions.com/blog/2010/mar/23/nonprofit_marketing_plan_template

This template, prepared by Getting Attention's Nancy Schwartz, features a nine-component plan that includes the following:

- Goal—This is the main goal you hope to achieve with this plan, and goals relating to communications needed to achieve that. An example would be to increase the net revenue of a Jewish Community Center (JCC) without compromising quality.

- Objectives—This includes 3-5 specific and measurable steps you wish to take to achieve that goal. Examples might be to capture more market share for the JCC's fitness facility, improve the reputation and quality of the organization, and increase the registration of children in the JCC's day care program, using an aggressive social media campaign.

- Target Audience—This section covers who the JCC is trying to reach, and what it wants them to do. Examples might be to reach those in the area who have children under six, young professionals who are looking to keep fit and meet people in the area who share their interests, and seniors who have a strong connection to their ethnic community and who may be interested in providing donations to the Center and the community.

- Best Strategies—Examples might be to communicate with every household in a 10-mile radius that has a child under 6, update the exercise equipment in the fitness center, and offer a package of membership fees that will offer free fitness classes to parents with children who are cared for in the day care center.

- Tactics—This includes actual actions that could be taken to meet the goals and objectives, and is where good brainstorming sessions can pay dividends. Examples might include advertising day care services in the local parenting magazine, having a wine and cheese party every Thursday evening following the evening spin classes and offering discounts to members of the Young Professionals organization, and having health fairs for seniors at the JCC. Tactics also include shaping the message to reach the target audience, using the most appropriate mix of media. For example, communicating with the young people about the fitness center would involve totally different tactics than communicating with the seniors, considering research validates the obvious conclusion that these groups of people typically receive their information in divergently different ways.

- Roles and Responsibilities—Executing a marketing plan takes substantial staff time. This aspect of the plan includes who will be responsible for composing the communications, placing the advertisements, updating the Web site, preparing intake, and training staff to carry out the plan.

- Step-by-Step Work Plan—This is the guts of the marketing plan—what has to happen, when, and by whom.

- Budget—This spells out in detail how much this plan will cost for staff training, print and Web advertising, Web site management, consulting, and so on.

- Evaluation—This final component considers how the results of implementing the plan will be evaluated and what data will be collected and analyzed.

See the following Web sites for additional resources on developing a marketing plan:

http://www.fundraising123.org/article/organizing-your-nonprofit-marketing-plan#.U6u7BLHBfwA
http://www.entrepreneur.com/article/43026
http://www.quickmba.com/marketing/plan/
http://www.marketingplan.net/sample-marketing-plan/

Some Strategies Included in a Marketing Plan

Among the more generic strategies that might typically be found in a marketing plan are the following:

- redesigning the logo to make it more recognizable and memorable

- targeting a specific demographic group that otherwise is underrepresented in accessing the organization's services

- offering a different menu of the organization's services at different locations

- changing the services offered to respond to changes in demand

- pricing services to be more competitive and offering discounts

- having a conference with an exhibit hall or offering workshops to not only generate revenue, but also to improve the visibility of the organization

- expanding the service area where a program is being offered

- bundling the offering of services (e.g., purchase a gym membership and also receive free access to the swimming pool)

- approaching businesses with preferential partnerships for their employees to access the service

- offering long-term contracts for selected organizations that benefit from the services offered

- changing the delivery of the service to make it more convenient for those who might otherwise not be able to access the service.

Strategic Planning and SWOT Analysis

Marketing planning needs to be a part of an organization's strategic planning process, if it has one (see Chapter 16). Many organizations will engage in one particular planning exercise called SWOT Analysis, an acronym for Strengths, Weaknesses, Opportunities, and Threats (Berry, T., n.d., Ogunjimi, A., n.d.). The first two are analyses of aspects that are internal to the organization. This part of the process looks at the organization's "capabilities, expertise, technology, financial stability, staff stability, donor base, volunteer base, board of directors, public image, social impact, program effectiveness, leadership, history, relationships, successes and failures" (Grau, p. 68). The last two analyze the environment in which the organization funds itself, and include factors that are external to the organization—such as the regulatory and legal climate, the organization's competition, changes in demographics, potential partners and collaborators, culture, and the advance of technology and how they affect the organization. For more on how a SWOT analysis is performed, see:

http://articles.bplans.com/business/how-to-perform-swot-analysis/116
http://www.ehow.com/about_6588184_nonprofit-swot-analysis.html

Cause-Related Marketing

Many nonprofits partner with for-profit organizations to endorse products and services that are consistent with the mission of the nonprofit organization, and which may provide substantial revenue. The term "cause-related marketing" was first used in 1983 by American Express, which engaged in this strategy to improve its market reach and raise funds for the Statue of Liberty restoration project (GrantSpace, n.d.). Cause-related marketing is discussed in more detail in Chapter 20. The benefits to the for-profit organization are well-documented. There are additional benefits that accrue to participating nonprofits beyond any financial remuneration they might receive, such as additional exposure for the organization. Organizations should be careful, however, to assure that any agreements they sign explicitly spell out what is expected from each partner.

Discussion Questions

1. Discuss how a perceived trend of nonprofit organizations hiring CEOs with MBAs to run social service organizations, as contrasted to those with MSW degrees, has changed attitudes with respect to marketing by these organizations. Are there any downsides to this?

2. Consider the pros and cons of the ways nonprofit organizations communicate with you about their marketing efforts. Are there particular ways they do this that you find annoying?

3. What are the similarities and differences that you might expect to find in a strategic plan, a marketing plan, a fundraising plan, and a technology plan? How might you structure these plans to avoid duplication of effort?

4. How has technology changed the face of nonprofit marketing over the past five, ten, and 30 years? What advances in technology can you anticipate in the near future that will affect how marketing messages will be delivered?

5. Discuss how pricing of nonprofit goods and services creates controversy. For example, if a nonprofit prices a product lower than market rate, a competing for-profit business might accuse that nonprofit of using its tax exemptions and other advantages to compete unfairly. And if it prices a product at a market rate, the for-profit business might suggest that the nonprofit does not deserve any government benefits, because it is operating just as any other business.

Activities

1. Create a database of nonprofit marketing efforts that are targeted to you. Are there any patterns you can identify?

2. Research recent nonprofit organization scandals and document how the nonprofit addressed the damage to its brand.

3. Research how your nonprofit management education program markets itself to prospective students. What appeals are effective? How would you suggest the program improve its communications and the way they are delivered?

Tips for Practitioners

1. If you are using interactive media such as YouTube to market a controversial message, be prepared for comments, either orchestrated or not, that respond negatively to your message, such as is the case with the Commonwealth Foundation message illustrated on page 166.

2. Consider whether your organization has the capacity to serve all of those who want to participate if your marketing plan is wildly successful.

3. Setting up an organization's Facebook page is a good first step in using social media. It is free and easy to do. A step-by-step guide can be found at: *http://www.ehow.com/how_8582699_successfully-design-facebook-nonprofit-organization.html*

4. Make sure you are in compliance with do-not call laws if you are using the telephone to sell goods and services. Typically, these laws provide exemptions for charities soliciting donations, but do not for calls selling goods and services.

5. Beware of mission drift with marketing efforts. Consider whether it makes sense to market the organization's goods and services to those who are most likely to be able to afford them while neglecting those who may not.

References

American Marketing Association. (July 2013). About AMA. Retrieved from *https://www.ama.org/AboutAMA/Pages/Definition-of-Marketing.aspx*

Anderson, L. (1998). Save the children reacts to probe, plans reforms. Retrieved from *http://articles.chicagotribune.com/1998-03-18/news/9803220001_1_special-report-child-sponsorship-children-federation*

Berry, T. (n.d.). What is a SWOT analysis? Retrieved June 27, 2014 Retrieved from *http://articles.bplans.com/business/how-to-perform-swot-analysis/116*

Commonwealth Foundation. (June 2014). We need our voices back. Retrieved from *http://www.youtube.com/watch?v=XYOV8N2SnV4*

Gaedeke, R. (1977). *Marketing in private and nonprofit organizations.* Santa Monica, CA: Goodyear Publishing Company.

Grau, S. (2014). *Marketing for Nonprofit Organizations.* Chicago, IL: Lyceum Books.

GrantSpace. (n.d.). What is cause-related marketing? Retrieved from *http://grantspace.org/Tools/Knowledge-Base/Funding-Resources/Corporations/cause-related-marketing*

Hrywna, M. (June 2014). Giving estimated at $335.17 Billion for 2013. *The Nonprofit Times.* June 14, 2014. Retrieved from *http://www.thenonprofittimes.com/news-articles/giving-usa-2013/*

Intangible Business. (2009). Nonprofit power brands 2009. Retrieved from *http://www.intangiblebusiness.com/news/marketing/2009/06/nonprofit-power-brands-2009*

Kotler, P. And Levy, S. (January 1969). Broadening the concept of marketing (in Gaedeke, R., *Marketing in Private and Public Nonprofit Organizations*, Santa Monica, CA: Goodyear Publishing Co.

MacLaggan, C. (2012). Exclusive: Livestrong cancer charity drops Lance Armstrong name from title. Retrieved from *http://articles.chicagotribune.com/2012-11-14/sports/sns-rt-us-cycling-armstrong-livestrongbre8ae000-20121114_1_lance-armstrong-foundation-livestrong-cancer-charity-yellow-wristbands*

Manktelow, J. & Carlson, A. (n.d.). The marketing mix and 4 Ps: Understanding how to position your market offering. Retrieved from http://www.mindtools.com/pages/article/newSTR_94.htm

Mathews, M. (2006). Marketing strategy—Product, place, price and promotion. Retrieved from *http://voices.yahoo.com/marketing-strategy-product-place-price-promotion-41520.html*

McKinsey Quarterly (2011). The power of storytelling: What nonprofits can teach the private sector about social media. Retrieved from *http://www.mckinsey.com/insights/marketing_sales/the_power_of_storytelling_what_nonprofits_can_teach_the_private_sector_about_social_media*

Mindak, W. & Bybee, H. M. (1977). Marketing's application to fundraising. In Marketing in private and public nonprofit organizations. Gaedeke, R. Santa Monica, CA: Goodyear Publishing Company.

Ogunjimi, A. (n.d.). Nonprofit SWOT analysis. Retrieved from *http://www.ehow.com/about_6588184_nonprofit-swot-analysis.html*

Panepento, P. (May 2007). Critics dispute claim that charities lose money on special events. *Chronicle of Philanthropy,* May 17, 2014. Retrieved from *http://philanthropy.com/article/Critics-Dispute-Claim-That/55107)*

Pava, A. (n.d.). Nonprofit marketing plan template. Retrieved from *http://www.civicactions.com/blog/2010/mar/23/nonprofit_marketing_plan_template*

Roeger, K., Blackwood, A. & Pettijohn, S. (2013). The nonprofit almanac. Washington, D.C.: Urban Institute.

Save the Children Foundation. (n.d.). Sponsor a child around the world. Retrieved from *https://sponsor.savethechildren.org/*

Wing, K., Pollak, T. & Blackwood, A. (2008). *The nonprofit almanac.* Washington, DC: Urban Institute.

YMCA. (2014). History: The YMCA in the United States. Retrieved from: http://www.ymca.net/history

Chapter 10
Grant Management

by Michael A. Sand

> **Synopsis:** Grant applicants should research the grantor before applying. They should not deviate from the format of the grant application except with express permission. There is a formula to follow for effective grant applications that, among other components, emphasizes the needs of the community rather than the needs of the applicant.

Introduction

Competition for government, corporate, and foundation grants is increasing. At the same time, funding from government sources for human services is shrinking, and the demand for human services is skyrocketing.

In response, charities are becoming more sophisticated in the ways they seek alternative sources of funding. Many are hiring development staff with specialized training and experience in obtaining grants. Others without the resources to make such a major investment are forced to do what they can. The purpose of this chapter is to provide a framework for the preparation of proposals for those without substantial grantsmanship experience.

It is often useful for grant seekers to develop the attitude that the relationship between them and the grantors is collaborative. True, all of the wonderful plans you have in mind will never come to fruition without the funds. However, the grantor needs the creativity, dedication, staff resources, and vision provided by the grant recipient. A grant proposal that is seen as simple begging is not as likely to be as successful as one that encourages the grantor to become a partner in an effort that will have substantial benefits to the community.

Before embarking on a costly and time-consuming search for grants, verify that the purpose of the grant is consistent with the organization's mission. Some organizations apply for grants simply because the money is available and obtainable, and they have a plan to win it. However, a successful grant application may result in the organization losing its focus if the grant is inconsistent with its direction.

Even if the grant's purpose is consistent with the mission, consider whether the project is viewed as constructive by an organization's stakeholders, such as members of the board, clients, and staff. It may be useful to convene a focus group to gauge whether the grant would truly be beneficial to the organization and its clients.

In addition, organizations should consider cash-flow issues, grant eligibility, the politics of the grant, and the source of the grant. The check from the funder may arrive months after the organization has committed itself to hiring staff and paying other project costs. Is a source of funds available until the grant funds are received? Are there laws or other grant requirements that must be adhered to that, for any reason, you are unable or unwilling to honor? Have the grants being applied for been promised informally in advance to other organizations? Does the grantor have a reputation for making unreasonable demands on the organizations it funds?

Researching the Grantor

Once you believe a funding source may have funds available, do not begin to write the grant application until you have tried to find out the answer to several questions. Try to obtain an interview with a representative of the funder before beginning to fill in the funding application. In any case, you should have the following information before beginning the proposal-writing stage:

1. The application format

Why write a 30-page application when a three-page application would have been funded? Why write a three-page application and not get funded when a 10-page proposal would have been accepted? Many government agencies will send you a *Request for Proposal* (RFP) that will outline exactly what should be included in the application. Many larger foundations will provide specific instructions.

If you are given written instructions by a funding source, do not deviate from these instructions without permission. One major reason grants do not get funded is that the writer does not follow the instructions to the letter. Even minor deviations can make the proposal ineligible. If you believe a particular instruction does not apply to your situation, request written permission from the funder to make changes.

2. Motivation of the funding source

Many funding sources specialize in awarding grants for specific purposes. An organization will not receive a grant from such a funder unless the proposal clearly is responsive to the vision and mission of the funding organization. When applying for a government grant, for example, obtain and study the legislative history that led to a funding appropriation. When applying for foundation funds, be sure to obtain the donor's funding instructions. Many corporate and family foundations have a priority listing of the types of programs they fund and will be glad to share this information.

3. The amount of funds awarded by the grantor per award, and the amount of total funds awarded

This will be extremely helpful information if you can obtain it. In many instances, a government agency has a specific allocation of funds for a particular program. Large foundations set specific priority areas and make general allocations in the priority area. Foundation directories provide information about the priority areas of grantors and are available in most public libraries. It is senseless to develop a grant application if the funds awarded by the source are too small for the organization's program needs.

4. Successful applications that were funded in previous funding cycles

Perhaps the best indicator of the types of funding applications that will be successful is a review of actual applications that have been funded. A strong argument can be made that government agencies have an obligation to provide you (as a taxpayer) with copies of funded applications. Although you may have to review the applications at the agency's headquarters or pay for duplication, you should be able to review past grants.

Many foundations will provide a list of the previous year's grants and the total of each. You can contact a funded organization and ask for a copy of its application. Although lists of past grants are often difficult to obtain from businesses, many annual reports and business newsletters include a list of grants that have been awarded as well as their sources.

5. The names of individuals making the funding decisions and their backgrounds

When writing a grant application, it is important to know who will be reviewing it. If the reviewers have extensive expertise in your field, you will not have to define every term. In many instances, however, a foundation trustee or a business official on the allocations committee will not have any knowledge of your particular field. You will then have to carefully explain your services in layman's terms, spell out every abbreviation, and define each technical term you use.

6. The criteria used in making the grant selection

Knowing the selection criteria can be crucial in determining how to write a grant. Many grantor agencies have limited amounts of funds and will give preference to smaller grants. Others will make the selection based on non-cost factors and then negotiate the cost of the proposal. Knowing whether it will be helpful or harmful to have political officials contact the grantor agency is important information.

Sections of a Grant Application

1. Cover Letter

Many grant applications specifically request a cover letter and define what information should be included. If this is not expressly prohibited by the grant application format, write a short cover letter on the organization's stationery that:

- Is addressed to the appropriate individual at the grantor agency, making sure the name, title, agency name, and address are absolutely correct

- Contains a one-sentence description of the proposal

- Provides the number of participants, jobs obtained, or other units to be funded by the grant

- Lists the total amount of funds requested

- Provides the name, address, and telephone number of the individual at the requesting organization the grantor can contact to request additional information.

2. Executive Summary

Include in this section a succinct summary of the entire proposal.

3. Introduction

Provide important information that may not otherwise appear anywhere else in the grant application. Items you might include are—

- Your organization's mission
- How long you have been providing the type of service included in this program
- A brief history of your organization
- Your capability of operating the kind of programs they fund efficiently and effectively
- If there are eligibility requirements in the proposal, a statement that you are eligible to receive the funds
- IRS Section 501(c) tax-exempt status determination letter
- Outline of letters of support from past clients, representatives of

cooperating agencies, and legislative officials (The letters themselves should be included as appendices to the application.)
- Statement of how you will obtain funding for the program at the end of the grant period.

4. Need

For a grant to be funded, the organization must demonstrate the need of individuals in the community for the service to be provided. What is the extent of the need and how is the need documented? The need described should be the need of the individuals in the community for the services, not the need of the organization. Rather than stating, "We need a counselor because our organization doesn't have one," or "The funds for the one we had were cut back by the government," estimate the number of individuals who need counseling services. The need should be the need in your coverage area. Although national or statewide figures might be given, if you serve a particular county, the estimate of need for that county should be provided.

The need should be the need for the particular service you are providing. If you provide services for victims of domestic violence, for example, the estimated number of victims of domestic violence should be provided, rather than unemployment figures or other available statistics. The need should be quantified. How many individuals do you believe are eligible for the particular service you provide in your coverage area?

Common sources of data are—

a. **Census Data**—Make certain you are using data from the most recent census. In most cases, earlier data are outdated.

b. **County Planning Departments**—Call the office of your county government to find the telephone number of your county's planning department.

c. **State Agencies**—The Departments of Education, Health, Labor, and Human Services, or their equivalents, are all excellent sources of data.

d. **Local Governments**—Local police departments are excellent sources of crime data, and local school districts can provide educational information.

e. **Self-generated Data**—In many cases, you can provide the data from sources within your organization. Sources might include—

- Waiting lists
- Letters from potential clients requesting a service
- Letters complaining that a particular service is not in existence
- Testimony at public hearings
- Information obtained from questionnaires administered to present clients asking them to list other services they might like
- Community surveys.

5. Objectives

Objectives are the proposed results of the project. Objectives should have the following characteristics:

- They are measurable. How many individuals do you estimate will participate in your program?

- They are time-based. How many individuals do you estimate will participate in your program in the next three months? In the next year?

- They are realistic.

The information needed to measure objectives can be obtained as part of the program funded by the grant. Do not list objectives in your proposal that are impossible to measure.

6. Project Description

Here is where you will outline your program. An easy way to remember what to include are the 6 W's of program writing:

- **Who?** Who are the clients? How are they selected? What are the restrictions (e.g., age, income, geographic)? Who are the staff members?

  If you are asking the funding source to pay for new staff members, include a job description and a qualifications statement that lists the education, experience, and other job requirements. If you are applying for funds to continue existing staff, include a résumé and a biographical statement for each staff member.

- **What?** What services will be provided? What will be the benefits of this program? What are the expected outcomes? For educational programs, include a course outline. You may include relevant sections of an operations manual. For other programs, a narrative outlining the services would be appropriate. Still others might provide a "day in the life of a client." What outreach efforts will be made?

- **Where?** Where will the services be provided? Give the addresses of all main and field offices. If you will be obtaining new space with the program funds, what type of space are you seeking?

- **When?** What are the hours that services will be provided? On which days during the year will services be provided? It is also useful to provide a timetable for project implementation.

- **With whom?** What other agencies are participating with you in the provision of services? For example, include agencies referring clients to you. Outline the agencies to which you refer clients. It is important to obtain letters from the other agencies confirming any relationships you describe.

- **Why?** Why are you providing these services rather than alternatives? Are you utilizing any unique approaches to the provision of services?

7. Budget

If it is not clear from the grant application forms, ask the funding source how much financial detail is required. Many businesses, for example, may only require the total amount you are going to spend. On the other hand, most government agencies require a line-item budget that includes a detailed estimate of all funds to be spent. Such a budget might be set up to include the following:

- Personnel costs (salaries, fringe benefits, consultant and contract services)

- Non-personnel costs (travel, office space, equipment, consumable supplies, and other costs such as telephone, postage, and indirect costs)

Some grantors may require your organization to contribute a matching share. If you are permitted to include in-kind or non-cash expenditures, use the same budget categories as above. In the personnel category, for example, you would list the worth of the time volunteers are contributing to your program. In the non-personnel category, you would include the market value of the equipment donated to your program.

8. Evaluation

Inform the funding source that you will be conducting an evaluation of the services you are providing.

- **Detail who will participate in the evaluation process.** Outline the participation of board members, staff members, clients, experts in the substantive field, and representatives of the community in the evaluation process. Some grantors require an independent evaluator.

- **Explain what will be evaluated.** List some of the issues the evaluation team will consider. For example, the evaluators will review whether the need was reduced as a result of providing the services. Were the objectives met? Were the services provided as outlined in the Project Description section? Will the budget be audited by an outside firm and, if not, who will review the receipts and expenditures?

- **Specify what type of evaluation will be provided.** Provide in as much detail as you can how the program will be evaluated. If formal classes are provided, include the pre- and post-test you will use to evaluate them.

If a client questionnaire will be used, attach a copy to the application. Describe how the program data will be reviewed in the evaluation process. Include a description of the audit or the process you will use to review the budget items.

9. Conclusion

In no more than two or three paragraphs, summarize the proposal's main points and the reasons the community will be improved as a result of successful completion of the project.

When you have finished writing your grant application, ask yourself the following questions before you send it to the funding source:

- Is the application free of the jargon of your field?
- Are all abbreviations spelled out the first time you use them?

- Have you followed all of the instructions in the Request for Proposal (RFP)?
- Are all words spelled correctly? Remember that your computer's spell-checker only tells you that the words you use are spelled correctly and in English, not that they are the correct words for the context.
- Is your application interesting to read?
- If you were the grantor agency, would you fund it?

Finally, get the application in the hands of the grantor well before the deadline. The fundraising field is replete with horror stories about multi-million dollar proposals that were not even considered because someone put the application in the mail and it did not arrive until well after the deadline.

If the application is mailed, make sure there is enough postage. It is highly recommended that applications be either hand-delivered or sent by a trackable, overnight courier, such as FedEx, UPS, or Airborne Express. Make several office copies before submitting the original, and be sure that you provide the number of copies requested by the grantor.

Discussion Questions

1. What are some of the shortcomings of grant applications for worthy new programs that result in funders rejecting them?

2. Some feel that nonprofit organizations are doing funders a favor by seeking their donations rather than the other way around. The justification is that the organization is providing its reputation, its expertise, its staff, and its resources to provide a service, and the funder is simply providing a check and "taking credit" for what is being accomplished by the organization being funded. Do you agree or disagree with this perspective? Why?

3. How much influence should a funder have over the general management of the funded organization, beyond the program being funded?

4. Is there too much pressure on nonprofit organizations to apply for grants based on the availability of the funding, rather than by sticking to the mission and purpose of the organization? Explain.

Activities

1. Download from the Internet ten foundation fundraising applications. What features do they have in common? Find a common grant application form that can be used to apply for grants from a range of funders that have agreed to accept this form.

2. Research the legal requirements that apply to foundations with respect to allocating a minimum amount of their assets each year. Then research a representative sample of foundation annual reports that are available online or otherwise, and determine how many allocate more funding than is required by law.

3. Research information about the largest private foundations in your area. Find out information such as their assets, number of staff, how many grants they fund annually, the amount awarded annually, the names and descriptions of the organizations funded, who serves on their board, and other information that you would consider useful in the event you decided to submit an application for funding.

Tips for Practitioners

1. Before applying for a grant, check to see if the grantor has a Web site, which will not only tell you something about that organization and contact information, but may also provide information about prior grants approved, what procedures are required to apply for funds, and, often, the application forms in downloadable format.

2. Double-check your proposal for spelling and grammar, that all pages are included in the proposal (i.e., the last page was not left in the copy machine as a result of making a copy of the submission for your files), that the correct number of copies is provided, and that all attachments are included.

3. Hand deliver your grant proposal, or use a trackable, reliable delivery service. Track the package to see if it has arrived prior to the deadline. This is not the time to save a few dollars by putting your proposal in the mail.

4. Even if your proposal is rejected, send a short thank-you letter to the funder for the opportunity to submit the proposal. Express a willingness to maintain a relationship with respect to future funding opportunities.

5. Be careful what you wish for; you might get it. Begin thinking about how to administer a grant even before you apply for it. You may decide that the stress of winning a particular grant might be too much for your organization.

Online Resources to Explore

Forum of Regional Associations of Grantmakers
    https://www.givingforum.org/

USA.Gov
> *http://www.usa.gov/Business/Nonprofit.shtml*

Grants.gov
> *http://www.grants.gov*

The Grantsmanship Center—Funding Resources
> *http://www.tgci.com/funding-sources*

Council on Foundations
> *http://www.cof.org*

The Foundation Center
> *http://foundationcenter.org/*

For Further Reading

Brown, L. G., & Brown, M. (2001). *Demystifying grant seeking: What you really need to do to get grants.* San Francisco: Jossey-Bass.

Browning, B. A. (2008). *Perfect phrases for writing grant proposals.* New York: McGraw Hill.

Browning, B. A. (2014). *Grant writing for dummies.* (5th Ed.). New York: Wiley & Sons.

Carlson, M. & O'Neal-McElrath, T. (2009). *Winning grants step by step* (3rd Ed.). San Francisco: Jossey-Bass.

Chelekis, G. C. (1993). *The action guide to government grants, loans and giveaways.* New York: Perigee Books.

Dermer, J. (1984). *How to write successful foundation presentations.* New York: Public Service Materials Center.

Geever, J. C. (2007). *The foundation center's guide to proposal writing.* (5th Ed.). New York: The Foundation Center.

Grobman, G. & Grant, G. (2006). *Fundraising online: Using the Internet to raise serious money for your nonprofit organization.* Harrisburg, PA: White Hat Communications.

Harris, D. (2008). *The complete guide to writing effective & award-winning grants: Step-by-step instructions with companion CD.* Ocala, Fl: Atlantic Publishing Company.

Karsh, E. & Fox, A. S. (2014). *The only grant-writing book you'll ever need: Top grant writers and grant givers share their secrets.* (4th Ed). New York: Basic Books.

Omnigraphics. (2013). *Government assistance almanac 2013: The guide to federal domestic financial and other programs.* Washington (22nd Ed.). DC: Author.

Schladweiler, K. (2004). *Foundation fundamentals: A guide for grantseekers.* (7th Ed). New York: Foundation Center.

Chapter 11
Financial Management

> **Synopsis:** All nonprofit corporations must keep certain financial records and create reports of their financial condition. There are three standards of financial verification used by accountants to verify financial data—audit, review, and compilation, with the audit being the highest level of scrutiny. *Line-item* and *program* budgets are the two major forms of budgeting utilized by nonprofit corporations. Nonprofit organizations must institute financial management systems to assure they will operate efficiently and effectively, and to minimize waste, fraud, and abuse.

The Importance of Financial Management to Nonprofits

Some of the most critically important duties of an organization's board and staff are to take steps to pay its obligations, invest its money, and plan for its financial future. Imagine the consequences that may occur if an otherwise "perfect," respected organization finds itself unable to meet its payroll because a large check anticipated from a funder failed to arrive in time before it could be deposited. An organizational culture that condones stealing—whether in the form of allowing office supplies to be requisitioned for personal use, using credit cards to make personal purchases, or even not penalizing the use of an organization's cell phones for personal texting—may experience a hemorrhage of organizational resources that could be fatal during tough economic times. Buyers who steer purchases to their relatives and friends rather than make dispassionate business decisions that are in the organization's best interest are subjecting the organization to a hidden "tax." Both board and staff leadership have a fiduciary duty to act in the best interests of the organization rather than in their own personal interest, and to manage the financial affairs of the organization prudently. To do otherwise is not only dangerous to the long term health of the organization, but is both unethical and illegal as well.

An organization's board and staff leadership are not the only sources of pressure to make its operations more "business-like," and assure that each dollar expended is necessary and used effectively to further the organization's mission. Government and private funders are increasingly demanding efficiency, cost effectiveness, and outcomes that demonstrate real, measurable progress toward achieving program goals. The press has perhaps become more vigilant about monitoring the voluntary sector since high profile scandals involving respected institutions such as American University, the United Way of New York City, the Association for Volunteer Administration, and the American Red Cross have made recent headlines. The Madoff financial scandal of 2008 resulted in the crippling or demise of hundreds of nonprofit organizations (Associated Press, 2009).

Nonprofit organizations are increasingly operating in a competitive environment not dissimilar to their for-profit counterparts. They compete for grants and donations, for board members, contracts, volunteers, media coverage, and qualified staff. Failure to manage the financial affairs of an organization can be catastrophic, resulting in bankruptcy, cutbacks of services, layoffs, involuntary merger/takeovers, and dissolution.

Where the transfer of money is involved, there are always ethics and accountability issues of which to be aware. As a result of high profile financial scandals in the nonprofit sector, the elimination of waste, fraud, and abuse in nonprofit organizations is not simply a public relations problem. In 2004, the Finance Committee of the U. S. Senate launched an initiative focusing on devising changes to laws that affect how the sector will develop, whether its historical tax exemptions will be secure, and what disclosure will be required to assure the highest level of ethics and accountability of these organizations that are ostensibly formed for the public good rather than any individual pecuniary interest. Obviously, the financial management practices of the sector are among the prominent areas under scrutiny.

As this is being written, there is a climate of increased demand for human services and fewer resources to pay for them from all levels of government (see Chapter 20). Competent financial management is the glue that can hold a nonprofit organization together during tough times.

How Nonprofit Financial Management Differs From the Private Sector

The private sector's general goal is to make a profit for the organization with the highest return on investment (ROI), and it uses financial management as a tool for that purpose. In contrast, a nonprofit organization uses financial management to make the optimal use of resources to achieve its mission(s) and accomplish its goals. Rather than trying to maximize profit, a nonprofit organization seeks to maximize the production and delivery of goods and services, consistent with demand, to those who for one reason or another, cannot receive those goods and services from either government or the marketplace. It may be that this is because they cannot afford the market cost of the services. Or it could be because the organization provides collective goods that the government either chooses not to provide, or chooses to subsidize nonprofit organizations that will. (See Chapter 3 for a discussion of why these organizations exist.) Nonprofit organizations also advocate for various causes, knowing that they will never generate any direct income from providing advocacy services.

Generally, nonprofit organizations experience more of a political process in virtually every aspect of financial management compared to a private sector organization.

Those involved in that political process are typically more diverse demographically and are not always on the same page with respect to the principal goal of the organization. In theory, the goal of for-profit organizations is to make as much profit as possible. A nonprofit organization may have many competing goals, some of which may be in conflict with each other. For example, a nursing home may want to increase its share of private-pay patients compared to those whose care is financed by Medicaid, but want to become the institution of choice for those who need care for Alzheimer's disease.

Because of the public benefits granted to nonprofit organizations, particularly those with 501(c)(3) tax-exempt status, the degree of accountability for funds is somewhat higher than for for-profit organizations. Because such organizations are entrusted with the care of people, many of whom are vulnerable and who have not voluntarily chosen that organization to receive services in the marketplace, there is an implicit acceptance by the public and government agencies that ethical standards are higher for such organizations than would apply to their for-profit counterparts (although many would argue that all organizations should have equally high ethical standards, regardless of their sector). Even with this being the case, there is no federal government regulatory authority over the financial management of nonprofit organizations comparable to that which the Securities and Exchange Commission (SEC) has over stock-issuing corporations. Such an agency might "impose uniform accounting standards on public charities, disseminate information on the financial conditions of organizations, and create channels through which donors, volunteers, clients, and community members could access and use this information" (Frumkin, 2002, p. 159).

Components of Financial Management

Among the activities encompassed by financial management, are a sequence of related activities, including planning, programming, budgeting, financing, controlling, and evaluating (McKinney, 2004).

Planning involves assessing the organization's current and likely future situation, surveying its strengths and weaknesses, setting out its goals and objectives, and developing a roadmap to achieve them. See Chapter 16 for an in-depth discussion of strategic planning. There are financial implications to changes in market conditions, new competitors, new laws and regulations, additional paperwork requirements (such as might be required by a new government or foundation funder), and an increase in the demand for services—both an increase in the number of clients and an increase in the level of services required by each client—resulting from changing social, economic, or political conditions.

Programming is the scheduling of the activities the organization needs to engage in to make its goals become a reality. In this phase, the organization creates distinct programs. A program is defined as "a collection of organizational resources that is geared to accomplish a certain major goal or set of goals" (McNamara, 2003). Prudent financial management requires that financial data be segregated by program, so that the performance of each program can be independently evaluated. This is particularly important to nonprofit organizations, as funders—and to an increasing degree, donors as well—want their grants and donations used for a particular purpose that may be only one small part of the overall operations of the organization.

The "program" is intended to achieve a particular outcome. Resources are sought from government, foundations, and the public to finance any net loss that the agency would incur by conducting that program, whether or not fees are charged to those who benefit directly from program services.

Budgeting is the process for allocating expenditures to each program. A budget is defined as an itemized summary of estimated or intended expenditures for a given period, often for a given fiscal year. A "fiscal year" is a one-year period at the end of which all accounts are reconciled, and for which the one-year budget applies. It does not necessarily coincide with a calendar year. For example, the federal government's fiscal year begins on October 1. Many states begin their fiscal year on July 1.

Typically, an organization's budget is not only a document to control the activities of subordinates, but it is also a political document. A budget, either directly or indirectly, indicates the priorities of the organization. Annual budget documents in all three sectors usually indicate what was spent during the previous fiscal year, what is being spent during the current year, and what is proposed to be spent for the next fiscal year. Stakeholders reading the budget get a sense of the direction the organization is heading with respect to each of its programs, whether it is growing or declining, from where it is planning to get its funds, and its general financial health. One gets a sense from the budget about whether the organization is more comfortable outsourcing or performing tasks with its own personnel. Those who prepare organizational budgets should look at it in its entirety and think about what message it is sending. For more details about budgeting, see pages 206-208.

Financing includes the activities necessary to obtain the resources needed in the budget. It may include borrowing from financial institutions to start new entrepreneurial ventures, or perhaps using endowment funds to serve as startup capital. It typically involves managing cash flow to assure that the organization has enough funds to pay its obligations, and policies relating to managing its cash and other assets. Fundraising, investment of surplus revenues, management of endowment funds, and use of funds generated by for-profit subsidiaries are among the activities that are included in the financing phase of the financial management cycle.

Controlling includes the development of a system that assures that the programs envisioned in the plans are being carried out appropriately. It also provides for feedback to warn when a program does not measure up to its expectations so that mid-course corrections can be implemented to get it back on track. Included in this phase of operations are policies to assure that the organization's assets—such as equipment and supplies, inventory of goods, and cash—are protected from inappropriate use or distribution. Most importantly, this includes systems that are designed to measure whether the implementation of programs is consistent with budget plans and projections, and to have procedures in place to expand, contract, or otherwise modify program operations when their performance differs from what was anticipated by the budget and planning documents. The basic accounting system; expense account policies; policies designed to minimize waste, fraud, and abuse; and the general Management Information System (MIS), if the organization has one, are among the systems that fall under this phase.

According to McLaughlin (2002), there are six elements of an internal control system.

1. *Control Cues.* This involves management and leadership sending signals, both overt and covert, of proper ethical behavior, and training staff in appropriate control policies that promote accountability.

2. *Policy Communication.* This entails having written policies and procedures for accountability and ethics related issues when you can, but in the absence of that, being able to communicate to employees what is acceptable and what is not by e-mail, fax, interoffice memo, or voice mail.

3. *Segregation of Duties.* This involves breaking up work duties so that one person does not have total dominance over a portion of the financial system. For example, it might make sense for the person ordering the good or service, filling out the purchase order, writing the check, signing the check, mailing the check, and receiving the ordered goods to be different people within the organization. This becomes a challenge for organizations with only a few employees, but even for a one-person office, a system of checks and balances needs to be developed.

4. *Record-keeping.* This relates to documentation and recording of all financial transactions. Among ways nonprofits try to minimize their vulnerability to internal fraud and abuse is by using a reliable payroll service, contracting out accounts receivable, and taking advantage of those financial institutions willing to do cash management for organizations. Of course, doing so increases the organization's vulnerability to external fraud and abuse.

5. *Budgets.* The budget is perhaps the best strategy to control behavior, since if there are no funds in the budget, it is difficult for spending to occur that has not been preauthorized and planned for.

6. *Reporting.* McLaughlin's view is that "you only need five financial reports to control the average nonprofit corporation" (p. 207): the balance sheet, revenue and expenses, aged accounts receivables, cash flow projection, and utilization reporting (which generally, refers to how many people are using the organization's services, and to what extent). By looking at these reports periodically, a manager ostensibly can see trouble spots.

Evaluation provides data on whether the programs are accomplishing what they set out to do. It involves validating the efforts of what is working and providing enough information to eliminate components of programs, or entire programs, when it is determined that they are not working. Many funders require the independent evaluation of the specific programs they fund as a condition of the grant. Since the popularity of the "reinventing government" movement and outcome-based management, nonprofit organizations are under increasing pressure to evaluate programs based on outcomes rather than the more easily measured outputs (see Chapter 16 for more on this topic). Regardless, systems to collect data that facilitate evaluation that are in place at the beginning before a program starts operating make evaluation easier than having to start from scratch after the program has been operating.

Generally, it is considered more efficient if all of the functions described in this financial management cycle are administered by one person. In smaller organizations, the executive director is responsible for all of the tasks involved that are described above. Larger organizations, however, will have one person (typically with the title of Chief Operating Officer or Chief Financial Officer) who will have these duties. In the case of the latter, as some high-profile criminal and civil cases have shown with respect to the for-profit sector, it is expected that there will be sufficient communication between the CEO and the CFO or equivalent. The CEO is ultimately responsible for the health of the organization, and simple ethics require that the CEO maintain a close watch over the financial affairs of the organization even if a subordinate staff member maintains day-to-day control over the financial operation of the organization.

Controls for Waste, Fraud, and Abuse

There are two general classifications of systems that are used to control waste, fraud, and abuse in nonprofit organizations. The first is to discourage these before they occur. The second is to assist in discovering them after they have occurred.

The traditional method of thwarting waste, fraud, and abuse *before* they occur consists of—

1. *The independent auditor's annual audit and the annual management letter.* The management letter is an opportunity by the auditor(s) to point out any

deficiencies seen in the operations of the organization that affect financial accountability and ethical concerns directly to the board. When you get a management letter that cites chapter and verse with respect to internal control problems, you need to deal with it (and quickly!). This requires a plan of corrective action that is approved by the board before implementation.

2. *Internal controls of the organization.* This consists of a system of checks and balances to assure that no one person (or perhaps even more than one) can control assets without appropriate accountability. This involves the requirement that expenditures be preauthorized by a responsible organization official in accordance with predetermined policies affecting disbursements. All expenditures are recorded by the accountant/bookkeeper, with appropriate documentation for the expenditure becoming part of the file. That financial officer has the responsibility to raise any questions about the expenditure. Oversight might include pre-audit checks of all purchase orders and vouchers, and review by someone other than the person requesting them before a payment is made, and separating those who order goods and services from the organization from those who receive the goods and services. It also might include spot checks of credit card transactions, long distance telephone bills, and cell phone accounts to assure that no personal expenses are charged to the organization.

3. *Policies requiring large orders of goods and services to be put out for bid.* This includes related policies that discourage purchasers from dividing up orders into small increments in order to undermine this policy. This does not necessarily mean that the organization must prepare a formal *Request for Proposal* (RFP) for every large purchase. But it should mean that quotes should be obtained from several qualified vendors and contractors for large purchases.

4. *Ethics policies that apply to organization resources are distributed to individuals.* These policies might apply to credit cards, copying machines, telephones, Internet accounts, cell phones, and organization vehicles, for example. Those authorized to make purchases need to have an arms-length relationship to the vender. These ethics policies would also include what is acceptable with respect to receiving gifts. For example, those who authorize company purchases would be prohibited from accepting gifts from suppliers other than *de minimus* gifts such as calendars. More substantial gifts, such as a box of cookies, would have to be shared with everyone in the organization. (The free vacation to Las Vegas as a thanks from the vendor to the organization's purchaser would have to be declined.) An ethics policy should also cover the issue of gifts made to staff members from those who receive services. All ethics policies should be reviewed at least annually and updated as appropriate.

5. *Training all employees on how to deal with the elimination of waste, fraud, and abuse.* The philosophy inherent in this method is that it is difficult to deal with a "bad" behavior when an individual might not have a clear sense as to what that might be in every case. The training should include procedures for staff to report suspected cases of fraud.

6. *Severe penalties for violating the organization's policies.* This involves written policies that require those found to have stolen from the organization be fired and referred to criminal authorities, or otherwise appropriately sanctioned by reprimand or suspension if the violation is in a gray area.

7. *Record keeping about all assets and taking a periodic inventory.* This is important so that when something is missing (such as a lap-top computer), an investigation can commence quickly.

8. *Electronic protection of records.* The purpose of maintaining backups is so that there remains an electronic trail, if not a paper trail, in the event of a fire or flood that destroys paper records.

Methods used to find occurrences *after* they have occurred include—

1. Determining when an employee has suddenly adopted a high lifestyle beyond his/her known income.

2. Investigating when it becomes suspected that purchasers are funneling purchases to personal friends or relatives, or receiving expensive gifts from suppliers.

3. Taking swift action when there appears to be missing documentation, "lost" organization checks, or an increased backlog in recording transactions.

4. Randomly reviewing credit card transactions and organization telephone bills for personal expenses charged to the organization's account.

5. Determining which expenses seem too high compared to what they have been historically, particularly when it is difficult to account for that with a reasonable explanation.

Basic Financial Statements

For a sample, actual document that summarizes the financial position of a nonprofit, the Association for Research on Nonprofit Organizations and Voluntary Action (ARNOVA) see Appendix 5. There are three basic financial statements that are prepared by the organization's accountant:

1. *Balance sheet (Statement of Financial Position).* The purpose of the balance sheet is to demonstrate the financial position of the organization at a certain point, typically the end of a fiscal year, by comparing its assets (what the organization owns) to liabilities (what the organization owes). Current assets consist of the monetary value of what is owned by the organization other than long-term assets, including the cash in the checking account and cash equivalents such as certificates of deposit; accounts receivable (minus the value of those receivables that are not likely to be collected, called "bad debts"); pledges receivable; grants receivable; the current value of its investments (stocks, bonds, and other marketable financial assets); inventories of goods; and prepaid expenses and other deferred charges (such as, for example, a fully-paid life insurance policy that covers more than one fiscal year). Fixed assets (including the value of land, buildings, and equipment owned by the organization that has a life of more than a year) are those that are not likely to be converted into cash at any time in the near future, such as stocks and bonds or real property owned by the organization.

   Liabilities are debts that the organization owes to those outside of the organization. Current short-term liabilities include accounts payable, grants payable (for those nonprofits that make such grants), taxes owed but not yet paid (such as sales taxes collected and UBIT—unrelated business income taxes— that apply even to those organizations that are tax-exempt), and current loans. Long term liabilities include long term loans, bonds, and mortgages. The report is called a balance sheet because assets and liabilities are brought into balance in the "bottom line" as a result of merging liabilities with the "net assets," also referred to as "fund balance"—the net value, the net worth, or the equity of the organization at that point in time.

2. *Income Statement.* Income statements consist of three parts, showing revenues, expenses, and the net difference between these two (positive if there is a profit, negative if there is a loss). That net difference can be distorted when an organization is on a cash basis of accounting, and there are either expenses or revenue paid out (or taken in, as the case may be), in a different accounting period. The accrual method of accounting overcomes this flaw (see page 203). Categories of income may include grants; donations; income from fees for services; income from for-profit subsidiaries; and sales of land, buildings, and equipment. Expense categories may include salaries, supplies, depreciation on buildings and equipment, administrative, general and fundraising expenses, and other expenses. The statement usually includes a line at the bottom comparing the net profit of the current year to the previous year, and the amount of this profit that has aggregated over time (called the "fund balance").

3. *Statement of Changes in Financial Position.* This statement typically includes the amount of cash from revenues; the amount of cash expenditures (and the difference between the two as net revenue or net loss); expenses from purchases of land, equipment, and income from the sale of these; and income from loans and bonds. The "bottom line" on this statement shows the net profit or loss and the cash balance, as well as how that cash balance compares to the previous year.

4. *Form 990—Return of Organization Exempt From Income Tax.* This annual information form has been required by the Internal Revenue Service since the 1940s. It applies to most federally tax-exempt organizations with gross revenues of $25,000 or more. Organizations with gross revenues of less than $100,000 and total assets of less than $250,000 may elect to file the short version of the form, 990-EZ. And smaller organizations are required to file a 990-N, which provides contact information, but does not disclose any financial data.

The filing deadline is four and a half months following the organization's fiscal year. Organizations are required by law to provide a copy of their Form 990 to anyone who requests it, although organizations that make their returns "widely available," such as by posting their 990s online, are exempt from this requirement. The organization may charge a reasonable copying fee (none if the requester provides his or her own copying equipment on site) and actual postage costs. Form 990, last revised in 2009, requires detailed disclosure relating to Revenue, Expenses, Changes in Net Assets or Fund Balances (Part 1); Statement of Functional Expenses (Part 2); Statement of Program Service Accomplishments (Part 3); Balance Sheets (Part 4); a list of officers, directors, trustees and key employees that includes salary information (Part 5); and "Other" information that includes information about lobbying, fundraising, unrelated business income, in-kind donations, among other issues (Part 6). The fine for not filing this return is $20 per day, not to exceed the lesser of $10,000 or 5% of the gross receipts of the organization for the year. For large organizations (those with annual gross receipts exceeding $1 million), the penalty is $100 per day up to $50,000.

Small organizations (those with revenue under $25,000 annually) must file a 990-N e-postcard at least once every three years, or they will automatically lose their federal tax exemptions, a requirement of a 2006 federal law.

Fund Accounting

Separate accounting records are maintained for each fund of a nonprofit organization. The nonprofit establishes each of these funds to meet a specified purpose. A small-sized nonprofit may only have a single fund, called the general fund, operating fund, or unrestricted fund. Larger nonprofits may have several funds in addition to this general fund. Among the most common are—

Endowment Fund. A permanent endowment fund assumes that the financial principal remains unspent, but that the interest earned on this fund may be spent for either any purpose or a restricted, specified purpose.

Fixed Asset Fund. This fund includes the fixed assets of the organization and liabilities associated with the physical plant (both purchase and maintenance). Pledges to construct new facilities are included in this fund.

Restricted Funds. It is not unusual for donors to specify how their donations must be used. If the board does not have the power to use donations for any purpose it chooses, the donations are placed in a restricted fund and reported in a separate accounting statement of Income, Expenses, and Changes in Net Assets. Some nonprofits have funds established for each major donor.

Accounting rules tend to get somewhat complex and legalistic. Some donations have conditions attached before they can be counted on by the charity. Two examples of these are bequests and matching pledges. Rather than being included as assets in fund accounting, these donations are often disclosed as footnotes in the financial reports.

Cash-Flow Analysis

Nonprofit organizations, as with other organizations, benefit from performing a cash flow analysis. The analysis is designed to answer the questions of how much cash the organization needs to pay its obligations at each point in time, and when and from where is it coming at each such point in time. This analysis is necessary because revenue, such as that coming from grants, is not always received before expenses need to be paid. A year-long grant may be paid in monthly installments. For organizations that write paychecks every two weeks, there are three payrolls rather than two every third month.

Utility bills (such as for heating in the winter and cooling in the summer), may be seasonal. The organization's annual fundraiser may create a spike in donations in May, a month or so before the end of the fiscal year. In short, a budget may balance appropriately based on a year of revenue and expenses. If the expenses are incurred mostly before the income is received, the organization may find itself unable to pay its obligations. A cash-flow analysis will look at how revenues and expenses project each month, and determines whether there is a problem with having enough cash in the bank to write checks for obligations when they need to be written. When there is a problem identified, there are often strategies for dealing with it. Some payments can be made in installments. Purchases can be put on a credit card until enough cash comes in. Accounts payable could be delayed a month or so in order to catch up or the organization could seek a loan.

What is the FASB?

The Financial Accounting Standards Board is a private-sector organization founded in 1973 with the mission "to establish and improve standards of financial accounting and reporting for the guidance and education of the public, including issuers, auditors and users of financial information" (FASB, 2005). Its accounting standards are promulgated with an open, participatory process, and are recognized by government agencies with statutory authority to enforce organizational accountability, including the Securities and Exchange Commission, and professional associations such as the *American Institute of Certified Public Accountants.* Indeed, although the board is independent of all government and professional associations, the FASB Board consists of fifteen representatives from eight membership associations with an interest in financial reporting.

There are two important standards issued by the FASB that apply to nonprofit organizations.

FASB Statement 116 and Statement 117 were issued in June 1993, and apply to all charities with at least $5 million in assets and $1 million in annual expenses and generally is required to be adopted for financial statements for fiscal years beginning after December 15, 1995. Statement 116 sets standards with respect to accounting for contributions made and received. Among changes in policy made by this statement is that donor pledges that are unconditional are counted as assets even though no actual payment on the pledges has been received (Shim and Siegel, 1997). For a summary, see: *http://www.fasb.org/st/summary/stsum116.shtml*

FASB Statement117 establishes standards for financial statements of nonprofit organizations. It requires, among other standards, that nonprofit organizations provide a statement of financial position, a statement of activities, and a cash-flow statement. Organizations must report total assets, liabilities, and net assets in a statement of financial position; report the change in an organization's net assets in a statement of activities; and report the change in cash and cash equivalents in a statement of cash flows. The main theme of SFAS 117 is to take into account the presence or absence of donor restrictions, and group an organization's funds into three categories: permanently restricted, temporarily restricted, and unrestricted, applicable only to the organization's net assets (McLaughlin, 2002). For a summary, see: *http://www.fasb.org/st/summary/stsum117.shtml*

Sarbanes-Oxley

The *American Competitiveness and Corporate Accountability Act,* commonly known as the Sarbanes-Oxley Act, was enacted by the Congress in 2002 as a response to corporate financial scandals, such as those at Enron, Arthur Anderson, and Global Crossing (Silk, 2004). Generally, this act does not apply to nonprofit corporations, although two provisions—those relating to protecting whistle-blowers and the destruction of litigation-related documents—do apply to both for-profit and nonprofit corporations (Board Source & Independent Sector, 2003). See pages 353-354 for more on efforts by the Congress and state legislatures to apply more provisions of this law to nonprofit organizations.

Bookkeeping

Both state and federal law require corporations to record all expenses and income in an organized format. This can be done manually or by using one of many popular computer programs.

Several basic decisions must be made with respect to record-keeping. First, the corporation must decide on the period of its fiscal year. Federal law requires the Form 990 nonprofit tax return to be filed within four-and-a-half months after the end of the fiscal year (technically, by the 15th day of the fifth month after the end of the fiscal year), that alone can determine when to begin the fiscal year. Other factors to consider are the fiscal years or the announcement dates of grants of major funding sources, using a calendar year for simplicity, or beginning the fiscal year as soon as the first corporate income has been received.

A second issue is in deciding whether the bookkeeping system will be on a "cash" or "accrual" basis. Cash basis financial reporting recognizes a transaction the date income was actually received and deposited and when expenditures were made. The "accrual" method recognizes a transaction when it is made, i.e., when supplies are ordered, not when they are received. The "accrual" method factors in "accounts payable" (when the organization owes someone money, but has not actually sent them a payment) and "accounts receivable" (when there is a legal obligation to pay the organization something in the future, but the organization has not yet received payment). Most novices find the cash basis easier and simpler. The accrual method, on the other hand, gives a more realistic picture of the actual financial situation of the organization, and thus complies with generally accepted accounting principles.

The "cash" vs. "accrual" decision should be discussed with the organization's accountant, or whoever is likely to prepare the tax returns and annual financial report. This is the time when the foresight of placing a certified public accountant or two on the board of directors can pay dividends.

Some funding agencies may have their own unique financial reporting requirements to qualify for grants.

Levels of Financial Verification

There are three levels of financial verification. In descending levels of scope and scrutiny, they are audits, reviews, and compilations. The level of financial verification required is often determined by the nature and source of funding for the organization. Many government grants explicitly require a minimum level of financial verification in their contracts. Such a contract may be a "pass-through" of funds from another source, and the original source may need to be tracked down to determine whether it has its own requirements. For example, a nonprofit organization may receive a grant from a United Way, but the funding is provided by a state government. As a result, the United Way may require financial reports from the nonprofit organization that will permit it to comply with its own reporting requirements to that state government grantor.

It is wise to request all financial reporting information, in writing, from any contracting agency that provides the organization with grant funds.

All of the three financial verification levels require that all organizational funds be segregated by the appropriate organizational accounts (and, of course, from the accounts of other organizations) and all transactions be accounted for. It is never good organizational policy to sign over an incoming check payment to a third party. Instead, deposit the check into the organization's account and then write a new check to the third party. Although ignoring this advice may save the time of making a deposit and writing a check, it will result in a loss of "paper trail" necessary to determine who paid what to whom, when, and for what.

In the absence of an overriding requirement in a contract, federal, state, and local governments require an audit report when the funds in the contract are $100,000 or more in any single year. State and local governments generally require a review if funding is between $25,000 and $100,000 annually. If funding is less than $25,000, a compilation report is usually acceptable.

Audit Report

The highest level of financial verification, an audit, is a complete arm's-length verification of the accuracy and reliability of account statements and financial reports. Records are systematically examined and checked to determine how they adhere to generally accepted accounting principles, management policies, and other stated policies. The purpose of independent audits is to eliminate bias, self-interest, fraud, and unintentional errors. What does the auditor do?

The auditor will request information from individuals and institutions to confirm bank balances, contribution amounts, conditions and restrictions, contractual obligations, and monies owed to and by your organization. The auditor will review physical assets, journals and ledgers, and board minutes to ensure that all activity with significant financial implications is adequately disclosed in the financial statements. In addition, the auditor will select a sample of financial transactions to determine whether there is proper documentation and whether the transaction was posted correctly into the books. In addition, the auditor will interview key personnel and read the procedures manual, if one exists, to determine whether or not the organization's internal accounting control system is adequate. The auditor usually spends several days at the organization's office looking over records and checking for completeness (National Council of Nonprofits, 2014).

Although an auditor can never obtain *absolute* proof of the representations made in a financial statement, the standard used is that of a "reasonable man" (or woman) who has "adequate technical training and proficiency as an auditor," according to the American Institute of Certified Public Accountants. Auditors have a professional code of ethics to ensure their independence from the management of the nonprofit organization they are auditing. Although they are paid a fee by the corporation, they are considered to be responsible to the public rather than to their corporate clients.

Many government agencies have audit requirements for recipients of their grants, as do many foundations and other umbrella fundraising organizations, such as United Ways and Jewish federations. Audits are often required by major umbrella fundraising organizations unless the revenues are relatively small.

Review

A second standard of financial verification, called a "review," is the application of analytical procedures by the accountant to the financial data supplied by the corporation. It is substantially narrower in scope than an audit. Much of the information supplied by the corporation is accepted at face value, although there may be a spot check to see if there are any glaring errors or inconsistencies between expenses recorded and the checks that are written. The examination of internal control and the proper allocation of income and expenses is similar to that of an audit report. Unlike an audit, the review will not include a formal auditor's "opinion" as to the compliance with generally accepted accounting principles.

Compilation

The third level of financial reporting/verification, a "compilation," calls only for the proper classification of assets, liabilities, fund balances, income, and expenses, from information supplied by management. Third-party verification of assets and liabilities is not required, although internal supporting documents may be used in their place. "Spot checks" are employed only when the accountant is aware of inconsistencies in other areas of the examination. As in a review, the accountant will not render an "opinion" on the accuracy of the report.

In the absence of legal requirements, it is good policy for nonprofits that expend more than a few thousand dollars to have at least a review. Many nonprofits have certified public accountants on their boards who may be willing to arrange for a review of the corporation on a *pro bono* basis.

Budgeting

Some nonprofits can exist for years using volunteer labor, donations of stamps, in-kind printing and other services, and have no need to raise money or make any expenditures. Others are more likely to have some staff and pay office rent or, if not, still have expenditures for workshops, postage, printing, telephone, and other typical corporate expenses.

The annual budget document is the blueprint for both spending and income. A poorly conceived budget can lead to the corporation's demise. On the other hand, a well-conceived, realistic budget can be the catalyst for program planning that provides a corporate life for many fruitful years.

Line-item and program budgets are the two major types of budgeting used by nonprofit corporations. Each has its advantages and disadvantages.

Line-Item Budget

The line-item budget is as it says—a list of various categories and the amount the corporation expects to spend for each category. Corporations, from the largest to the smallest, have some of the same categories in a line-item budget. Among the most common are:

- salaries
- consulting services
- professional services
- taxes
- fringe benefits
- telephone/wireless
- postage
- printing and photocopying
- travel
- workshops and conferences
- bank fees

- dues
- subscriptions and publications
- data processing
- equipment
- equipment maintenance and repair
- legal services
- insurance
- rent
- office supplies
- maintenance and repairs
- security services
- utilities
- bookkeeping and payroll services
- Web hosting services
- advertising
- miscellaneous

As an expense is incurred, its amount is entered in a journal prepared for this purpose, coded by its expense category. At the end of each month, the amounts of each category are aggregated on a ledger sheet called a "monthly summary." The monthly totals should be compared with the budget for each category to determine whether spending patterns are consistent with the budget. For example, an organization can have "annual conference" as a program, and include all expenses associated with it included, such as printing, postage, advertising, travel, consulting, and so on. Or as an alternative, the individual expenses of the conference for printing and postage could be included in the organization's regular printing and postage line-items.

The advantage of a line-item budget is the ease of assigning every expenditure. A dollar spent on paper clips is an expense for "supplies," and a dollar spent on Web hosting is an expense for "Web hosting." The disadvantage is that it is not always clear how much can be saved by eliminating any particular program of an organization, because the expenses of that program are subsumed within many different line-items, such as would be the case with the example of an annual conference.

Program Budget

The second type of budget is called a program budget. The program budget also contains various line-items, but the difference is that each program of a nonprofit, such as conferences, newsletter, membership, or publications, has its own budget within it.

For example, if the organization is having a conference, then the conference itself has a budget. Printing, postage, and telephone costs are attributed to the conference. Printing and postage costs may be associated with another program as well, such as a newsletter.

The advantage of the program budget is that one can quickly determine the incremental savings that will accrue to the organization if a particular program is eliminated. The disadvantage is that it is not easy to allocate overhead costs—such as the CEO's salary and rent—to various programs.

It is not unusual for nonprofits to combine the two types of budgeting—to have a general line-item budget, but to allocate some spending in all categories to certain programs. For small nonprofits, line-item budgets are the easiest to prepare and follow, but program budgets provide better information.

The Budget Process

Each organization is likely to develop its own budgeting process, which evolves over time based on the personalities of its staff and board, the stability of its funding streams, the needs of outside stakeholders, and other factors. The following is one possible model.

Step 1. Begin the budgeting process at least three months before the start of the organization's fiscal year, allowing enough time for the board to approve the final budget after having the opportunity to provide feedback.

Step 2. Review all programs and management achievements. Compile a comparison of estimated costs to actual costs, which is called a "variance."

Step 3. Make estimates of expenses for commitments made for the upcoming year (in salaries, new programs, capital expenses) that did not require funding for the current year, such as new programs and the expansion of existing programs approved in the organization's strategic plan.

Step 4. Make estimates of expenditure increases resulting from predictable budget items, such as salary inflation adjustments and merit increases, rent, utilities, insurance, and other categories that grow as a result of inflation rather than expansion of services or programs.

Step 5. Make estimates of income—including estimated contributions, grants, fees, the sale of goods and services, and investment income.

Step 6. Adjust spending and income based on the organization's ability to build surpluses or incur deficits, but avoid making adjustments in income based on the need to balance a budget. The reason is that spending is more likely to be controllable compared to income.

Step 7. Submit the budget to the board for approval.

Step 8. Periodically adjust the organization's budget and resubmit changes to the board as new information is received.

Expense Reimbursement

Organizations incur expenses. Many of these can be paid conveniently by corporate check. Many others can be paid by corporate credit card, which is particularly useful for travel expenses. For reasons of good financial management, it is not atypical for newly formed organizations to require two signatures on checks. This is not unreasonable for recurring expenses that can be processed well in advance, such as paychecks, rent, major equipment purchases, and taxes.

Requiring two signatures does present problems when making small, but reasonable, on-the-spot purchases. An expense reimbursement system should be designed to provide protection against one person making unilateral, capricious decisions on spending, but needs to be flexible enough to keep the organization from being hamstrung when trying to pay $25 for office supplies.

One suggestion is to set up an "imprest account" to pay routine office expenses, requiring only one signature. The authorized person (such as the executive director) has a reasonable sum to disburse from this checking account, which is entirely separate from the "master" checking account. The imprest account is replenished from the master checking account using a check that requires the usual two signatures, only upon a review by the chairperson or treasurer (or both) of what was expended—including supporting documentation, such as receipts. This account should provide an amount needed not only to pay reasonable expenses for the month, but enough to cover expenses for part of the following month, since several days or weeks may elapse during the processing of the expense report.

The organization's leadership should provide general guidelines as to what types of expenses are acceptable for reimbursement and what expenses should be absorbed by the staff. For example, hotel accommodations in any city can range from $60-$300. A dinner can be purchased for $5 or $75. Many organizations refuse to make decisions concerning what is appropriate, and instead provide a per diem allowance—a flat payment that is expected to pay reasonable travel expenses for each one-day period. The staff member then must absorb costs that go beyond this amount.

Many other expense issues arise that require board policies. How much should staff be reimbursed for mileage? What if a spouse attends a conference with a staff member and shares a room, resulting in an incremental cost increase? How will expenses be reimbursed that cannot be directly documented with a receipt, such as tips or parking meter expenses?

All of these issues can be resolved on an ad hoc basis, but it is useful to think about the nature of expense reimbursement before it creates problems. Many organizations have failed because their budgets were depleted by discretionary spending in the absence of an expense policy.

Investment Policy

According to the National Center for Charitable Statistics, the nonprofit sector earns 2.8% of its revenues from investments, providing a small, yet significant supplement to revenues from service fees and donations (Urban Institute, 2012). There are thousands of organizations that live hand-to-mouth, struggling day-to-day with making ends meet, and allocating virtually all of their meager resources to keeping the organization afloat. They may only have a checking account, often not bearing any interest. They can only dream of a day, which may never come, when the organization can move beyond that to have a steady source of income from investments with a diverse portfolio of stocks and bonds. At the other end of the spectrum is Harvard University, which, through the Harvard Management Corporation, manages an endowment valued at $32.7 billion as of June 2014, and other investments (Alden, 2014).

Most nonprofits fall somewhere between these two extremes. They may have a nest egg of modest revenue surpluses, which are certainly appropriate to have for times when costs exceed revenues. Putting surplus revenue into a certificate of deposit is safe, but over the long term, other strategies have shown to provide a much better return. Many nonprofits receive gifts of assets in the form of bonds, equities, royalties from intellectual property, real estate, valuable goods that can appreciate in value, and other investment instruments. It takes work to manage them. Lots of issues arise in how these assets are managed.

It simply makes sense for organizations to have a formal investment policy that spells out the board's policy with respect to the following:

1. Goals and Objectives—What rate of return are we expecting to achieve from investments?
2. Payout—How will we be using the return from investment for the operating budget of the organization?

3. Diversification—What is our philosophy with respect to "asset allocation," the extent to which we do not put all of our investment eggs in one basket?
4. Management—Who will be responsible for investment management, for reporting and updating the status of investments, and for overseeing/evaluating the results achieved?
5. Risk—How much risk are we willing to accept to meet the goals and objectives we have in #1?
6. Ethics and Values—Are there certain investments we will consider prohibited because they are not consistent with our organization's values?

For a comprehensive sample organization investment policy, see: *http://www.mtnonprofit.org/uploadedFiles/Files/Org-Dev/Principles_and_Practices/MNA_Sample_Docs/Sample-Investment-Policy-2.pdf*

Discussion Questions

1. If a nonprofit organization has only one employee, what controls might be instituted to minimize waste, fraud, and abuse?

2. What dollar amount of abuse should trigger sanctions against an employee with respect to discovering that such an employee has made personal calls using the organization's telephone account, or making copies on the office copier?

3. What control should the board have over the ability of nonprofit executives to spend funds to accomplish organizational objectives? Should nonprofit executives have flexibility to adjust their budgets in response to new conditions without obtaining board approval?

4. Why should nonprofit organizations consider adopting any of the provisions of Sarbanes-Oxley that are not mandatory?

5. Imagine you are the CFO of the ALS Association in the summer of 2014. What adjustments in financial management might you have considered when you realized that your organization was likely to receive more than $100 million in unanticipated contributions in a single month as a result of the "ice bucket challenge"? How might these adjustments have differed had the $100 million come in the form of a one-time contribution from a wealthy donor?

Activities

1. Construct a line-item budget for a new nonprofit organization that expects revenues of $250,000 each year, whose mission is to promote ethical conduct within the nonprofit sector.

2. Research actual cases of fraud involving nonprofit organizations and draft policies that might have either prevented the scandals or uncovered them sooner.

3. Read the full text of Sarbanes-Oxley, and write up a report on which provisions that are not mandatory for nonprofit organizations could apply equally to them, and whether doing so makes any sense from a public policy perspective.

Tips for Practitioners

1. Before choosing either a cash or accrual basis of accounting, verify that your organization is not required to adopt the accrual method because of government or funder requirements.

2. If you are not the individual performing the accounting, yet are legally responsible for their accuracy, periodically examine the organization's books to see if there are any inconsistencies, or whether they are being kept sloppily.

3. Have clear, written policies that inform staff about how they need to avoid diverting organizational resources for personal use and the penalties for doing so.

4. Keep duplicate paper and electronic copies of important financial records, and store them at an alternative physical site.

Online Resources to Explore

Business Owner's Toolkit: Small Business Guide
    http://www.toolkit.com/

Guidestar—Nonprofit Reports
    http://www2.guidestar.org/RequestForProfileInstructions.aspx

Carter McNamara's Basic Guide to Non-Profit Financial Management
    http://www.managementhelp.org/finance/np_fnce/np_fnce.htm

Nonprofit Good Practice Guide
    http://www.npgoodpractice.org/

Idealist.org's Nonprofit FAQ—General Management
    http://www.idealist.org/if/i/en/faqcat/27-94

Board Source/Independent Sector: The Sarbanes-Oxley Act and Implications for Nonprofit Organizations
http://www.independentsector.org/sarbanes_oxley

References and Further Reading

Alden, W. (2014). Endowment chief to exit at Harvard. Retrieved from *http://dealbook.nytimes.com/2014/06/10/harvard-endowment-chief-to-step-down/?_php=true&_type=blogs&_r=0*

Associated Press. (2009). *Madoff's scandal still plaguing charities like American Jewish Congress a full year later.* December 11, 2009. Retrieved from *http://www.nydailynews.com/money/2009/12/11/2009-12-11_madoffs_scandal_still_plaguing_charities_a_year_later.html*

Board Source & Independent Sector. (2003). *The Sarbanes-Oxley and implications for nonprofit organizations.* Author. Retrieved from *http://www.independentsector.org/sarbanes_oxley*

Coe, C. (2011). Nonprofit financial management: A practical guide. New York: Wiley.

Dropkin, M., Halpin, J. & La Tiouche, B. (2007). The budget-building book for nonprofits: A step-by-step guide for managers and board. San Francisco, CA: Jossey-Bass.

FASB. (2005). Facts about FASB. Retrieved from *http://www.fasb.org/facts/index.shtml*

Frumkin, P. (2002). *On being nonprofit: A primer.* Cambridge, MA: Harvard University Press.

McKinney, J. (2004). *Effective financial management in public and nonprofit agencies* (3rd Ed.). Westport, CT: Praeger Publishing.

McLaughlin, T. (2002). *Streetsmart financial basics for nonprofit managers.* New York: Wiley and Sons.

McNamara, C. (1999). *Program planning and management.* Retrieved from *http://www.managementhelp.org/prog_mng/prog_mng.htm#anchor1676854*

National Council of Nonprofits. (2014) *Audit guide for charitable nonprofits.* Retrieved from *http://www.councilofnonprofits.org/nonprofit-audit-guide*

Shim, J. & Siegel, J. (1997). *Financial management for nonprofits: The complete guide to maximizing resources and managing assets.* New York: McGraw-Hill.

Silk, T. (2004). Ten emerging principles of governance of nonprofit corporations. *The Exempt Organization Tax Review.* 43(1), pp. 35-39, January 2004.

Urban Institute. (2012). The nonprofit sector in brief: Public charities, giving and volunteering, 2012. Retrieved from *http://www.urban.org/publications/412674.html*

Chapter 12
Personnel

> **Synopsis:** Nonprofits have options for staffing their agencies. A planning process is necessary when hiring and firing employees, and there are legal requirements for doing so. There is a continuum for disciplining employees short of termination. Volunteers are a crucial strength for nonprofits. They can be highly motivated and can save organizational resources. There are significant disadvantages, as well. Managing volunteers requires many of the same responsibilities as managing paid staff.

Introduction

Few can argue with the view that a nonprofit's human capital is its most important resource.

The executive director influences the direction, morale, image, and financial stability of an organization. Yet, even the least senior employee can have a significant impact, negative or positive, on the organization. Employees can be creative, nurturing, versatile, ingenious, inspiring, and team-building. Or they can be disruptive and destructive—infecting morale, and creating scandal that can ruin the reputation of a charity that took decades to foster.

The scandal involving the United Way of America's CEO, William Aramony— convicted in 1995 on 25 counts of engaging in fraudulent practices and generally living lavishly at the organization's expense— is just one example of how a single individual can stain an entire sector. The shock waves from the New Era Philanthropy scandal are continuing to be felt. The forced resignation of the American Red Cross's chief executive in 2001, blamed in part on an alleged policy of deceptive fundraising, made front page news.

As our society becomes more litigious, poor performance by an employee can have disastrous consequences. Many human services nonprofits that work closely with aging populations, children, and people with disabilities have had experience defending the actions of their employees in court, and they are at risk for damage suits that run in the millions of dollars. In some cases, poor staff performance may be a matter of life and death for at-risk clients. The responsibility for choosing staff in a nonprofit should not be taken lightly.

Each hired employee is an investment by a nonprofit not only in the salary paid to him or her. The chemistry of an organization is changed by a new hire, and bad hiring decisions can haunt an organization for many years or destroy it completely.

In recent years, nonprofits have lost the image of having certain characteristics, compared with their for-profit counterparts. That image often viewed nonprofits as—

- less hierarchically structured
- less willing or able to fire non-productive employees
- more informally managed
- paying less and providing fewer benefits for longer hours
- more altruistically managed, with less emphasis on the bottom line
- more interested in their employees' personal satisfaction

Evidence shows that this stereotype is no longer valid, or that it is at least becoming frayed at the edges. Nonprofits today face the same competitive and financial pressures to succeed as their for-profit counterparts. Nonprofits are becoming more comfortable hiring MBAs and those with for-profit business experience to manage their enterprises, whereas once social science degrees were the educational pedigree of choice.

Hiring Employees

Many of the jobs available in the nonprofit sector are equally available in the for-profit sector. For example, both often require a CEO, accountants, legal staff, supervisors, receptionists, Webmasters, human resources specialists, social media managers, government relations personnel, public relations officers, administrative assistants, and secretaries. In many of these jobs, the actual tasks performed by nonprofit employees are quite similar to those performed by for-profit employees.

Regardless, it is important to recognize that those who apply for jobs offered by nonprofits may retain the stereotypical image. It is useful to consider whether a prospective employee may have an unreasonable expectation of working for a nonprofit organization. This can be assessed during the job interview.

Hiring requires a positive attitude, which is often missing on the part of the hirer. First, if the hiring is being done to replace an employee who was fired or resigned, the hirer often is distracted by the disruption caused by the separation. The hirer often is in a position of having to perform a task that is not pleasant—putting aside current responsibilities to conduct the job search and interview. Few, if any, managers enjoy this process.

Before embarking on hiring a new employee, it is useful to do some planning that addresses some considerations:

- What are the tasks and duties the new employee will perform?
- Are these tasks absolutely necessary?

- Could someone already in the organization perform these tasks? Do these tasks require special education, professional credentials, and/or experience that are currently lacking in the staff?
- Can we obtain these services through means other than hiring an employee?
- How long will it take to hire a new employee, and will these duties still be required after that time?
- How will these tasks change over time?
- What can we expect in productivity of this new hire?
- Which support services will this person require? For example, will we also have to hire a secretary or administrative assistant?

Options—Advantages, Disadvantages, Legal Considerations

Organizations must choose among various staffing options, and each has its advantages and disadvantages. Among these options are—

Hired Staff—The Sunday paper classifieds and online job boards are usually filled with hundreds of job listings from nonprofit organizations that have decided to hire full-time staff.

>**Advantages**: Employees have the most stake in the organization; they tend to be loyal, may work additional hours, and can be flexible in doing tasks not in the job description when necessary.

>**Disadvantages**: Employees must be paid even when work is not needed, require payroll taxes and expensive benefits, and are paid for vacations and when sick—possibly disrupting work flow.

Paid Contractors—private for-profit companies and individuals market their services to nonprofits to perform tasks that are intended to obviate the need for hiring full-time workers.

>**Advantages:** The nonprofit does not have to withhold employee income, Social Security, Medicare, state and local taxes, or pay unemployment and Social Security taxes. Contractors can be hired for short-term or long-term projects and can be terminated easily, do not require year-round benefits (although the equivalent is often built into the contract price), and do not obligate payment by the nonprofit unless the job is completed successfully. The contractor may have skills and resources that the nonprofit would not otherwise be able to afford, except on a temporary basis.

Disadvantages: Hiring a paid contractor may be legal only under certain limited circumstances. The Internal Revenue Service Publication 15-A *(Employer's Supplemental Tax Guide)* provides details on the 20 factors that indicate whether an individual is considered an employee or an independent contractor. This publication is available for download from the IRS *(http://www.irs.gov/pub/irs-pdf/p15a.pdf)*. Independent contractors sometimes charge steeply in that they must cover overhead and marketing, as well as make a profit.

Volunteers—Unsalaried workers, some of whom may be there not solely because they are altruistic and want to help, but because they may be fulfilling educational requirements or disciplinary requirements ordered by a court.

Advantages: They do not require a salary, and they are there not for a paycheck but, with some exceptions, because they want to be.

Disadvantages: They do not have the paycheck as motivation, generally work fewer hours than employees, and may leave the organization on short notice.

Temporary Hires— hiring people for short-term employment without a promise that the employment will continue beyond a certain date.

Advantages: They permit the organization to respond to short-term or seasonal fluctuations in workload.

Disadvantages: The recruitment and administrative burden of temp workers can be substantial.

Outsourcing to another organization—either contracting with an employment service for temporary workers, or contracting with an outside organization to perform the functions. One example is a payroll and accounting service, which could perform services otherwise done by a staff bookkeeper.

Advantages—The organization can avoid the expense and administrative burden of hiring employees.

Disadvantages—Outsourcing is often more expensive on an hourly basis than would be the case if a person were hired temporarily.

Process in Hiring

Search Process. Many nonprofits, through their personnel committees, develop a procedure for hiring new employees. Search committees are often authorized by the board to develop job descriptions, prepare job notices, cull through résumés to identify several candidates to interview, and recommend a candidate to the board. Others delegate the process entirely to the executive director—unless, of course, the search is for an executive director. In either case, the basic steps remain the same:

1. **Prepare a job description.** The job description is a useful planning document for the organization. It also allows prospective employees to decide if they are interested in, and capable of, performing the duties expected of them.

2. **Prepare a job notice.** The job notice provides standard information, such as job title, description of the job, education and/or work experience required, salary range, deadline for application, and the person to contact. Decide whether the notice will request applicants to send résumés or file applications provided by the organization.

3. **Advertise the job.** Jobs may be advertised in daily newspapers, trade journals and publications, the newsletter of a state association, through the State Job Service, with educational institutions, online through the Internet at general employment sites such as Monster *(http://www.monster.com) and Career Builder (http://www.careerbuilder.com)*, and, most importantly, internally. There are online job boards that target nonprofit sector employment, such as Idealist *(http://www.idealist.org), The Chronicle of Philanthropy (http://philanthropy.org)*, and the Foundation Center *(http://foundationcenter.org/pnd/jobs/)*. Many nonprofit organizations also include a current job opportunities listing on their own Web sites and social networking pages, as well.

4. **Review the applications.** Develop a process for reviewing and ranking applications to decide who will be invited to interview. Remember to send a letter to those not interviewed, informing them that they were unsuccessful.

5. **Interview candidates.** The interview should be a dialogue, not a monologue by the interviewer. Let the candidate talk, so the interviewer can make judgments about how articulate the candidate is. It is useful to be friendly, ask a few softball questions first, and perhaps make a comment about something interesting on the résumé, such as a hobby, professional association membership, or award. Ask about any years that appear to be missing from the résumé.

There are questions that should be asked by the interviewers, and questions that by law cannot be asked. Among the questions that may be asked are:

- What background and experience make you feel you would be suitable for this particular position?

- What has attracted you to apply for a position with this organization?

- What experience, education, or background prepares you for this position that makes you feel you would be suitable for this position, and would separate you from other applicants?

- Do you have experience using the software packages used by this organization?

- What former employers or teachers may be consulted concerning your abilities?

- What are your long-term professional goals?

- What are the two or three things that are most important to you in a new professional setting?

- What motivates you to perform? How do you motivate those who work with you or for you?

- What were some of the most important accomplishments in your previous position, and what did you do that was special to achieve them?

- Describe a situation in which you had a conflict with another individual, and explain what you did to resolve it.

- Are you more comfortable working with a team on a group assignment, or by yourself?

- What are your significant strengths and weaknesses?

- Why are you shifting direction in employment?

- Where do you see yourself professionally in five years?

- How do you feel about your current/previous employer(s)?

Among questions that may *not* be asked are:

- questions relating to an applicant's race, sex, sexual orientation, national origin, religion, or age

- questions relating to the applicant's physical and mental condition that are unrelated to performing the job

- questions that provide an indication of the above, such as the number of children the applicant has, the applicant's maiden name, child care arrangements, height/weight, whether the applicant is pregnant or planning to have children, the date the applicant graduated from high school, and whether the applicant is a Sabbath observer

- whether the applicant has ever been arrested or convicted of a crime, without proof of business necessity for asking.

6. **Select the best-qualified candidate.** This is different from selecting the best candidate. The best candidate within the pool of applicants may be identified easily, but if that person is not quite up to the task, it is a mistake to hire him or her. It is better to begin the search again, or try to find another way to have those duties performed without taking a chance that a bad hiring decision will harm the organization, perhaps irreparably.

7. **Verify information from the résumé and interviews; investigate references.** By law in some states, employers may not refuse to hire an employee based on a prior criminal conviction, unless that conviction specifically relates to the prospective employee's suitability for employment.

   Even in that case, the applicant must be informed in writing of a decision based on that, in whole or in part. For some nonprofit jobs, particularly those involving children, state law requires a State Police background check.

   It is not unusual for job candidates desperate to make their résumés stand out to embellish their educational or professional qualifications. A few telephone calls can ferret out many of these. This is a wise investment; someone who is dishonest enough to falsify qualifications on a résumé is likely to be just as dishonest when it comes to other professional issues. Investigating references can often turn up reasons for not hiring someone. It is good practice to request permission from the applicant to check references and to contact previous employers.

Although a candidate may refuse for personal reasons to permit contact with a previous employer, it is sometimes, but not always, an indication of a flawed relationship.

Among the questions that are appropriate when contacting prior employers are:

- How long did the applicant work for you?
- What was the quality of work of this applicant?
- What level of responsibility was the applicant given?
- How did the applicant get along with coworkers?
- Did the applicant show initiative and creativity? In what ways?
- Was the applicant a self-starter, or did he or she require constant supervision and direction?
- Was the applicant punctual?
- Is there anything you can tell me that would be relevant to my decision to hire or not hire the applicant?

8. **Make an offer to the candidate and negotiate salary, benefits, and other terms of the offer.**

9. **Put the offer in writing once the offer is successful.** Use a contract, if necessary or desirable. Once the contract is signed or the offer is otherwise accepted, notify other candidates that they were not successful, and arrange to orient the successful candidate.

Firing Employees

The loss of one's job is often the most stressful and traumatic event in a worker's life, with the exceptions of the death of a close family member or divorce. For most managers, having to fire someone is unpleasant at best, and can be traumatic. In many cases, it represents a failure not just by the affected worker but also by the organization.

Managers must be careful about how the firing is done; employee lawsuits over firings are becoming more common. When a nonprofit is unionized, even firings for the most egregious offenses may be challenged. It is also important to make sure that there is authority to fire. For example, the board chairperson may not fire the executive director without authority from the board, unless the bylaws provide for that. The executive director may not fire the communications director, for example, unless the organization's bylaws, policy of the board, and/or job description of the executive director make it clear that he or she has this authority.

Planning Issues

Before firing an employee, it is important to do some planning. Among the issues to consider are how to deal with the workload performed by the fired employee; the effective date of the termination; what to tell coworkers about the action; how to ensure that the employee will not take away sensitive files and other materials; what to tell the employee about health and life insurance continuity, pension, and other benefits; how to deal with separating personal property and organizational property; how and when to terminate e-mail addresses and passwords; how much severance pay to offer; and whether any letter of recommendation will be provided.

When to Fire

It is usually appropriate to summarily (without warning) fire an employee for gross misconduct that threatens the organization. Examples of this are drinking on the job, being convicted of a serious criminal offense, the willful destruction of organizational property, stealing from the organization, or causing harm to others (such as clients or other employees).

Most unacceptable behaviors that eventually result in dismissal are not as abrupt, and it is only after the manager has attempted a series of mitigation efforts that have failed that the employee is told to leave. Among these behaviors are unexplained absences, chronic tardiness, insubordination, laziness, and general poor job performance. Many nonprofit managers are close to their employees and shy away from taking appropriate disciplinary action. They need to realize that the health of the organization requires discipline and that they are getting paid to ensure that the organization functions. Problem employees inhibit otherwise productive coworkers.

Discipline Short of Firing

Poor performance on the job may be the result of many factors. These might include personal problems of the employee, miscommunication by the manager, or the employee's lack of skills—for whatever reason—required to perform the task. Each of these has a remedy and, if the manager is flexible, dismissal can be avoided.

For example, the birth of a child or serious illness of a spouse or other close family member can leave a valued employee temporarily unable or unavailable to perform job duties. Some time off, flextime, counseling, or temporarily decreasing duties can all help. Continuing education can improve job skills. Improving communication from the manager, either through "coaching" on how to do the job better, or at least providing some feedback on what is going wrong, can prevent the necessity to terminate an employee. Most employees want to do well, and many believe they are doing well but are never told that their professional work is actually considered poor by those who evaluate and manage them. For some employees, however, discipline is required.

Discipline Continuum

1. **Verbal communication.** Short of the gross misconduct referred to in the beginning of this section, this should always take the form of informal communication by the manager. It should be verbal, one-on-one, and definitely not in front of coworkers. The manager should explain the problem and seek an explanation from the employee of what the manager can do to help improve the worker's ability to perform. In many cases, this will be enough. Make a notation in your records when this communication occurred and what was said, and whether the employee acknowledged the problem and agreed to improve his or her performance.

2. **Written warning.** If there is no appropriate response to the verbal communication (e.g., the employee continues to show up to work late or misses reasonable deadlines), a written memo outlining the problem should be shared with the employee. It should not be accusatory, but should state that the employee is engaging in behavior that is unacceptable, needs to be changed, and that this memo follows up on a verbal communication.

3. **Written formal warning.** This involves a formal memo to the employee from his or her immediate supervisor, similar to the written warning, but notes that this new memo will become a part of the employee's permanent personnel file. The memo should make clear that the person's job may be in jeopardy unless there is significant progress measured by a certain date, and that this progress will be evaluated on or shortly after that date.

4. **Suspension without pay.** Some employees just will not comprehend the seriousness of being late or being disruptive unless there is a real financial penalty attached. A one-day suspension, without pay, makes it clear that the manager has authority to take action and that permanent suspension (i.e., firing) is possible.

5. **Firing.** This is the last resort. In the larger nonprofit, this may actually have a beneficial effect on other employees if they feel that the employee being fired is hurting the organization. In the smaller organization, firing is rarely beneficial in the short term; a poor employee is often much more productive than no employee at all.

In a nonprofit organization, firing should always be for cause. It is not appropriate to fire your administrative assistant who has been faithful, loyal, and productive for 10 years just because the daughter of your college professor moved to town and needs a job, even if the administrative assistant has a contract that provides for employment "at will."

Even if there is no avenue for the fired employee to appeal, a nonprofit manager should be convinced that the firing is called for and could be defended in a court of law, if necessary. Some managers may actually have to defend the firing in court or before a grievance panel of some kind, such as a human relations commission. In recent years, courts have considered "wrongful discharge" suits and have awarded damages to fired employees who were dismissed unfairly.

How to Fire

1. It is common courtesy to make sure that the fired employee is the first to know, other than those up the chain of command who must know or be consulted first to obtain dismissal authority.

2. Fire the person in private, in a one-on-one situation or with other supervisors present, as appropriate.

3. Explain to the person why he or she is being fired, and point out the previous attempts to reach accommodation. Do not turn the meeting into a debate or let the person plead for his or her job. By this time, it is counterproductive to rescind the decision. Explain that the purpose of the meeting, in addition to letting the person know about the firing, is to share important information about policies, procedures, and benefits.

4. Explain applicable company policies, procedures, and benefits, such as severance pay, outplacement services, the effective date of the firing, when to turn over keys and files, and COBRA benefits. COBRA (the Consolidated Omnibus Budget Reconciliation Act of 1985) per-

mits employees who retire, are laid off, who quit, or who are fired for reasons other than gross misconduct to continue to qualify for group health coverage for up to 18 months after termination, provided they pay the premiums. At this time, the manager may make suggestions about other jobs.

5. If appropriate, arrange for an exit interview, permitting the employee the opportunity to share information about the organization, job description, coworkers, job function, and so on. Although this exit interview may not always be pleasant, the information provided may be invaluable.

Personnel Policies

Whether a nonprofit corporation has one salaried employee or hundreds, a written personnel policy can prevent disputes that, in some cases, can destroy an organization even before it gets off the ground. Obviously, a personnel policy for a small organization will be less complex than that of a large one. It is advisable to review personnel policies of several organizations of similar scope and choose among the provisions that are most sensitive to your organizational needs. It is not necessary to reinvent the wheel, but *having* a wheel is important.

Qualified and trained personnel are an organization's most prized assets. Staff members need to feel that the organization is flexible enough to respond to their individual needs. Conversely, the organization must have the ability to operate efficiently, effectively, and economically, and to treat all employees fairly and equally. A balance must be attained, and each organization can best determine for itself where the balance lies.

Before hiring the first employee, among the issues to consider and to develop policies for are:

- Should staff be paid employees of the corporation, or should the corporation hire a consultant? (See page 217.)
- What will be included in staff job descriptions?
- How much should each staff member be compensated? Should a staff person be paid on a salaried basis or by the hour?
- If an office is established, what should the office hours be, and where should the office be located?

It may be advisable for the organization to have a personnel committee. Its role is to study the issues raised in this section; develop a personnel policy for ratification by the board, if appropriate; and to serve as the adjudicating body to resolve grievances by employees.

After a decision is made to hire employees, some of the issues to consider for inclusion in a personnel policy are the following:

1. **Hiring policies**—How should job vacancies be advertised? Will there be affirmative action to recruit minorities? Should the search be national, statewide, regional, or local? Should current employees be given preference in hiring for vacant positions? Is a pre-hiring physical examination required?

2. **Firing policies**—What are the conditions that permit dismissal without appeal, such as "for cause"? Will there be severance pay? Will placement services be provided? Will notice be given of unsatisfactory job performance before dismissal?

3. **Probationary periods of employment**—Should there be a period of probation during which an employee can be terminated without access to any grievance procedure or will not be entitled to receive benefits, including leave?

4. **Sick leave and vacation**—How many days will be allowed? Can they be accumulated and, if so, how? Will a doctor's note verifying illness be required?

5. **Holidays**—Which holidays are paid holidays and which are optional? What is the policy with respect to the observance of religious holidays?

6. **Personal days**—How many personal days will be permitted, and will they be accumulated? If not taken, will they carry over? Can they be "cashed in" upon retirement?

7. **Overtime policies**—Which classes of employees are eligible for overtime pay? Is overtime mandatory if requested by the organization? Will overtime be compensated in salary or compensatory time?

8. **Compensatory ("Comp") time**—Should comp time be granted in lieu of overtime pay? Should surplus comp time be required to be used for routine doctor and dentist appointments rather than for sick leave?

9. **Full-time vs. part-time status**—How many hours per week qualify the employee for benefits?

10. **Health insurance**—What *must* be offered to comply with the *Affordable Care Act*? Is there a group plan? Will gross salary be increased if

an employee is covered by the health insurance policy of a spouse and elects not to be covered by the organization?

11. **Pension**—How long does it take for an employee to be vested? What is the employer and employee contribution required?

12. **Life insurance and other benefits**—Is there a menu from which to choose?

13. **Employee evaluation**—Who performs the evaluation? How often will the evaluation be performed? Under what conditions may employees exercise their legal rights to examine their files? Who has access to personnel files?

14. **Merit salary increases; cost-of-living increases**—What are the criteria used for salary increases, and how often and by whom are salaries reviewed?

15. **Continuing education benefits**—Are they offered? Who has authority to approve requests? What are the time and cost limitations? When do employees become eligible?

16. **Staff training/orientation**—Is there a formal review for new employees concerning staff personnel policies? What type of training will be provided and who will provide it?

17. **Maternity leave**—What documentation is required? What is the maximum leave the employee may take without losing her job?

18. **Bereavement leave**—How long will such leave be, and which relatives will be included in the policy?

19. **Family and medical leave**—For what purposes will this leave be granted? What documentation is required to accompany a leave request? Will the leave be paid or unpaid? What will be the effect on unused sick leave and vacation (see #17)?

20. **Pay for jury duty, military leave**—What is the organization's policy?

21. **Sabbatical leave**—After how many years will employees qualify, for how long, and will this be paid or unpaid leave?

22. **Expense reimbursement documentation**—How will expenses be filed and what expenses are eligible? Is there a flat per diem rate for out-

of-town travel or reimbursement? What amount will be reimbursed for mileage?

23. **Notice required for resignation**—What is the minimum notice required, and what are the sanctions for not complying?

24. **System for resolution of employee grievances**—May employees appeal to the board of directors? Is there a committee for this purpose?

25. **Disciplinary sanctions for rule-breaking**—Is there provision for suspension with or without pay?

26. **Prohibition against secondary employment**—What types of outside earned income are prohibited or permitted?

27. **Telephone policy**—What is company policy concerning personal calls at work, including reimbursement by the employee for toll calls or personal use of cell phones provided by the organization?

28. **Payroll**—Will salary be provided weekly, every other week, or monthly?

29. **Use of the Internet**—What is the policy for using the organization's Internet account for personal use, during working hours, and after working hours? Are there limitations on what employees may post on their personal social networking sites about work-related issues?

30. **Personal Relationships**—What types of personal relationships are not permitted among staff, or which may need to be reported to determine if there is a conflict of interest?

31. **Dress Code**—Is there a dress code? What is and is not permitted?

Although the issues may seem overwhelming, a small organization may only need basic policies such as hours of operation, vacation and sick leave policy, benefits provided, and holidays. The rest can be determined on an ad hoc basis by the executive director, in consultation with the board's chairperson and/or the personnel committee, if there is one.

Major Federal Laws Affecting Employers

Taxpayer Bill of Rights 2 (P. L. 104-168)
This law was enacted on July 30, 1996, but its provisions relating to excessive income are retroactive to September 1995. It includes "intermediate sanctions" provisions that authorize the Internal Revenue Service to levy excise taxes on excessive compensation paid out by 501(c)(3) and (c)(4) organizations, and to penalize nonprofit managers who authorize such compensation. The law also provides for increased public disclosure of financial documents.

Fair Labor Standards Act of 1938 (52 Stat. 1060, 29 §201 et seq.)
Enacted in 1938, the law provides for a minimum wage, controls child labor, and requires premium pay for overtime.

Equal Pay Act of 1963 (P.L. 88-38, 29 § 206)
Requires that men and women performing equal work be paid equally.

Civil Rights Act of 1964 (P.L. 88-352, 28 §1447, 42 §1971, 1975a-1975-d, 2000 et seq.)
Prohibits discrimination, including employment discrimination, on the basis of race, color, religion, sex or national origin. Includes prohibition of certain questions being asked by prospective employers at job interviews.

Equal Employment Opportunity Act of 1972 (P.L. 92-2615 §5108, 5314-5316, 42 §2000e)
Amends the Civil Rights Act by expanding anti-discrimination protection.

Age Discrimination in Employment Act of 1967 (P.L. 90-202, 29 §621 et seq.)
Prohibits discrimination against persons age 40-70, as revised by the 1978 amendments.

Immigration Reform and Control Act of 1986 (P.L. 99-603, 7 §2025 and other references)
Requires employers to certify that their workers are not illegal aliens, and prevents discrimination on the basis of national origin.

Employee Retirement Income Security Act of 1974 (ERISA) (P.L. 93-406, 26 § 37 et seq., 29 §1001 et seq., and other references)
Requires accountability and reporting related to employer pension plans.

National Labor Relations Act of 1935 (49 Stat 449, 29 §151 et seq.)
Authorizes workers to form unions and other collective bargaining units.

Pregnancy Discrimination Act of 1978 (P.L. 95-555, 42 §2000e(k))

Amends the Civil Rights Act (which prohibits discrimination on the basis of sex) to change the definition of "sex" to include "because of or on the basis of pregnancy, childbirth, or related medical conditions."

Drug-Free Workplace Act of 1988 (P.L. 100-690, 41 §701 et seq.)

Requires organizations receiving federal contracts valued at $25,000 or more to certify that they will provide a drug-free workplace, notify their employees of actions taken against those who violate drug laws, and establish a drug-free awareness program.

Americans With Disabilities Act of 1990 (P.L. 101-336, 29 §706, 42 §12101 et seq., 47 §152, 221, 225, 611)

Prohibits employers with 15 or more workers from discriminating on the basis of disability.

Family and Medical Leave Act (P.L. 103-3, 29§2601 et seq.)

Requires businesses with 50 or more employees to provide certain workers with up to 12 weeks annually of family or medical leave to care for a sick spouse, child, or parent, or to care for a new child.

Uniformed Services Employment and Re-Employment Rights Act of 1994 (P.L. 103-353, 38§4301-4304).

Protects the job rights of individuals who voluntarily or involuntarily leave employment positions to undertake military service and prohibits employers from discriminating against past and present members of the uniformed services and applicants to the uniformed services.

The Patient Protection and Affordable Care Act (P.L.111-148, 29§1558).

Among many other requirements, requires employers to report the value of health care benefits to employees on W-2s, requires nonprofit hospitals to meet certain criteria to maintain their federal tax exemptions, and provides small tax-exempt organizations with a refundable tax credit to subsidize the cost of providing health insurance to their employees, specifically targeted for low- and moderate-income individuals. Most of the provisions apply to employers of 50 or more full time equivalent employees. See: *http://www.councilofnonprofits.org/how-will-affordable-care-act-impact-nonprofit*

Sample State Laws Affecting Nonprofit Employers (examples from Pennsylvania)

Solicitation of Funds for Charitable Purposes Act (10 §161.1 et seq.)
Provides for regulation and disclosure of organizations that raise funds from the public for charitable purposes.

Child Labor Law (43 §41 et seq.)
Prohibits the employment of persons under 16 with limited exceptions, and provides labor standards for the employment of persons 16-18.

Corporation Not-for-Profit Code (Nonprofit Corporation Law of 1972 and Nonprofit Corporation Law of 1988—15 Pa. C.S.A. §7101 et seq.; §7301 et seq.; and 15 Pa. C.S.A. §5101 et seq.)
Contains codified statutes that apply to all nonprofit corporations in Pennsylvania.

Directors' Liability Act (42 §8361 et seq.)
Reduces the liability for directors of nonprofit corporations.

Equal Pay Law (43 §336.1 et seq.)
Requires employers to provide fair wages for women and persons 16-21, and to keep records of hours worked and wages paid to their employees.

Pennsylvania Labor Relations Act (43 §211.1 et seq.)
Protects the right of employees to organize and bargain collectively.

Human Relations Act (43 §951 et seq.)
Prohibits discrimination because of race, color, religious creed, ancestry, age, or national origin.

Employee Records Inspection Law (43 §1321)
Requires employers to make employee records with respect to qualifications for employment, promotion, additional compensation, termination, or disciplinary action available for inspection by the employee or his or her agent during business hours, and permits the employer to require that the inspection take place during the free time of the employee or agent, as the case may be.

Lobbying Disclosure Act (Act 134 of 2006)
Requires persons receiving compensation to advocate the passage or defeat of legislation to register with the State Ethics Commission, and to disclose certain expenditures and contacts.

Minimum Wage Act (43 §333.101 et seq.)
Sets the Pennsylvania minimum wage.

Pennsylvania Workmen's Compensation Act (77 §1 et seq.)
Provides for a worker's compensation program.

Unemployment Compensation Law (43 §751 et seq.)
Provides for unemployment compensation to workers who lose their jobs through no fault of their own.

Standard Federal Paperwork for Corporations with Employees

1. Form SS-4, Application for Employer Identification Number—This is the first form to be filed when starting a corporation. Once this form is filed, the Internal Revenue Service will establish an account for the organization and assign a federal tax number (EIN). This number will be the organization's account for paying taxes and is requested by other government authorities for tax purposes. It is requested by most foundations and grant makers, as well. This form should be filed at least a month before the number is needed. To obtain this form, call the IRS toll-free at 1-800-829-3676 or access it at: *http://www.irs.gov/ http://www.irs.gov/pub/irs-pdf/fss4.pdf*

2. Form W-4—Employee's Withholding Allowance Certificate—Each employee must file with the employer a copy of form W-4, which documents the number of exemptions and additional federal withholding. The information in the W-4 enables the employer to calculate how much should be withheld from gross salary (not including state and local withholding).

3. Circular E—Employer's Tax Guide—Employers need to obtain a copy of this publication (call toll-free 1-800-829-3676 to request this guide or access it at: *http://www.irs.gov/publications/p15/index.html*) to calculate the amount of federal income tax withholding, Social Security withholding (for calendar year 2014 set at 6.2% of gross wages up to $117,000), and Medicare withholding (for calendar year 2014 set at 1.45% of gross wages, without any ceiling). In addition to withholding Medicare tax at 1.45%, employers must withhold a 0.9% Additional Medicare Tax from wages they pay to an employee in excess of $200,000 in a calendar year. The amount of wages needed to earn a Social Security credit is $1,200 in 2014. Workers thus will need to earn $4,800 in 2014 to earn the maximum four credits for the year. Most workers need 40 credits to be eligible for retirement benefits (see www.ssa.gov/pubs/EN-05-10072.pdf for more information about Social Security credits).

4. Electronic Federal Tax Payment System (EFTPS)—As of 2011, employers must use electronic funds transfer to make all federal tax deposits (such as deposits of employment tax, excise tax, and corporate income tax). Generally, electronic fund transfers are made using the Electronic Federal Tax Payment System (EFTPS). Employers may arrange for a tax professional, financial institution, payroll service, or other trusted third party to make electronic deposits on their behalf. For more information on what forms are required and how they are electronically submitted with payments, see: https://www.eftps.gov/eftps/

5. Form 941—Employer's Quarterly Federal Tax Return—Each quarter, the IRS requires reconciling federal tax payments that were deposited for the previous quarter. The final line will indicate if the corporation owes any payments to the IRS. With limited exceptions, employers must submit their return and payment using the Electronic Federal Tax Payment System (EFTPS) unless their total payment for the current quarter or previous quarter is not more than $2,500.

6. Form 940—Employer's Annual Federal Unemployment (FUTA) Tax Return— Nonprofit organizations other than those with 501(c)(3) status are subject to FUTA taxes. This form must be filed if more than $1,500 was paid in wages during any calendar quarter or if the organization had one or more employees at any time in each of 20 calendar weeks during the previous two calendar years. The tax rate for 2014 was 6.0% of the first $7,000 paid to each employee. Businesses receive a credit on the amount of unemployment taxes paid to their state. Quarterly tax deposits may be necessary, depending on the amount owed. These deposits are made in the same way as federal quarterly withholding deposits. If payments are more than $500, the payment must be submitted using the Electronic Federal Tax Payment System (EFTPS).

7. Form W-2—Wage and Tax Statement—This statement is given to all employees on or before January 31. It details their gross salary and amounts withheld in federal, state, and local taxes during the previous year.

8. Form W-3—Transmittal of Income and Tax Statement—This return looks like a Master W-2, and aggregates information for all employees. It is filed with the Social Security Administration, accompanied by one copy of each employee's W-2.

9. Form 990—This is the tax-exempt nonprofit corporation's tax return.

10. Form 990-T—This is a supplement to the tax-exempt nonprofit corporation's 990 tax return that reports gross income of $1,000 or more from unrelated business income during the fiscal year.

11. Form I-9—This form is kept by the employer for each worker to certify that the worker is a citizen, national, or alien legally authorized to work in the United States.

12. Form 1099 MISC—This form must be filed if the organization pays more than $600 in the calendar year to those who are not direct employees, such as independent contractors. One copy is given to the individual on or before January 31. The other is sent with similar forms to the IRS on or before February 28, using **Form 1096** as a transmittal form.

Volunteers

Nonprofit organizations rely on volunteers to perform organizational functions, ranging from receptionist to board chairperson. Indeed, the term "voluntary sector" is a working synonym for "nonprofit charities."

Nonprofit organization budgets rarely permit salaries for all needed employees. During times of economic uncertainty, nonprofit organizations are particularly vulnerable to budget cutbacks, ironically at the very same time that the demand for their services increases. Using volunteers is an effective way to stretch limited organizational resources, build community support, improve communications, and tap hard-to-find skills.

The changing demographics in recent decades—more single-parent households, more two-parent working families, more women in the workforce, an increased incentive to continue working to maintain income rather than retiring—demand that volunteer recruitment, training, support, and recognition change to meet new realities.

National statistics validate the view that volunteering continues to be popular, despite a slightly declining trend. The Urban Institute estimates that about 64.5 million Americans, or 26.5 percent of the adult population, averaged 193 hours of volunteer service during 2012 worth an estimated $259.6 billion, based on an estimate that each hour is worth $22.55 for 2013 (Pettijohn, 2013, Independent Sector, n.d).

Figure 9—Volunteering Trends—Number of Volunteers 2002-2013 (in thousands)

	Sep-02	% of Pop.	Sep-09	% of Pop.	Sep. 2013	% of Pop.
Total #	59,783	27.4	63,361	26.8	62,615	25.4
Men	24,706	23.6	26,655	23.3	26,404	22.2
Women	35,076	31.0	36,706	30.1	36,211	28.4

Source: U.S. Dept. of Labor, Bureau of Labor Statistics, Volunteering in the United States (released 12/9/2005; retrieved from *http://www.bls.gov/news.release/volun.nr0.htm*) and Volunteering in the United States (released 2/25/14; retrieved from *http://www.bls.gov/news.release/volun.nr0.htm*).

Figure 10: Volunteers by Age (in millions): 2009 and 2013				
	2009		2013	
Age	Number	% of population	Number	% of population
16-24	8,290	22.0	8,466	21.8
25-34	9,511	23.5	9,118	21.9
35-44	12,835	31.5	12,098	30.6
45-54	13,703	30.8	12,184	28.2
55-65	9,894	28.3	10,191	26.0
>65	9,129	23.9	10,558	24.1

Source: U.S. Dept. of Labor, Bureau of Labor Statistics, *Volunteering in the United States*. Retrieved from *http://www.bls.gov/news.release/volun.nr0.htm (released 1/26/2010 and 2/25/14)*.

Volunteerism is alive and well in the United States. New public-private sector initiatives are strengthening the institutions that promote volunteerism. Partnerships are developing in schools, colleges, religious institutions, and the private sector. Successful volunteer programs tap "non-traditional" sources of volunteer strength. More and more, these partnerships are being directly encouraged by government.

Federal legislation signed on September 21, 1993, the *National and Community Service Trust Act* (P.L.103-82), provides incentives to promote volunteerism among the young and not-so-young, and to pay them living and educational stipends, as well.

President Bush spoke to the nation about changes to the federal budget he would propose in the wake of the September 11th terrorist attacks. In his January 29, 2002 State of the Union address, the President proposed establishing a new "U.S. Freedom Corps," which would also expand volunteer opportunities (see the Corporation for National and Community Service Web site at: *http://www.serve.gov/*). On April 27, 2006, President Bush issued an Executive Order requiring every federal agency to designate one staff member to serve as a liaison for volunteer community service.

In April 2009, President Obama signed into law the *Edward M. Kennedy Service America Act*. It authorizes a 5-year, $5.7 billion national and community service bill that triples the AmeriCorps program over an 8-year period. The law also authorizes transferable $1,000 education grants to those 55 years of age and older who perform community service activities. See: *http://www.nationalservice.gov/about/legislation/edward-m-kennedy-serve-america-act*

Benefits and Considerations of Having Volunteers

Among the benefits of using volunteers are:

1. They do not require salaries or fringe benefits. Although this is the most obvious advantage, there may be other financial savings, as well.

2. They are often highly motivated. Volunteers are there because they want to be, not because it is their livelihood. If it was "just a job," volunteers might be somewhere else.

3. They can speak their minds without fear of loss of a livelihood. Volunteers can often be a useful sounding board. They are often less shy about speaking out than a paid employee might be.

4. They may bring skills to the organization that it otherwise may not be able to find or afford.

5. They may have a network of community contacts who may be a source of contributions, expertise, prospective staff, or additional volunteers.

Other considerations are:

1. Just because volunteers are not on the payroll does not mean that the organization incurs no costs. Volunteers need telephones, work space, equipment, supplies, desks, and virtually everything else besides a paycheck. Training and orientation costs are just as high as for salaried workers.

2. Volunteer retention is often a problem. The opportunity for paid employment elsewhere may influence a volunteer to leave, and family commitments or other duties may intervene. A volunteer can be easily captured by competing interests.

3. Volunteers, just like paid staff, dislike dull, repetitive, uninteresting work. They are more likely to do something about it quickly than would paid staff.

4. Volunteers are generally available for fewer hours per day. Many, such as students, volunteer for specific time periods and for short terms. They often require more hours of training and supervision per hour of productive work than employees.

Volunteer Job Description

Individuals are more likely to volunteer to assist an organization if they have specific information about the tasks they are being asked to perform. Before requesting volunteer assistance, develop a detailed job description that includes at least the following information:

- Examples of duties to be performed
- Specific skills or training needed
- The location where the duties will be performed
- The hours per week required
- The time period (e.g., weeks, months) the duties will be performed
- The supervision or assistance that will be provided
- The training that will be provided.

Volunteer Recruitment

McCurley & Lynch (2011) provide a typology of volunteer recruiting strategies:

1. Warm body recruitment—seeking volunteers from as wide a pool as possible. This is done by distributing brochures and posters, using PSAs, using the organization's Web site, and contacting organizations who have lots of members. Advantage: This technique is good for finding volunteers for short-term assignments, such as a running race fundraiser. Disadvantage: You typically do not have much time to learn whether the prospective volunteer is honest, dependable, or otherwise suitable for the job. Example: Putting up posters around town seeking volunteers to hand out water for a YMCA-sponsored 5K.

2. Targeted recruitment—identifying a particular group of people who are most likely to be suitable for the volunteer position. These groups are targeted both by the message in the communication and the media by which it is communicated to maximize the probability that they will be exposed to it and respond. Advantage: You are more likely to identify someone with the right combination of skills. Disadvantage: You are limiting the pool of individuals from which to recruit. Example: Approaching a local computer club to find a volunteer to create a Web site for the YMCA's 5K road race.

3. Concentric circles recruitment—using current volunteers to find replacements and/or additions. Advantage: It does not require much work on the part of the volunteer coordinator to ask the person opting out to find someone who will take over. Disadvantage: The person who did the volunteer job last year may have a really good reason why he/she would not encourage someone to do that this year! Example: Asking last year's race director to find a replacement for this year's race.

4. Ambient recruitment—recruiting volunteers through a particular group who have a high affinity for that group, such as a particular school, business organization, religious congregation, or profession. Advantage: A group of volunteers from one particular organization will feel a bond, and would likely feel that volunteering on behalf of their group will improve the image of their organization. Disadvantage: Someone still must work with the group to make sure everyone understands their roles, will work together, and will not spend their entire time socializing with each other rather than performing the work for which they volunteered. Example: Sending an e-mail to everyone who is a member of the local Young Professionals Association asking for race volunteers.

5. Brokered recruitment—finding volunteers through a third party, such as a local volunteer center, a Web site that has volunteer listings, a corporate volunteer office, or a similar office whose responsibility is to coordinate the placement of individuals willing to volunteer. Advantage: The organization gets exposure to a pool of willing volunteers, who are likely searching for an assignment that fits their needs with respect to type of work, geographical location, and cause. Disadvantage: You may get folks volunteering for a specific task who are not suitable to the organization. Example: Partnering with the local running club, and offering its members a $5 discount on race registration if the organization provides 40 volunteers.

Active recruiting is required to maintain a dedicated volunteer pool. Some strategies nonprofit organizations use to recruit volunteers are—

- They pass around a sign-up sheet at community speaking engagements where potential volunteers can indicate their interest. Be sure to provide space for addresses, telephone numbers, and e-mail addresses, as well as to indicate specific skills or interests.

- They include information about volunteer opportunities in any public relations brochures, media stories, newsletters, and public service announcements. Many local newspapers have a regular column devoted to nonprofit organization volunteer opportunities.

- They ask users of the organization's services if they would like to volunteer, if this is appropriate.

- They target solicitation of potential volunteers to groups in the community that are likely to have time to share. Retired people, schoolchildren, and groups sponsored by places of worship are excellent sources for volunteers.

- They post volunteer opportunities on their Web sites and on general sites that permit the posting of volunteer opportunities, such as IdeaList *(http://www.idealist.com)*.

Interview potential volunteers as you would potential employees. Be sure their interests are compatible with the organization's. Find out what their motivation is for volunteering. Is it to perform a service or advance a cause? Is it to develop marketable job skills and make contacts? Is it to have a place to "hang out"?

A volunteer can have the same organizational impact, negative or positive, as a paid staff member.

Tell potential volunteers about the organization and obtain basic information about them, such as their skills, training, and interests. Ask about their time availability. Once satisfied that the right volunteer is matched with the right job, review the volunteer job descriptions with them and ask them if they are ready to volunteer for specific assignments.

The fact that a person is willing to work for free does not automatically make him or her the best candidate for the "job." The organization should not lower its standards in any way. Make sure that expectations are clear and the volunteer's performance is reviewed.

Where practical, organizations should screen volunteers thoroughly and require references, including police background checks, particularly for those positions where the volunteer might be in close contact with children. Organizations should seek diversity in their volunteer mix for the same reasons this is desirable for paid staff. And it goes without saying that organizations should avoid discrimination on the basis of any aspect of individuals that are protected by laws relating to paid employment. Organizations should avoid giving volunteers only the work that paid staff feel it is beneath them to perform. Paid staff should be a part of the process for recruiting and supervising volunteers, and making sure that the volunteer job description is meaningful to potential volunteers.

Organizations should have written volunteer policies and share them with volunteers during the recruitment/interview process. See *http://www.serviceleader.org/virtual/sample* for a sample volunteer policy that was developed by Jayne Cravins.

Volunteer Orientation

Make certain every volunteer receives a complete orientation before starting to work. In some instances, a group of volunteers may participate in a formal volunteer orientation program. In other situations, a one-on-one orientation at the work site is appropriate. Make sure to include—

- An overview of the organization's mission.
- A description of the specific task to be performed.
- Confirmation of the hours required.
- A statement of whom to contact if help is needed.
- The individual to contact if an assignment cannot be completed as scheduled.

Rewards

Although volunteers do not receive a paycheck for their services, they should receive other types of payment. Remember to thank them for the work they perform. Both informal thanks and periodic formal award and recognition ceremonies for volunteers are appropriate. Encourage volunteers to attend training programs to update their skills. Include them in the organization's social events. Remember that extra "payments" to volunteers will pay off in effective service to the organization.

Virtual Volunteering

A growing number of organizations are harnessing a new source of volunteers—those unable or unwilling to work on site, but who are eager to work for their favorite cause from their home or work computer. Virtual volunteering has obvious advantages for those who are elderly, disabled, caretakers, or those who otherwise are restricted in their mobility or willingness to travel to a volunteer site. For many others who are too busy or otherwise unable to commit to a specific time and place for their volunteering, this non-traditional method opens up opportunities. Virtual volunteering has appeal to those who are too busy to make a commitment, but have the ability to fit in volunteer work from home on an ad hoc basis—provided they have a computer and Internet access.

Virtual volunteers are being used to design and update Web sites, prepare newsletters, manage social media, respond to requests for information, research reports, and prepare advocacy materials. Although there are some limitations involved in virtual volunteering (such as no hands-on supervision or the lack of face-to-face interaction), advances in technology are providing opportunities for people who otherwise would not make a commitment to volunteer. An eye-opening feature by Jayne Cravens on virtual volunteering can be found at: *http://www.coyotecommunications.com/volunteer/ovmyths.html*

Impact Online, an organization founded in 1994, administers a Virtual Volunteering Project. You can find information about how to begin, and you can even locate volunteers at this site, which can be found at: *http://www.volunteermatch.org/*

Discussion Questions

1. Should volunteers be treated any differently by the organization and its employees than paid staff members?

2. Should volunteers be held to a lower standard of job performance than their paid counterparts?

3. What are the pros and cons of building a diverse staff in a nonprofit organization? Are these different than in a for-profit organization?

4. How has technology changed over the past five years with respect to recruiting new staff?

5. Is the stereotype of the nonprofit organization job seeker described on page 216 still valid? If not, how does this affect the task of the nonprofit manager?

6. Is it appropriate for volunteers of nonprofit organizations to be "paid" by the government?

7. What are the implications of students volunteering for nonprofit organizations to satisfy a service learning requirement of their educational institution?

8. Do you think that a nonprofit organization should have a different standard with respect to firing an unproductive employee compared to a for-profit organization?

Activities

1. Visit a nonprofit online job board such as NonprofitOyster.com. Compile a list of job titles that are being recruited by participating organizations.

2. Contact your state Human Relations Commission and determine if there is any literature available about laws that affect hiring and interview questions.

3. Research the paperwork that is required to hire a new employee.

4. Contact a sample of nonprofit organizations in your area. Determine what types of services they outsource.

Tips for Practitioners

1. Make sure that those who hire employees are familiar with the questions they can and cannot legally ask.

2. Perform an Internet search on the names of prospective employees. You may find information that could be helpful in making hiring decisions.

3. Consult an attorney to resolve particularly sticky personnel matters.

4. Keep good records of employee misconduct and what you did at every step to address the problem.

5. Treat all employees as you would like to be treated if you were in the same position.

6. Keep calm, even if the employee you are disciplining starts yelling, screaming, or crying.

7. Interview all prospective volunteers.

8. Make sure the duties of all paid staff and volunteers are clearly defined, expectations are understood, and their performance is reviewed.

9. Have a policy for volunteer termination or reassignment just as you would for paid employees.

10. Consider having a formal awards or recognition ceremony for volunteers.

11. Perform an "exit interview" with paid staff and volunteers who leave or are terminated.

Online Resources to Explore

Idealist.org
http://www.idealist.org/

Carter McNamara's Online Guide to Staffing
http://www.managementhelp.org/staffing/staffing.htm

Carter McNamara's Developing and Managing Volunteer Programs
http://www.managementhelp.org/staffing/outsrcng/volnteer/volnteer.htm

Nonprofit Good Practice Guide
http://www.npgoodpractice.org/

Volunteer Match/Impact Online
   http://www.volunteermatch.org/

For Further Reading

Bagley, B. (1996, April). Necessary v. nosey—Guidelines and strategies for hiring. PA Society of Association Executives Society News, 20.

Barbeito, C. (2006). *Human resource policies and procedures for nonprofit organizations.* New York: Wiley.

Broder, D. (2003, June 15). Empty promises for AmeriCorps. *The Washington Post,* p. B07.

Conners, T. D. (Ed.). (1988). *The nonprofit organization handbook.* New York: McGraw-Hill.

Denhardt, R., Denhardt, J., and Aristiguesta, M. (2012). *Managing human behavior in public and nonprofit organizations.* (3rd Ed.). Thousand Oaks, CA: Sage.

Dresang, D. (2009). *Personnel management in government agencies and nonprofit organizations.* Upper Saddle River, NJ: Longman.

Drucker, P. F. (1990). *Managing the nonprofit organization.* New York: Harper Collins.

Flanagan, J. (1984). *The successful volunteer organization: Getting started and getting results in nonprofit, charitable, grassroots and community groups.* Chicago: Contemporary Books.

Fletcher, K. B. (1987). *The 9 keys to successful volunteer programs.* Rockville, MD: Taft Group.

Gelatt, J. P. (1992). *Managing nonprofit organizations in the 21st century.* Phoenix, AZ: The Oryx Press.

Glickman, R. (2010). Update on FY 2011 national service budget. August 5, 2010. Retrieved from *http://www.americorps.gov/about/newsroom/statements_detail.asp?tbl_pr_id=1842*

Independent Sector. (n.d.). Independent Sector's value of volunteer time. Retrieved from *http://independentsector.org/volunteer_time*

Internal Revenue Service. (2014). Independent contractor (self-employed) or employee? Retrieved from *http://www.irs.gov/Businesses/Small-Businesses-%26-Self-Employed/Independent-Contractor-Self-Employed-or-Employee*

Lipp, J. (2010). *The complete idiot's guide to recruiting and managing volunteers.* Indianapolis, IN: Alpha.

McCurley, S. H. (1987, Spring-Summer). Protecting volunteers from suit: A look at state legislation. *Voluntary Action Leadership.*

McCurley, S. & Lynch, R. (2011). *Volunteer Management.* (3rd Ed.). Plattsburgh, NY: Interpub Group.

O'Connell, B. (1983). *America's voluntary spirit.* New York: The Foundation Center.

Pennsylvania Human Relations Commission. (n.d.). Pre-employment inquiries: What may I ask? What must I answer? Harrisburg, PA: Author.

Pettijohn, S. (2013). *The Nonprofit sector in brief.* Washington, DC.: Urban Institute. Retrieved on-from *http://www.urban.org/publications/412674.html*

Pynes, J. (2013). *Human resources management for public and nonprofit organizations: A strategic approach (4th Ed.).* San Francisco: Jossey-Bass.

Tschirhart, M. & Bielefeld, W. (2012). *Managing nonprofit organizations.* San Francisco: Jossey-Bass.

Chapter 13
Communications and Public Relations

> **Synopsis:** Organizations need to effectively communicate their objectives, activities, and accomplishments to attract funding, participation, and public support. Print and electronic publications, media contacts, and workshops are among the accepted methods used to do so.

Introduction

A well-planned public relations/communications strategy is important for two reasons. First, the organizational leadership has made a major investment in forming a nonprofit corporation, and a solid public relations effort will promote the organization's purposes. Second, few newly formed nonprofits begin with a silver spoon in their mouths. The first few years are often a fight for financial survival. Sound intraorganizational communications and building a solid public image through a public relations strategy are instrumental in building and maintaining a donor base and attracting grants and contracts.

But there is often a "Catch-22" at work here. New organizations must accomplish something useful quickly to obtain the credibility necessary to attract financial assistance. Yet, the organizations often need this financial assistance to accomplish something useful.

Public relations serves an important function. It puts the organization in a positive light and generates the essential public support needed to perpetuate it. An organization may be quietly successful in changing public opinion, advancing a legislative agenda, or providing vital services to worthy clients and its members. But if the right people—the board, funders, and potential funders and leadership—are unaware of the organization's successes, then its continued existence may be at risk.

There are thousands of creative ways to get the name of an organization in front of the public in a positive context.

Menu of Nonprofit Communication Tools

Among the conventional techniques nonprofits use are—

1. Organizational Brochure

Each nonprofit organization, from the largest to the smallest, should have a brochure. The brochure should clearly include the organization's name, address, telephone number, e-mail address, Web site and social networking addresses; its mission, its purposes and principal interests, its affiliations (if any); its federal tax-exempt status, and ways to make contributions; the names of its board members, advisory committee, and key staff people; and its major accomplishments. The organization's logo should appear on the brochure. If the organization is a membership organization, the brochure should provide information on dues and how to join.

The brochure should be distributed with all major fundraising solicitations. It should be a standard component of press packets, and should be distributed at speaking engagements made on behalf of the organization. All board members should have a supply of brochures to distribute to their friends and colleagues who may be interested in joining, contributing, volunteering, or assisting in other ways.

2. Print and Electronic Newsletter

No less than quarterly, the organization should publish a newsletter and distribute it free of charge to all board members, all dues-paying members, significant opinion leaders on the issue(s) of interest to the organization, political leadership (such as members of the state legislature, local members of Congress, and local elected officials), the media, current and potential funders, and colleagues in the field.

Among the items the newsletter may contain are—

- Recent board decisions
- The organization's "wish list" of in-kind donations
- Legislative action in Washington, the state capital, and municipal government of interest to the membership and clients
- Planned giving information
- Schedules of upcoming meetings, workshops, conferences, and training sessions
- Messages from the executive director and/or board president
- Articles contributed by experts on the board or the membership about issues of interest to the readership

- Articles about organizational accomplishments, such as grants received, advocacy accomplished, coalitions joined, and letters of commendation received
- Profiles of people involved in the organization
- General information about the status of issues of interest to the organization
- New features of the organization's Web site
- Names of new donors
- A list of all board members and staff
- A form to join the organization, volunteer, or make a donation
- Information on services and publications available from the organization.

The newsletter need not be fancy, but it should be as current as possible. It is advisable to select a creative and descriptive name for the publication and establish a master layout, so that subsequent issues will have the continuity of similar design.

The newsletter is often the only contact hundreds of influential people will have with an organization. As such, it is vitally important to present a professional, accurate, and eye-pleasing format. The newsletter should be carefully proofread and *all* typographical and grammatical errors eliminated. Make sure articles on one page continue correctly on subsequent pages.

Headlines should help busy readers find their way through the newsletter. Tricky headlines can be annoying. Double-check all headlines for appropriateness. Double check all names, telephone numbers, addresses, and Web site addresses.

3. News Releases

The media annually provide millions of dollars in free publicity to nonprofit organizations. The typical mode of communicating with the media is through the mailing, faxing, or e-mailing of a standard news release.

The news release is a pre-written "news" article that includes the name, organization, work telephone number, and e-mail address of the key organizational contact person at the top. If the release is *really* important, include the home telephone number, as well. The release should be dated, along with "For Immediate Release" or "Embargoed Until (insert date/time)" as appropriate.

Examples of topics for news releases are—

- The initial formation of the organization
- An organization's official comment on a new law, legislative proposal, new regulation, or court decision affecting the organization's clients or members
- An accomplishment of the organization
- The release of a study or survey commissioned by the organization
- The hiring or promotion of a staff member, or change of leadership within the organization
- Awards given by or to the organization.

News releases are distributed to those who are most likely to print or broadcast them. A news release to a TV or radio station should be no more than six or seven sentences, and no more than two double-spaced pages for the print media. Most news releases will be edited before final publication or broadcast, although many neighborhood newspapers will print news releases word-for-word.

The basic style of the body of a press release is—

- Precede the text with a catchy, descriptive headline.
- Put the most important sentence first.
- Place subsequent facts in descending order of importance.
- Include suitable quotes from organizational leadership when appropriate. The quotes should express a view/opinion, rather than providing a fact that could appear in the release narrative.
- Make sure the text answers the basic questions of "who," "what," "where," "when," "why," and "how."

4. Press Conferences

Organizations with a story of major interest to the public may want to consider holding a press conference. To do so, a media advisory is distributed in the same manner as a news release, telling the press where and when the press conference will be held, the subject, and speakers. It may be helpful to make follow-up calls to the news desks of local newspapers and broadcast stations.

At the press conference, written materials (a press packet consisting of a copy of a written statement, the organization's brochure, and materials relating to the topic of the press conference) should be distributed.

Another good idea is to arrange for a high resolution photo to be taken of the organizational representative speaking at the press conference. The photograph may be accompanied by a picture caption and sent in a press packet to media outlets not covering the press conference.

Digital cameras have eliminated some of the frustration of having to wait for a picture to be developed commercially. The files of these pictures can be sent conveniently through the Internet as e-mail attachments to newspapers on deadline, or can be posted on the organization's Web site and social networking pages.

A banner with the organization's logo, draped in front of the podium, creates a photograph that is useful for future annual reports, newsletters, and related publicity.

5. Public Service Announcements

Many TV and radio broadcasters regularly broadcast public service announcements (PSAs) for nonprofit organizations without cost. PSAs are an excellent and cost-effective way to get an organization's message, and its name, across to thousands of viewers and listeners.

The last line of such an announcement can be: "This message is brought to you by (the name of the organization) and this station as a public service." The rest of the announcement can be a 30-second sound bite of information of interest to people—how to obtain a free service, how to avoid health and safety risks, or even how to join or volunteer for the organization while accomplishing some vital objective in the public interest.

Before preparing a PSA, check with a potential broadcaster for the technical specifications for the form and format of the announcement. Some stations may be willing to produce your announcement without charge, as well as broadcast it.

6. Conferences and Workshops

Well-planned conferences and workshops can serve a useful public relations function. A one-day conference can bring together interested volunteer leadership and professionals in a shared field of interest, introduce them to the organization, increase networking among the participants, and advance the organization's interests. The charge for the workshop can be set to cover all anticipated costs, or even generate net revenue—provided it is planned well in advance and the plan is executed properly.

There are scores of major decisions to make in planning a conference, such as choosing speakers who will generate attendance and excitement, preparing and distributing the conference brochure, selecting the site for the conference, and arranging for exhibit space and advertising. There are hundreds of minor decisions that need to be made as well, such as choosing the type of name tag to use, deciding who staffs the registration table, and choosing the luncheon menu. There are many sources of advice on how to run a successful conference, many of which can be borrowed from the local library.

7. Intraorganizational Communication

Board and key contacts need to know what is happening beyond what they read in the organization's newsletter. Periodically, it is useful to send out "Action Alerts" or "Background Briefings" by mail or e-mail that describe the status of a problem and what they can do to participate in its resolution.

Some organizations have specially printed stationery for these messages. A sample letter may be included if the organization is encouraging its constituency to write advocacy letters. However, the organization should urge writers to use their own words rather than copy the sample exactly. The address or telephone number of the person they should contact should always be included.

Many organizations are sponsoring conference calls to update their stakeholders, using toll-free numbers. Or they are using free services like Google Hangout for videoconferencing, although this is limited to ten participants (15 with purchase of a premium service). Skype, a similar videoconference app, can be accessed free by up to 25 participants at a time.

8. Annual Report

Among the typical publications produced by nonprofit organizations is the annual report. Many nonprofits use this opportunity to supplement the financial information provided to stakeholders with a report on the operations of the nonprofit during the fiscal year. Many organizations produce both a print and electronic version (typically PDF format) of their annual reports.

The annual report can be professionally designed with a fancy layout, fonts, charts, graphics, and color pictures, which imply progress and success in meeting organizational goals and objectives. It can also be a word-processed report photocopied on plain paper. In either case, the annual report offers the opportunity to communicate what the organization has been doing on behalf of its board and membership, clients, funders, and the public, as well as its goals and plans.

9. Other Publications

Many nonprofits publish small booklets about various issues of concern, which are disseminated to their constituents and other interested parties. This is one more way to get the name of the organization in front of additional people, and it is another effective way to communicate the organization's views to those whose opinions count. Subjects of such publications include—

- The latest developments on issues of interest
- How to contact government offices
- How to lobby on behalf of the organization's issues
- Information about the state legislature, and who serves on committees of interest to the organization.

These publications can also be considered the written equivalent of the public service announcement. Many institutions, such as hospitals, community centers, nursing homes, day care providers, and libraries, will distribute these public relations booklets without charge to the organization's target audience.

10. Membership/Board Surveys

Membership and board surveys can be, but may not always be, a useful tool to obtain information and feedback. The target of the survey may feel a sense of connection to the organization, and the survey will provide useful input from the membership.

Member surveys can be tailored to suit the needs of the organization. For example, many advocacy nonprofits periodically survey their boards and/or membership to determine who among the board and membership has influence or personal relationships with key public policy decision-makers. Surveys can be used to gauge the effectiveness of organizational programs and activities.

Free or low-cost software is available to administer online surveys. There are also free and low-cost commercial services that provide high-quality surveys, but may include advertising. Among the services to check out (features change quickly in the dot-com environment) are Survey Monkey.com *(http://www.surveymonkey.com),* Free Online Surveys *(http://www.freeonlinesurveys.com),* and BraveNet Web Services *(http://www.bravenet.net).*

11. Speakers' Bureaus

Many groups, such as men's and women's clubs, fraternal organizations, educational organizations, membership organizations, and places of worship, have speakers at their regular meetings. Organizational leaders may wish to proactively seek invitations to discuss the activities of their organizations with these groups.

Such meetings may be the source of volunteers, donations, ideas, or simply good will and public support. Local newspapers (do not forget the "Shopper" newspapers) list many of these club meetings and their leaders. Addresses can be found in the telephone book, if they are not listed in the newspaper announcement. Members of the board can be deputized to speak on behalf of the organization. Many of them have associations with other organizations and clubs that would be delighted to host a speaker.

12. Newspaper Op-Ed Articles

Virtually all newspapers print feature-length opinion articles on their Opinion/Editorial (Op-Ed) pages. Many will include a picture and a line of biographical material about the author. The Op-Ed page is usually the page most widely read by a newspaper's readership, along with the Letters to the Editor page. It is an excellent forum to share an organization's ideas on an issue and bring attention to the organization.

There are many cases in which a thoughtful Op-Ed article resulted in legislation being enacted by Congress or the state legislature to address the issue raised by the Op-Ed piece.

13. Letters to the Editor

Letters to the Editor are an effective way to "talk back" to a newspaper when the organization believes an article or editorial unfairly and erroneously shapes an issue. They can also be an effective medium for reinforcing a position and permitting the writer to expand on that position from the perspective of the organization.

The general guidelines for writing letters to the editor vary from paper to paper, but they usually provide for writing on a single issue, being concise (no more than three paragraphs), using non-threatening language, and providing information that might not be available to the readers from any other source.

Many, if not most, newspapers with online access provide for the ability for readers to post comments about each article. This provides a targeted opportunity to reach those individuals who have an interest in a particular topic covered by the newspaper.

14. Web Sites

Thousands of nonprofit organizations use their Web pages to communicate information about donations; volunteer opportunities; products, services, and publications; and general facts about the organization (see Chapter 15). These Web sites can be prepared and maintained for very little cost and permit the general public to access information by computer from the privacy of their own homes and offices. Podcasts, blogs, wikis, message boards, and chatrooms are some of the techniques nonprofit organizations are using to build online communities to generate support.

15. Coalitions

There is strength in numbers. Two heads are better than one. Whatever the cliché, many organizations find a benefit to pooling their resources to accomplish an objective. One strategy is to form a coalition with other organizations to address an issue of vital importance (See Chapter 19).

16. Social Networking Sites

Facebook, Twitter, Pinterest and LinkedIn are among the social networking sites that thousands of nonprofit organizations are using to advantage. These free platforms are raising money, finding volunteers, coordinating advocacy, providing forums for interaction and relationship building, and serving as a quick and inexpensive means to communicate with stakeholders. Each of these sites, and there are hundreds of them, has its own personality and features. For more on this, see Chapter 15.

Discussion Questions

1. Discuss the differences in content and style between a print and electronic newsletter.

2. What are the pros and cons of nonprofits having an active presence on the social networking sites with which you are familiar?

3. What kind of information should be available on a nonprofit organization's Web site and social networking pages? What information should be available for public access, and what should remain available only to the organization's members and/or board of directors?

4. Should an organization's board meetings be open to the public? What are the pros and cons of permitting this?

Activities

1. Design a brochure for a mock nonprofit organization that advocates for an increase in the state minimum wage.

2. Attend a press conference held by a nonprofit organization and make a report about who was there, who spoke, what questions were asked, whether the event accomplished what was expected and desired by the organization, and the press coverage that occurred as a result of the event.

3. Visit the Web sites and social networking sites of a sample of local nonprofit organizations, and survey the types of content that are available on these sites. Is there any content missing that you feel should be provided?

Tips for Practitioners

1. Use the power of the Internet to reach a global audience to foster relationships between your organization and potential future stakeholders. Review Chapter 15 for more ideas.

2. Do not hold a press conference unless you feel that the information being shared is truly newsworthy. Be prepared for every reasonable question (and

perhaps unreasonable ones, as well) that may not have any direct relationship to the subject matter discussed.

Online Resources to Explore

Carter McNamara's Public and Media Relations
  http://www.managementhelp.org/pblc_rel/pblc_rel.htm

Jayne Cravens's Community Relations With and Without Technology
  http://www.coyotecom.com/tips2.html

Media Relations for Small Non-Profit Organizations
  http://pdfcast.org/pdf/media-relations-for-small-non-profit-organizations

The Nonprofit FAQ: Communications and PR
  http://www.idealist.org/if/i/en/faqcat/32-41

Further Reading

Bonk, T., Tynes, E. Griggs, H. & Sparks, P. (2008). *Strategic communications for nonprofits: A step-by-step guide to working with the media* (2nd Ed.). San Francisco: Jossey-Bass.

Committee to Defend Reproductive Rights of the Coalition for the Medical Rights of Women. (1981). *The media book: Making the media work for your grassroots group.* San Francisco: Author

Drucker, P. F. (1990). *Managing the nonprofit organization.* New York: Harper Collins.

Durham, S. (2010). *Brandraising: How nonprofits raise visibility and money through smart communications.* San Francisco: Jossey-Bass.

Feinglass, A. (2005). *The public relations handbook for nonprofits: A comprehensive and practical guide.* San Francisco: Jossey-Bass.

Patterson, S. & Radtke, J. (2009). *Strategic communications for nonprofit organizations: Seven steps to creating a successful plan.* New York: Wiley.

Salzman, J. (2003). *Making the news: A guide for nonprofits and activists.* (Revised & Updated Edition). Boulder, CO: Westview Press.

Taylor, C. (2009). *Publishing the nonprofit annual report: Tips, traps, and tricks of the trade.* San Francisco: Jossey-Bass

Williams, E. (2012). *The essential non-profit public relations guide: Tips on great public relations for non-profits.* CreateSpace.

Chapter 14
Lobbying

> **Synopsis:** Lobbying by nonprofit corporations is not only legal, but should be encouraged. There are effective strategies for communicating with legislators in person, by letter, or by telephone. All states require lobbyists to be registered and report expenditures.

Lobbying is the time-honored tradition of communicating with elected or appointed officials for the purpose of influencing legislation and other public policy. The word itself derives from the tenure of President Ulysses S. Grant, who used to hang out in the lobby of the Willard Hotel a few blocks from the White House, and listen to individuals seeking favors.

In recent years, the term has developed a pejorative character as the public, justified or not, perceives special interest lobbyists as using their influence to work against the public interest. This general mistrust of lobbyists has been exacerbated by a corruption scandal that rocked the nation's Capital in 2006 involving the lobbying efforts of Jack Abramoff, an independent lobbyist, with close ties to Congressional leaders and the White House.

Organized lobbying is an effective way to communicate an organization's views on a pending issue, to promote a favorable climate for those served, and to directly influence the outcome of decision-making. Lobbyists are employed by organizations who view themselves as working in the public interest—speaking for the poor and disenfranchised, improving the environment, establishing programs to serve the disabled, or expanding government support for vital human service and community needs.

Whether referred to as "advocacy," "government relations," or "lobbying," it is a right afforded by the First Amendment to the U.S. Constitution relating to freedom of speech, as well as the right to petition to redress grievances. Many of the public policy decisions made in Washington, state capitals, and cities and towns have a direct effect on nonprofit organizations and the client interests they serve.

Many nonprofits are expressly created to advance one cause or another whose fate is considered by a government body.

Legal Requirements for Lobbying

Lobbying is regulated at both the state and federal levels. Although there may be similarities between state and federal requirements, lobbyists must register separately with federal and state regulatory offices.

Federal Requirements

The *Lobbying Disclosure Act,* PL 104-65, was enacted on December 19, 1995, and provides major changes in registration and reporting requirements for lobbying the Congress and the Executive Branch. The law also includes a provision (Section 18) that places restrictions on the lobbying by nonprofit civic leagues and social welfare organizations, among others, which receive federal funds. The effective date of the act was January 1, 1996. Minor changes were made by the *Lobbying Disclosure Technical Amendments Act of 1998*. On September 14, 2007, President George Bush signed into law the *Honest Leadership and Open Government Act,* which made substantive reforms affecting lobbying, a response to a major scandal. The new law makes major changes in lobbying reporting requirements, gift disclosure, and travel financed by lobbyists. Of particular importance are the following:

- Lobbying disclosure forms are now required to be filed quarterly rather than semi-annually.
- Thresholds for reporting lobbying expenses have been reduced.
- Information requirements for reporting and disclosure have been expanded.
- New reports are required relating to political contributions made by, or transferred to politicians by, lobbyists.
- With some exceptions, gifts to members of Congress and their staff from lobbyists are prohibited.
- With some exceptions, lobbyists, or organizations that employ them, may not pay for the private travel of members of Congress or their staff.
- Lobbyists may not participate in privately funded Congressional travel.

The *Lobbying Disclosure Act* defines "lobbying contact" as—

any oral or written communication (including an electronic communication) to a covered executive branch official or a covered legislative branch official that is made on behalf of a client with regard to—

(i) *the formulation, modification, or adoption of Federal legislation (including legislative proposals);*
(ii) *the formulation, modification, or adoption of a Federal rule, regulation, Executive order, or any other program, policy, or position of the United States Government;*
(iii) *the administration or execution of a Federal program or policy (including the negotiation, award, or administration of a Federal contract, grant, loan, permit, or license); or*
(iv) *the nomination or confirmation of a person for a position subject to confirmation by the Senate.*

It defines "lobbyist" as—

any individual who is employed or retained by a client for financial or other compensation for services that include more than one lobbying contact, other than an individual whose lobbying activities constitute less than 20 percent of the time engaged in the services provided by such individual to that client over a six month period.

A packet of materials, including a copy of the *Lobbying Disclosure Act,* registration and expense reporting forms, instruction booklets for filling out the forms, and answers to frequently asked questions, can be obtained by contacting—

Secretary of the Senate
Office of Public Records
232 Hart Senate Office Building
Washington, D.C. 20510
(202) 224-0758

Unless they are self-employed, individual lobbyists do not register with the House and Senate. The law requires registration by lobbying firms, defined as entities with one or more employees who act as lobbyists for outside clients. A separate registration is required for each client. A typical nonprofit that has one or more employees who engage in lobbying activities is required to register, provided that its expenses attributable to lobbying exceed $10,000 in a semi-annual period (either January 1-June 30 or July 1-December 31). Registration is required no later than 45 days after a lobbyist first makes a lobbying contact or is employed to do so, whichever comes earlier. To register, the organization must electronically file a Form LD-1 in duplicate with the Secretary of the Senate and the Clerk of the House:

Secretary of the Senate	Clerk of the House
Office of Public Records	Legislative Resource Center
232 Hart Senate Office Building	B106 Cannon House Office Building
Washington, D.C. 20510	Washington, D.C. 20515
(202) 224-0758	(202) 226-5200

Registration discloses general information, a description of the registrant's business or activities (e.g., social welfare organization), and a list of employees who act or are expected to act as lobbyists (an employee is not considered to be a lobbyist if he/she spends less than 20% of his or her time lobbying). Also disclosed are an indication of the issues to be lobbied (selected from a list of 74 general categories, such as "welfare"), and the specific issues to be addressed, including specific bill numbers or executive branch activities.

Online forms and instructions can be found at: *http://lobbyingdisclosure.house.gov/*

Expense Reporting Requirements

Registered organizations are required to file four quarterly reports each year. The reports are due 20 days after each quarter. One copy each must be filed with the Secretary of the Senate and the Clerk of the House. Organizations employing lobbyists must report whether their lobbying expenses were less than $5,000, or more. If lobbying expenses were more than $5,000, the organization must make a good-faith estimate, rounded to the nearest $10,000, of its lobbying expenses during the reporting period.

Organizations must also file a separate sheet on each general lobbying issue that was engaged, specific information about each bill or executive branch action, houses of Congress and federal agencies contacted, and the name and title of each employee who acted as a lobbyist. Online forms and instructions can be found at: *http://lobbyingdisclosure.house.gov/lda.html*

State requirements

Each state has its own registration and reporting requirements for lobbyists and organizations that employee them. The requirements for each state may be found on the Web sites for each state government.

Effective Strategies for Lobbying and Advocacy

- Get to Know Legislators—Give them the information they need to help the nonprofit organization meet its objectives.

- Identify Key Contacts—Survey the organization's network to discover who has a personal or professional relationship with key public policy decision-makers, and who contributes to political campaigns.

- Target Decision-Makers—Pay special attention to legislative leadership, the majority and minority chairpersons of relevant committees, and their staffs.

- Use Local Resources—Identify constituents connected to the organization, such as board members and organization members. Match them with their legislators, and assign them to meet with these particular legislators on issues of concern to the organization.

- Schedule Lobby Days—Many nonprofit organizations and other groups schedule a Capitol Lobby Day. Such events typically include a briefing on an important pending issue by the organization's executive director, a rally and/or press conference in the Capitol, scheduled office visits to local legislators and legislative leadership, and a closing session conducted by the organization's staff to exchange information gleaned from those visited.

- Schedule Press Conferences—Nongovernmental organizations can hold press conferences in the Capitol or on the steps of the Capitol.

- Circulate Petitions—Although viewed as one of the least effective forms of lobbying, the presentation to a legislator or government official of a petition signed by thousands of persons is a worthy "photo opportunity" and may get some coverage.

- Present Awards—Many nonprofit organizations present a "Legislator of the Year" or similar award to recognize key legislators for their interest in the issues of concern to that nonprofit. These awards further cement a positive relationship and ensure continued access to that legislator.

- Arrange Speaking Engagements—Most legislators are delighted to receive invitations to address groups of their constituents. Such gatherings provide opportunities to educate the legislator on issues of interest to the organization through questions and comments from the audience.

- Provide Contributions—Organizations exempt under Section 501(c)(3) may not establish political action committees. Other exempt organizations may do so and pay administrative and other indirect expenses of their affiliated Political Action Committees (PACs). However, money is still considered to be the mother's milk of politics. Although corporations, by law, cannot make contributions themselves, individuals and corporation-affiliated PACs may and do. Those who make contributions find their access to public policy makers is vastly improved. As a general rule, the more an organization's activities are perceived to be in the public interest, the less need there is to rely on making political contributions to develop access and to deliver the organization's message. The third edition of a publication of the Alliance for Justice, *The Connection: Strategies for Creating and Operating 501(c)(3)s, 501(c)(4)s, and PACs* is available for free download at: *http://www.issuelab.org/click/download2/connection_strategies_for_creating_and_operating_501c3s_501c4s_and_political_organizations_-_third_edition_the*. It is an excellent guide for charities and social welfare organizations that want to influence the political process without violating federal laws and regulations.

- Request Public Hearings—Public hearings held by a legislative committee provide an opportunity for media coverage, a forum for an organization's point of view, and a way to galvanize support for an issue. Having an organization's clients fill a hearing room sends a clear message to the committee members and staff. Although it is true that the suggestion by a committee chairperson to hold hearings on an issue may be a strategy to delay or kill a bill, public hearings can nevertheless be utilized by the organization to focus attention on an issue. A hearing can generate public and media support. It can provide a forum for improving the proposal, thereby minimizing opposition to the legislation.

501(h) Election

The U.S. Congress in 1976 enacted a law that expanded the rights of nonprofits to lobby. However, it was not until August 30, 1990, that the IRS and Treasury Department promulgated final regulations to implement this law. In the preceding 14 years, there had been a pitched battle between nonprofits and the Congress. Nonprofits fought diligently to preserve their rights to lobby under the Constitution and the 1976 law. Some in the executive branch also sought to deny those rights. The principal issue is the definition of the term "substantial," since the law prohibits 501(c)(3) nonprofits from carrying on "substantial" lobbying activities.

The regulations permit electing organizations to spend on lobbying, on a sliding scale, up to 20% of their first $500,000 in expenditures, and up to 5% of expenditures over $1.5 million—with a $1 million ceiling in each year. Organizations can spend no more than a quarter of their lobbying expenses on grass-roots lobbying (communications to the general public that attempt to influence legislation through changing public opinion).

These regulations exclude certain expenditures from lobbying, including—

1. Communications to members of an organization that brief them on provisions of legislation, but do not urge that they take action to change those provisions.

2. Communications to legislators on issues that directly affect the organization's own existence, such as changes to tax-exempt status law, or lobbying law.

Of major importance to nonprofits, the organization would no longer be subject to the "death penalty" (i.e., the total revoking of their tax-exempt status) for violations. There is a system of sanctions replacing that.

All 501(c)(3)s must report the amount they spend on lobbying on their Form 990 annual federal tax returns.

IRS Regulations on Lobbying

The August 1990 regulations of the Treasury Department with respect to lobbying are quite complicated. An excellent 42-page publication, *Being a Player: A Guide to the IRS Lobbying Regulations for Advocacy Charities,* is available from The Alliance for Justice *(http://www.afj.org; 202-822-6070)*. The guide explains in clear and precise terms what is permitted under these regulations, and includes many sample forms and worksheets. The publication, last updated in 2011, can be downloaded free at: *http://bolderadvocacy.org/resource/being-a-player-a-guide-to-the-irs-lobbying-regulations-for-advocacy-charities*

Contacts With Legislators

1. When visiting a legislator—

- Make an appointment, if at all possible.

- Arrive promptly, be warm and courteous, smile, and speak for five minutes or less on a single issue.

- Do not threaten or exaggerate your political influence. If you are really influential, the legislator will already know.

- Listen carefully to the legislator's response and take notes; be polite, but keep the legislator on the subject.

- Leave the legislator with something in writing on the issue, if possible.

- Request that the legislator do something to respond to the organization's position—vote in a specific way, take action on a problem, or send a letter to legislative leadership requesting action.

- Follow up the meeting with a thank-you note, taking advantage of this second opportunity to reinforce the organization's views and remind the legislator of the action requested.

- Do not feel slighted if referred to a staff member—legislators often have last-minute important meetings or unscheduled votes. Staff members are valued advisors who, in some cases, have as much or more influence than the legislator in the process and may have more time to help.

2. When writing to or e-mailing a legislator—

- Restrict letters/e-mail to one issue; be brief and concise.

- Clearly indicate the issue of concern, the organization's position on it, and the bill number, if known.

- Write the letter/e-mail in a manner that will require a written response and include a return address.

- Use facts to support positions, and explain how the issue affects the organization, its members, and the community.

- If a letter, use professional letterhead, if appropriate.

- Try not to indicate that the letter or e-mail, as the case may be, may be a form letter/e-mail sent to scores of other legislators.

- Make the letter/e-mail positive—do not threaten the loss of votes or campaign contributions.

- Follow up after the vote on the issue to indicate to the legislator that the organization is following his or her actions with interest and that it appreciated or was disappointed by that vote.

3. When telephoning a legislator—

- Speak clearly and slowly.

- Make sure that callers identify themselves in a way that will permit the legislator to reach them or the organization by letter or telephone.

- Follow the guidelines listed above for writing and visiting that are equally appropriate for telephoning.

Discussion Questions

1. Why do you think some members of Congress seek to muzzle the voices of the nonprofit sector by trying to pass restrictions on advocacy by these organizations?

2. Some states require registered lobbyists to wear badges indicating registration status. Why do you think this is required, and do you feel this policy is justified?

3. Discuss the pros and cons of nonprofit organizations having their own in-house lobbyists rather than contracting out lobbying responsibilities to an outside firm that represents other clients.

4. What are some of the strategies nonprofits use to convince a public official to change his or her vote on a public policy issue? Discuss the effectiveness of each of these strategies.

5. Should nonprofit executives make personal political contributions and volunteer on campaigns, or simply not participate in the electoral process?

Activities

1. Write a letter to a public official about a public policy issue of interest to you, and share with the class the response you receive.

2. Invite the lobbyist for your school to meet with the class and discuss his or her role, what issues he or she is lobbying currently, the strategies used to influence actions by public officials, and the general issue of advocacy on behalf of nonprofit organizations.

3. Research the lobbying laws in your state and discuss how you would change them to make them more fair and/or more responsive to the public's right to know how private funds are being used to influence public policy.

4. Invite an elected official to meet with your class to explain the importance of advocacy, how the nonprofit sector is involved in advocacy, what issues are on the agenda that affect the nonprofit sector, and what are the best ways to influence the public policy process in support of the nonprofit sector.

5. Research past and current legislative proposals to restrict the ability of nonprofit organizations to lobby, such as amendments sponsored by Rep. Ernest Istook (R-OK).

Tips for Practitioners

1. Those who expect to spend a substantial amount of time in legislators' offices should register as lobbyists, even if they feel the law may not require them to do so. The judge of whether a person doing advocacy is in compliance with lobbying laws will not be that advocate, but rather a regulator.

2. Comply with all state and federal reporting requirements.

3. If the nonprofit corporation is a human service provider, invite local legislators to tour the facility and observe the services being provided.

4. If the organization has members, invite local legislators to speak to the membership.

5. Encourage members to make individual contributions (but, of course, not to anyone specific). It is good advice not to get involved in partisan politics, particularly if the organization has 501(c)(3) status. Those who do choose to participate in partisan politics should be scrupulous about separating personal political activities from those of the organization and not using organizational resources for partisan political activities.

6. Consider an e-mail advocacy campaign. Many organization members are more comfortable sending an e-mail to a legislator based on a sample provided on an organizational Web site than writing a conventional letter.

Online Resources to Explore

Institute for Sustainable Communities
http://www.iscvt.org/

Center for Lobbying in the Public Interest
http://www.clpi.org/

Independent Sector
http://www.independentsector.org

Center for Effective Government (formerly OMBWatch)
http://www.foreffectivegov.org/npadv

The Virtual Activist's Virtual Activist 2.0 Training Guide
http://www.netaction.org/training/

For Further Reading

Arons, D. & Berry, J. (2005). *A voice for nonprofits.* Washington, DC: Brookings Institution Press.

Avner, M., Wise, J., Narabrook, J. & Fox, J. (2013). *Lobbying and advocacy handbook for nonprofit organizations: Shaping public policy at the state and local level.* (Second Ed.). St. Paul, MN: Fieldstone Alliance.

deKieffer, D. (2007). *The citizen's guide to lobbying Congress.* Chicago, IL: Chicago Review Press.

Gelek, D. (2008). *Lobbying and advocacy: Winning strategies, resources, recommendations, ethics and ongoing compliance for lobbyists and Washington advocates.* Alexandria, VA: TheCapitol.Net, Inc.

Guyer, R. L., & Guyer, L. K. (1999). *Guide to state legislative lobbying.* (Third Ed.).Gainesville, FL: Engineering the Law.

Maskell, J. (2009). *Lobbyist registration and compliance handbook: The Honest Leadership and Open Government Act of 2007 (HLOGA) and the Lobbying Disclosure Act Guide.* Alexandria, VA: TheCapitol.Net, Inc.

Pekkanen, R., Smith, S. & Tsujinaka, Y. (2014). *Nonprofits and advocacy: Engaging community and government in an era of retrenchment.* Baltimore, MD: Johns Hopkins Univ. Press.

Smucker, B. (1999). *The nonprofit lobbying guide: Advocating your cause—and getting results.* (2nd Ed.). San Francisco: Jossey-Bass.

Chapter 15
The Internet for Nonprofits

Synopsis: Nonprofits have an exciting, versatile resource in the Internet. Once connected, organizations can share information inexpensively and quickly, and they can use search engines to find information. Nonprofits can set up their own Web sites, utilize social media to have their messages go viral, and generate donations and other revenue.

Introduction

In 2013, the ALS Association raised a total of $19.4 million for its programs to provide research and education about amyotrophic lateral sclerosis, also known as Lou Gehrig's disease. Amyotrophic lateral sclerosis (ALS) is a progressive neurodegenerative disease that affects nerve cells in the brain and the spinal cord of about 30,000 Americans at any one time, according to the home page of the organization *(http://www.alsa.org)*. This is a much smaller number of people than those affected by "high profile" diseases such as heart disease, which is the cause of death of one in four Americans, or cancer, which kills almost 600,000 annually.

Almost three million new donors contributed to the organization in August 2014 alone, providing more than $100 million, compared to about $2.5 million the ALS Association raised during the same month the previous year. An online fundraising campaign called the "ice bucket challenge" went viral, perhaps fundamentally changing the way charities view the power of the Internet. Interesting enough, the campaign to pour a bucket of ice water over one's head or make a donation to the ALS Association came from a single individual from outside of the organization. The rest is history. Hundreds of thousands of individuals participated in the challenge, posted videos of their participation on Facebook and other social media sites, challenged their friends to do the same, and also made a donation to the ALS Association. Some chose to simply make a donation.

Among the participants were hundreds of celebrities. Many donors were young people who may never have contributed before to an established national charity. And even those who took the challenge and did so to avoid the peer pressure to make a financial contribution participated in encouraging others to participate in the campaign, a contribution in itself, which also served to raise awareness about ALS.

The recent explosion of useful resources for nonprofits on the Internet is perhaps the most exciting positive development for this sector in years. Twenty years ago, many nonprofit leaders had barely heard of the Internet. Now, it is an almost essential part of our daily lives. Our children have grown up with it. And today, nonprofit organizations are not only connected, but have their own Web sites, pages on Facebook, podcasts, blogs, and wikis. They tweet the latest happenings on Twitter, hold virtual board meetings using Skype, and create online communities to build organizational support.

Practical Applications of the Internet

Among the most popular services and applications of the Internet for nonprofits are e-mail, text messaging, electronic mailing lists, e-newsletters, videoconferencing, chat, blogs, social media, podcasts, and wikis.

E-mail: Nonprofit organizations typically use e-mail as their prime method of communication with their stakeholders. Many organizations use it for direct fundraising appeals, although using e-mail to communicate with those who have no previous relationship to the organization is frowned upon. Because e-mail has become so important, nonprofit organizations should make every effort to obtain and update the e-mail addresses of their stakeholders. Recipients should be given an opportunity to request that they be removed from the organization's mailings, often facilitated by an "unsubscribe" procedure at the bottom of each e-mail.

Text Messaging: Texting is becoming the preferred mode of communication, particularly among the millennial generation. Text messages typically have more impact than e-mail. However, they are annoying to many recipients (and even expensive) if/when they are paying for each message sent and received. Organizations can ask their supporters to enter a code into their cell phones with a text message, authorizing a small donation that appears on the donors' telephone bills. Utilizing this technique, the American Red Cross raised more than $30 million during a 10-day period for relief efforts in Haiti following the January 2010 earthquake.

Electronic Mailing Lists: Mailing lists provide a way to have a discussion or distribute information to a group using e-mail. Users who subscribe to a particular list may send a message on a topic of interest to that list. That message is automatically distributed as e-mail to every subscriber on the list. Some mailing lists generate hundreds of messages a day. Others publish one or less each day. Subscriptions to almost all electronic mailing lists are free. To subscribe to a mailing list, the subscriber generally sends an e-mail message to an administrative address, or simply clicks on a button on the Web site of the organization that offers subscriptions. See *http://www.arnova.org/?section=sections&subsection=listserve #Join* for instructions on how to join the mailing list of the Association for Research on Nonprofit Organizations and Voluntary Action (ARNOVA).

E-Newsletters. These are the electronic version of an organizational newsletter, going out on a regular schedule by e-mail to stakeholders who subscribe to them. Among what one might find in a nonprofit e-newsletter might be information about an upcoming conference, changes in staff, new features of the organization's Web site, full-text articles written by staff, links to articles of interest that can be found on the Web, and upcoming programs sponsored by the organization.

Videoconferencing: Using free applications such as Skype or Google Hangouts, nonprofits are engaging their stakeholders in virtual meetings in which the participants can see each other and share documents. Or they can pay for commercial alternatives that include more bells and whistles, such as GoToMeeting, *(http://www.gotomeeting.com),* which can accommodate up to 100 participants. Most applications feature the ability to record the session for later use.

Chat: Using chat software, you can have a text-based, real-time conversation with an individual or a group. What you type and the response of the other participant(s) appears on your screen simultaneously. It is possible to have a nonprofit board meeting entirely by chat. Most commercial providers provide for privacy among those who participate. Many Web sites, including those of nonprofit groups, use software, often provided free by commercial providers, that permits visitors to participate in chats related to their mission. In return for the use of free chat rooms, the visitors often see advertising messages controlled by the software provider, not under the control of the organization that is sponsoring the individual chat room. For an example, see the chat site sponsored by the American Cancer Society's Cancer Survivor Network at: *http://csn.cancer.org/about*

Blogs: Short for "Web Log," a blog is a Web site that consists of a frequently updated journal or diary by an individual. The style of commentary is typically informal and personal—although in the years since the term "blog" was first used (in the late 1990s), these sites have become more sophisticated, with some of them resembling online magazines.

Blog entries are typically in reverse chronological order—the latest entry is placed on top. Each dated entry has its own Web address (called a "permalink"), making it easy for other blogs and search engines to link to any particular entry (rather than to the entire blog). Most allow comments, and many have an RSS (Really Simple Syndication) feed, a software application that lets viewers subscribe to blog updates by using an RSS reader or receiving the feed by e-mail.

For the nonprofit community, blogs provide another mechanism to improve interaction with an organization's stakeholders, enhance the bond with donors, and create a dialogue with outsiders while giving them an inside look at what the organization is trying to accomplish. The technical tools are easily accessible. Blogs can be created free with Blogger, Word Press, and similar tools. Blogs serve many purposes for a nonprofit organization. If they are interesting or provocative, they draw readership—not only from the general public, but from the media and political leadership, as well. And these site visits often translate to new and more productive current donors, volunteers, advocates, and friends. Bloggers need to vigilantly monitor all comments, routinely deleting "comment spam" and inappropriate comments. You can find an example of a nonprofit blog at: *http://blog.redcross.org/#sthash.KRmu7qZH.dpbs* (American Red Cross).

Social Media: Today, with more than a billion accounts on Facebook alone, almost everyone with access to a computer either has one or more of these accounts, or has at least visited one or more social networking sites. Nonprofit organizations have recognized that online social networking can be an effective technique to drive traffic to its Web site and blog, raise awareness of its mission and programs, encourage people to take action (such as participating in advocacy efforts), find volunteers, market their services, increase donations, and enhance already-created relationships they have with their stakeholders. Although initial results of using these sites to generate donations have been disappointing, so was online fundraising in general when organizations first began using it. Technology that promotes micro donations has improved substantially since then, as the Obama for President campaign proved in 2008. We are in the midst of a major change in culture, and sites such as YouTube, Twitter, Pinterist, LinkedIn, Instagram, and Facebook are changing the landscape. Nonprofit organizations are often slow to respond to such culture shifts, but those that proactively take advantage of new technology can benefit. The intent of these sites is to provide links that help connect individuals and groups to others that share some common interest or objective. And, by and large, they do this with unqualified success. Evidence of this is the fact that a search of jobs using the search term "social media" on the Idealist.com site I conducted in August 2014 identified more than 1,700 nonprofit organization job listings that included job duties involving social media management tasks. For some ideas on how to creatively use social media for fundraising, volunteer recruitment, and building cause awareness, download BluePrint Creative Group's white paper at: http://www.blueprintcreativegroup.com/a-case-study-of-how-nonprofits-are-using-social-media-to-build-cause-awareness-and-fundraise

Podcasts: Podcasting refers to the creation of audio files that can be uploaded to the Internet and listened to at a later time by subscribers who are informed when the audio program is available. These files are typically in MP3 format and 5 to 60 minutes in duration, making them suitable for hearing on the subscriber's computer or personal audio player, such as an iPOD or other MP3 player. Podcasting permits the organization's staff to be the producer of a radio show (or TV show) rather than a third party, and gives them the ability to reach their target audience when they are most perceptive to hearing what the organization wants to say about itself. What makes podcasting an incredibly powerful means of communication is that anyone in the world with an Internet connection can listen to podcasts at any time he or she chooses. This compares to traditional TV and radio shows, which are on at a specific time and require action on the part of the viewer/listener to first know that there is a program of interest and then take steps to either listen to it in real time or record it. Usually, there is no advertising to listen to, although there is no law against a charity making a subtle plea for donations to support its mission. The broadcaster's costs for equipment are negligible, and the subscriber pays nothing for the service. For examples of a nonprofit organization podcast, see: *http://www.podfeed.net/tags/Salvation%20Army* (Salvation Army).

Wikis: A wiki is a feature of a Web site that facilitates collaboration and participatory contribution among its users, who can add, remove, or edit content quickly and easily. Perhaps the best known example is Wikipedia, which is supported by the nonprofit Wikipedia Foundation (*http://wikimediafoundation.org/wiki/Home*). Following Hurricane Katrina, a wiki was established permitting the public to create a master database of messages from those who were seeking information about missing friends and relatives, consolidating the message boards of dozens of those established by media outlets, disaster relief organizations, and others. Hundreds of volunteers, including the author of this book, participated in the project and were delighted by the convenient opportunity to respond to the tragedy in a more tangible way than by simply donating money. Wikis can be public or password-protected, and software supporting this feature can be accessed for free or at minimal cost. For more details, read the *Exploring the World of Wikis* article at Digital Divide Network: *http://www.digitaldivide.net/articles/view.php?ArticleID=605*

Mobile Applications

Wireless phones are almost universal in this country, and nearly everyone has, or will soon have, a "smart" phone, such as an iPhone, Android, or BlackBerry, that can easily access the Web and customized applications ("apps"). At a minimum, nonprofits are finding it essential to develop mobile-friendly versions of their Web sites to facilitate access by those who depend on their smartphones. Many major nonprofits are recognizing that they can develop apps themselves that will assist them in their marketing efforts. Sophisticated, custom mobile apps currently cost about $5,000-$10,000 to develop, but this amount is spiraling downward quickly. Simple smartphone apps can now be created for a few hundred dollars using free templates. Looking for where to start? See a tutorial, updated in 2012, at: *http://www.smashingmagazine.com/2009/08/11/how-to-create-your-first-iphone-application/*

For example, the American Museum of Natural History has developed a free app to assist visitors exploring its collections. The Detroit Zoo's iPhone app, which sells for $1.95, tracks a visitor's location within the zoo and shares information about attractions nearby, can create a personalized schedule to make one's visit more efficient, and provides a photo gallery.

The Web

The sophistication of Web sites has evolved substantially in just the last few years. Organizations that started in the 1990s with static billboards now have interactive, dynamic sites.

The number of Web sites grew from just a single one in 1991 to a billion in 2014 *(http://www.internetlivestats.com/total-number-of-websites/)*. In 2008, Google engineers announced that they had achieved a milestone: access to more than one trillion unique Web pages (see: *http://googleblog.blogspot.com/2008/07/we-knew-web-was-big.html*), and this is only a fraction of those available.

Among the types of information that can be found on typical Web sites of nonprofits are:

> breaking news, blogs, newsletter, annual report, press releases, brochure, how to contribute or volunteer, financial data, action alerts, job openings, information about board and staff members, publications, upcoming conferences and seminars, product catalogs and order forms, a link to e-mail the organization, links to connect to the organization via social media, and links to other organizations and government-based sites related to the mission and purpose of the organization.

Domain Names

A domain name is the part of the e-mail address after the "@" sign or the part of a Web address after the "www." For example, the personal e-mail address of the author of this book is: gary.grobman@paonline.com. Paonline is his Internet Service Provider (ISP), and "com" indicates that it is a commercial provider. *Paonline.com* is the domain name. If you are just starting to develop a Web site for your organization, you will need to choose and register a domain name. Most organizations prefer to use "my organization.org" where "my organization" is the name of the organization. Go to a registrar's site (such as *register.com* or *networksolutions.com*) and follow the directions, which include steps to make sure the name you want is available.

Domain Extensions (also known as gTLDs)

You have registered yourorganization.org. Should you register domains with other generic top level domains (gTLDs—the letters to the right of the dot in the address), as well, such as yourorganization.com and yourorganization.info? One advantage of doing so is that anyone looking on the Web for "yourorganization" will be more likely to find you. Another is that it prevents someone else from setting up a Web site using your organization's name. Until recently, gTLDs were limited. In July 2014, scores of new top-level domain extensions became available. Many experts have suggested that this will cause more confusion, as for example, nonprofits may have to choose among several hundred possible extensions that have their name to the left of the dot. Registering for all of these is likely to be cost-prohibitive for most nonprofit organizations. For a list of new top-level domains either available now or likely to be soon, see: *http://www.newgtldsite.com/new-gtld-list/*

Developing Your Web Site

There are thousands of commercial services offering to design and administer Web sites for a fee. With a minimum of technical background, you can do it yourself. The days when you needed to learn the HTML language and hand-code your Web site are long gone. Open source content management systems, such as Joomla and WordPress, are available free of charge and allow you to use templates to make your site look professional.

Simply having a Web site is clearly not enough to bring your organization fame, friends, and fortune. The "build it and they will come" philosophy may work well for Hollywood baseball movies, but you need to take proactive steps to build a base of loyal visitors and keep them returning. See Chapter 9 for some ideas on how to do this.

Nonprofit E-Commerce

The term *e-commerce* refers to business that is conducted electronically. It includes the marketing of goods and services, using the Internet to join an organization or subscribe to a publication, and automated customer service.

The business models and strategies used by for-profits can be adapted by nonprofits to generate revenue that will finance the expansion of nonprofit organizational programs and activities. At the very least, these techniques make it a bit easier to raise funds and thus reduce what must be one of the leading causes of stress and burnout among nonprofit executives and staff—the constant battle to raise dollars to balance organizational budgets.

For years, charities have generated income through a variety of programs and activities, such as selling newsletter subscriptions and other publications, collecting fees at conferences and workshops, operating thrift shops, conducting flea markets and running races, renting mailing lists, having auctions, scheduling fundraising dinners, and selling group outings to sporting events or theater performances.

The Web has made all of this easier, at least for many organizations, in two significant ways. First, it has provided organizations with a way to reach almost everyone, and to do this quickly and inexpensively. Using a combination of strategies, such as conventional mail, telephone, and media advertising, along with Web site and social media posts, mailing list postings, broadcast e-mail, and Web advertising, an organization can reach its target market and expand its reach. Second, using sophisticated technology, organizations can take advantage of homebound volunteers (at one end of the scale) and pricey, professional "back end" providers (at the other end of the scale) to do much of the work.

As a result of e-mail, the Web, electronic mailing lists, and social media, the velocity of business transactions has made a quantum leap. The Internet has salient advantages over conventional sales marketing, such as—

- Overall marketing and order processing costs are lower using the Web.
- Organizations can reach a global, targeted market virtually instantaneously.
- A Web-based "store" is open 24 hours/day, seven days/week, and always has free parking.
- The playing field is leveled between small organizations and those with many more resources.
- Business transactions can be consummated electronically without the need for expensive labor or intermediaries, such as brokers.
- Internet search engines and directories bring potential customers to organizations without unreasonably expensive marketing efforts.
- Customer service can be almost completely automated.
- "Back office" for-profit organizations with substantial expertise, labor, and sophisticated software will do the necessary work and make it appear to customers that the nonprofit organization is performing the work.

Build, Buy, or Rent

An organization's Web site is the most visible ingredient of its e-commerce strategy. Organizations have three basic choices in deciding which direction to go. Making the choice depends on factors such as—

- The amount of financial investment they are prepared to make
- The amount of staff time they are willing to devote to building, maintaining, and troubleshooting
- Whether they are comfortable with "off the rack" features or want a site that is state-of-the-art and custom-made
- Their comfort level with outside vendors having access to their financial transactions
- Whether they want to have complete control over their Web sites so, for example, they do not have to depend on private companies to update files when they have the time
- Whether they are comfortable with paying an outside firm based on the amount of revenue that is transacted on their sites
- The importance to them of having all visitors stay on their sites rather than being routed to a private vendor who may subject the visitor to advertising that the nonprofit organization cannot control, or may be inconsistent with the organization's values.

Build: Almost all of the tools a nonprofit needs to build a credible e-commerce site can be found by searching Google using the terms "shopping cart" or "online store." Much of the software can be downloaded for free.

Buy: If an organization is as well-heeled as the Metropolitan Museum of Art *(http://www.metmuseum.org)*, it can afford to buy the very best. From the appearance of this site, one can expect this organization's investment in hiring a private firm to custom-design a Web site will result in long-term financial dividends. This site was custom-designed by a locally-based outside firm, IconNicholson. Everything about this site is, pardon the pun, state of the art.

Rent: Application Service Providers (ASPs) advertise in the nonprofit national media about the availability of their services. In this context, renting involves purchasing services from a firm that will, for a monthly or annual fee, provide nonprofit organizations a customized, "hosted" e-commerce (and donation processing) site based on a template. The pages usually reside on the server of the ASP.

Setting Up an Online Store

If your organization sells products and services, you can enhance these sales by adding a secure online store to your organization's Web site. Before opening your store, you should consider costs, how you will handle online transactions, customer service issues, receipts and invoices, tax issues, and shipping.

Handling Online Financial Transactions

Qualifying for merchant status to accept popular credit cards such as Visa, MasterCard, American Express, and Discover is often routine. An organization typically approaches its bank to set up a merchant account. One can find hundreds, if not thousands, of financial institutions willing to establish merchant accounts on the Web. One way to find them is to search under the terms "credit cards" and "merchant accounts."

Startup fees, account maintenance fees, per transaction fees, and the bank's percentage of sales fee for processing each transaction varies by financial institution and may be negotiable.

An alternative to setting up a merchant account for credit card sales is to utilize the services of a third-party payment processor that will accept credit cards for you by using a secure, online platform. One such popular provider, PayPal *(https://www.paypal.com)*, not only provides this service but also gives access to tools that you can use to build your online store, such as shopping carts, invoices, and shipping/tracking management services. From the home page, click on "Merchant Tools" for details about these services. There are no setup fees to establish an account as a merchant. PayPal charges a fee of from 1.9% to 2.9% (depending on sales volume) plus 30 cents per transaction. There are additional fees for foreign currency transactions. More than a hundred million individuals worldwide have PayPal accounts. The company was purchased by eBay in 2002 and is quickly becoming the standard for making and receiving online payments, with $56 billion processed in 2010 (Statistic Brain, 2014).

In June 2005, PayPal established Web site Payments Pro to accept credit cards directly on your site without having a merchant account.

Customer Service

Depending on what products and services are offered, many of the issues relating to customer service will be the same for a nonprofit as for a for-profit organization. Organizations will need to have policies for, and routines for, processing returns, exchanges, refunds, and shipping.

One obvious disadvantage of shopping over the Internet is that shoppers cannot touch and feel the product, or try it on or try it out. People are more willing to make purchases over the Internet when they feel that they can return the products if they are not completely satisfied. A refunds and returns policy should be posted on your site, and it should be a more liberal policy than one would expect to find at the local mall. This is good business practice; nonprofits certainly do not want to alienate a customer who is also a donor or potential donor. Among the issues that should be addressed are:

1. Will refunds be given in cash or credit for a future purchase?
2. What is the time limit for returns?
3. Can returns be made unconditionally, or only for defective products?
4. Is there a restocking fee?
5. Must the product be returned in salable condition in the original packaging?
6. Will shipping and handling also be refunded, or only the product purchase price?
7. Will the organization pay for shipping back returns?
8. Will certain products not be returnable (such as publications, electronics, or jewelry)?

Receipts and Invoices

Products should be shipped with a receipt if pre-paid, or an invoice if payment is due. If they were not prepaid, the invoice should state the terms of payment, such as when the bill is due, and the percentage added to the bill per month for any outstanding balance. The receipt should include the name of the purchaser; the name of the organization; the description of the product(s); the price of each purchase; and the amount of tax, shipping, and handling. Generic accounting software programs such as Quickbooks, Quicken, MYOB Accounting, or Peachtree provide forms for standard invoices and receipts.

Collecting Taxes

Only the states of Alaska, Delaware, Montana, New Hampshire, and Oregon do not have a state sales and use tax. The sales tax applies to sales made within a state to a purchaser from that same state. The use tax applies to sales of products bought in one state and taken into another. The use tax is intended to be paid by the purchaser and goes to the purchaser's state treasury, although this requirement is rarely, if ever, enforced. Generally, organizations are obligated to collect sales and use taxes on sales they make to customers within their own states.

There is a general moratorium on Internet sales taxes until November 1, 2014, courtesy of enactment of the *Internet Tax Freedom Act Amendments Act of 2007. S. 743, The Marketplace Fairness Act,* with the support of the Obama Administration, passed the Senate in June 2013. It would establish a system whereby states could collect and remit sales taxes for remote sales from sellers with remote sales exceeding $1 million (See: *http://thomas.loc.gov/cgi-bin/bdquery/z?d113:SN00743:@@@L&summ2=m&)*. A House committee in June 2014 passed a bill, the *Permanent Internet Tax Freedom Act* [PITFA], to extend the moratorium permanently (Gross, 2014).

Sales taxes still must be collected for intrastate purchases in states with sales taxes, although enforcement of this requirement is spotty. Even if an organization is tax exempt, most states still require nonprofit organizations to collect sales taxes on sales they make to customers within the state.

Typically, states require organizations to obtain a sales tax license, and to transmit the collected taxes to the state using a provided form. It is advisable to check with a reputable local business organization, such as the Chamber of Commerce, to find out what the requirements are for collecting and transmitting state sales taxes in a particular state before engaging in the sale of goods and services there.

Shipping and Handling

Organizations need to decide how much they will charge for shipping and handling and display that information prominently on the site. Some shopping cart software provides for letting the customer decide how the product is to be shipped—automatically adjusting the amount for shipping and handling (such as by using a database provided by UPS or other shippers), based on how much the organization wants to add over the actual cost. They can charge a flat fee for shipping, charge by weight, charge by the number of products ordered, or provide for free shipping if the order exceeds a certain amount. Organizations should also consider policies with respect to out-of-country sales, which raise issues concerning payment, shipping, and customs duties.

Affiliate Marketing

Business models have emerged that permit nonprofit organizations to take advantage of technology and raise funds that would not have otherwise come their way. Even if your organization does not sell products or services of its own, you can generate revenue by marketing products and services of others through "affiliate" or "associate" programs.

The "affiliate" model was pioneered by Amazon.com. The Seattle-based company simply announced to the world that by placing specially coded links on your Web site, you can earn a commission on purchases of books, CDs, DVDs, videos, electronics, software, video games, toys, home improvement items, and many other products that are generated by those links.

Joining the Amazon Associates program involves visiting the Amazon.com site, clicking on the "Join Associates" link at the bottom of the home page, electronically submitting a form provided on the site (after reading and agreeing to the operating agreement), and using tools provided on the site to set up your links to Amazon.com and promote products. Each link has your Associate ID code embedded in it, so when someone buys something from Amazon.com through a link on your site, your organization gets a commission.

An effective way to take advantage of this program is to have a book review section or recommended books section on your organization's Web site. For each book mentioned, include your Amazon Associate link to that book's page on Amazon.com. For an example, see: *http://cpnl.rice.edu/book-reviews*

More than 2,000,000 Web sites have become Amazon.com associates. For nonprofits and for-profits alike, this simple, yet revolutionary, business model is generating valuable revenue without the need for any investment or exposure to risk.

Similarly, affiliate programs exist for many other online retailers and online services. Your organization can become an affiliate of eBay, Buy.com, allPosters.com, or CareerBuilder.com, for example. Typically, if a site offers an affiliate program, there will be a link for it somewhere near the bottom of the page, leading to an explanation of how to join and how the program works.

When considering whether to join an affiliate marketing program, think about how the site with which you will be affiliating fits with your organization's mission, as well as how you will incorporate the affiliate program into your own site. For example, if you are joining an affiliate program of an online bookstore (such as

Amazon.com), will you place reviews and links to carefully selected books that are in line with your mission? Or will you set up a complete store where your site's visitors can buy anything that is available in the affiliated store, encouraging your visitors to do all their shopping through your site, as a way of supporting your organization? Each of these approaches has its pros and cons.

Let's say your organization is an animal shelter. Using the first approach, you can create links to (and perhaps reviews of) books on animal care. This will keep the focus on your mission and promote products that your site's visitors are likely to be interested in. You can target these links to the visitor's interests, so a person who is reading an article about German shepherds will see a link on that page to a book on German shepherds. The conversion rate (from seeing the link to clicking on it to purchasing the item) on such links will be higher than that for random links that are unrelated to your site's content. You will need to monitor the links to make sure that they are up-to-date and the items are still available for purchase.

Using the second approach, you can build a store on your site using an automated data feed (if one is provided), and then "educate" your visitors to "support this site" by shopping there. If your visitors get in the habit of going through your site to make their purchases, you can do well with this method. They may buy animal care books, or they may buy office products, or both. Either way, you will earn the commission. However, keep in mind that you do not have complete control over the items that are shown through the data feed, and some items may not be consistent with the mission or character of your organization.

Advertising

Another way you can generate revenue from your organization's Web site is to allow advertisements to be placed on it. The quickest and easiest way to earn money through advertising is to join Google AdSense or a similar program. Once you join, you will be able to log in to Google's AdSense site and generate HTML code to put on your site. Then ads will begin to appear on your site that correspond with key words in the content of your site. Google will send you a monthly check or automatic deposit for a portion of the advertising revenue from these ads.

One downside to this is that you do not have complete control over the content of the ads that appear on your site. You can filter the ads to a certain extent, but it will take some staff or volunteer time to monitor the ads to make sure they are appropriate.

Instead of or in addition to this approach, your organization may decide to sell classified and/or banner advertising directly on your site. You will need to develop a policy stating what types of ads you will accept, your advertising rates, and so forth. And you will need to develop a "media kit" telling advertisers the benefits to them of advertising on your site, the amount of traffic the site experiences, the procedure for placing an ad, technical specifications, and how to make payment. If your site is a popular one that is getting a significant amount of traffic in your niche, this can be an excellent way to use your site to generate revenue.

Security and Privacy

Even putting e-commerce transactions aside, nonprofit organizations have many reasons to protect the security and privacy of the computer files they generate and the communications they send over the Internet. Human service organizations, for example, routinely use client files that, if disclosed in an unauthorized manner, could cause irreparable harm to their clients and result in lawsuits.

E-mail exchanges may involve sensitive personnel matters or contract negotiations with unions and other entities. Even if nothing sensitive is discussed in a file or e-mail message, an organization still does not want any prying person, within the organization or outside of it, to be able to browse through its business.

SSL and other Encryption Technology

Virtually every survey on Internet security has demonstrated the pervasive fear of providing credit card numbers over the Internet. The concern that unscrupulous merchants (or those who pretend to be merchants) will use the credit card information is mostly unfounded; even if this happened (and it does occasionally), there are limits on the amount of loss the consumer sustains (typically $50), and there is no exposure to loss if the problem is reported promptly.

The principal concern tends to be that hackers will tap into the transaction and steal the credit card data. Recent high-profile hacking incidents involving otherwise trusted for-profit retailers have made the front pages and have made many individuals wary of sharing valuable and personal data over the Internet. Considerable effort has gone into making financial transactions over the Internet safe by encrypting (that is, disguising) the data so that only the intended sender and receiver can read it.

Although there are several protocols for encryption, the industry standard for e-commerce has become Secure Sockets Layer, or SSL. SSL was created by Netscape and is a feature of the company's Web browser software. The Netscape program uses what's known as a public and private key system and a digital certificate.

Without having both the public and private keys, a message that is encrypted looks like gobbledygook. Each person has his or her own private key, which is kept very secret, and a public key, which is shared with others.

Certification/Authentication

Organizations that are serious about e-commerce should obtain an SSL certificate from a certifying authority to assure purchasers that they are who they say they are. A purchaser can see a lock icon or other indicator on his or her browser that authenticates encryption software if the organization has one of these certificates.

Many people will refuse to send their credit card information over the Internet unless the organization has a valid certificate. Server certificates are available commercially from many different companies, and the cost varies. Some free certificates are available, but there may be problems using free versions on some browsers and these are best used for testing purposes only.

The most widely-used certificate authority in the United States is Symantec *(http://www.symantec.com)*. ComodoGroup *(http://www.comodo.com)*, GoDaddy *(http://www.godaddy.com)*, and GlobalSign *(http://www.globalsign.com)* are among its competitors. One recurring problem is that the certificates may not work on all browsers, so make sure to inquire about this information.

Protection of Customer Data

Organizations can have all of the sophisticated encryption systems in place, but it would not do any good if employees keep the printouts on their desks or put them in an accessible file on their computers. Employees should take reasonable precautions to keep all customer data protected.

Firewalls

A firewall is a type of Internet security software that limits access to Web sites, allowing approved traffic in and out through a secure gateway. Firewalls can be downloaded for free (for example, find one at: *http://pfsense.com)* or obtained for thousands of dollars. See *http://www.interhack.net/pubs/fwfaq/* for a complete guide to firewalls.

Privacy Policies

Many commercial Web sites address privacy concerns by having a privacy policy posted online. The policy generally includes—

1. What information will be collected on the site.

2. What information will be shared with others, and under what circumstances. For example, many organizations sell or rent their mailing lists.

3. What information will not be shared with others. For example, obtaining a telephone number is helpful in the event of a problem with a customer's

transaction. Although many business organizations will request the telephone number for that purpose, they will keep the customer's telephone number confidential.

4. What customers can do to keep their name, mailing address, and e-mail address confidential. This may entail simply clicking a box on an electronic form.

TRUSTe is an organization established to set up privacy standards and to provide sanctions against participants who violate the standards. Web sites that meet TRUSTe's strict privacy standards in the areas of notice, choice, access, and security and submit to TRUSTe's oversight program may display the organization's seal for a fee. This has become the Web privacy equivalent of the "Good Housekeeping Seal of Approval."

Cookies

One feature of the Internet that has contributed to fears about privacy violation is the cookie, a feature created by Netscape as part of its browser. Cookies are ASCII files (plain text) that can be created and accessed by a Web site visited by the browser. The file is stored in the browser directory, so using another browser results in the cookie not being readable by the originating Web site.

Cookies can be deleted, or the feature in the browser that creates them can be disabled. The benefit of the feature is that the cookie file lets the site being visited know something about the visitor and the visitor's interests by accessing it and permits the site to provide custom-designed information based on the cookie. Having a cookie can save a lot of time and keystrokes, because the site will "recognize" the visitor as a repeat visitor and "remember" what was done on previous visits. The downside is that the visitor may not wish to share this information.

Charity Portals

Scores of for-profit and nonprofit dot-com companies have sprouted up, promising to take donations over the Internet by credit card, and funneling the donation—sometimes after deducting an administrative fee—to the charity. For charities that receive an unsolicited check in the mail from one of these portal companies, this is a windfall. For the donor, using a charity portal can be convenient and often provides anonymity, if requested.

The donor can use the site search engine to find a suitable charity, and there is often other content on the portal site to influence donation decisions. The administrative fee pays the bills and provides a profit to the service provider who runs the portal. Some make money by selling advertising on their sites. Others charge charities to be listed.

Some of these portals may not be legitimate. Many others are, but it is difficult to tell simply by visiting the Web site.

For many charities, being listed on these portals is a way to publicize the existence of the organization and the importance of its mission, even if donations received through participation are minimal. For others, being associated with a firm that takes a commission on donations is unacceptable. According to a report that appeared in *The Chronicle of Philanthropy,* the World Wildlife Fund sent "cease and desist" letters threatening to take legal action if the sites did not remove its name from the list of organizations eligible to receive donations.

The Internal Revenue Service has raised questions about whether donations made through charity portals can be deductible for federal income tax purposes. Many are not likely to survive, since it takes a lot of marketing capital to draw people to the site to donate. In general, a site that requires charities to pay any kind of up-front fee is likely to be a scam.

How all of this will shake out is anybody's guess, but as more and more charities use their own Web sites to routinely accept donations by secure credit card forms, donations made through portals are likely to be a small slice of the online donation pie.

Perhaps the leading charity portal is Network For Good *(http://www1.networkforgood.org/),* founded by America Online, AOL-Time Warner Foundation, Cisco Systems, the Cisco Foundation, and other cooperating charities. Its Web site boasts that it has distributed more than $1 billion in donations so far to more than 100,000 charities, as of July 2014.

Online Shopping Malls

For-profit dot-coms have established agreements with national retailers willing to offer discounts to online shoppers. These brokers will sign up charitable organizations for the purpose of driving traffic to the Web site of the retailers. Typically, the shoppers receive the same discount when they visit the retailer via the online shopping mall, and a percentage of the purchase is split between the charity and the broker. The charity encourages its stakeholders to shop at the online shopping mall by placing a link on its Web site. To find links to these sites, Google "charity shopping malls" or use the Yahoo Directory *(http://dir.yahoo.com)* and follow this path:

Directory > Business and Economy > Shopping and Services > Retailers > Virtual Malls > Charity and Fundraising Malls

Charity Auctions

The Internet provides many advantages if an organization has goods and services to auction off, particularly those obtained from celebrities. Many people will be interested in what an organization has to offer, even if they have never heard of the organization or do not care about its mission, if the goods and services are attractive.

An almost infinite number of items can be offered, and the auction can be conducted 24 hours each day year-round with the participation of people down the street or on the other side of the world. Innovative software makes the process relatively easy, and there are Web sites that help organizations seeking to harness this strategy. To find links to these sites, Google "charity auctions" or use the Yahoo Directory *(http://www.yahoo.com)* and follow this path:

Directory > Business and Economy > Shopping and Services > Auctions > Charity

One application service provider that is gaining a reputation as the leader in online charity auctions is PayPal Giving Fund, which changed its name from Missionfish *(https://www.paypalgivingfund.org/index.html).* Missionfish, formed in 2000, was a program of the Points of Light Foundation. Charities can register and run a charity auction using the tools on this site in the same way that members of the public do.

In November 2003, Missionfish launched eBay Giving Works, a program that permits hundreds of millions of eBay users to donate from 10-100% of their proceeds from eBay sales to a favorite 501(c)(3) organization. As of July 2014, this site had raised more than $389 million for U.S. charities. The charity must register to be eligible to receive these donations, but registration is free. According to the Web site, more than 21,860 nonprofits have registered as of July 2014.

Participating charities have online tools to review the types of goods being auctioned. Why is this a useful feature? As one Missionfish press release pointed out, a charity that is dedicated to the protection of animals would not want to be the beneficiary of an auction of fur coats! A charity benefits not only from the donation, but also from the exposure of having its name listed at the auction site. There are administrative fees involved for processing, but it is possible for a charity to encourage its stakeholders to participate in this form of auction, which requires no work for the charity other than cashing the donations.

Online Communities

An online community is any Web site or application that attracts people who have something in common, and allows them to contribute to content or discussions at the site. The types of services that are typically available are real time chat, blogs, forums or message boards, member directories, instant messaging, job/career information, shopping, and news and information. What members of the site have in common can be anything: their age, their social status, their profession, their religion, their politics, some health concern, or interest in a particular public policy issue.

What distinguishes online communities from other Web sites is that much of the content is contributed by visitors. This content may be moderated by the Web site host, although in many cases, it is not.

Challenges of Online Communities

1. Creating and maintaining an online community requires substantial time and effort.

2. Some visitors post inappropriate content, such as putting slanderous or libelous messages on the message board, posting commercial messages, violating confidentiality, or infringing on a copyright.

3. Some words used in real-time posting may be offensive, requiring the use of filtering software. It is difficult to choose which words to ban.

4. Online communities need an effective Code of Conduct.

Even when an online community is free, most require members to register and to select a user name and password. Doing so ensures that the organization has at least minimal control and can deny access to those who consistently violate the site's Code of Conduct. There are also marketing reasons to have a password-protected site, such as having access to information about those who visit.

Online communities with powerful features can be created using third-party services such as those available at *http://www.ning.com*. But more and more, nonprofits are taking advantage of the opportunity to build free online communities through social media, such as Facebook, Twitter, and Google+. And, as evidenced by the number of jobs available for this type of work on the Idealist Web site (see page 274), many nonprofits are hiring specialists to manage their social media duties.

Legal Issues

Establishing an online community exposes an organization to legal liability in a number of areas that are unsettled, chiefly because many technology issues are new and have not been tested in the courts.

A Code of Conduct is a necessity, as is a privacy statement. The Code should include a declaration of what behaviors are not permitted by site users, such as flaming; obscene, sexist, anti-Semitic, or racist postings; the posting of copyrighted material without permission from the copyright owner; the uploading of files, such as software or other materials that are a violation of intellectual property laws; and engaging in fraudulent conduct or the harassment of other users.

Discussion Questions

1. Should employees of a nonprofit organization be permitted to use their organization's e-mail account as a personal account, as well? What are the pros and cons of such a policy?

2. Discuss how organizational Web sites have "leveled the playing field" between large and small organizations, and between those with varying degrees of access to resources, with respect to communication with potential stakeholders.

3. What are some arguments against nonprofit organizations becoming too invested in e-commerce activities?

4. How has the Internet affected fundraising, both online and offline?

5. Do you think that nonprofit organizations are significantly behind their for-profit counterparts with respect to the adoption of technology? Why or why not?

6. What can nonprofit organizations do to close the digital divide? Do you think that the nonprofit sector has a responsibility to do so?

7. How have social networking sites such as Facebook added to the challenge of managing nonprofit organizations?

Activities

1. Design a Web site for a mock nonprofit organization that engages in advocacy on behalf of abused and neglected children.

2. Research Web sites that help nonprofit organizations that engage in prospect research.

3. Compile a list of Web site addresses that you feel provide useful information with respect to the scope of the nonprofit sector, nonprofit advocacy, technology, management, legal and regulatory, and ethics/accountability. Create a one-paragraph summary of each Web site, exchange your list with

your classmates, and create a master list of these sites. Use the Internet to distribute this list.

4. Visit online shopping mall sites and read the agreements the owners of these sites ask affiliate nonprofit organizations to sign. Discuss various agreement provisions that you might not fully understand.

5. Organize a class online charity auction, with the proceeds going toward a charity or charities selected by the class.

Tips for Practitioners

1. Subscribe to a general nonprofit electronic mailing list to keep current with what your colleagues in the field are thinking and discussing.

2. Using popular search engines, perform searches on your own organization's name, and take steps to ensure that what you find is accurate and up to date.

3. Protect your domain names by keeping your fees paid.

4. Look at the Web sites of similar organizations and see how they are harnessing the power of the Internet.

5. Make sure you are comfortable with the legal ramifications of e-commerce applications—such as privacy, security, copyright, and tax collection—before launching an e-commerce initiative.

Online Resources to Explore

Carter McNamara's Computers, Internet and Web
http://www.managementhelp.org/infomgnt/infomgnt.htm

The Nonprofit Matrix
http://www.nonprofitmatrix.com

Technology Works for Good
http://www.npowergdcr.org/

Beth's Blog: How Nonprofit Organizations Can Use Social Media to Power Social Networks for Change
http://bethkanter.org/

TechSoup
   http://www.techsoup.org

Network for Good Web Site 101
   http://www.fundraising123.org/web-site-101

For Further Reading

Allen, A., Warwick, M., & Hart, T. (Eds.). (2001). *Fundraising on the internet: The ePhilanthropy Foundation.org's guide to success online.* San Francisco: Jossey Bass.

Greene, S. (2003, June 12). Online-donation group shuts its doors. *The Chronicle of Philanthropy, 17, p. 25.*

Grobman, G. and Grant, G. (2007). *Fundraising on the internet.* Harrisburg, PA: White Hat Communications.

Gross, G. (2014). House committee approves permanent internet tax moratorium. PC World, June 18, 2014. Retrieved from *http://www.pcworld.com/article/2365120/house-committee-approves-permanent-internet-tax-moratorium.html*

Hart, T., Greenfield, J. & Haji, S. (2008). *People to people fundraising: Social networking and web 2.0 for charities.* New York: Wiley.

Hart, T., Greenfield, J., MacLaughlin, S. & Geier, Jr., P. (2010). *Internet management for nonprofits: Strategies, tools and trade secrets.* New York: Wiley.

Kanter, B. & Fine, A. (2010). *The networked nonprofit: Connecting with social media to drive change.* San Francisco: Jossey-Bass.

Marwick, T. & Allen, N. (Eds.).(2009). *Fundraising on the internet: The ePhilanthropyFoundation.org's guide to success online* (2nd Ed.) San Francisco: Jossey-Bass.

Statistic Brain. (2014). PayPal statistics. Retrieved from *http://www.statisticbrain.com/paypal-statistics/*

Watson, T. (2009). *Changing the world.* New York: Wiley.

Chapter 16
Strategic Planning and Change Management

> **Synopsis:** Formal strategic planning is not for every organization. All stakeholders must be committed to successfully develop and implement a strategic plan. Although such plans require a major investment in money and time and have other institutional costs and risks, the benefits include enhancing the organization's ability to respond to internal and external threats. Total Quality Management, Reengineering, Benchmarking, Outcome-Based Management, and Large Group Intervention are potential ways to improve nonprofit organizational quality and performance.

Introduction

Strategic planning is a formalized process by which an organization makes a study of its vision for the future, typically for three years or more from the present. A strategic plan is an important management tool that can help an organization's leaders to consider the effects of advances in technology; changing markets for its services; government funding cutbacks; or the emergence of other organizations (both for-profits and nonprofits) that provide similar, competing services.

An organization's CEO often is frequently so involved with putting out fires and responding to the exigencies of day-to-day operations that it is a luxury to set aside time to think about the position of the organization even a year into the future. An organization's board is often ill equipped to consider changes in structure and operations in the context of a regular board meeting.

Purpose of Strategic Planning

In his 1994 book *The Rise and Fall of Strategic Planning*, Henry Mintzberg lists four reasons organizations do strategic planning: to coordinate their activities, to ensure that the future is taken into account, to be rational, and to control. Strategic planning is designed to suggest remedies for organizational problems before they escalate. Deep cuts in government grants, changes in markets, advances in technology, competition from for-profit businesses, and changes in demographics in an organization's service area all crystallize the need to change the basic way an organization does business. Strategic planning is also a technique to systematically provide an institutionalized process to respond to changes in an organizational environment, whether or not there is a specific problem that needs to be addressed.

Virtually all successful large for-profit businesses engage in a formal strategic planning process. The conventional wisdom is that businesses that do so, regardless of whether they are for-profit or nonprofit, are more successful over time than those that do not. However, Mintzberg cites scores of academic studies that show mixed results as to the benefits of strategic planning in business and industry, and concludes that the value of strategic planning is nebulous at best.

Putting that aside, a periodic strategic planning process provides the framework for a long-term assessment of emerging threats, and the opportunity to develop creative strategies to respond to them. The intent here is not to encourage or discourage nonprofits from engaging in a formal strategic planning process; rather, it is to raise issues to consider in the event that this endeavor, for whatever reason, is under consideration.

Strategic planning requires the investment of both time and money. For most nonprofits, both are scarce. Thus, it is important that an organization's leaders systematically evaluate whether the benefits of preparing, updating, and implementing a periodic strategic plan outweigh the costs. Strategic plan preparation often involves the hiring of an outside consultant; resource-consuming meetings; and the involvement of board members, staff, and other stakeholders for an extended period of time.

The strategic planning process is fraught with danger. The contents of a final strategic plan often are totally at odds with the vision of the organization leader who first suggested preparing one. The planning committee dynamics are often uncontrollable by the people who provide the organization with leadership. An organization's leaders may be uncomfortable sharing with a professional outside consultant the organization's dreams and aspirations, its "dirty little secrets," and proprietary financial projections, and may be even more reticent with community members of the planning committee. Yet, many organizations that successfully complete a strategic planning process improve their performance. Participating board members feel a renewed connection and bond to both the organization and their colleagues. Organizations that do not plan for the future, whether in a formalized process or informal board retreats, often suffer the consequences.

Strategic planning in the for-profit sector has been popular for several decades. In the for-profit world, strategic planning has the advantage of having each member of the committee, virtually by definition, already in agreement on the basic mission of the organization; that is, in short, to make as much profit as possible. There will be differences, of course, as to the methods used to accomplish this. In a nonprofit, there is not always agreement on the mission from the outset. In a hospital situation, for example, some planning committee members may view the mission as providing quality health care to the community. Others may feel it is to teach medical students, advance life-saving technology, increase "market share" by gobbling up other health care institutions, or serve populations not served by other institutions.

In a for-profit setting, the outcomes are easily measurable—net profit and market share are statistics easily compiled. In the nonprofit sector, consumer satisfaction, community benefit, and image in the community often are considered more important than bottom-line net revenue, and they are difficult to measure satisfactorily. In the nonprofit sector, board members may actually be concerned if the institution is making too much net revenue and not providing services to sectors of the market that would clearly result in revenue shortfalls. It is the nature of nonprofits that the institution is not motivated by private profit motive and, in theory, this can create conflicts. As a result of government cutbacks, tensions are mounting within nonprofit boards as they wrestle with difficult decisions concerning how to ease the financial crunch while maintaining traditional markets.

Making the Decision to Develop a Strategic Plan

The motivation for initiating a strategic plan comes from many sources:

Board Members. Board members who have participated in successful strategic planning as a result of their service on other nonprofit boards are often the source for initiating a strategic plan. Board members who run their own businesses or work for for-profit companies that routinely develop strategic plans also may raise this issue. Many who serve on nonprofit boards see strategic planning as a management and governance tool equal in importance to budgeting, and they cannot imagine an organization that does not initiate a formal process to look inward at least once every half-decade.

Funders. Some funders require the development of a strategic plan before they make grants to nonprofit charities. These funders want evidence that their contributions will be used prudently and cost-effectively and will influence the direction of the organization. A strategic plan developed as a result of such a requirement by a funder would obviously highlight changes in the organization's programs that are the direct result of the contribution.

Retirement of a Long-Term CEO. Many nonprofits were started by visionary leaders who ran the organizations from the seat of their pants. This "old school" of doing business may no longer be valid. New leaders, many with MBAs, believe that nonprofit organizations are businesses, and the same management techniques they learned in business school are applicable to the philanthropic sector. The "new school" of doing business recognizes that the bottom line remains the principal concern of the organization, whether or not the bottom line is interpreted as the net revenue at the end of the year or the number of satisfied clients served. The old school organization executive is often skeptical, if not fearful, of strategic planning. Perhaps his or her vision has never been challenged, and a formal process to evaluate from top to bottom, from the mission statement on down, is a threat to executive autonomy. In some cases, that skepticism is justified.

Once a new generation assumes the mantle of leadership, there is motivation to rebuild from the ground up, starting with the mission statement and proceeding, in some extreme cases, to changing the model of the copying machine. A strategic plan is often the vehicle for the new leadership to assert its authority and provide a mechanism for a higher level of executive accountability.

Organization Trauma. More often than not, it is an organizational crisis that triggers the decision for a strategic plan when an organization has no regular process to prepare one. The resignation or firing of a CEO is a traumatic event for any nonprofit. Sometimes, this event has occurred because of underlying unresolved issues and problems that may have developed and been inadequately addressed over many years. In the case of the involuntary separation, the organization's leadership has the opportunity to reshape the organization before a new executive takes over and molds its direction. Other traumatic events that may trigger the initiation of a strategic plan are the loss of a major funder; the establishment of competition from another nonprofit or for-profit; major damage to, or aging of, the organization's physical plant; liability suits; or quantum advances in technology that call into question the future demand for services.

Benefits of Strategic Planning

1. **It permits discussion of issues in a proactive rather than reactive mode.** Usually developed in an atmosphere that encourages creativity and brainstorming, the strategic plan may not only include concrete directions, but also provide an institutional set of core values. In a typical board meeting, there is simply no time to engage in a meaningful discussion about the long-term future of an organization. Many nonprofits are operating on the edge of financial chaos, often one failed grant application away from having to lay off staff or fold entirely.

2. **It requires an action plan to solve real problems faced by an organization.** The action plan is a template that the staff can use to implement the policies and desires of the board. Many CEOs complain that the board helps with solving problems, but fails to provide direction on the core values of the organization. A strategic plan explicitly includes those core values, and assists the CEO in creative strategies for solving current problems and anticipating future ones.

3. **It provides a formal mandate for the reallocation of resources to respond to changing conditions, and the means to obtain additional resources if required.** A successful strategic planning process that develops an aggressive plan to attack problems often energizes a moribund board.

4. **It builds inter-board relationships that might not otherwise exist, and creates a partnership among the board chairperson, board members, staff, funders, and other stakeholders.** Each has a role that is defined in the plan and, if bought into, the added responsibilities increase the available resources of the organization. The social contact that occurs at many board retreats, particularly those designed in bucolic settings away from the hustle and bustle of the organization, cement personal relationships among participants. This improves the bond between the organization and its leadership.

5. **It provides a mechanism for the board, staff, and organization stakeholders to become more informed about the activities and problems faced by the organization.** It promotes, in many cases, a frank discussion by the organization's chief executive of problems that might not be shared in a conventional board meeting context. Many CEOs welcome the process in that it takes a burden off their shoulders and shares it with the organization's "owners" and constituents.

6. **It provides an opportunity to focus on the forest rather than the trees.** It is easy for a CEO to become lost in the mundane issues of personnel, budgeting, fundraising, office management, board relations, and public relations, and virtually ignore issues relating to the actual purpose and mission of the nonprofit.

Costs of Strategic Planning

1. **Money.** Serious strategic planning costs money, a scarce resource for most nonprofits. Many nonprofits recognize that it is useful to have a trained, dispassionate consultant to assist in the planning process. There are costs to schedule planning meetings and travel to those meetings. Many organizations recognize the value of eliminating outside distractions to aid brainstorming, and thus schedule planning meetings at staff retreats held at attractive, isolated campgrounds, conference centers, business resorts, or hotels. There are costs of photocopying and printing all of the planning documents. There are opportunity costs, as well, because staff and board resources are diverted from other duties.

2. **Time.** Any realistic strategic planning process requires the allocation of precious staff and board resources. Meeting preparation, meeting attendance, minutes, preparation of draft and final strategic plans, and hiring a consultant all take time. It is not uncommon for a strategic planning process to take more than a year.

3. **Potential bad will.** As with any process, things can go wrong. Bad group dynamics can result in painful meetings and destructive outcomes. A group may spend an entire four-hour meeting arguing over trivial words in a mission statement. This can be painfully frustrating for committee members more interested in developing an action plan to solve problems. Strategic planning may bring board factions into collision, and meetings can degenerate into a test of wills. This may be healthy in the context of a committee rather than having a drag-out fight at a board meeting, but it means that to have a constructive planning process, personal baggage must be dealt with first. If the final strategic plan is not implemented, board members who participated may feel that the organization wasted their time, and may not be as likely to participate in future efforts, or even may resign from the board. Current staff members may feel threatened that their jobs are at risk, and may look for other employment.

4. **Loss of Initiative.** A formal strategic plan may diminish an executive's initiative and quick response to changing conditions, because the preferred course of action is not in the strategic plan. The strategic plan may become outdated quickly and stifle a more appropriate response to changing conditions that were not anticipated in the plan. In addition, strategic planning often involves the board not just in setting objectives and outcomes, but also in determining the methods that should be used to achieve those objectives and outcomes. Many feel that this is the role of staff, not the board, and making it the role of the board takes away the flexibility necessary for executive staff to function effectively.

A Sample Strategic Planning Model

This chapter gives a cursory review of what a strategic plan is, its costs and benefits, some advantages and disadvantages, and some issues that often arise when nonprofits consider initiating a strategic plan. It is recommended that other specific resources be consulted when exploring the need for a strategic planning process, and several excellent sources are included in the bibliography. The following is one model for developing a strategic plan and is a hybrid put together from several theoretical models.

Step 1. Decide whether to develop a strategic plan.

Consider the costs and benefits mentioned earlier in this chapter, and also the following questions:

- Is there enough time and money to allocate for this planning process now?
- Is the organization prepared to implement whatever plan eventually is approved, or will it sit on the shelf?
- Do we have a commitment from the executive director, board chairperson, board members, and other stakeholders to develop a plan, or will we just be going through the motions?
- Are the organization's short-term problems so overwhelming that the organization is wasting time planning for the future when its continued existence is seriously threatened by current problems?

Step 2. Build the infrastructure necessary to develop a plan.

- **Appoint a planning committee of the board.** Include creative board members, funders, the CEO, chief financial officer, clients, and opinion makers from the community. Consider that any committee of more than 10 becomes unmanageable. Some strategic planners recommend that the entire board serve on the committee.

- **Compile and distribute articles and related material on strategic planning to the entire board.** (For information on reprints or rights to photocopy this chapter or other copyrighted materials, contact the publisher of the material.)

- **Decide on whether the facilitator/consultant will be a board member or a paid or volunteer consultant.** A board member already knows a lot about the organization, its strengths and weaknesses, its personnel, and all other members of the committee. On the other hand, that board member brings with him or her prejudices about colleagues and staff, and often has a point of view or hidden agenda that is not objective. A private strategic planning consultant has the experience to keep the discussion focused and follow the agenda. There are many consultants who have experience working with nonprofit agencies in designing the planning process itself, participating in orientation sessions for the planning committee, serving as a referee for dispute resolution, helping the committee reach consensus when that is desired, neutralizing oppositional or disruptive participants, and providing technical assistance.

A good consultant can organize the process and provide logistical support so the board and staff will not be absorbed by the planning process mechanics. On the other hand, a bad consultant may influence the process beyond what is desirable, and constrain the participation of committee members. One must be careful to ensure that the plan, if written by a consultant, is not a tepid re-write of the plan the consultant developed for a previous client, which may have only minimal relevance to the current client.

It is a good idea to informally survey comparable organizations to check out potential strategic planning consultants. Statewide associations may also be helpful in identifying consultants. Of course, it is vital that any contract between the organization and the consultant spell out exactly what services are required, the timetable, and the level of participation required by the consultant.

Step 3. Decide how many years the strategic plan will cover.

In general, small nonprofits choose a shorter time frame than larger nonprofits, perhaps two-to-four years for smaller agencies, compared to larger institutions, which prepare five-year plans.

Step 4. Put in writing the timetable and the process.

This includes the steps that are required and who is responsible for accomplishing each task. Among the tasks are:

- Appointing the committee
- Hiring a consultant or facilitator
- Leading the orientation of the planning committee
- Choosing the meeting site
- Scheduling the meetings
- Writing the first draft of the plan
- Providing the procedures to review and revise the draft
- Writing the final plan
- Developing the process for the planning committee to approve the final plan
- Formulating the review and the process for the full board's approval of the final plan.

Step 5. Prepare a memo on what is expected of the strategic planning process.

This memo to the planning committee should highlight the major problems that are to be resolved by the strategic plan, such as how to review and update the mission statement, how to respond to potential cuts in government funding, how to respond to the new location of a for-profit competitor, how to deal with a change in the demographics of the people in the area served by the organization, and so on. The memo should note whether the planning report should be a consensus document (which does not require unanimity) or if majority rules after all points of view are heard.

Step 6. Have the board endorse the planning process, and allocate funds necessary for it to proceed.

Step 7. Appoint the committee, appoint or hire the facilitator/consultant, send out orientation materials, and schedule the first meeting.

The first meeting

The first meeting is usually an orientation session, which includes some of the following five components:

1. A review of the purpose of the committee, the timetable, future meeting schedule, and meeting the facilitator.

2. A review of the organization's current mission, history, short-term problems, long-term threats, staff resources, programs, activities, strengths and weaknesses, major successes and failures, core values of the organization, financial status, and future commitments. The CEO and CFO should be present to answer questions from the planning committee and to ask questions of the facilitator to establish ground rules for the planning process.

3. An analysis of the needs of the stakeholders, including those currently receiving service, and scenarios about how those needs may change. For example, is the population served by the organization changing demographically? Is government funding likely to drop? Is the community becoming poorer, limiting future fee-for-service revenue and requiring more non-fee revenue?

4. An analysis of institutional limits: population served by geography, age group, and income level.

5. An identification of what in the above can be changed by the organization as a result of strategic planning and what is the result of forces beyond the control of the organization.

The second meeting

The second meeting begins the brainstorming of the committee. This meeting examines the mission statement and reviews potential changes to that statement which—in some cases—might have been unrevised for decades. The facilitator may list various problems on the horizon, with the planning committee serving as a focus group—such as funding problems, changes in markets, competitors, outside threats from changing social, economic, political, or technological conditions, or demand for services. The planning committee is given a homework assignment to come to the third meeting with suggestions for solving these problems.

The third meeting

The third meeting consists of brainstorming on action strategies that will solve the problems identified at the first and second meetings. The facilitator lists each strategy and includes a table with the costs and benefits of each, the probability of success, and the pros and cons. Each strategy for each problem may be ranked based on the committee's assessment as to the value of the strategy.

The fourth meeting

The committee develops an action plan, with a timetable for implementation that includes coming up with the resources necessary to implement the action plan. The plan also includes a procedure to review the progress made in implementing the plan.

In the above model, a draft strategic plan can be accomplished with four three-hour meetings.

In *Managing a Nonprofit Organization,* Thomas Wolff outlines six levels in the linear model of strategic planning. In the linear model, the planning committee considers one level before proceeding to the next. This contrasts with the integrated planning model, which provides for many of these levels to be considered simultaneously, recognizing that the end result is interdependent upon each of the earlier levels.

> **Level 1.** The planners consider the mission statement, which describes the purpose the organization is trying to achieve.
>
> **Level 2.** Organization goals are developed, providing the general direction in which the organization intends to go.
>
> **Level 3.** Objectives and targets are set, indicating the outcomes the organization hopes to achieve.

Level 4. Strategies are formulated to meet the objectives and targets. These are the methods and ways the organization plans to achieve those outcomes.

Level 5. An action plan is developed to implement the strategies.

Level 6. An evaluation is performed after implementation, to review whether the outcomes were achieved and whether the strategies were successful.

For example, a hypothetical nursing home might have a planning document that, in an abridged form, is as follows:

Level 1. To provide quality long-term care services to the aging population of Anytown, for the purpose of improving the quality of life for those who need institutional care.

Level 2. To reduce the operating deficit and become the long-term care institution of choice in the community by improving quality of care.

Level 3. Increase non-fee revenue by 50%, and improve the cash-flow situation by taking advantage of accounting productivity. Improve government reimbursement by 25% within three years.

Increase the number of private pay residents from 30% to 50% within the next five years.

Level 4. Hire a development staff member.

Hire a lobbyist to assist the statewide association to advocate for increases in Medicaid reimbursement.

Hire a marketing associate to place advertisements in publications read by active, upscale, middle-aged persons whose parents may be in need of long-term care services.

Level 5. Investigate the feasibility of marketing charitable gift annuities, and hire a consultant by July 15 to develop a program for residents and their families.

Aggressively go after accounts receivable, delay accounts payable for an additional 30 days, eliminate programs that are not profitable, increase fee-for-service revenues; increase fundraising; become entrepreneurial by selling clothing and health care equipment on the organization's Web site.

Place an advertisement in the newsletter of the state chapter of the American Society of Association Executives to hire a registered lobbyist.

Hire a marketing associate by June 15, and use endowment funds for seed money. Assume the new staff member will generate at least enough income to finance his or her salary.

Level 6. One year after final approval of this report, require the executive director to prepare a progress report on whether the goals outlined in Level 2 are being achieved, and what mid-course corrections to Level 5 are required in order to meet the targets of Level 3.

The process of planning each level can be discussed and refined for two hours or nine months. The parameters differ, obviously, for a hospital with a half-billion dollars in gross revenue, compared to a charity with $50,000 in gross revenue.

The actual plan may be written by the facilitator, the chairperson of the planning committee, or staff in consultation with the board and facilitator. In every case, the planning committee should review a draft of the plan before submitting its final version to the board. The board reserves the power to approve, disapprove, approve with changes, or send the plan back for revision.

Some of the changes that may be recommended by a nonprofit organization strategic plan are:

1. A mission change
2. A change in the character of services provided
3. A plan to expand or downsize staff
4. A plan to expand or sell capital equipment and/or physical plant
5. A plan to expand fundraising
6. A plan to retrain staff
7. A plan to move the organization's location
8. A plan to seek a merger with similar organizations
9. A communications plan to improve or renovate the organization's public image
10. A plan to hire a lobbyist, or form a statewide association representing agencies with similar problems or uncertainties
11. A plan to establish a for-profit subsidiary
12. A plan to seek, or refuse, government grants

13. A plan to liquidate the organization
14. A plan to professionalize the organization, or deprofessionalize it—e.g., a decision by a hospital to substitute nurse aides where registered nurses were used formerly
15. A plan to change the governance of the organization—increase or decrease board membership, change quorum requirements, change voting requirements, change committee structure, change the powers of officers
16. A plan to change the compensation structure to reward and improve productivity
17. A plan to change the organization's market niche
18. A plan to change into a for-profit
19. A plan to modernize the name of the organization.

Some components of a strategic plan may be:

1. a five-year projection of staffing patterns
2. a five-year projected budget
3. sources of revenue to implement changes required by the plan
4. a marketing strategy
5. a schedule for periodically updating the strategic plan
6. a schedule for evaluating whether the plan is being implemented effectively and whether the strategies provided in the plan are successful
7. a physical plant/equipment plan.

Change Management

In the context of this chapter, "change management" does not refer to a prescription for getting rid of the people who run the organization. Rather, it is a menu of strategies to change the philosophy of management to accomplish an objective or set of objectives such as, for example, improving efficiency and competitiveness, motivating employees and increasing their job satisfaction, or reducing absenteeism. In this sense, "change" is used as an adjective rather than a verb.

There is general agreement among scholars, practitioners, and management experts that organizations must adapt to changing conditions to survive. Technology advances; markets change; the requirements and expectations of customers evolve; and the needs of workers are altered as a result of demographics, economic conditions, and changes in culture, among other things.

Businesses, both for-profit and nonprofit, go out of existence every day. This is attributable to many causes. There may be an organizational scandal that causes the public to lose confidence or the government to take action. There may be quality lapses. The services provided by an organization may no longer be needed, or a competitor skims off a lucrative market share. The organization's operations may be too economically inefficient to support it. Government funding priorities or regulatory requirements may shift, leaving an organization in the lurch. The list of possible causes goes on.

For years, the for-profit business community has utilized formal change management strategies to improve operations and keep organizations competitive and vibrant, improve efficiency, generate loyalty, and maintain or expand support from customers. One time-tested change management strategy, strategic planning, is described in more detail in the beginning of this chapter. It has only been recently that the nonprofit community, with health care institutions leading the way, started implementing some of these newer, more unconventional strategies.

Among the most popular change management strategies being considered by nonprofit organizations are Total Quality Management (TQM), Business Process Reengineering (BPR), Benchmarking, Outcome-Based Management (OBM), and Large Group Intervention (LGI).

Total Quality Management (TQM)

TQM is an innovative, humanistic, general approach to management that seeks to improve quality, reduce costs, and increase customer satisfaction by restructuring traditional management practices. It requires a continuous and systematic approach to gathering, evaluating, and acting on data about what is occurring in an organization. The TQM management philosophy includes the following:

1. It asserts that the primary objective of an organization is to meet the needs of its "customers" by providing quality goods and services, and to continually improve them. In the nonprofit organizational context, customers include not only the direct recipients of services, such as clients, but the organization's board, elected and appointed government officials, the media, and the general public.

2. It instills in all of the organization's members an *esprit de corps,* assuring them that having quality as the number one goal is an important tenet. Every organizational member is responsible for quality, even if it is related to an issue beyond the scope of his or her job. Eliminating the "It's not my job" mentality becomes an achievable organizational objective.

3. It continuously searches for ways to improve every activity, program, and process. It does so by constantly seeking feedback from the organization's customers and promoting suggestions from all sources, both external and internal, on how to improve.

4. It rewards quality, not only internally, but from its suppliers. It recognizes that poor quality from an organization's collaborators, be they suppliers or other organizations, affects its own quality.

5. It recognizes that all staff members must receive continuous training to improve their work performance.

6. It encourages all components of the organization to work as a team to solve problems and meet customer needs rather than compete against each other.

7. It empowers workers at every level. It permits them to be actively engaged in decisions that affect the organization and to constantly look for ways to improve it.

8. It permits employees the opportunity to have pride in what they produce for the organization and to see the fruits of their labor measured in the quality of the service they provide, rather than just receiving a paycheck.

9. It promotes a planning process geared toward continuously improving quality in everything the organization does.

In 1992, the United Way of America developed the *Excellence in Service Quality Award* (ESQA) for nonprofit human service agencies. The purpose was to recognize that quality improvement is just as important, if not more so, in charities as in private business. 501(c)(3) charities were eligible for four levels of recognition. Judging and criteria were patterned after the Baldrige Award, which is given to for-profit corporations. The United Way of America discontinued this program in 1999. In 2004, the Congress enacted legislation authorizing nonprofit organizations to apply for the Baldrige Award beginning in 2007, with a one-year pilot program commencing in 2006. Two nonprofit organizations were among the five awardees in 2007, one nonprofit was among the three awardees in 2008, and two nonprofits were among the five awardees in 2009. A nonprofit hospital won a Baldrige in 2013 in the health provider category.

TQM principles are finding their way into nonprofit settings other than health care, such as community centers, arts organizations, and human services agencies. Focusing on the needs of the "customer" rather than on the "bottom line" is a value with which the nonprofit sector should feel comfortable compared with its for-profit counterpart. When a nonprofit organization's leadership becomes excited about TQM, the excitement can become contagious, provided that the behaviors of the leaders are consistent with their words. When it "happens," those in a TQM environment notice the difference, whether they work there or benefit from the organization's services. Workers feel empowered. Clients notice a positive difference in staff attitudes. Everyone associated with the organization feels good about it.

Business Process Reengineering (BPR)

If your heart stops beating and you keel over breathlessly, a professionally trained medical professional often can revive you by administering CPR. But if it's your *organization's* heart that fails, BPR, administered by professionally trained consultants or by those within an organization, is increasingly becoming the TLA ("three-letter acronym") of choice for cutting-edge managers. BPR is a successor to TQM as the latest management bromide for reviving comatose organizations.

Business Process Reengineering is defined by Michael Hammer (1948-2008), BPR's leading guru, as "the fundamental rethinking and radical redesign of business processes to achieve dramatic improvements in critical measures of performance (cost, quality, capital, service and speed)."

Fanatical interest in Total Quality Management peaked in the 1980s, but its once-pervasive influence seems to have waned in recent years. One of the reasons often given for TQM's apparent decline in the United States is that the philosophy of slow, incremental, and continuous improvement is generally inconsistent with American culture. Perhaps this is so; American organizational leaders are perceived as more impatient to see the tangible results of their business management interventions compared with their Asian, African, and European counterparts. They want to see quantum leaps of measurable improvement rather than the tortoise-paced improvement promised by TQM advocates. The tenure of many organizational leaders is short; several CEOs may come and go before TQM had had the time to be fully implemented to show results.

A major strategy involved with BPR efforts is to look at a business process involving many tasks that have been performed by several specialists. Then, the specialists are replaced with generalists (or the specialists are retrained to become generalists) who can handle all of the tasks of the process and have access to all of the information they need to do so.

BPR requires a new way of thinking. Unlike TQM, which requires the involvement of everyone in the organization, BPR is necessarily implemented from the top. It is the zero-based budgeting of business processes, contending that, at least theoretically, the past should have no bearing on what is planned for the future. It makes the assumption that organizations have evolved incrementally, reflecting a history of culture, tradition, technology, and customer needs that may not be particularly relevant today. BPR suggests that managers step out of the constraints of their current physical plant, work processes, organizational charts, and procedures and rules, and look at how the work would be performed if they were starting from scratch.

BPR requires an organizational leader to step back and answer the question: If I were building this organization today from scratch, knew what I know now, had the technology and human resources that I have now, and knew the customer needs that I have now, would I still be doing things the same way? More often than not, the answer is a resounding "no"! In the nonprofit environment, this might mean redesigning data collection and reporting, client intake, billing, purchasing, and every other process.

In many cases, new and more efficient technology is available. For example, a human service agency may receive a telephone call from a client requesting even a minimal change in service as a result of some change in circumstances. The person answering the telephone may have to put the person on hold and call the client's caseworker, who has the client's case file. The caseworker may have to put the person on hold and check with the supervisor for a decision on whether to waive a rule, and the supervisor may have to meet with the caseworker to make the decision.

Following BPR, the person answering the telephone may be able to pull up the case file on a computer screen and be preauthorized to approve a change in services within a constraint programmed into the computer. Or the person answering the telephone may be able to give the caller technical advice on how to solve a problem by searching a "frequently asked questions" file on a computer screen, instead of transferring him or her to a technical specialist.

Another way of looking at this is that everyone in the organization is conventionally functioning solely as his or her part of a process rather than on the actual mission of the organization. The receptionist answers the telephone. The case manager holds the file for a particular set of clients. The supervisor makes decisions authorizing variances from the organization's rules. BPR permits a work process to change so that the true objective of the process—responding to the client's needs—does not require the intervention of several people in the organization. The revolutionary advances in information technology permit this.

With the use of networked computers and an educated labor force, it is possible for a single person to process and troubleshoot an entire client request that previously may have required being passed serially from person to person in the organization, taking many days to complete. And the less hands involved in a process, the lower probability of an error.

Among the major principles of BPR are:

1. Use modern technology to redesign work processes rather than work tasks, concentrating on permitting a single person to achieve a desired outcome/objective.

2. Let the worker who uses the output of a process also perform the process. For example, instead of having a purchasing department make purchases of pencils and paper clips for the accounting department and other departments, the accounting department orders its own pencils and paper clips and other "inexpensive and nonstrategic" purchases.

3. Let those in the organization who collect information be the ones who process it. For example, when the public relations department wants to send out its newsletter to a mailing list, it should be able to generate the mailing labels itself rather than having to make a request to a data processing department.

4. Treat decentralized organizational resources as centralized, utilizing information technology to bring them together. A college with several satellite campuses, for example, could link its bursars so that a student making a payment at either the main office or a satellite campus would have the payment show up in the records of the registrars of all of the campuses.

5. Electronically link disparate parts of an organization to promote coordination.

6. Let those who perform the work make the decisions, thereby flattening the pyramidal management layers and eliminating the bureaucracy and delay that slow down a decision-making process.

7. Use relational databases and other technology to collect and store information only once, eliminating both redundancy and error.

Generally, BPR often enables a single person to perform all of the steps in a process by using information technology. One advantage of BPR is that the need for many employees may be eliminated. This saves a lot of money for organizations. One downside is that implementing BPR, in some cases, has been known to terrorize a work force.

Benchmarking

Benchmarking refers to the process by which organizations study how organizations similar to theirs perform the same business processes and learn how to adapt those that are most efficient, innovative, and successful. Obviously, no two organizations are alike, and there is no guarantee that copying something from another organization will automatically work well in another. But certainly there is value in exploring how various organizations perform some of the same tasks and discussing what efficiencies they may have found that would improve business operations of similar organizations. For-profit organizations have been doing this in a formalized way for many years. Nonprofit organizations are only recently recognizing the value of benchmarking.

There are two types of benchmarking that nonprofit organizations might wish to consider. The first, internal benchmarking, looks at an organization and projects future goals, including a process by which employees are encouraged to meet performance targets. External benchmarking, on the other hand, tries to determine the "best practices" of similar organizations. Rather than reinventing the wheel, external benchmarking permits the allocation of minimal resources to finding how others have solved a problem, or have exponentially increased productivity with respect to some process, rather than having to discover that by themselves.

Many nonprofit organizations are not only willing to share this information, but are quite proud to do so. The fact that competition among nonprofit organizations is almost always either friendly or nonexistent promotes benchmarking in a manner that avoids some of the troublesome potential conflicts and ethical dilemmas in the for-profit context.

Jason Saul, writing in *Benchmarking for Nonprofits: How to Measure and Improve Performance*, says that nonprofits should typically consider benchmarking in three general categories: A *process* (such as screening job applicants or organizing inventory in a food bank), a *policy* (such as a salary structure or incentive plan), or a *program* (such as welfare-to-work or educational incentives).

Three approaches taken to benchmarking include:

- *technical approach*—using computer models, statistics, spreadsheets, and other quantitative methods

- *committee approach*—bringing in a team of experts from outside the organization to gather data and make judgments about which changes would be beneficial to it

- *survey approach*—combining the above two models by creating a team of individuals from within the organization to identify which processes should be benchmarked, define the measures and organizational performance, obtain the "best practices" information, and implement these practices.

Saul, who is the co-founder of The Center for What Works, a Chicago-based clearinghouse for those studying solutions to social problems, recommends a seven-step process for benchmarking. It includes self-assessment, measuring performance, assembling the team, data collection, evaluating practices, translating best practices, and continuously repeating the process.

Outcome-Based Management (OBM)

To improve quality in a larger organization, simply adopting a progressive management philosophy such as TQM or BPR is not going to suffice in today's modern competitive business climate. As an organization grows, there are more pressures for accountability, not only internally from a board of directors, but externally from elected officials, government funders, foundation funders, individual donors and volunteers, and the public. Leaders of large organizations generally do not have the ability to visualize every aspect of their organization's operations and assess what is going on just by looking out their office windows or by engaging in informal conversations with their staff and clients. The proverbial "one-minute manager" is an ideal construct that is not particularly well suited to crystallizing the information a CEO needs to make judgments on how to allocate precious resources.

To accomplish the important task of determining what is really going on, most large organizations have a Management Information System (MIS). An MIS permits the aggregation of data in a form that can be analyzed by a manager, enabling him or her to see trouble spots and make adjustments in operations and to generate reports required by the government, funders, auditors, and the board of directors.

For many larger nonprofits, particularly those that depend on government and foundation grants rather than private donations, the objective of "meeting clients' needs" has become a more formalized process. Times have changed within just the last decade or so. Traditionally, measures of organizational performance for human service organizations were based on a model more appropriate for industrial processes, where raw materials were turned into finished products. In the language of industrial systems analysis, inputs (the raw material) were processed into outputs (the finished product).

In adopting an analogous frame of reference to industry, the conventional thinking was that human service agencies took in unserved clients (input), provided services (process), and changed them into served clients (output). In this way of thinking, organizations improved their output by increasing the number of clients served.

An exciting new way of looking at the output of an organization is called outcome-based management (OBM) or "results-oriented accountability" (ROA). Most recently, results-oriented management and accountability (ROMA) has become the buzzword describing this general tool. OBM focuses on program outcomes rather than by simply quantifying services delivered. Program outcomes can be defined as "benefits or changes for participants during or after their involvement with a program" (from *Measuring Program Outcomes: A Practical Approach, United Way of America*).

For example, an organization that deals with reducing drug abuse may have a stellar record of attracting clients through a flashy outreach program. It may be exemplary in convincing doctors in the community to donate thousands of hours of free services to the program, thereby reducing unit costs per client. It may have few complaints from the clients, who feel the staff are competent and treat them with dignity. An analysis of conventional data might indicate that there is little room for improvement. But, perhaps, no data were collected on whether those treated for drug abuse by the organization are successfully able to become independent, avoid future interactions with the criminal justice system, and abstain from drug use for an extended period of time—all measurable outcomes for a successful substance abuse program. If most of these clients are back on the street and abusing drugs, is that organization providing successful treatment, even if drug abuse services are being provided? Are funders and taxpayers getting a fair return on their investment?

In the outcome-based management model, the number of clients served is an input. The outcome is considered to be a measurement of the change in the condition of the clients after receiving the services. For example, if thousands of clients are served, but the condition of the clients has not improved, then the outcome is zero, even if the services were provided 100% on time, every client received a satisfactory number of hours of services, and there were no client complaints. It is no longer indicative of the effectiveness and value of an organization to only collect data on how many clients sought services, how many of these were accepted into the client stream rather than being referred or turned down, how many hours of service were provided, and how much each service cost and was reimbursed. Outcome data, together with the above process data, are needed to measure the effectiveness and value of an organization.

In addition to a significant change in attitude about the accountability of the private nonprofit sector, the passage in 1993 of the *Government Performance and Results Act,* PL 103-62, changed the way federal agencies plan, budget, evaluate, and account for federal spending. The intent of the act is to improve public confidence in federal agency performance by holding agencies accountable for program results and improving congressional decision-making. The act seeks to accomplish this by clarifying and stating program performance goals, measures, and costs "up front." These changes were implemented beginning in September 1997.

For some organizations, the shift to outcome-based management will have modest cost implications. It may mean more data being collected from clients during intake. It may mean follow-up surveys to see what happens to clients after they have availed themselves of the organization's services. When this information is available, it is of extraordinary value to those who design, administer, and deliver those services.

What makes outcome-based management attractive to the human services sector is that it is common sense. What is the point of investing thousands, if not millions, of dollars of an organization's resources if the end result is not accomplishing what is intended by the investment—improving the lives of the organization's clients?

Our human service organizations have been established to make our lives better. When our organizations change their focus to concentrate on doing what it takes to do this, as opposed to simply providing human services, it is much more likely that this worthy goal can be accomplished successfully. Outcome-based management is compatible with the values of most in the sector, who often make financial sacrifices to make a difference in the lives of those who need human services.

In cases in which the data show that an organization is successfully providing services, but those services are not having the intended effect on the clients, the leadership should be the first to recognize that it is wasteful to continue business as usual. Outcome-based management is a powerful tool that allows organizations to allocate their precious resources to do the most good. If successfully implemented, it also can provide the ammunition to fight the increasing public cynicism about what is often perceived to be a poor return on investment of tax dollars and a competitive edge to organizations that adopt it.

Large Group Intervention (LGI)

Large Group Intervention (LGI) is the generic term given to a family of formal change management strategies that involve placing large parts of an organization, or even the entire organization, in simultaneous contact with one another to plan how the organization is going to change.

Proponents and users of LGIs believe these methods are particularly well suited to organizations seeking to establish a shared vision of their future and to build a road to get there. Some LGI models are designed specifically for organizations that seek to change the way their work is done (e.g., through reengineering or business process redesign).

Although many different LGI models have been developed and are in current use, they generally have common origins and are rooted in similar principles. Among these principles are getting the "whole system" into interactive discussion, using a carefully designed mixture of communication elements and processes designed to make effective use of participants' emotions as well as thoughts, and facilitating effective dialogue while validating differing perspectives.

Strategies such as TQM and BPR, as well as strategic planning itself, demand that each member of the organization thinks about the needs of the entire organization rather than his or her piece of it. "Democratic," participatory efforts by organizations may facilitate their members to see beyond the borders of their individual organizational niche and develop the spirit required to make TQM not simply a "program" but a working philosophy.

The general philosophy inherent in planning change is recognizing that there is resistance to change within organizations. Change is more likely to be successfully implemented when people affected can participate in the process, influence the process, and prepare for its consequences.

Much more than a device for overcoming psychological resistance, LGI is an effective approach to substantially improve the probability that a planned change will achieve its objectives, and have more desirable results for the organization. One dimension of additional benefits is more effective communication about the planned changes. Plans become far less distorted when everyone affected is hearing the same message at the same time, rather than having it communicated through the grapevine, through regular hierarchical channels, or not at all.

Another advantage of LGI is that those affected by the changes can provide invaluable input. It is rare that a few layers of management (or a subset of the full breadth of functions) within an organization can have an adequately detailed grasp of the whole. In most change management strategies, those at the bottom of the hierarchy—usually the most aware of the "nuts and bolts" of current reality—are often frozen out of the planning process. Most LGI models bring in a broad base of stakeholders to brainstorm together and weed out problems and unintended consequences that typically are invisible to the unrepresentative group of employees on the planning staff.

A third advantage of LGI is that it builds a diverse and broad base of support for planned changes. Useful in all cases, this advantage becomes particularly powerful when circumstances alter, planned changes need to be modified, and time is of the essence. Circumstances that otherwise could be expected to derail well-laid plans can be addressed by a robust and already engaged subset of the organization. Plans are far more open to effective alteration midstream when developed via an LGI approach.

LGIs tend to bring together people from various hierarchical levels within the organization, who otherwise may have minimal direct interaction. Many organizational development experts believe that this pays an additional dividend of creating positive social linkages among organizational members that otherwise would not have been created. Large Group Interventions create a new and different organizational bonding, which increases networks of informal communication within an organization and provides for more flexible and adaptive capabilities.

All of this can occur in a three-day period, significantly curtailing the process time of conventional change management planning.

Permitting workers affected by planning to participate in the planning process is one strategy to erode resistance to organizational change. LGIs also generate fresh ideas from people who have expertise as a result of doing their jobs every day. They may have shied away from making valid, responsible suggestions, not only because "no one ever asked us," but because they may feel that their views are not important, or that management does not have an interest in listening to them.

Large Group Interventions are usually staged in a setting away from the workplace, where participants can focus on the objective at hand without the distractions of the normal work environment. Artificial boundaries within organizations, such as functional departments, are routinely and intentionally fractured to facilitate communication and participation. These boundaries often get in the way of addressing important needs of organizations.

Among the most popular models for LGIs are the Search Conference, Future Search Conference, and Real-Time Strategic Change.

Discussion Questions

1. Discuss why there is often resistance to implementing the recommendations of a strategic plan.

2. When would a strategic plan be considered an appropriate organizational change strategy, and when might it not be?

3. Why do many organizational change experts consider formal strategic planning to be an anachronism?

4. How much influence do you think each of the players that participates in putting together a strategic plan has in its conception, writing, and implementation: the facilitator, the executive director, the board chair, funders, the board of directors, others?

5. Discuss some of the technical and political difficulties nonprofit organizations might have in moving from an output-based evaluation system to one that is based on outcomes.

6. Some who have read about Total Quality Management dismiss it as simple common sense and common courtesy. Others see it as a totally new paradigm with respect to business relationships where there is an information dissymmetry. Discuss your views.

7. Why is TQM considered a "bottom up" strategy and Business Process Reengineering a "top down" strategy? In general, which strategies are more likely to be successful in a large organization? A small organization?

8. Is it possible to implement TQM and BPR in an organization simultaneously?

Activities

1. Research the term "strategic thinking" and compare and contrast it to strategic planning.

2. Use an Internet search engine to find the full text of at least 10 strategic plans of nonprofit organizations. Compile a list of their common features.

3. Make a list of what your university, school, department, or library might do differently if it operated consistently with the principles of TQM. Do the same exercise with BPR.

4. Research what the actual paperwork would look like for an organization that wanted to establish a formal TQM program that is consistent with the ISO 9000 Quality System standards.

5. Look at empirical research that has been conducted about the effects change management strategies such as TQM and BPR have had on nonprofit and other organizations. Consider research that also looks at the limitations of these strategies in effecting change.

6. Using a database such as ProQuest, research articles in the popular press about the effectiveness of the change management strategies considered in this chapter.

7. Visit Web sites such as the American Productivity and Quality Center *(http://www.apqc.org)*, the American Society for Quality *(http://www.asq.org)*, and

the Benchmarking Exchange *(http://www.benchnet.com)*. These provide information about how benchmarking strategies are being used by nonprofit organizations.

8. Research the text of the *Government Performance and Review Act of 1993* and other legislation that is directly and indirectly encouraging the adoption of outcome-based management in both government and the nonprofit sector.

Tips for Practitioners

1. Do not let a strategic plan sit on the shelf after investing time and money developing it.

2. Know when to let a strategic plan sit on the shelf when conditions have become so turbulent or changed that following it blindly simply does not make sense.

3. Do not fall into the "goal displacement" trap by concentrating more on the paperwork involved in making a TQM program run than on the actual change in culture and staff attitudes that make TQM an attractive change management strategy.

4. Consider the steps that might be necessary to undo a change management strategy in the event that it simply does not work for one reason or another.

5. Make sure your change management strategy does not bring about the undesirable outcome of making your organization more streamlined, efficient, and effective, but with employees who cannot stand to be there anymore.

6. Incorporate useful concepts in this chapter, such as benchmarking and outcome-based management, into your strategic planning process in the event your organization engages in such planning.

Online Resources to Explore

Carter McNamara's Strategic Planning
http://www.managementhelp.org/plan_dec/str_plan/str_plan.htm

Nonprofit Leadership and Administration Faculty, Western Michigan University: Strategic Planning in Smaller Nonprofit Organizations
http://501cweb.wordpress.com/2006/11/06/strategic-planning-in-smaller-nonprofit-0rganizations/

Carter McNamara's Business Planning for Nonprofits, For-profits, and Hybrid Organizations
http://managementhelp.org/businessplanning/index.htm

Idealist.com's Strategic Planning FAQ
http://www.idealist.org/if/idealist/en/FAQ/QuestionViewer/default?section=03&item=22

Nonprofit Expert.com—Strategic Planning
http://www.nonprofitexpert.com/strategic_planning.htm

For Further Reading

Allison, M., & Kaye, J. (2003). *Strategic planning for nonprofit organizations: A practical guide and workbook.* (Second Ed.). New York: John Wiley & Sons.

Beitler, M. (2013). *Strategic organizational change.* (3rd Ed.). Greensboro, NC: Practitioner Press International.

Bryson, J. & Alston, F. (2011). *Creating and implementing your strategic plan: A workbook for public and nonprofit organizations.* (3rd Ed.). San Francisco: Jossey-Bass.

Bunker, B. B., & Alban, B. T. (1992). What makes large group interventions effective? *Journal of Applied Behavioral Science, 28*(4).

Bunker, B. B., & Alban, B. T. (2007). *Large group interventions: Engaging the whole system for rapid change.* (Kindle Ed.). San Francisco: Jossey-Bass.

Cameron, E. & Green, M. (2012). *Making sense of change management: A complete guide to the models, tools and techniques of organizational change.* (3rd Ed.). London: Kogan Page.

Deming, W. E. (1975). On some statistical aids toward economic production. *Interfaces,* 4, Aug. 1975, pp.1-15. The Operations Research Society of America and the Institute of Management Sciences.

Evans, J. & Lindsay, W. (2013). *Managing for quality and performance excellence.* (9th Ed.). KY: South-Western College Pub.

Friedman, M. (1997). *A guide to developing and using performance measures in results-based budgeting.* Washington, DC: The Finance Project.

Greenway, M. T. (1996). *The status of research and indicators on nonprofit performance in human services.* Alexandria, VA: United Way of America.

Hammer, M. (1990, July-August). Reengineering work: Don't automate: obliterate. *Harvard Business Review,* 104-112.

Hammer, M., & Champy, J. (2007). *Reengineering the corporation: A manifesto for business.* (Revised and Updated Edition). New York: HarperBusiness.

Hammer, M., & Stanton, S. A. (1994). *The reengineering revolution: A handbook.* New York: HarperBusiness.

Hiatt, J. & Creasey, T. (2013). *Change management.* (Second Ed.). Loveland, CO: Prosci Research.

La Piana, D. (2008). *Nonprofit strategy revolution: Real-time strategic planning in a rapid-response world.* St. Paul, MN: Fieldstone Alliance.

La Pianca, D. (2010). *Play to win: The nonprofit guide to competitive strategy.* St. Paul, MN: Fieldstone Alliance.

McNamara, C. (2008). *Field guide to nonprofit strategic planning and facilitation* (3rd Ed.) Minneapolis, MN: Authenticity Consulting.

Mintzburg, H. (1994). *The rise and fall of strategic planning.* New York: MacMillan.

Nelson, K. & Aaron, S. (2005). *The change management pocket guide.* Cincinnati, OH: Change Guides, LLC.

Richmond, F., & Hunnemann, E. (1996). What every board member needs to know about outcomes. Management and Technical Assistance Publication Series No. 2, Harrisburg, PA: Positive Outcomes.

Rouda, R., & Kusy, Jr., M. (1995). Organization development—The management of change. *Tappi Journal* 78(8), 253.

Watson, G. H. (1992). *The benchmarking workbook: Adapting best practices for performance improvement.* Portland, OR: Productivity Press.

Chapter 17
Quality Issues

> **Synopsis:** Quality is as important to nonprofit organizations as it is to for-profit businesses, if not more so. Nonprofits need quality programs to compete for donations, clients, board members, workers, and political support.

Introduction

Those who govern and manage nonprofit organizations are increasingly finding them subject to many of the same economic pressures as their for-profit counterparts. Their operations often resemble their for-profit competitors in both organizational structure and corporate culture. They are increasingly led by those trained in business rather than the social sciences, and their mentality and administrative style often reflect this. Stereotypically, managers trained in business school often make the "bottom line" paramount above the needs of clients.

In many cases, the products and services once provided solely by nonprofit, charitable organizations are now being provided by for-profits. One can often find health clubs, hospitals, online schools and universities, nursing homes, and day care centers—both for-profit and nonprofit—competing for clients on an equal basis within communities. When there is this direct competition, particularly in the delivery of human and educational services, cost is just one factor in a customer's decision. Quality of service is often even more important, and nonprofits that offer high-quality products and services obviously have a competitive edge. Those that cannot offer quality may find themselves out of business.

Many thousands of other nonprofit organizations do not have direct economic competition from others providing the same service. There is only one United Way affiliate in each community, one Arts Council, one Arthritis Foundation, one AARP affiliate, and one Special Olympics affiliate. Except under unusual circumstances, it is unlikely that another organization will sprout up to directly challenge one of these. It would be easy to jump to the conclusion that having a monopoly of this nature would mean that quality and performance are not as important as they are to those with direct, head-to-head competition for providing a particular product or service. That conclusion would be flawed.

Why Quality is Important to Nonprofit Organizations

Quality is important to all nonprofit organizations. None is immune from the consequences of neglecting it. Charities rely on loyal "customer" support, particularly at a time when there is an increasing reliance on fee-for-service revenues (see

Chapter 9). Even if a nonprofit is not involved in direct economic competition, there is substantial competition for things that indirectly affect the viability of organizations. Among them are:

1. **Competition for government and foundation grants.** Most charitable nonprofits depend on grants to supplement any client fees they receive. Foundations are acutely aware of organizations that have poor reputations with respect to skimping on service quality. No one wants to be associated with such an organization. It is no wonder that first-class organizations often have little trouble attracting funding, because everyone wants to be associated with them.

2. **Competition for private donations.** Would you make a donation to a charity that had a reputation of treating its clients like animals? Unless that organization is the Society for Prevention of Cruelty to Animals (SPCA), you are more likely to look elsewhere for a charity worthy of your donation.

3. **Competition for board members.** Why would anyone want to serve on the board of a second-class nonprofit and risk being condemned or otherwise embarrassed by the media, the political hierarchy, and clients? There are only so many skilled, committed civic leaders in each community who are willing to donate their time and expertise to serve on nonprofit boards, and it is clearly not attractive to serve on the board of a charity with a reputation for poor quality.

4. **Competition for volunteers.** What can be said for board members goes double for service delivery and other volunteers. No one wants to be associated with an organization with a reputation for poor quality. Many volunteers see their volunteer work as a springboard for a career, and volunteering for a pariah in the community does not serve their interests.

5. **Competition for media.** The media play an important role in helping a nonprofit charity promote its fundraising, encourage clients to utilize its services, and improve employee morale. Poor quality can result in the media ignoring an organization or, worse, highlighting its shortcomings for the entire world to see.

6. **Competition for legislative and other political support.** Nonprofit charities have benefited from the support of political leaders—directly through the provision of government grants, and indirectly

through the provision of favors such as cutting government red tape and legislation to help solve the problems of the organization and those of its clients. Political leaders are certainly not going to be responsive to an organization if they receive letters of complaint about the organization's poor quality.

7. **Competition for qualified employees.** Quality nonprofits have less employee turnover and find it easier to attract employees to fill vacancies and for expansion. Considering the high transaction costs of recruiting, training and retaining workers, this continues to be an important consideration.

The consequences of poor quality, or the reputation (public perception) of having it, can result in the board of directors throwing up its hands and deciding to liquidate the organization. Or, in extreme cases, a state government agency might step in and liquidate the organization. Imagine the aftermath of a child care agency that failed to perform a quality background check on an employee who later was found to be a child abuser, or the hospital that failed to adequately verify whether a staff member it hired was adequately board-certified.

As pointed out by Dr. John McNutt of the University of Delaware, most, if not all, states look at the community benefit provided by a nonprofit organization in considering whether it is eligible for nonprofit status in the first place. Quality and community benefit are inextricably linked (Grobman, 1999).

In 1998, an investigation by *The Chicago Tribune* uncovered that some international relief nonprofit organizations were asking donors to sponsor specific children, and failed to inform their donors that their sponsored child had died (see: *http://www.christianitytoday.com/ct/2001/december3/5.50.html*). Who knows how many millions of dollars will not be contributed because one official from one such organization did not feel it was important to inform donor sponsors that their sponsored child had died several years earlier?

The Cost of Poor Quality

An *Associated Press* article on January 8, 2002 reported that the American Red Cross disposed of 49,000 pints of blood collected after the September 11th disaster because of a lack of storage space. Many still think twice before responding to an urgent future call from that organization for blood donations, despite the obvious need to continually replenish the nation's blood reserves.

The cost to organizations with poor quality standards can be substantial. Just read the newspapers and you can find many more examples. Owners of assisted-living residences have failed to see the value of installing sprinkler systems and, as a result, have seen the loss of life and of their properties. Doctors have mistakenly removed the wrong kidney from a patient. Hospital maternity ward staff have given the wrong newborn to the wrong parents. The consequences of such lapses far exceed the financial loss and loss of prestige to the organization—human suffering for the clients and potentially huge, successful lawsuits against the nonprofit organization.

Quality in the Nonprofit Organizational Context

For the typical nonprofit that does not deliver client services, quality should mean much more than the ability to answer the telephone on the first ring. It means having a newsletter without typographical errors. It means having an attractive, periodically updated Web site. It means spelling the names of donors correctly in letters acknowledging donor gifts. It means delivering on promises made to legislators for follow-up materials. It means having conferences at which participants feel they get their money's worth. It means ensuring that each board member has all of the necessary and appropriate information to make governing decisions. It means that volunteers know in advance what is expected of them.

For those who deliver direct human services, it means, among other things:

- Treating each client with the dignity he or she deserves
- Respecting confidentiality
- Providing on-time services
- Providing timely resolution to legitimate complaints
- Providing services in a safe and secure setting
- Providing services in a facility that is accessible, clean, and functional
- Delivering services provided by competent, trained personnel
- Ensuring that services meet high standards and respond to the clients' needs
- Obtaining informed consent from clients before services are provided
- Seeking constant feedback from clients to improve the delivery of services
- Using advances in technology to improve communication between the organization and its clients.

Discussion Questions

1. How can nonprofit organizations maintain quality when budget cuts, decreases in foundation funding, declining interest in volunteering, and the burgeoning increase in the demand for services places pressures to cut corners wherever possible?

2. Do nonprofit organizations that consistently provide poor quality services really go out of business? If they do, how would this happen, and who would provide the services?

3. Should nonprofit organizations be held to a higher standard in providing quality services than their for-profit counterparts?

4. Why might it be more difficult for a nonprofit organization to recover from a lapse in quality service provision than a for-profit counterpart?

5. Do you know of any nonprofit organizations with a reputation for poor quality? What could they do to reverse that reputation?

Activities

1. Invite a staff member from your local United Way to meet with the class to discuss the importance of quality in the nonprofit environment.

2. Research how episodes of poor quality have affected various nonprofit organizations, and find out what these organizations did to respond to quality scandals.

3. Download grant application forms from various large private foundations that make grants to nonprofit organizations, and research what questions are asked that relate to quality of services.

4. Review the requirements for applying for the Baldrige Award and the application form *(http://www.nist.gov/baldrige/enter/how_to_apply.cfm)* and fill it in for a mock organization.

Tips for Practitioners

1. Consider providing all organizational staff with training that focuses on improving quality.

2. Make it organizational policy to promote "continuous quality improvement" of every program, activity, and work process.

3. Continually seek feedback from the organization's funders, clients, and staff to identify problems before they evolve into serious quality deficits.

Online Resources to Explore

National Institute of Standards and Technology's Baldrige National Quality Program
http://www.nist.gov/baldrige//

University of Wisconsin's Center for Quality and Productivity Improvement
http://cqpi.engr.wisc.edu/

American Society for Quality
http://asq.org/

The W. Edwards Deming Institute
http://deming.org/

For Further Reading

Creech, B. (1994). *The five pillars of TQM: How to make total quality management work for you.* New York: Penguin Books.

Crosby, P. B. (1979). *Quality is free.* New York: McGraw Hill.

Garvin, D. A. (1988). *Management quality: The strategic and competitive edge.* New York: Free Press.

Goetsch, D. & Davis, S. (2012). *Quality management for organizational excellence: Introduction to total quality.* (7th Ed.). New York: Prentice Hall.

Grobman, G. (1999). *Improving quality and performance in your non-profit organization: Change management strategies for the 21st century.* Harrisburg, PA: White Hat Communications.

Martin, L. (1993). *TQM in human service organizations.* San Francisco: Jossey-Bass.

WagMPB. (2013). *Quality management.* Seattle, Washington: Amazon Digital Services.

Webber, L. & Wallace, M. (2007). *Quality control for dummies.* (Updated Ed.). New York: For Dummies.

Chapter 18
Liability, Risk Management, and Insurance

> **Synopsis:** Nonprofit organizations, like all others, are exposed to risk in a variety of areas. Staff members, volunteers, clients, and members of the general public may suffer injuries while participating in or attending an organization's activities. The nonprofit may be sued for a variety of alleged wrongful acts, from unemployment discrimination to negligent supervision to breach of fiduciary duty. Every nonprofit organization should consider how it will minimize its risks, even though state and federal laws provide some protection to nonprofit organizations.

Murphy's Law has many variations and corollaries. In its simplest form, it states, "If something can go wrong, it will." And at the worst possible time. No one can foresee catastrophic events, and even if one could, it is virtually impossible to protect a corporation against all possible eventualities.

A nonprofit corporation, like a business corporation, should do everything in its power to mitigate the effect of claims against it. Like any other type of business, nonprofits could suffer personal injury or property damage claims caused by floods, fire, theft, earthquake, wind damage, building collapse, and slips and falls, just to name a few possibilities.

Legal claims against corporations tend to be of the low-incidence, high risk variety. These claims do not happen very often, but when they do, the results can be disastrous for the organization and its leadership.

Nonprofits are exposed to legal risks in many other areas. They engage in typical business transactions on a routine basis. They post on social media sites. They arrange for conventions, seminars, and other meetings. They publish newsletters. They also are employers with the attendant risk that hiring, advancement, or firing decisions may be challenged based on contract rights, discrimination, or fraud.

A nonprofit corporation could be exposed to the antitrust laws if its membership has a competitive advantage. Such nonprofit corporations could conduct various kinds of programs that permit their members to self-regulate, such as by business or professional codes, product standards and certification, or professional or academic credentialing, to use but a few examples. Such self-regulation increases exposure to liability because, among other reasons, a member may feel that a decision made about him or her was not fair.

Liability of Officers, Directors, and Other Volunteers

Nonprofit corporation volunteers may suffer from the same potential liability for actions in performance of their duties as individuals involved with business corporations. Furthermore, as managerial people, volunteer officers and directors of nonprofit corporations are bound by the same basic principles governing conduct as are directors and officers of profit-making business corporations. They owe a fiduciary duty of reasonable care and the duty to act in the best interests of the corporation and its members. This involves a duty of loyalty or good faith in managing the affairs of the corporation (see Chapter 4).

Generally, this duty requires individuals to use due care in the performance of their duties for the corporation, to act in good faith in the best interest of the corporation as a whole and not for the interests of some but not all of the members. It also entails a requirement to avoid activity or transactions in which the individual has a personal interest.

In short, in this litigious society, courts are tending more and more to impose responsibility on officers, directors, and volunteers of nonprofit corporations—including hospitals, charities, and educational institutions—for anti-trust problems, tort liability, and similar areas of liability exposure.

Several other factors contribute to increasing liability exposure for nonprofit organizations.

First, federal and state laws, such as the 1988 *Drug-Free Workplace Act* and the 1990 *Americans With Disabilities Act,* have fueled an increase in lawsuits against organizations.

Second, the increased use of technology by nonprofits has resulted in new techniques for the collection and dissemination of personal and/or confidential information. Many feel that the techniques for preserving privacy and security in the nonprofit organization environment are not keeping pace with the technology for collecting and storing information, making organizations vulnerable.

Third, nonprofits are engaging in business activities to an increasing degree to fund their programs. These activities, such as selling mailing lists, engaging in e-commerce, and publishing documents and selling them on the Internet, expose organizations to increased liability.

And fourth, but related to the three above, nonprofit organizations are more frequently partnering with for-profit organizations, making agreements by contract and delegating some of their authority to third parties that may not have the same interest in preserving the integrity of the nonprofit's brand as that nonprofit.

Civil and Criminal Liability

Nonprofit organizations have two types of liability to worry about. The first, tort liability, is intended to require someone who causes damages to another person to "make them whole" by compensating them. The damage may have been intentional or unintentional, but the action that caused the damage usually, but not always, does not fall to the level of being a crime. An example might be subjecting a potential employee to employment discrimination. If the aggrieved person can prove in court that he or she was not hired because of unlawful discrimination, a judge can award monetary damages.

A second type is criminal liability. An organization's treasurer who embezzles funds may be charged with a crime and prosecuted in the criminal courts. In contrast to a civil trial that has a standard of "preponderance of the evidence," the criminal trial has a standard of "beyond a reasonable doubt." In contrast to a civil judgment, punishment for those found guilty of a crime may include a prison sentence and/or restitution.

A perpetrator of sexual harassment, for example, may be liable for both tort liability and criminal liability. The first is intended to compensate the victim for damages. The second is intended to punish the perpetrator.

In dealing with liability suits, the courts generally consider the degree to which the action that caused the damage was intentional, and whether the damage would have been avoided if the defendant had acted in a reasonable manner. Courts also consider the context of the action—for example, even a nonprofit organization has a higher standard with respect to avoiding harm that may result in the transportation of their clients. A court may consider a higher standard to apply if the client is paying for a service.

Strategies to Minimize Exposure to Lawsuits

What can a nonprofit organization do to minimize its exposure to lawsuits? Among the strategies are—

1. *Do not offer programs and activities that impose too high a risk on the organization.* This may be the strategy of choice if your organization does not have the funds to adequately train and supervise workers or if you typically hire low-salary, entry-level workers rather than those with experience who require higher salaries. Can you afford state-of-the-art safety equipment, and are you willing to make this investment? When the nature of the service you want to deliver is simply "an accident waiting to happen," it may be best simply to

avoid sticking your neck out. Of course, many nonprofits make society better for all of us *because* they are willing to stick their necks out and provide a needed service when neither government nor the private sector is willing to do so.

2. *Change the activity or the procedures involved to reduce your organization's exposure.* This may take the form of doing background checks on potential employees. It may include periodically certifying that your workers are capable of performing their jobs, and providing them continuing education and training. Or it may simply be reducing the chances of criminal activity against one of the program participants by changing the time or venue of an event, or providing additional security personnel.

3. *Pool the risk by passing it on to insurance companies.* Respond to risk exposure by purchasing insurance to cover potential losses of specific programs and activities, or general activities of the organization and its employees and leaders.

4. *Share the risk, or pass it on to another organization that is better prepared to deal with the increased liability exposure.* For example, an organization may choose to outsource client transportation to a for-profit provider that already has sufficient insurance to cover potential losses, and has experienced, licensed, and trained personnel (e.g., professional drivers rather than volunteers).

Regardless of the strategy chosen, having basic general liability insurance to cover personal injury and property damage claims is an advantage. Consideration also should be given to purchasing directors' and officers' (D&O) insurance to protect volunteer leadership from personal legal claims.

Finally, a similar but broader type of insurance policy dealing with general professional liability protects not only officers and directors, but all association volunteers and staff, as well. Fortunately, federal and state laws have been enacted to limit the liability exposure to those who volunteer for nonprofit organizations.

Volunteer Protection Act

Although few successful lawsuits have been brought against nonprofit corporation volunteers, the possibility that lawsuits can occur presents a "perception problem." At the federal level, the *Volunteer Protection Act* (VPA) was signed into law by President Clinton in July of 1997, with an effective date of September 16, 1997.

The intent of the law is to provide limited legal immunity for the volunteers of charities who are involved in accidents that occur in connection with their charitable service. The VPA provides some protection, but there are some limitations to its applicability. Among these limitations are—

- protection applies only to volunteers—those who do not receive compensation for their services other than reasonable reimbursement of their expenses. Directors and officers are covered if their compensation is $500 annually or less.

- protection applies only in cases in which the volunteer was acting within the scope of his or her volunteer responsibilities at the time of the incident.

- the liability limit does not apply if the volunteer was required to be licensed or certified to perform an activity, and that volunteer lacked such certification or licensing.

- the liability limit does not apply if the person intentionally caused harm to others or showed flagrant indifference to the safety of those who were injured.

The immunity does not extend to harm caused by the operation of a motor vehicle, crimes of violence, activities not authorized by the charity, hate crimes, civil rights violations, damage resulting from the use of alcohol or drugs, or sexual offenses. The law encourages states to grant liability immunity to nonprofit organization volunteers who are acting in good faith and within the scope of their official duties.

Even if a nonprofit organization is liable for injuries caused by its volunteers, there is nothing in the act that prohibits the nonprofit from taking action against a volunteer who was directly responsible for damages, and recovering money paid by the nonprofit organization in claims. The act does provide for some limits of non-economic losses, such as punitive damages, that may apply to the volunteer, unless the damage caused was the result of willful or criminal misconduct, or conscious, flagrant indifference.

Personal or Professional Individual Insurance Coverage

These federal statutory provisions and many state laws provide some protection to individuals involved with nonprofit corporations. Nonetheless, many nonprofit corporations purchase either directors' and officers' (D&O) insurance to cover directors and officers, or a broader type of policy sometimes referred to as professional liability insurance, to protect not only officers and directors but all association volunteers and staff. The value of this insurance is not only to pay for substantiated claims that arise against the organization and its leadership. It also will provide the funds to defend against frivolous or otherwise unsuccessful lawsuits.

There is not much standardization with respect to what D&O insurance covers or does not cover. Consequently, organizations need to review every provision carefully and understand what they are buying. They need to consider deductibles and other out-of-pocket expenses they may have to incur before receiving benefits. Some of the more common exclusions are—

- *Dishonesty exclusion:* This is a provision that excludes coverage when a "finding in fact" is that the director or officer engaged in dishonest, fraudulent, or criminal conduct. Some policies may trigger this exclusion even when there are simply allegations of such conduct rather than a "final adjudication" by the court that such conduct did occur.

- *Insured vs. insured exclusion:* This provision excludes coverage when one director of an organization sues another director of that organization in many, but not all, cases. The intent of this provision is to limit fraudulent collusion between directors to tap insurance benefits.

- *Reimbursement after the fact:* Some D&O insurance policies only provide benefits after the claim has been resolved. Some policies will advance the funds needed to defend a claim, which can be vital in mounting an effective defense.

Although premiums for this type of insurance continue to be high, it is expected that the decrease in exposure afforded by recent state and federal laws will result in lower claims, and, eventually, lower premiums. How much should you expect to pay? According to a 2008 article posted at *http://www.blueavocado.org/content/board-members-guide-nonprofit-insurance)*, organizations without employees should expect to pay about $600 for $1 million in coverage, and those with up to 50 employees should expect to pay $4,000-$5000, but premiums vary widely.

Board Member Decision-Making

The Board of a nonprofit organization "owns" the organization in trust for the public. Ultimately, the board is responsible for assuring that the organization complies with all laws, and it is the board, not staff, that is responsible for protecting the assets of the organization. There are few cases in which board members have been found liable for making reasonable, good-faith, arm's length decisions even when hindsight has demonstrated such decisions were "bad." More likely, board members have been liable for decisions that involved self-dealing, obviously taken with criminal intent, or were just plain "stupid." As Dr. Carter McNamara writes in *Some Legal Considerations for Board Members (http://www.mapnp.org/library/legal/lgl_thot.htm)*, "Directors must attend most board meetings, not just on occasion. Absence from a board meeting does not release the director from responsibility for decisions made. A pattern of absence may indeed be presumed to increase an individual's liability because she/he cannot demonstrate a serious dedication to the obligations of the position."

McNamara further states that board members are more liable for taking no action than for taking the wrong action for the right reasons. His advice is sage when he suggests that board members should be vigilant against something that smells "fishy" and should not always assume that the information they receive is accurate.

Risk Management

The term "risk management" refers to management strategies an organization can use to enhance the safety of its stakeholders, such as clients and employees; minimize its exposure to litigation; protect its assets; and maintain its reputation. One step is to engage in a continuing planning process and implement a risk management program. Among the steps of a typical planning process are—

1. Identify potential exposure and risk to the organization's personnel, property, clients, funding, and reputation.

2. Evaluate and prioritize potential risks.

3. Develop strategies to minimize these risks.

4. Periodically evaluate and update a risk management plan.

The Nonprofit Risk Management Center has developed resources to help nonprofits assess and manage their risks. See: *http://www.nonprofitrisk.org/*

General Business Insurance

Employee lawsuits, floods, fire, theft, earthquakes, wind damage, building collapse, loss of business income, pollution, riot, lightning, war, landslides, nuclear contamination, power failures, falls, electrocution…the possibilities for natural disasters, accidents, and crime are endless. Fortunately, generic business insurance policies will protect a corporation from all of these, plus scores of other potential but unlikely occurrences.

If the organization is willing to accept a reasonable deductible (an amount of damages the corporation pays before benefits are provided on the remaining amount of damages), a policy may cost as little as a few hundred dollars. It is a worthwhile investment to make, if only for peace of mind.

Most policies include paying for defending corporate leaders in the event they are sued for whatever reason relating to business activity. Prices for basic insurance are competitive. A nonprofit organization should have liability and medical expenses coverage of at least $500,000, and the policy should cover the legal costs of defending and settling suits against the corporation and its staff.

Workers' Compensation Insurance

Every state has a workers' compensation law, which has as its purpose to provide income to workers injured on the job and to pay their medical bills. In exchange, the employee gives up the right to sue the employer. Each state's Department of Labor or the equivalent can provide information about the requirements for purchasing this insurance, which is typically obtained through a commercial insurance agency.

Unemployment Compensation Insurance

The state unemployment compensation program is a job insurance program. Its purpose is to provide some limited protection against loss of income for workers who lose their jobs through no fault of their own. The state Department of Labor or the equivalent can provide information about the requirements for participating in this program.

Discussion Questions

1. Why should nonprofit organizations be held accountable for the negligence of their employees? Can an argument be made to justify granting nonprofit organizations and their staff the same immunity that government organizations have?

2. Discuss the advantages and disadvantages of placing caps on damage awards resulting from medical malpractice.

3. Should nonprofit organizations be willing, as a matter of principle, to accept a higher level of risk of liability than their for-profit counterparts, simply because of an obligation to serve the public rather than operate out of self-interest?

4. How might a nonprofit organization's use of social media increase its exposure to liability?

Activities

1. Obtain an actual Directors' and Officers' Insurance policy from a provider, and discuss issues relating to what is covered and what is not, as well as any terms or conditions that you do not understand.

2. Use Lexis/Nexis to research actual cases involving the Volunteer Protection Act, the liability of nonprofit board members, and other liability issues involving nonprofit boards and staffs.

Tips for Practitioners

1. This chapter provides a general summary of liability issues that affect nonprofit organizations. Seek legal counsel before making any corporate decisions with respect to liability suits and claims.

2. Make sure you have an up-to-date personnel policy manual and that it includes a sexual harassment policy. Take steps to enforce these policies. Although the policies should be customized to the needs of your organization, templates can be found on the Web.

3. Provide detailed job descriptions, even for volunteers. Some provisions of the federal immunity law apply only in cases in which volunteers are engaged in activities within the scope of their duties.

4. Make sure all volunteers are certified or licensed if they engage in activities that require such certification or licensing for paid staff.

5. If your organization transports clients, make sure volunteers have vehicle insurance, and verify that all insurance policies for vehicles owned by the organization will cover damages caused by volunteers while driving those vehicles.

6. If you serve on a board and disagree with a decision made at a board meeting that you feel may result in unreasonable increased liability exposure to you or your organization, ask that your objections be recorded in the minutes.

7. Shop around for directors' and officers' insurance. Check to see if any policy you are considering will insure directors and officers for more than civil lawsuits.

Online Resources to Explore

Carter McNamara's Guide to Business Insurance
   http://www.managementhelp.org/insurnce/insurnce.htm

Idealist.com Insurance Pages
   http://www.idealist.org/if/i/en/faqcat/40-8

The Grantsmanship Center's Managing Risks in Hiring and Firing
http://www.tgci.com/articles/managing-risks-hiring-and-firing

Nonprofit Risk Management Center
http://www.nonprofitrisk.org

For Further Reading

Chapman, T. S., Lai, M. L., & Steinbock, E. L. (1984). *Am I covered for? A guide to insurance for nonprofit organizations.* San Jose, CA: Consortium for Human Resources.

Herman, M., Head, G., Fogarty, T. & Jackson, P. (2004). *Managing risk in nonprofit organizations: A comprehensive guide.* New York: Wiley.

Herman, M. (2009). *Ready...or not: A risk management guide for nonprofit executives.* Leesburg, VA: Nonprofit Risk Management Center.

Herman, M. (2003). *Ready in Defense: A liability, litigation and legal guide for nonprofits.* Leesburg, VA: Nonprofit Risk Management Center.

Jackson, P. (2006). *Nonprofit risk management & contingency planning: Done in a day strategies.* New York: Wiley.

O'Leary, M., Scheiner, E., & Smerdon, E. (2012). *Directors & officers liability insurance deskbook.* (3rd Ed.). Washington, DC: American Bar Association.

Patterson, J. & Oliver, B. (2002). *The season of hope: A risk management guide for youth-serving nonprofits.* Leesburg, VA: Nonprofit Risk Management Center.

Chapter 19
Forming and Running A Coalition

> **Synopsis:** Many nonprofit organizations form and participate in coalitions to accomplish objectives that would be difficult to achieve by themselves. There are significant advantages and considerations to forming a coalition, and the fact that they flourish is indicative of their value. This chapter discusses the advantages and disadvantages of creating and/or participating in coalitions.

Introduction

The tapestry of advocacy efforts at the international, national, state, and local levels is replete with collaborative initiatives that bring together diverse interests to accomplish a common goal. As a nonprofit organization seeks to accomplish its mission, its leadership often finds the value of creating formal and informal partnerships among like-minded organizations. As in any endeavor, there are traps and pitfalls in creating and running a coalition.

Although it is often said that "two heads are better than one," it is equally rejoined that "too many cooks spoil the broth." Both of these clichés are often equally valid when applied to a coalition, and it is important for an organizational leader to be able to assess which one applies predominantly before embarking on coalition-forming.

The Coalition

A coalition is a group of diverse organizations that join together to accomplish a specific objective that is likely to be achieved more quickly and effectively than if the organizations acted independently. There are many types of coalitions, and the structure is often dictated by political as well as financial considerations. The prototypical coalition involving state government issues starts with a convener coalition partner who has identified an issue, usually of direct importance to the convener's organizational membership.

The convener then "rounds up the usual suspects" by soliciting membership in the coalition from constituencies that will participate in the coalition. He or she schedules periodic meetings of the coalition at which members share information about the issue and develop a strategy to accomplish a specific goal of the coalition that, as is often the case, is the passage of legislation to solve the problem. It is not unusual for the coalition to continue even after the legislation upon which it focused on is enacted into law.

Structures of Coalitions

- *Formal organization.* Some coalitions structure formally, creating a distinct nonprofit corporate structure, such as a 501(c)(3), which will permit the coalition to hire staff, seek tax-deductible contributions from the public, rent office space, and have a system of governance that parallels, in many respects, the constituent organizations that comprise the coalition. Obviously, one would not seek to create such a complex legal entity if the objective of the coalition was to be achieved in the short term. It is not atypical for a new 501(c)(3) coalition staff to spend much of its efforts raising funds to keep it in business rather than focusing on the actual mission of the coalition. Even if funding is stable, many formal coalitions spend an inordinate amount of time on intra-organizational issues, compared to achieving their stated purposes. An example of a formal coalition is the REACH Alliance, formed in 1991 to coordinate advocacy relating to private school tuition vouchers (see: *http://www.paschoolchoice.org/*).

- *Semi-formal coalition.* These coalitions consist of organizations that have some financial resources themselves and are able to fund the activities of the coalition. Although not incorporated as separate legal entities, these coalitions nevertheless may have office space and staff. The office space may be provided as an in-kind contribution from one of the coalition members, and the staff may or may not be employees of one of the member organizations. An example of such a coalition is the Public Education Coalition to Oppose Tuition Vouchers.

- *Informal coalition.* Most coalitions are informal, with a convener organizational leader, but with no dedicated organizational staff or budget, or separate bank account. The convener organization convenes the coalition, sends out meeting notices, holds the meeting in the convener's office, and staffs the coalition as a part of its routine organizational duties. Costs can be shared among coalition members, and the convener duty can be rotated among members. In general, member organizations are not bound by the positions taken by the coalition. An example of such a coalition in Pennsylvania is the Charities Build Communities Coalition, sponsored by the Pennsylvania Association of Nonprofit Organizations.

- *Group networks.* A group network is a type of informal coalition that has been formed to serve an information-sharing function with less emphasis on coordinated action. These networks have no staff, no budget, take no positions, and are useful in raising the consciousness of participants about a particular issue or set of issues. These networks also are valuable in bringing people together to "network," and to build trust among organizational leadership.

Although efforts to coordinate action on an issue are often the result of a network-based coalition, the network itself often does not take a formal role in the coordination; rather, the discussions among the participants during and after the meeting result in the synergistic effects of the network. Among examples of these coalitions in Pennsylvania have been coalitions formed to ban corporal punishment, increase welfare grants, support minimum wage increases, and expand the school breakfast program.

Advantages of Forming a Coalition

- Coalitions focus attention among the media, opinion leaders, and those with advocacy resources on a specific issue. Any organization, no matter how large and powerful, has a limited ability to get its message across to the public, government officials, and the media. Building a coalition is an effective strategy to call attention to an issue, since messages not perceived to be important when heard from one organization may be considered important from another.

- Coalitions bring together experts on a particular issue. A convener of a coalition often has a burning desire to solve a particular public-policy problem and has well-developed organizational skills, but may lack the technical expertise to develop the solution. Creating a coalition is a strategy to bring together experts in the field who collegially can participate in developing a solution.

- Coalitions provide a forum to resolve turf issues and to limit destructive competition. Very few important public policy issues are so narrow that a single organization is the only one with a direct interest in their resolution. Virtually any public policy issue, particularly one that influences human services, affects a broad range of advocacy organizations, whether it impinges on children, schools, the environment, business, the disabled, or the aged. Trying to solve a problem without the "buying in" of key decision-makers is a recipe for disaster. Coalitions provide the framework for obtaining the cooperation of opinion makers who otherwise would be threatened by any effort to change public policy that violates their political turf.

- Coalitions provide credibility to an issue and to the convener organization. One obvious application of this principle is the effort, often unsuccessful, of various extremist organizations not accepted in society, such as the KKK, to try to form or participate in coalitions that have a goal consistent with a community consensus. Another principle is that organizational messages viewed as self-interest are viewed negatively. When coalitions include organizations that are viewed to be acting in the public interest (such as those affiliated with the religious community or the League of Women Voters), it is more beneficial to have the organization's message delivered by a coalition.

- Coalitions permit resources to be shared. Coalitions benefit by the resources of their membership, including money, volunteers, staff, office equipment, and meeting space. It is more cost-effective for an organization to form a coalition to permit resources to be shared, rather than having to pay the entire bill itself.

- Coalitions provide a path to inform new constituencies about an emerging issue. For example, the religious-based advocacy community's constituency may not have access to detailed information about a specific state budget problem, other than seeing an occasional newspaper article. It is one thing for welfare recipients to write to their legislators requesting a grant increase, and another for middle-class taxpayers to write advocating for an increase based on economic justice, not self-interest. Coalitions provide a framework for expanding constituencies beyond those of the convener.

- Coalitions result in positive public relations for a convener coalition-builder. New organizations build respect by forming and running a successful coalition. Although the "credit" for a success achieved single-handedly can be savored, achieving that success is often much more difficult than with help from a coalition. By bringing other organizations together and working for a common goal, those organizations learn to work with the convener, to build trust, to get visibility for the new organization, and to make it more likely that the convening organization will be invited to participate in other coalitions.

Disadvantages of Coalitions

- It is often difficult for members of a coalition to focus on an issue that is usually not the priority issue for any member of the coalition other than the convener.

- Coalition members who are not the convener often have an agenda that differs from that of the convener. They may seek to exploit the coalition for their own goals in a manner that may be inconsistent with the purpose for which the coalition was formed.

- Coalitions usually reach agreement on issues by consensus, which is sometimes difficult to achieve. When it is achieved, the result is often the lowest common denominator and dilutes the aggressiveness that might have been necessary to solve a problem.

- Coalitions require considerably more time to make decisions than would be required by the convener acting alone. Many coalition members require major decisions to be discussed by their own boards. There is a lag time between when a decision is requested and when a decision can be made by a coalition, compared with an individual organization. Even scheduling a coalition meeting to discuss when a coalition consensus can be developed can be extremely difficult at times.

- Many important coalition partners have organizational difficulties that make them accustomed to working independently rather than in coalition.

- Coalitions can require substantial organizational work, such as preparing agendas, mailing materials, and coordinating meeting times.

To Form a Coalition or Not

There are many questions that should be answered, and an honest assessment made, in determining whether forming a coalition to solve a problem is constructive. Among them are:

- What is the outcome I wish to achieve with this coalition? Is it realistic to achieve it by myself? Are the chances for success improved with a coalition?

- Whose turf am I treading on by trying to solve this issue alone? Is there a more appropriate organization to form this coalition?

- Are there constituencies in my own organization that will react negatively if I form this coalition?

- How much will a coalition cost me in terms of money, time, and focus?

- Who should be invited to participate; who should not be invited?

- Will I have better access to outside experts if I form a coalition?

- Will my prospective coalition participants get along?

- How will the coalition dissolve after my goals are achieved?

- What kind of commitment do I need from participants, and is it realistic to expect to receive these commitments?

How to Form a Coalition

- Make sure that there are no major irreconcilable differences between coalition participants, either as a result of ideology or personal enmities.

- Identify all organizations that have a direct or indirect interest in the issue.

- Invite, if appropriate, organizations that would enhance the credibility of the coalition.

- Make sure that the effort is not perceived to be partisan.

- Invite outside experts to either serve on the coalition or speak to it.

- Consider business, labor, education, religious advocacy, good government citizen groups, health, local government, state government, federal government, beneficiaries of success of the coalition's objective, provider associations, lobbyists, experts on the issue, community leaders, foundation and other grantmaker representatives, charities, and religious leaders as coalition members.

Discussion Questions

1. What do you think would be the lifecycle of a typical statewide coalition? What factors might contribute to a coalition dissolving prematurely?

2. Do you think it is possible for coalition membership to include two organizations that have diametrically opposed views on some important issue, such as pro-Choice and anti-abortion organizations, labor unions and the chamber of business and industry, and the trial lawyers association and insurance industry representatives?

3. When do you think it might be more appropriate to form a formal 501(c) organization to fulfill the tasks of a coalition compared to simply keeping the coalition informal?

4. What are some of the differences between a coalition and an association?

Activities

1. Research what coalitions are currently collaborating on advocacy issues in your State's capital city. Hint: Good sources for this information are lobbyists from groups that serve on many of these coalitions, such as those from religious advocacy organizations, labor unions, chambers of commerce, and public interest groups.

2. Put together a mock statewide coalition formed to increase the share of the state's budget that is provided for human services. Develop a list of coalition invitees, a letter of invitation, an agenda for the first meeting, a press release announcing the coalition's formation, and a statement of principles of the goals and objectives of the coalition.

3. Perform a Google search on the terms "Coalition for" and "Coalition against" paired with the name of your state. Compile a list of such organizations that you can find from telephone books in the state capital and major metropolitan areas of the state. Research these organizations by finding information from the coalitions' Web sites, by telephoning, or sending a mail survey. Compare and contrast them with respect to tax-exempt status, number of paid staff, whether their members are organizations or individuals, whether membership is free, how long they have existed, the type of coalition they are, and so on.

Tips for Practitioners

1. Remember that if the objective of the coalition were the most central focus of all members of the coalition, they would have formed it first.

2. Respect the fact that your coalition is perhaps one of many, and keep meetings short with the agenda focused. Encourage all in attendance to participate, but do not dominate the discussion yourself or let any other participant dominate. Reach consensus as quickly as possible, and then move on.

3. Delegate the work of the coalition to participants (such as by forming committees when necessary to develop a consensus).

4. Make the meeting pleasant by being hospitable (such as providing soft drinks or lunch).

Online Resources to Explore

Wisconsin Clearinghouse for Prevention Resources—Community Change Tools
http://healthinpractice.org/communications/tech-tools

Community How To Guide on Coalition Building
http://www.hungerfreecommunities.org/resource-library/community-how-to-guide-on-coalition-building/

National Coalition Building Institute
http://ncbi.org/

University of Kansas Coalition Building Community Toolbox
http://ctb.ku.edu/en/tablecontents/sub_section_main_1057.aspx

Institute for Sustainable Communities
http://www.iscvt.org/

For Further Reading

Brown, C. R. (1984). *The art of coalition building— A guide for community leaders.* New York: American Jewish Committee.

Kahn, S. (1991). *Organizing: A guide for grassroots leaders.* Washington, DC: NASW Press.

Roberts, J. (2005). *Alliances, coalitions and partnerships: Building collaborative organizations.* British Columbia, CA: New Society Publishers.

Van Dyke, N. & McCammon, H. (2010). *Strategic alliances: Coalition building and social movements.* Minneapolis, MN: University of Minnesota Press.

Wolff, T. (1997). *From the ground up! A workbook on coalition building & community development.* Amhurst, MA: AHEC/Community Partners.

Chapter 20
The Future of the Nonprofit Sector

> **Synopsis:** The nonprofit sector is facing transformational challenges. Among the trends identified to watch are the threat of terrorism, changing demographics, advancing technology, increased government scrutiny, government cutbacks, donor attitude changes, the blurring of the sectors, and increasing professionalism of the sector.

Introduction

Serious challenges currently face the nonprofit sector. Yet when has there been a time when this was not so? Those who lead nonprofit organizations have always been on the front lines of the battle to improve the human condition. If there were no problems that people could not adequately address themselves or with the help of government alone, then the sector may well have dissolved by itself. That being said, many feel, including me, that the nonprofit sector is undergoing a revolutionary transformation, the result of massive changes in society with respect to demographics, economic instability, technology advancement, cultural and attitudinal shifts, and increasing competition for shrinking resources.

The purpose of this chapter is to focus not on these generic challenges particularly, but to look at what transformational trends, both for good and for bad, point to potential major restructuring of the sector. This is done from the standpoint of how it is perceived by the media, contractors, government regulators, donors, and the public. In this chapter, I identify and discuss eight major trends that have the potential to transform the sector.

Trend 1: Terrorism and the Fear of Terrorism are affecting the way charities do business.

At this very moment, scores, if not hundreds, of well-financed and well-trained terrorists are dedicating their lives, both literally and figuratively, to attacking America, its citizens, and its institutions, and to bringing an end to our way of life. It is not a question of whether they would do the unthinkable—kill as many of us as they can with weapons of mass destruction. It is understood that the limitation is not motivation, but rather the means and ability to do so. As the September 11th terrorist attacks demonstrated, no one is immune. And it is not as if we did not have any warning, since the previous attack on the World Trade Center was intended to have the same result.

Since 9/11, we have seen a public reaction ranging from acceptance to panic, and back to complacency. Duct tape and plastic sheeting sales skyrocketed in the weeks after 9/11 (Isidore, 2003; Reaves, 2003). Potassium iodide tablets were being distributed by local governments, including my own municipality of Harrisburg, Pennsylvania, just ten miles from the Three Mile Island (TMI) nuclear plant (Pennsylvania Department of Health, 2002).

Yet, since 9/11, major foreign threats to the homeland were either thwarted or never materialized, and the American public again has been lulled into the feelings of invulnerability it had before that attack. We are reminded of the threat of terrorism only from annual commemorations of the worst domestic terrorist incident in our history and the legal fallout from the 2013 terrorist bombings at the Boston Marathon, an event sponsored by a nonprofit organization, the Boston Athletic Association.

As a runner, I was an eyewitness to the Boston bombings that traumatized our nation and resulted in a virtual lockdown of a major U.S. city for four days. I also saw firsthand how the threat of terrorism influenced the operations of the event at the following year's marathon, in which I also participated. Security, which had always been present (there had been bomb-sniffing dogs patrolling the Athlete's Village even in years prior to the bombings), was quite visible throughout the course at the 2014 Boston Marathon.

As I write this, the American public sleeps soundly, undisturbed. There appears to be no lasting effect of the 9/11 tragedy on the nonprofit sector, unless one factors in the indirect effects of the wars in Iraq and Afghanistan. The threat of single-day losses of billions of dollars in the value of nonprofit organization endowments due to terrorism has been supplanted by the reality of single-day losses exceeding $1 trillion (Twin, 2008) attributed to the self-inflicted precariousness of the financial markets that cannot be traced in any way to terrorism or the fear of terrorism. But 9/11 and the Boston bombings served to illustrate the vulnerability of an open and free society—even as new towers are being built and occupied on the 16 acres that comprise "ground zero," and one of America's most prestigious sporting events continues to be held each year.

Cyber-terrorism, defined as "an assault on electronic communications networks" (Webster's, 2004), is a related issue that affects the behavior of the public. In 2000, the "I Love You" virus caused an estimated $15 billion loss in data (Schumer, 2000). Dan Verton, a former intelligence officer and a *ComputerWorld* senior staff writer, writes that our computer systems are not only vulnerable, but are already being targeted by hackers with the ability to cause physical death and destruction—such as by flooding 911 call centers with phantom calls, disabling power grids, wreaking havoc with the distribution of food supplies, and disrupting communications of first responders (Verton, 2003). A September 2010 study of the Council of Foreign Relations reported that the annual cost of cyber-crime has now reached an astounding $1 trillion (Knake, 2010). A more recent study (June 2014) calculated it at between $400 billion and $675 billion annually (Lawrence, 2014).

How will terrorism and the fear of terrorism affect the nonprofit sector in the long term? Here are some mini-trends:

a. There will likely be less travel outside of the home and less large group aggregation. After a high profile terrorist incident or during a time of high terrorism alert—which can be a weekend or last for months—we could expect that there will be a hesitation to travel outside one's home, except for essential purposes, in the immediate hours following such an attack. Government officials shut down the city of Boston and implored their citizens to stay inside following the search for the perpetrators of the Boston Marathon bombings (DeLuca, 2013).

We saw this phenomenon immediately after the 9/11 attacks, when airline travel plummeted. Airports and airplanes now have increased security, and we now have reports that potential targets of terrorists include "softer" targets, such as ports, shopping malls, hotels, apartment buildings, and train stations. The bombing of trains in Madrid on March 11, 2004, highlighted the vulnerability of our own passenger rail system. At a time of high terrorism alert (or in the wake of an attack), it would seem logical that simply staying in one's own home would decrease the exposure to risking personal safety. People would be more likely to stay connected via the telephone, radio, cable television, and the Internet rather than by meeting together. This could hamper group activities relied upon by the nonprofit community, such as face-to-face board meetings, holding group fundraising events at a centralized site, organizing advocacy days in the state and national capitals, scheduling conferences and annual meetings, and other activities that bring people together to support the work of a nonprofit organization. In response, nonprofits are likely to utilize new technologies to permit people to "come together" while safely in their own homes or offices (see Trend #3).

b. There may be a potential depression in charitable giving, based on a belief that the future is uncertain and unstable. When trading on the New York stock exchange resumed on September 17, 2001, the DOW Industrial Average recorded a drop of 684 points, the largest point decline of the Dow in history at the time, and the third largest ever (Morning, 2014). Are Americans less likely to share their wealth if they believe that the wealth they feel they have, and need to provide security for themselves and their families, could "disappear" in the wake of another attack that some predict could dwarf the 9/11 tragedy? Although some of this can be attributed to a flagging economy, some attribute the flagging economy to the after-effects of 9/11.

c. Foundations and nonprofit organizations will suffer directly from the collapse of equity markets in the wake of any terrorist attack. When the equity markets collapsed post 9/11, it was not only individual investors and corporations that suffered. Foundations and nonprofit organization endowments also were devastated, reducing the capital that was available for investing in charitable organizations.

d. Nonprofit organizations will be urged to devote more of their resources for security and emergency-preparedness. They will need to make sure that those who access physical and virtual facilities are who they say they are and do not have weapons. More funds will need to be budgeted and spent for building security, computer security, emergency planning and equipment (such as generators and emergency kits), backup for sensitive electronic data, training, and the staff to manage these issues. Organizations can expect to experience disruptions resulting from computer worms and viruses. They will spend time and money backing up data, printing out hard copies to ensure that data are available in the event of electronic disruptions, storing vital records in protected environments, and other tasks that have increased the transaction costs of running an organization. Since 2007, nonprofit 501(c)(3) organizations in high-risk cities have been eligible for grants of up to $75,000 to improve the security of their buildings as part of the Department of Homeland Security's Urban Areas Security Initiative Nonprofit Security Grant Program. Thirteen million dollars were available for this program in FY 2014, a $3 million increase over previous years (FEMA, 2014).

Trend 2: The demographics of the United States population are changing.

Although America has always had the reputation of being a "melting pot," it has become increasingly popular to celebrate ethnic and religious diversity. It is understood that older people have different needs and attitudes compared to the "X" generation. Language differences result in more communication difficulties, and these can be accentuated when cultural differences are magnified. Older donors tend to have different views about charity than younger donors. These are some of the reasons nonprofit sector futurists keep a close eye on demographic trends.

What are some important demographic trends worth watching?

a. The nonprofit workforce, already more diverse in many respects than the general workforce, is becoming much more diverse. According to the U.S. Census, the non-Hispanic white population will be falling steadily, from 74% in 1995 to 72% in 2000, to 64% in 2020 and 53% in 2050 (U.S. Census Bureau, 1996). This trend, identified almost two decades ago, was confirmed by the 2010 census—of a total population of 281.4 million, 216.9 million, or 75%, were white (CBSNews.com, 2001). According to the latest census, the U.S. population was 316.1 million, and the Census Bureau classified only 196.8 million, 63.7%, as "white" and not Hispanic or Latino. This decreased to 62.6% by 2013 (U.S. Census Bureau, 2014a). Nonprofit organization managers must be more sensitive to cultural differences among those they manage and take steps to ensure that their staff will be culturally competent.

In the same way, the population being served by nonprofit organizations is becoming more diverse. Fundraisers can benefit by being sensitive to cultural differences among those they approach for gifts, taking into account the increasing capacity of minorities to make donations (Anft, 2001).

b. The U.S. population is aging. Census data confirm that Americans are growing older; the median age in the U.S. increased from 32.9 in 1990 to 35.3 in 2000 and to 37.2 in 2010 (U.S. Census Bureau, 2011). The U.S. Census Bureau predicts that between 2012 and 2050, the population aged 65 and over will be 83.7 million, almost double its estimated population of 43.1 million in 2012. Baby boomers make up a large part of this increase, as they began turning 65 in 2011 (Ortman, Velkoff, & Hogan, 2014).

The 2010 census did confirm that the fastest growing cohort of the aged was the group of those 90 and older, growing from 2.8% of the population 65 and over in 1980 to 4.5% in 2010. The Census Bureau reported that the 90 and older population reached 1.9 million in 2010, tripling over the past three decades (U.S. Census Bureau, 2011).

Older Americans need more health care and income to live on. Some of this will be provided by their children, who might otherwise have volunteered and donated to charities. According to the Family Caregiver Alliance, 65.7 million caregivers, 29% of the U.S. adult population, provide care to someone who is ill, disabled, or aged (Family Caregiver Alliance, 2012).

Thirty-five percent of workers reported that they had provided care for a relative or in-law 65 years or older within the past year (Bond, et al., 2002). On the other side of this ledger, conservative estimates are that $41 trillion will be transferred among the generations over the next 50 years with $12 trillion transferred by 2020 (Johnston, 1999; Community Foundation R&D Incubator, 2000). Even after many personal wealth portfolios were devastated by economic disaster, the study's author maintained that the $41 trillion figure was still valid (Schervish, 2009). And much of this wealth was recovered in the 2013-2014 period of record stock market highs. Even at its worst, wealthy individuals lost just 16% of the value of their investment portfolios (Grogan, 2013).

Nonprofits themselves are facing a potential internal leadership crisis as a result of the aging of our population. A study conducted by the School of Public Affairs of Baruch College, commissioned by the United Way of New York City, found that nearly half of all of the City's nonprofit executives plan to retire within the next five years. Little or nothing is being done to plan for their succession or to train the next generation of leadership (Gardyn, 2003).

In June 2007, the Conference Board issued a study following up on data compiled by the Bridgestone Group's study, *The Nonprofit Sector's Leadership Deficit*, which predicted massive leadership shortages in the sector. The Bridgestone Group study found that over the next decade, even excluding hospitals and institutions of higher learning, nonprofit organizations with revenues exceeding $250,000 annually—

> *will need to attract and develop some 640,000 new senior managers— the equivalent of 2.4 times the number currently employed. If the sector were to experience significant consolidation and lower-than-forecast turnover rates, this number might fall as low as 330,000. On the other hand, given historic trends, the total need could well increase to more than one million. By 2016, these organizations will need almost 80,000 new senior managers per year* (Tierney, 2005).

The Nonprofit Congress, which first convened in 2006, served as a forum bringing together nonprofit leaders to discuss the needs of the sector, as well as to consider its future. Among the working groups established by the Nonprofit Congress was a Leadership Working Group that issued a report of leadership programs around the country. Grantmakers for Effective Organizations also added its two cents. For more on this issue, see: *http://www.academia.edu/433609/Executive_Succession_An_Assessment_of_Nonprofit_Research*

c. There are more women in the workforce and more dual-earner couples. According to the Census Bureau, the number and percentage of women in the work force has skyrocketed, from 30.3 million in 1970 (38%) to 72.7 million (47.2%) during 2006-2010 (Baig, 2013). The proportion of men and women who are dual-earning couples has increased in the past from 66% in 1977 to 78% in 2002, according to the 2002 study, *National Study of the Changing Workforce*, from the Families and Work Institute (Bond, 2002). The findings showed that fathers in dual-earner couples spent 42 minutes more doing household chores on workdays than these same fathers in 1977. The time these couples spend caring for and doing things with their children on workdays actually increased by almost 20%. Precious little time (an average of 1.3 hours for dads and .9 hours for moms) is spent on themselves each workday. Left unsaid in the report is that there is a strain on leisure time that can be devoted to volunteer service with the voluntary sector.

d. There are more single-parent families. "One of the most striking changes in family structure over the last twenty years has been the increase in single-parent families. In 1970, the number of single-parent families with children under the age of 18 was 3.8 million. By 1990, the number had more than doubled to 9.7 million" (Kirby, 1995). As of 2013, there are approximately 12 million single-parent families in the U.S., about 10 million of them headed by the mother (U.S. Census Bureau, 2013a). Of these single-parent families, 34% of incomes fall below the poverty level

(Bosak, 2003). Although studies that show children from such families lagging behind on indicators such as achievement, intellectual development, and behavior have been challenged on methodological grounds, mother-only families are more likely to live in poverty. As the number of nontraditional families increases, nonprofit organizations that provide human services must make adjustments. Many banks are open on weekends—unthinkable a decade or two ago. This is a reflection of that industry's willingness to adjust to the times.

e. The number of Americans who report a disability is increasing. According to the U.S. government (U.S. Census Bureau, 2012), 56.7 million Americans have some type of long-lasting condition or disability. This constitutes 18.7% of the 303.9 million civilians aged five and older who were not living in prisons, nursing homes, or other institutions. Nonprofit organizations must ensure that their offices are accessible to people with disabilities, that their Web sites are accessible to those who are vision-impaired, and that their staffs are trained to accommodate special needs.

Trend 3: Most nonprofits are taking advantage of the technology revolution, but a digital divide threatens to divide the sector into "haves" and "have nots."

The nonprofit sector has been transformed by advances in technology. Obviously, nonprofits are benefiting by technology other than just the Internet. Smartphones, tablets, scanners, relational databases, and bar codes are just some examples of technological advances that are helping make the sector more efficient. Here, I will focus on some aspects of the Internet that are revolutionizing how nonprofit staff are doing their jobs.

Perhaps as much as $30 billion of what charities raise is consummated over the Internet (Agitator, 2010), and this amount has been increasing geometrically for some time (Wallace, 2004; Wallace 2006). Nonprofits use their own Web sites and specialized sites such as Idealist *(http://www.idealist.org)*, Nonprofit Oyster *(http://www.nonprofitoyster.com)*, and VolunteerMatch *(http://www.VolunteerMatch.org)* to hire staff and find volunteers. Prospect research may still involve going through dusty newspapers in libraries, but a few simple clicks using search engines such as Google *(http://www.google.com)* and online databases such as Melissa Data Corporation Lookups *(http://www.melissadata.com/Lookups/index.htm)* and Hoover's *(http://www.hoovers.com)* turn up more information about more potential prospects. A simple broadcast e-mail, text message, or Facebook post can instantly mobilize thousands of advocates for or against an important legislative bill or amendment. Millions of dollars of additional revenue are being raised online through the sale of goods and services, holding charity auctions, and partnering with for-profit retailers (Grobman, 2001; Grobman & Grant, 2006). Nonprofits instantly research and apply for government grants online, using sites such as Grants.gov *(http://www.*

grants.gov). Universities (and other types of nonprofits, as well) rely on the Internet for training, workshops, courses, and virtual meetings.

Here are some mini-trends:

a. Online fundraising is skyrocketing. Between July 29 and August 29, 2014, contributions to the ALS Association exceeded $100 million, most of it online, as a result of the viral, social media driven "ice bucket challenge"—with some days exceeding $10 million. The Leukemia and Lymphoma Society reported raising $98 million online in 2013 (Daniels and Narayanswami, 2014). Network for Good boasts on its Web site that it has distributed more than $1 billion to 100,000 charities since its founding in 2001, including $190 million in 2013 (Network for Good, 2014). Within days of the December 2004 tsunami disaster, the charity portal recorded at least $10 million in online donations made to tsunami relief organizations. The organization reported donations of more than $1 million by credit card on a single day. An analysis of donations made to 115,489 organizations in both 2011 and 2012 through the online-payment processors Blackbaud, Network for Good, and PayPal indicated that online giving grew at an annual rate of about 12% in 2012, totaling $2.13 billion (*Chronicle of Philanthropy,* 2014).

b. Advocacy efforts are harnessing the full power of technology. A description of the success of the Web site Moveon *(Moveon.org),* a group founded in 1998, in the April 17, 2003, issue of *The Chronicle of Philanthropy* provides a snapshot of the future of nonprofit advocacy (and, perhaps, fundraising as well). More than 550,000 people signed an online petition directed to the United Nations concerning the Iraq situation in less than two days, and eventually, the total number of signers of the petition exceeded one million.

Online advocacy efforts are resulting in much more than "virtual" advocacy that generates e-mail, petitions, telephone calls, and letters to public policy decision-makers. The Internet is being used to mobilize people to physically attend political demonstrations. Many analysts credit the use of the Internet for fundraising, volunteer recruitment, and advocacy as the decisive edge that won the presidency for Barack Obama in 2008 (Stirland, 2008; Granfield, 2008). Mr. Obama had 3 million Facebook friends on election day compared to 600,000 for Sen. John McCain, his Republican opponent. As of July 2014, President Obama had more than 41 million Facebook likers, through the nonprofit organization Organizing for Action (*Fanpagelist.com, 2014*).

c. The "digital divide" will become more pronounced with respect to nonprofit organizations. The mainstream media have focused attention on the so-called "digital divide." The term is typically used to describe the disparity of technology access not only among races and income levels, but also communities, regions, and countries. The generalized fear is that we are quickly becoming a society of two classes—those who have access to, and proficiency with, technology, and those who do not. Race, socio-economic status, and education level may soon take a back seat to whether or not each of us has the ability to download files from the Internet, use a smartphone, or submit a résumé electronically.

There is continuing evidence that the digital divide between the rich and poor is also applicable to the comparison of for-profit organizations and their nonprofit counterparts, as well as within the nonprofit sector itself (Greene, 2001). The interest of foundations in aggressively closing the sector digital divide has waned. For example, a review of the digital divide pages of the Benton Foundation *(http://benton.org/library#thedigitaldivide)* shows little evidence that this issue remains a high priority. Perhaps one reason for this is that the divide may indeed be closing, as the cost of technology has plunged. Computers, interactive Web sites, and smartphones are more accessible. Sophisticated software is becoming available for free or at minimal charge as a result of the "open source" movement (Grobman, 2008, Grobman & Grant, 2006). For more on recent literature concerning the digital divide, see: *http://www.digitaldivide.org/#!dd-redefined/c1cji*

One issue that might deserve some exploration four years from now is the human cost of having nonprofit staff tethered to their smartphones, laptops, and tablets, and having their personal boundaries encroached by the advance of technology. Will we be seeing more executive burnout in the sector exacerbated by this technology?

d. Social networking sites such as Facebook and Twitter are being exploited by nonprofit organizations to recruit volunteers, raise funds, and increase advocacy. Virtually every major nonprofit organization maintains an active presence on sites such as Facebook, LinkedIn, and Twitter. See Chapter 15 for more on this trend.

Trend 4: The nonprofit sector should expect increased government scrutiny, as well as more regulation and accountability requirements.

We should expect that increased regulation of charities is more likely in the future, as a result of real and perceived abuses by charities. Among areas of regulation likely to be the focus in the future include reform relating to engaging in political activity, paying excessive fees to board members, and expanding financial accountability requirements. We've recently seen the IRS crack down on organizations that applied for 501(c)(4) status whose names suggested a mission of substantial political activity. The IRS apologized for inappropriately singling out organizations solely based on their names, but generally defended its actions as an effort to keep political organizations from qualifying as social welfare organizations (Bump, 2013; Teaparty.org, 2013; Internal Revenue Service, 2013).

The following summarizes some of the areas of nonprofit regulation that are ripe for reform:

a. Financial accountability in the nonprofit sector. The *American Competitiveness and Corporate Accountability Act,* commonly known as the Sarbanes-Oxley Act, was enacted by the Congress in 2002 as a response to corporate financial scandals, such as those at Enron, Arthur Anderson, and Global Crossing (Silk, 2004). Generally, this act does not apply to nonprofit corporations, although two provisions—those relating to protecting whistle-blowers and the destruction of litigation-related documents—do apply to both for-profit and nonprofit corporations. Despite this, many of the requirements of the act could apply to nonprofit organizations. In September 2004, the California legislature enacted the *Nonprofit Integrity Act of 2004,* extending many of the federal requirements to California's nonprofit organizations. Other states are actively considering whether to apply some or all of the provisions relating to for-profit corporations to nonprofit organizations, including Massachusetts, New Hampshire, and Connecticut (Herwit Associates, 2014). Among other provisions, Sarbanes-Oxley requires an independent and competent audit committee, requires the lead and reviewing partner of the firm providing the audit to rotate off at least every five years, prohibits the auditing firm from providing non-auditing services to an organization concurrent with an audit, requires the CEO and the CFO to certify the appropriateness of financial statements and to verify that these statements fairly represent the financial condition of the company, prohibits loans to executives and directors, and increases financial disclosure requirements.

b. Payments to board members. A survey of 238 foundations conducted in 2003 disclosed that more than two-thirds paid their trustees, and such fees in 1998 amounted to $31.1 million to individual board members and $13.8 million to bank trustees (Lipman, 2003). Studies such as this, and scandals involving questionable payments and loans (Lipman & Williams, 2004a; Lipman & Williams, 2004b) by some foundations to their governance and management leadership, have focused the attention of state and federal regulators on changing the way foundations calculate the minimum 5% payout rate threshold (Kramer, 2003).

c. Advocating for public policy positions. Most of us take it for granted that part of the civic responsibility of nonprofit organizations is to advocate for changes in public policy that will support our important missions. This imperative is not necessarily accepted by some conservative members of Congress. The Istook Amendment, actually a series of amendments placing curbs on public advocacy and lobbying by organizations that receive federal grants, was successfully added by Rep. Ernest Istook (R-OK) in 1995 to appropriations legislation (Maskell, 1998). There was a lot of sympathy in Congress for the Congressman's view that charities, subsidized by federal tax exemptions, were using their funds for public advocacy, often advocating for policy changes that were out of the mainstream. The nonprofit advocacy community mobilized, and the amendments were never enacted. Years later, Rep. Istook was offended by an advertisement that appeared on District of Columbia-area Metro bus and subway system vehicles and facilities that suggested that marijuana should be legalized and taxed. An amendment by Rep. Istook to the conference report of H.R. 2673, the $373 billion Consolidated Appropriations Act, considered in December 2003, prohibited transit agencies receiving federal funds from running advertising from groups seeking to decriminalize marijuana and other Schedule I substances for medical or other purposes (OMB Watch, 2003; U.S. House of Representatives, 2003). In 2005, Rep. Istook added language to the proposed Federal Housing Finance Reform Act (H.R. 1461) that would have disqualified nonprofits from participating in the grant program envisioned by the legislation if they engaged in voter registration and other nonpartisan voter activities within 12 months of applying for the grant. The toxic effects of battling the amendments offered by Rep. Istook eventually became a dim memory. Rep. Istook is no longer offering these amendments, as he left Congress to run for governor of Oklahoma in 2006. Mr. Istook lost and is now a fellow at the Heritage Foundation, a conservative think tank in Washington, D.C., and also a radio talk show host. With Mr. Istook no longer involved, his cause was taken up by Rep. Virginia Foxx (R-NC) and Sen. Jim DeMint (R-SC), who offered amendments in 2009 to the *Serve America Act* designed to cripple the ability of nonprofits to lobby if they accepted funds under the bill (Stehle, 2009). The amendments did not succeed. However, it should be expected that nonprofits will need to remain vigilant against continuing attempts to muzzle their legitimate right (and duty) to advocate public policy changes. And it would not be unexpected if the Congress enacts some, perhaps mild, curbs on the advocacy rights of nonprofit organizations.

d. Churches and political activity. Current law proscribes tax-exempt organizations from participating in partisan political activity, including taking action in support of, or opposition to, any candidate. Until relatively recently, the IRS had a history of not enforcing this prohibition with any great diligence. In 1994, churches in Virginia that allowed candidates for the U.S. Senate to address political remarks to their congregations from the pulpit received an IRS warning to not do this again (Dye, 2002). Courts have upheld a ruling by the IRS to revoke the exemption of a New York church that purchased a newspaper advertisement containing negative references to a candidate during a campaign (Dye, 2002).

Beginning with the 2004 election cycle, the IRS established its Political Activities Compliance Initiative (PACI) to respond to allegations of violations. In February 2006, the IRS released a report that concluded that of the 110 churches it studied after accusations that they were illegally politicking, 59 of them were indeed violating the law and 28 of the cases were still being reviewed. According to the IRS, it was seeking to revoke the tax exemptions of three of these churches, was fining one other, and was sending a letter to the others requesting that the violations cease (Lenkowsky, 2006). The IRS has gotten much more aggressive about enforcing the law against tax-exempt organizations, including churches that are perceived as engaging in partisan political activity in support of candidates for office. In July 2006, the IRS sent 15,000 notices to tax-exempt organizations, including churches, to warn them that improper campaigning could put their tax exemptions at risk (*Philanthropy News Digest*, 2006). Despite this warning, the IRS recorded 237 public complaints alleging illegal campaign activities by tax-exempt organizations during the 2006 election cycle. An IRS audit of campaign finance reports found nearly $345,000 in illegal direct contributions to candidates from 269 organizations.

In June 2007, the IRS initiated investigations of more than 350 nonprofit organizations for illegal political activity and began gearing up to monitor charities for the 2008 election cycle (Panepento, 2007). A publication of the IRS, *Tax Guide for Churches and Other Religious Organizations* (Pub. 1828, revised November 2009), provides guidance about acceptable and unacceptable political activities by religious congregations. It is available at: *http://www.irs.gov/pub/irs-pdf/p1828.pdf*. Despite these rules, the IRS has apparently stopped enforcement of the law since 2009 (Zoll, 2012), but one might expect that as violators become more brazen, or if the Congress applies more pressure, the IRS may resume enforcement at any time.

Trend 5: Government funding for nonprofits is drying up at a time when demand for services will be increasing.

U.S. public benefit charities relied on government funding to provide about 31% of organization income in 1989, nearly twice the revenue these organizations received from private contributions (Salamon, 1999). The federal, state, and local governments that year spent nearly a trillion dollars on "social welfare services," about 53% of all government spending and almost a fifth of the entire U.S. gross domestic product, with about 59% of that total provided by the federal government (Salamon, 1999). Increasing percentages of these services are provided by the voluntary sector, and even when not, charities are often called upon to pick up the slack when people fall through the cracks and do not receive the government services to which they are entitled. The obvious implication is that the partnership between government and the nonprofit sector is vital.

As Lester Salamon points out, government growth in spending for social programs grew rapidly for a decade and a half prior to the inauguration of President Ronald Reagan. During the Reagan years, most of the cuts in federal domestic spending were targeted to programs for the poor (Salamon, 1999). Some of the cuts were motivated by ideology that expressed the view that "government is not the solution to our problem, government is the problem" (Reagan, 1981) and that individual initiative and the nonprofit sector can do a better job than government in improving the lives of the needy. But the budget cuts were also justified by the Congress and the Administration by the arithmetic of budgeting. Major increases in defense spending and a massive tax cut led to federal budget deficits. Entitlement spending and interest payments on the debt left little else to attack other than domestic spending, much of which was spent on programs that political conservatives found unpalatable anyway.

Today, some of the same dynamics are at work that militate for a repeat of the disastrous 1980s, which saw attempts to poke holes in the "safety net" that protects the needy. The September 11th attacks justified a quantum increase in expenditures for defense and homeland security. The war in Iraq created tens of billions of dollars in unbudgeted spending. A large tax cut was enacted for the purpose of pump-priming the moribund American economy, slashing government revenues. And huge budget deficits were incurred despite the fact that just months before, surpluses were predicted for the coming decades. On top of all this, a severe recession dried up federal revenues and created a burgeoning increase in the demand for services.

Brinckerhoff (1995) suggests that "demand will grow irrevocably, irreversibly, and faster than you anticipate, in almost every service area" for several reasons. First, society has steadily turned to nonprofits over the last 30 years. Second, the chronic underfunding of social services results in many homeless and "underclass" citizens seeking help. Third, the trend of relocation of some nonprofits (such as inner-city hospitals) to market their services to a more lucrative market leaves many unserved or underserved.

But these are far from the only reasons. New social problems surface, and government has always been slow to respond. The terrorist attacks of 2001 and natural disasters here and abroad created a demand for billions of charitable dollars. Americans responded generously, but many charities without missions related to helping the victims suffered fundraising decreases, some of which were attributable to the declining economy, but certainly not all. The number of families and individuals without health insurance has been steadily increasing. According to the U.S. Census Bureau, the number of persons without health insurance increased from 46.3 million in 2008 to 50.7 million in 2009 (U.S. Census Bureau, 2010). The number dipped only slightly in 2012, according to the U.S. Census Bureau, to about 48 million, mostly attributed to increased enrollment in Medicaid and Medicare (Galewitz, 2013). Presumably, this still bleak picture will be improved once the *Affordable Care Act* takes full effect.

Census data released in 2013 show that poverty is still a scourge in this country, with the poverty rate maintaining a steady 15% of individuals in 2012 and 2013, 2.5 points higher than in 2007 (U.S. Census Bureau, 2013b). There is nothing on the horizon that militates for reversing these trends.

And all of this has occurred during a period of relative "prosperity" for Wall Street, with the Dow Industrial Average reaching record highs in 2014. A few years prior to then, we saw a drying up of credit markets, viral bank failures, the fall 2008 stock market crash of about 40% of the value of the equity markets compared to its high for the year, and the subprime mortgage scandals. The public became more attuned to the sword of Damocles over the American habit of borrowing more than its individuals and organizations could possibly pay back. As an article in the *San Francisco Chronicle* portends, the worst is yet to come:

> *Think $700 billion to bail out Wall Street is expensive? Just wait. The mortgage meltdown is cheap compared with the coming fiscal firestorm fanned by unfunded Social Security and Medicare costs. Together, these programs hold unfunded obligations totaling $41 trillion—60 times larger than the proposed Wall Street bailout. And even this understates the difference, because $41 trillion is the current net value of the unfunded obligations over 75 years. The actual cumulative yearly deficits these programs face over the next 75 years are several magnitudes larger than $41 trillion* (Riedl, 2008).

As I update this chapter, even with the official unemployment rate down to a "manageable" 6.2% in August 2014 compared to 9.6% in September 2010, some of the same dynamics are at work that raise the specter of a repeat of the disastrous 1980s, which saw attempts to poke holes in the "safety net" that protects the needy.

An Associated Press article in mid-October 2008 focused public attention on the increase in the national debt:

> *A watched clock never moves—unless it's the National Debt Clock. In fact, the digital counter has been moving so much that it recently ran out of digits to display the ballooning figure: $10,150,603,734,720, or roughly $10.2 trillion, as of Saturday afternoon.*
>
> *The clock was put up by the late real estate mogul Seymour Durst in 1989 when the U.S. government's debt was a mere $2.7 trillion, and was even turned off during the 1990s when the debt decreased. It will be replaced in 2009 with a new clock, said Jordan Barowitz, a spokesman for the Durst Organization. The new clock will be able to track debt up to a quadrillion dollars, which is a "1" followed by 15 zeros* (Franklin, 2008).

As I write this, the clock reads $17.6 trillion (it was "only" $13.4 trillion when I last updated this statistic for the third edition of this book). In 2013, the federal government was shut down from October 1 to October 16, as there were not enough votes to pass budget-related legislation. The same political forces fought tooth and nail against legislation that would authorize an increase in the debt ceiling, which, if not enacted, would have sent the country into default on its fiscal obligations.

As pointed out by Jacqueline Pfeffer Merrill in an article posted online in *Philanthropy Daily* during the shutdown, many nonprofit organizations felt the effects directly. She wrote:

> *Nonprofits that rely on government funding are being shuttered or cutting back during the government shutdown, including charities that provide fuel assistance and meals and lunches to needy children. And it's not just beneficiaries of charities that are being hurt: nonprofit staff may be*

sent home without pay—and without the assurance given to furloughed federal employees that they will ultimately be paid for these days (Merrill, 2013).

Almost all states have suffered serious revenue shortfalls, with charities depending on state dollars experiencing additional rounds of reduced state support that began in 2009. The consequences of this for nonprofits were documented in a March 2010 report published by the Council on Nonprofit Organizations titled *State Budget Crises: Ripping the Safety Net Held by Nonprofits* (Council on Nonprofit Organizations, 2010). In the report, the Council charges that states have:

- cut funds for essential human services, shifting cost burdens to nonprofits;

- delayed payments they contractually owe nonprofits for delivering services, essentially forcing nonprofits to bankroll public programs; and

- extracted money from nonprofits by imposing new fees and circumventing constitutionally protected exemptions from various taxes.

Even with signs of an improving economy, the Tea Party Movement has influenced political discourse to the extent that neither major political party could possibly support tax increases for ANY reason and survive.

Global warming, undocumented immigration, AIDs, and teenage pregnancy are among emerging issues that demand help from the voluntary sector. This is because some of the political leadership in the U.S. does not accept that global warming is actually occurring, dealing with immigration is too politically hot to deal with, and many believe that barely little more than telling people to refrain from having sex is required to solve the other two problems. The same ideology supports keeping a high unemployment rate because of the fear that the economy would overheat and result in unacceptable inflation levels, and to keep the minimum wage rate too low to permit millions of workers to escape poverty. It is the role of the voluntary sector, in partnership with government, to provide a safety net, and it can be expected that if current policy continues, the lack of resources and a burgeoning demand for services will once again be the rule rather than the exception.

Trend 6: Donor attitude changes will profoundly affect how charities raise funds.

A November 2002 article in *The Washington Post* explored what may be a new attitude by donors toward nonprofit organizations. According to fundraisers interviewed for the article, donors are taking an "ask questions now, send money later" attitude (Salmon, 2002, p. H01). The trend seems to have started several years back with large donors, and now has filtered down to the point that even average donors are asking lots of questions before writing checks. The new attitude manifested itself just about the time that contributions overall were reported to drop slightly in real terms, influenced by a flat or declining economy, a lack of confidence in the management of charities as a result of scandal and mismanagement, and uncertainty about the future.

Whether called "the new donor," the "high tech donor," the "social entrepreneur," "venture philanthropist," or "high engagement philanthropists," today's contributors have something in common: they use the skills of entrepreneurs and apply them to the organizations they support. These skills include pursuing opportunities in innovative ways, leveraging new resources, assuming some risk, engaging in strategic thinking, and taking a hands-on approach to the organizations in which they invest (Wagner, 2002). Rather than simply writing a check, they do considerable research, participate in the organization's decision-making, require accountability, and expect measurable and positive results. As Wagner points out, these new philanthropists are success-oriented, achievement focused, mostly under 40, make decisions quickly, and often are willing to devote an extraordinary amount of time to ensure that their "investment" in a charity is not wasted. Although there has been criticism about the applicability of the venture capitalist model to the voluntary sector (Wagner, 2002; Kramer, 1999), the point is that billions of dollars in assets are accessible to the charitable community, with decisions being made by those who are adherents of this model of philanthropy. Because they are mostly young, it is not likely that this perspective will die any time soon.

In response to "customer demand," the United Way in the 1990s began permitting its donors to designate charitable donations made to the United Way to particular member agencies, and, in some cases, agencies not part of the United Way. Many donors have stopped giving to the United Way as a result, but simply use the organization as the administrative arm to distribute their gifts (Barman, 2005). There are alternative explanations for this phenomenon, but one is that many donors want to target their donations based on their personal preferences rather than to deputize a United Way allocation committee to make the decisions for them.

There appears to be a growing trend of donors changing their attitudes in the way they view charities. In the past, it was typical for donors to give to a charity based on its reputation, whether its mission was consistent with the donor's values, and (typically) to leave it to the charity's board to decide how the funds would be utilized. Today, donors are becoming much more involved in how their donations are being used. Two of the world's wealthiest individuals, Bill Gates and Warren Buffett, joined forces in 2006 to combine their philanthropy. They do not simply funnel money to existing charities, but rather have created their own programs, emphasizing accountability, outcomes, and results. To an increasing degree, donors are not only spelling out detailed requirements for how their donations are being used, but they are requiring charities to sign enforceable contracts that even permit the donor to sue if the funds are not used exactly in accordance with the donor's wishes.

In a March 2002 cover story, *The Chronicle of Philanthropy* (Blum, 2002) explored this trend, often tied to requirements that programs financed by these grants be evaluated to determine how much good is being done. Blum offers three explanations. Some see this trend as an extension of strategic philanthropy, the practice of concentrating dollars in a specific area and measuring the results. Others see it as a nonprofit sector application of venture capitalism, in which charity is an "investment" rather than a donation, and is expected to bring a "return on investment." A third explanation is simply that charitable giving is becoming more corporatized as a result of more professionals supervising how funds are donated (Blum, 2002). In any case, many donors seem to have changed their attitudes with respect to their donations, and if this trend continues, nonprofit governors will have significantly less flexibility to direct charitable dollars to the programs they feel need them the most.

Charities are being asked to justify their performance in a manner unprecedented in history, with funders requiring the collection of data on outcomes. As documented by Paul Light, the United Way of America embraced the outcomes measurement reform movement—

with gale force, issuing policy papers, authoring measurement manuals, promoting implementation, and generally cheerleading its local associates to adopt outcome measurement as its allocation tool...the United Way of America is unrelenting about its ultimate goal to convert the nonprofit sector to its image of outcomes management. The central indicator of its success will be nothing less than the adoption of outcomes measurement by every last one of its local partners, and, in turn their use of outcomes measurement to make all funding decisions (Light, 2000, p. 20-21).

Many Web sites have emerged that provide free, unbiased (relatively) information about charities, so donors can find out whether their potential support will be put to good use or will merely line the pockets of fundraisers. According to its Web site, more than seven million visitors consulted the CharityNavigator site in 2013 (Charity Navigator, 2014). Its more wizened competitor, GuideStar, boasts of more than 10 million visitors to its Web site annually (GuideStar, 2013).

In 2006, business journalist Matthew Bishop coined the term "philanthrocapitalist" in a 2006 article in *The Economist,* exploring in detail some of this change in donor attitude among the newly wealthy. As documented by an article in the October 2, 2008, *Chronicle of Philanthropy,* this new donor attitude emphasizes "results and business efficiencies" (Wilhelm, 2008, p. 35). The *Chronicle* article heralded the fact that Bishop has written a book with economist Michael Green, *Philanthrocapitalism: How the Rich Can Save the World.* One interesting observation made by Mr. Bishop in the *Chronicle* interview is that he sees the danger that there will be two parallel nonprofit worlds being created—one by the business-savvy philanthrocapitalists, and the other that relies on traditional government funding and mass funding (Wilhelm, 2008).

Another trend is that fundraising is becoming more transparent and democratized, as the technology of the Internet has permitted thousands of individuals making minimal donations to have the same impact as some of the "big boys" (and girls) who provide mega-gifts. The success of this relatively new form of fundraising (and business startup financing), dubbed "crowdfunding," was documented in a May 2014 report published by The Crowdfunding Centre, *eFunding & The State of The Crowdfunding Nation*. Hundreds of sites, such as Kickstarter *(http://www.kickstarter.com)* and Indiegogo *(http://www.indiegogo.com)* are raising more than $1 million daily in 2014, utilizing an innovative model that aggregates hundreds of modest donations to finance upwards of 75,000 current fundraising projects, 465 more on the average added each day. For more details about how crowdfunding works, see: *http://thecrowdfundingcentre.com/?page=datacenter*

Trend 7: The nonprofit, for-profit, and government sectors will continue to converge.

The convergence of the government, nonprofit, and for-profit sectors has been a subject of study and scrutiny by the academic community for more than a decade (see Saidel, 1991; Ferris, 1993; Weisbrod, 1997). As pointed out by Lester Salamon (1999), it is a myth that nonprofit organizations get most of their revenue from donations from individuals and foundations. According to the IRS, nearly three quarters of all tax-exempt nonprofit revenue in the 2010 tax year came from program services, and this funding source is increasing at a much more stable rate than either donations or investment income (Arnsberger, Winter 2014). There is substantial evidence that the trend of sector convergence is not only continuing, but accelerating. A report by the Kellogg Foundation (2003) documents this and concludes that "(T)here is no right or wrong conclusion about the value of blurring sectoral lines. It is a fact of the times. However, the blurring should be happening in the midst of a richer dialogue about the meaning and benefits of individual engagement for the common good" (p. 28).

The Kellogg report identified five "flashpoints" of change. These include the creation of hybrid organizations that are part nonprofit and part business organizations, social entrepreneurship (which means using charitable funds to provide private enterprises), the creation of private business organizations that have social missions virtually identical to their nonprofit counterparts, the formation of partnerships that involve the collaboration of the nonprofit sector and either one or both of the other two sectors, and the creation of educational and support systems that are designed to "improve the effectiveness of social entrepreneurs and business ventures that seek to benefit the common good" (Kellogg Foundation, 2003, p. 9).

Salamon (1999) points out that another factor driving sector convergence is that for-profit businesses are increasingly competing for "business" traditionally in the purview of nonprofits, such as day care, health care, and physical fitness. Using data provided by the U.S. Census, he informs us that between 1977 and 1992, for-profit firms captured 80% of the growth in day care centers and 90% of the growth in home health and clinic care.

The trend of nonprofit hospitals being bought up by for-profit hospital chains has been well-publicized, and it has been characterized by several commentators as "the largest redeployment of charitable assets in history" (Magat, 2004). Billions of dollars in assets received from the sale of nonprofit hospitals to for-profits have been placed in so-called "conversion" foundations, signaling a go-ahead for the new profit-oriented leadership of these institutions, many of them chains such as Columbia/HCA (162 hospitals) and Tenet (79 hospitals), to lay off staff, raise fees, and take steps that decrease quality of care (Piccone, Chou, & Sloan, 2002).

There has been an explosion in the construction of for-profit physical fitness centers competing head-to-head with YMCAs and Jewish Community Centers that have been around for more than 100 years. The number of fitness centers increased from 26,830 in 2005 to 30,500 in 2012, with revenues of $21.8 billion, according to the trade association that represents for-profit facilities (IHRSA, 2014).

Because for-profit and nonprofit service providers in the same community often must compete for the same revenue stream from the same market in order to survive, it is not unexpected that they will tend to make decisions in the same way, hire the same type of staff, market their products and services in a similar manner, have similar physical facilities, and start looking like each other in many aspects. The "iron law of emulation," a term coined by Daniel Patrick Moynihan (Rogers, Jr., 1999, p. 6 footnote), suggests that organizations in conflict will tend to become similar to one another.

Another driving force behind the blurring of the sectors is the increase in cause-related marketing, defined as "the public association of a for-profit company with a nonprofit organization, intended to promote the company's product or service and to raise money for the nonprofit" (Foundation Center, 2004). The term was first used by American Express in 1983, when the company pledged to donate a penny to the Statue of Liberty restoration project for each time someone used its charge card. According to American Express, the number of new card holders "soon grew by 45%, and card usage increased by 28%" (Foundation Center, 2004).

A 2010 study by Cone Marketing found that 80% of consumers would abandon a brand for another that supports a cause, quality being equal, and that 85% of respondents reported positive feelings toward the brand that supported a cause. Some critics charge that by promoting commercial products and services to attract charitable dollars, charities are becoming more like their for-profit counterparts, perhaps sacrificing their missions to serve the public good to increase their revenues.

With respect to cause-related marketing, the signs point to a continuing expansion (see Figure 11 on page 364), which is viewed as another trend contribut-

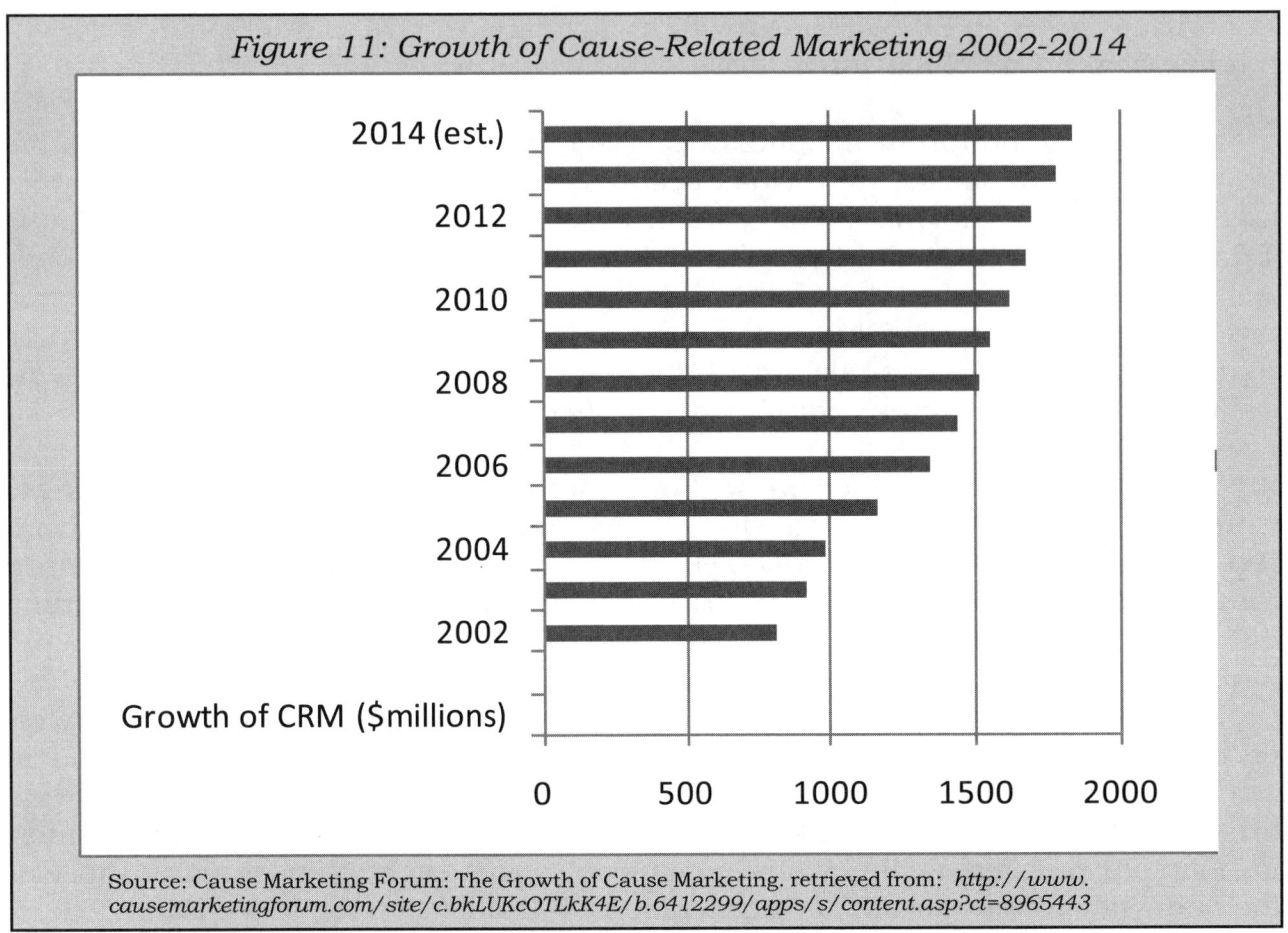

Figure 11: Growth of Cause-Related Marketing 2002-2014

Source: Cause Marketing Forum: The Growth of Cause Marketing. retrieved from: http://www.causemarketingforum.com/site/c.bkLUKcOTLkK4E/b.6412299/apps/s/content.asp?ct=8965443

ing to the blending of the sectors. In 1990, cause sponsorship spending was only $120 million (Cause Marketing Forum, 2008). U.S. sponsorship spending on cause marketing will hit $1.84 billion in 2014, according to the IEG Sponsorship Report, Chicago (Cause Marketing Forum, 2010, 2014). According to the Cause Marketing Forum, the sponsorship spending declined in 2009 to $1.51 billion because of the poor economy, but has increased every year since then.

The practical effect of the "Reinventing Government" reform movement of the early 1990s was to encourage an increase in outsourcing ("steer rather than row"), be results-oriented (require data on outcomes rather than outputs), encourage competition among the sectors, make government more "business-like," and generally blend and blur the three sectors (Osborne & Gaebler, 1992).

Jane Wales, Vice President for Philanthropy and Society at the Aspen Institute, touched on this from a perspective that this was not only a positive trend, but should be accelerated as a result of deteriorating economic conditions. In it, she said:

> *It's too early to see the effects of the economic downturn. Having said that, we have to anticipate them. Not only anticipate that endowment assets will shrink, but also that governments at all levels — state and*

city — are facing dramatically shrinking budgets at the same time that they face increased needs as portions of the population tumble into poverty. I think looking forward we will see a combination of much greater need in many areas at the same time we see shrinking resources. What that suggests is that the transformation already under way needs to accelerate, and this is the convergence of public, private, and philanthropic sectors (Wales, quoted in Henry, 2008).

One area where there has unquestionably been an increased blending of the sectors is in higher education. For-profit online universities have flourished and traditional nonprofit institutions of higher learning are imitating them in many respects. Relatively newly chartered for-profit universities—such as the University of Phoenix, Capella University, and Walden University—provide chiefly online educational programs and compete head-to-head with their traditional, bricks and mortar counterparts, many of which are just beginning to offer online degree programs. Founded in 1976, the University of Phoenix has already become the largest private university in the United States, serving as many as 600,000 students at its peak in 2010, but experiencing a 30% drop in enrollment between 2010 and 2014 (Wikipedia, 2014, Wikipedia, 2010). These for-profit schools exploit the obvious advantages of distance learning. They are being helped by trends in education that militate for traditional non-profit schools offering online courses, and a change in attitude by these traditional schools about the validity of online coursework, which views them more positively than much earlier (Allen & Seaman, 2007). Although their traditional target market is non-traditional aged students, they are increasingly going after the younger crowd (University Business, 2004). Of the 18.3 million Americans seeking higher education degrees, about 7.1 million are adults over 25 years old. About one-tenth of all college students (1.8 million) are in fully online degree programs, according to Capella founder Stephen Shank (Walden, 2008). During the 2010-11 academic year, for-profit institutions of higher learning enrolled 2.4 million students, about 12% of the entire number enrolled (National Conference of State Legislatures, 2013).

In 1983, when Medicare first provided a hospice benefit, most hospices were nonprofits affiliated with religious or community organizations. Today, the majority are for-profits. According to the Medicare Payment Advisory Commission, this has been a factor in facilities acting to maximize reimbursements and "to provide care in a manner not warranted by patients' clinical needs" (Medicare Payment Advisory Commission, 2008).

Where is all of this heading? In 2010, Russell Sullivan, staff director for the Senate Finance Committee, floated an idea during a speech to create what he termed "for-benefit corporations" that would be a hybrid of a nonprofit and a for-profit, with different tax rules applying to those entities than either a traditional for-profit or nonprofit (*Chronicle of Philanthropy,* 2010). The general idea is to permit corporations to consider the benefit to society of their operations, rather than to solely consider the amount of profit they need to make for their shareholders, as is the case with traditional corporations. In April 2010, Maryland became the first state to codify such a legal entity. A number of states—including Virginia, Vermont, New Jersey, Hawaii, California, New York, Washington, Louisiana, South Carolina, Massachusetts, Illinois, Pennsylvania, and Washington D.C.—have followed (Wikipedia, 2014b). If this trend catches on, it will clearly be another step in the convergence of the nonprofit and for-profit sectors.

Trend 8: The nonprofit sector workforce is professionalizing.

A profession can be defined as a class of workers who have their own body of knowledge, ethical standards, and educational credentials. "Profession" in Latin means "bound by an oath," deriving from the requirement of tax collectors in ancient Rome for taxpayers to declare under oath what their occupation was—because the tax was based on it. This tradition continues in modified form to this day with occupation taxes (Davis, 1999). One characteristic of a profession is that its members profess their loyalty to the profession over that of the organization that pays their salaries.

Many professions have licensing and certification requirements, continuing education requirements, specialized degrees with standardized curriculum requirements, accreditation bodies to set standards and evaluate educational programs, their own ethics code with committees to enforce it, and associations to further the interests of the profession.

Some professions are very organized; others are more informal. For example, social workers are licensed in every state; there is "practice protection" in some states so that those who do the work that is typically performed by social workers cannot legally call themselves "social workers" unless they have state social worker licenses. In order to qualify for licensing, one must have a degree from a university program accredited by the Council on Social Work Education, pass a licensing exam, have supervised experience, and take continuing education courses. Each state has its own credentialing requirements (NASW, 2005). Social workers who violate the Code of Ethics of the National Association of Social Workers can have their licenses revoked, in addition to other available sanctions.

Contrast this with the requirements of being a journalist, a government administrator, or a nonprofit manager. There is certainly a body of specialized knowledge and ethics codes for each of these three professions. There are curricula and accredited degrees one can obtain. But anyone can "come in off the street" and take such a position. This is not the case with a medical doctor, a dentist, an attorney, or, as previously noted, a social worker.

But, increasingly, the nonprofit management field is becoming more professionalized. Those in the field are putting letters after their names that designate advanced degrees in nonprofit management or certification as professional fundraisers.

Education

Perhaps the first credentialed program in nonprofit management was launched by Columbia University's Institute for Not-for-Profit Management in 1977. A Masters of Public Administration degree with a concentration in nonprofit management was offered by the University of Missouri-Kansas City as early as 1981. More and more, institutions of higher learning are offering degrees specializing in nonprofit management. Seton Hall's University's Nonprofit Management Education Web site *(http://academic.shu.edu/npo/)* reports that 292 colleges and universities currently offer courses in nonprofit management. There are 168 programs listed that offer a graduate degree with a nonprofit management concentration, defined as requiring three or more courses.

The Nonprofit Leadership Alliance, formerly known as American Humanics, was first conceived in 1947 by H. Roe Bartle, a former mayor of Kansas City, MO. The mission of the program is "to strengthen the social sector with a talented, prepared workforce" (Nonprofit Leadership Alliance, 2014a). Today, 37 institutions of higher learning have an affiliation with the program (Nonprofit Leadership Alliance, 2014b).

The National Association of Schools of Public Affairs and Administration (NASPAA) has looked at the issue of nonprofit management education. In a 2000 report co-sponsored by the Nonprofit Academic Centers Council (NACC), that organization recommended that a graduate program with a concentration in nonprofit management should consist of 36 credit hours with at least 12 of those hours focusing on the unique aspect of the nonprofit sector (Wilson & Larson 2002).

Typical courses offered by these programs include many of the same courses one might find in a business or public administration curriculum (e.g., strategic planning, marketing and communications, organization theory/behavior, budgeting/financial management, personnel management, ethics) but others that are unique to the sector (e.g., fundraising, grantsmanship, nonprofit law, volunteer management, and board-staff relations).

Accreditation of Fundraisers

CFRE International offers a certification to "fundraising professionals who demonstrate the knowledge, skills, and commitment to the highest standards of ethical and professional practice in serving the philanthropic sector" (CFRE International, 2010). The certification requires a written application, a written examination consisting of 200 multiple choice questions. There is a continuing education requirement.

An Advanced Certified Fundraising Executive credential is offered by the ACFRE Professional Certification Board to those who already have the CFRE credential. (For more information, visit the Web site of the Association of Fundraising Professionals *(http://www.afpnet.org)* and click on Education and Career Development/Certification and Career Management.

In 2013, the organization made its credential available throughout the globe (CFRE International, 2014).

Standards for Excellence

In 1998, the Maryland Association of Nonprofit Organizations initiated an ethics and accountability code for the nonprofit sector, *Standards for Excellence* (see Chapter 7). The program, modified substantially in April 2014, includes educational components and a voluntary certification process whereby charities can receive certification that they meet basic ethical and accountability standards in six general areas. If the peer-review panel affirms that the organization meets the standards, the organization receives a Seal of Excellence. The full set of standards can be found at: *http://www.standardsforexcellenceinstitute.org*

This credential for nonprofit organizations is another recent development that is promoting the professionalization of the nonprofit sector.

What does this trend mean for the future of the sector? Overall, this is a positive trend. Professionalization, with its emphasis on training, best practices, quality standards, ethics, and accountability, means that workers, managers, and executives will perform their jobs better. It also implies more public visibility and increased respect from not only the public, but from government and funders and those who receive services, which should improve the ability of the sector to attract qualified, committed applicants for positions.

Conclusion

It is difficult to find a time in the long and honored history of the nonprofit sector that was free of the generic challenges that it faces today. The most obvious—a difficulty in meeting legitimate and increasing needs for services as a result of limited resources—is a plague that will not likely disappear in our lifetime. As a sector that provides collective goods dependent on voluntary donations of time and money, there will be cycles of public trust and public participation. Government partnership with the nonprofit sector will also likely go through its ups and downs, influenced by the political ideology of elected officials, budget realities, and the level of confidence these officials have in the ability of the sector to deliver goods and services consonant with that ideology.

Throughout the history of the nonprofit sector, a spirit of optimism has prevailed. Many feel that people in nonprofit organizations, working collectively to better their society, can overcome whatever physical, economic, and psychological obstacles stand in their way. And it is usually the nonprofit sector that has recognized a need for collective action first—often decades before government mobilizes any action—and has devised creative solutions to respond to society's most complex and perplexing problems.

The challenges never end, and we should not expect them to. As I write this, the fear of AIDS is being replaced by a fear of the Ebola virus. The fear of global nuclear war between superpowers has been supplanted by a fear of terrorism fomented by religious fundamentalists using stolen or home-made weapons of mass destruction. The scourges of air and water pollution are being eclipsed as a focus of environmental concern by global warming and offshore oil spill disasters. And child neglect and abuse has been pushed off center stage by an obsession with dealing with kidnapped children. Obviously, AIDS, nuclear war, air and water pollution, and child abuse and neglect continue to pose serious threats to our quality of life. Whether the threats are old or new, nonprofit organizations will continue to be partners with government and the private sector in dealing with them, and will not be hesitant to go it alone when the other sectors shirk their responsibilities.

Stakeholders of these organizations (i.e., *all* of us) should expect to continue to be called upon to meet these challenges. If history is any guide, the millions of committed individuals and organizations will continue to successfully develop creative and aggressive responses in a way that makes the sector an essential component of a healthy, vibrant society.

Discussion Questions

1. What are the pros and cons of creating the hybrid organizations described on pages 365-366? How do you think this will change the sector, for the better or for the worse, if this option becomes widespread?

2. What steps might you take to organize the nonprofit sector leadership to create a professional credential for nonprofit managers that parallels that available to social workers?

3. How has the "ice bucket challenge" in 2014 changed the way fundraisers view social media? Is this really a new paradigm for fundraising and friendraising, or a passing fad that appeals to a narrow demographic of potential contributors?

4. What are the similarities and differences between cause-related marketing and the partnership of charities with celebrities to call attention to their mission? What can go wrong with each of these strategies?

5. Discuss whether the actions of the Internal Revenue Service with respect to approving applications for 501(c)(4) tax-exempt status in 2013 were politically motivated in any way.

Activities

1. Research how much your state has budgeted for a particular program in which a small number of nonprofits receive the bulk of the appropriations. How has the funding level varied over the past decade for this program? Consider the reasons for the funding level to be unstable over time.

2. Research whether any nonprofit organizations in your local area pay salaries to their board members, and discuss under what conditions, if any, such payments would be appropriate.

3. Download a copy of the application form for certification from the Standards of Excellence program described on page 368, and fill out the form as if you were applying for a Seal of Excellence, either using data from an existing organization or creating data for a hypothetical organization.

4. Research the new rules that the IRS proposed in November 2013 to clarify what activities are permissible with respect to qualifying for 501(c)(4) tax-exempt status. Then discuss how this changes the IRS's current policy.

Online Resources to Explore

Center for Effective Government
http://foreffectivegov.org

U.S. Census Bureau
http://www.census.gov/

James Irvine Foundation's Report on Sector Convergence
http://www.irvine.org/images/stories/pdf/eval/convergencereport.pdf

Center on Budget and Policy Priorities
http://www.cbpp.org

Duke Philanthropy Central
   http://cspcs.sanford.duke.edu/blog/cohen_nonprofit_policy_trends_under_obama

References

Abramson, Alan; Salamon, Lester; & John Russell (2006). *The nonprofit sector and the federal budget: Analysis of President Bush's FY 2007 budget.* Washington, DC: The Aspen Institute (Nonprofit Sector Research Fund). Retrieved from *http://search.yahoo.com/search?fr=mcafee &type=A111US0&p=%22The+Nonprofit+Sector+and+the+Federal+Budget%22+aspen+institute*

Agitator, The. (2010). *2009 Online fundraising trends.* Retrieved from *http://www.theagitator.net/hot-research/2009-online-fundraising-trends/*

Allen, I. E. & Seaman, J. (2007). Online nation: Five years of growth in online learning. Sloan Consortium. Needham, MA. Retrieved from *http://eric.ed.gov/?id=ED529699*

Anft, Michael. (2001). Raising money with sense and sensibility. *Chronicle of Philanthropy.* 14(1); October 18, 2001, p. 20-21.

Arnsberger, P. (Winter 2014). Nonprofit charitable organizations, 2010. Retrieved from *http://www.irs.gov/uac/SOI-Tax-Stats-SOI-Bulletin:-Winter-2014*

Baig, M. (2013). Women in the workforce: What changes have we made? Retrieved from *http://www.huffingtonpost.com/mehroz-baig/women-in-the-workforce-wh_b_4462455.html*

Barman, E. (2005). With strings attached: Nonprofits and the adoption of donor choice. *Nonprofit and Voluntary Sector Quarterly,* 37(1), March 2008 pp. 39-56.

Blum, D. E. (2002). Ties that bind: More donors specify terms for their gifts of charity. *Chronicle of Philanthropy.* 14(11), March 21, 2002; pp. 7-9.

Bond, J., Thompson, C., Galinsky, E. & Prottas, D. (2002). *Highlights of the national study of the changing workforce (Executive summary).* New York: Families and Work Institute.

Bosak, Susan V. (2004). Mother's Day activity kit. Retrieved from *http://www.somethingtoremembermeby.org*

Brinckerhoff, Peter C. (1995). What the next 10 years will bring and how to get ready. *Nonprofit World.* 13(2), pp. 19-25; March-April 1995.

Bump, P. (2013). The Tea Party gets an apology from the IRS. Retrieved from *http://news.yahoo.com/tea-party-gets-apology-irs-151751165.html;_ylt=A0LEVz7BPL9TggsAa9pXNyoA;_ylu=X3oDMTByODJtaWUzBHNlYwNzcgRwb3MDMwRjb2xvA2JmMQR2dGlkAw--*

Business in the Community. (2004). Brand benefits—Cause-related marketing. Retrieved from *http://www.bitc.org.uk/our-resources/report/brand-benefits-cause-related-marketing*

Cause Marketing Forum. (2014). Retrieved from IEG sponsorship report. *http://www.causemarketingforum.com/site/c.bkLUKcOTLkK4E/b.6449067/k.71C8/IEG_Sponsorship_Report.htm*

Cause Marketing Forum. (2010). The growth of cause marketing. Retrieved from *http://www.causemarketingforum.com/site/c.bkLUKcOTLkK4E/b.6412299/apps/s/content.asp?ct=8965443*

CBSNews.com. (2001). America's racial divide. August 13, 2001. Retrieved from *http://www.cbsnews.com/news/americas-racial-divide/*

Center for Health Policy. (1998). *A guide for communities considering hospital conversion.* Durham, NC: Duke University, Center for Health Policy, Law and Management. May 1998.

CFRE International. (2014). About us. Retrieved from *http://www.cfre.org/about.html*

Charity Navigator. (2014). Overview. Retrieved from *http://www.charitynavigator.org/index.cfm?bay=content.view&cpid=628#.U79NzkD-ItU*

Chronicle of Philanthropy. (2010). Congress could create new kind of group. *Chronicle of Philanthropy,* 23(12), May 6, 2010. p. 12.

Chronicle of Philanthropy. (2014). Facts and figures: Online fundraising by month. Posted July 10, 2014. Retrieved from *http://philanthropy.com/factfile/ofr_annual*

Community Foundation R&D Incubator. (2000). *Family philanthropy and the intergenerational transfer of wealth,* (Community Foundation R&D Incubator, 2000).

Council on Nonprofit Organizations. (2010). State budget crises: Ripping the safety net held by nonprofits. Retrieved from *http://www.councilofnonprofits.org/sites/default/files/Special-Report-State-Budget-Crises-Ripping-the-Safety-Net-Held-by-Nonprofits.pdf*

Daniels, A. and Narayanswami, A. (May 2014). Online fundraising goes mainstream. *Chronicle of Philanthropy,* May 18, 2014. Retrieved from *http://philanthropy.com/article/Online-Fundraising-Goes/146619/*

Davis, M. (1999). Perspectives on the professions. A periodical of the Center for the Study of Ethics in the Professions (CSEP), Illinois Institute of Technology. 19(1). Retrieved from *http://ethics.iit.edu/index.html*

DeLuca, M. (2013). Boston transit shut down, nearly 1 million sheltering in place amid terror hunt. MSNBC, April 19, 2013. Retrieved from *http://usnews.nbcnews.com/_news/2013/04/19/17822687-boston-transit-shut-down-nearly-1-million-sheltering-in-place-amid-terror-hunt?lite*

Dye, A. (2002). Political activity by clergymen. January 23, 2002. Christian Coalition of Iowa. Retrieved from *http://www.priestsforlife.org/government/dyememo.htm*

Family Caregiver Alliance. (May 2012). *Selected caregiver statistics.* Retrieved from *https://www.caregiver.org/selected-caregiver-statistics*

Fain, P. (2008). Senator Grassley wants new 990 tax form tailored to colleges. *Chronicle of Higher Education.* September 8, 2008. Retrieved from *http://chronicle.com/news/article/5104/senator-grassley-wants-new-990-tax-form-tailored-to-colleges*

Fanpagelist.com. (2014). Top 100 Facebook fan pages. Retrieved from *http://fanpagelist.com/category/top_users*

FEMA. (2014). FY 2014 Urban Areas Security Initiative (UASI) Nonprofit Security Grant Program (NSGP). Retrieved from *http://www.fema.gov/fy-2014-urban-areas-security-initiative-uasi-nonprofit-security-grant-program-nsgp*

Ferris, James M. (1993). The double-edged sword of social service contracting: Public accountability versus nonprofit accountability. In *The nature of the nonprofit sector*. Ott, J. Stephen (Ed.); (2001), Boulder, CO: Westview Press. pp. 391-398.

Foundation Center. (2004). Frequently asked questions: What is cause-related marketing? Retrieved from *http://foundationcenter.org/getstarted/faqs/html/cause_marketing.html*

Foxnews.com. (2008). Aide to former Rep. Istook charged in Abramoff-related fraud. June 2, 2008. Retrieved from *http://www.foxnews.com/story/0,2933,361781,00.html*

Franklin, M. (2008, October). *Debt clock draws confused looks, anger or nothing.* Associated Press. October 12, 2008. Retrieved from *http://www.nbcnews.com/id/27150961/ns/business-stocks_and_economy/t/national-debt-clock-runs-out-numbers/*

Galewitz, P. (2013). 48 million Americans remain uninsured, Census Bureau reports. September 17, 2013. Retrieved from *http://www.kaiserhealthnews.org/Stories/2013/September/17/census-numbers-uninsured-numbers-remain-nearly-unchanged.aspx*

Gardyn, R. (2003). New York groups could face leadership gap, study finds. *Chronicle of Philanthropy*; 16(3), November 13, 2003; p. 31.

Granfield, M. (2008). How social media won Obama the US Election. *Marketing Magazine.* Retrieved from *http://www.marketingmag.com.au/blogs/howsocialmediawonobamatheuselection-3565/*

Greene, S. (2001). Astride the Digital Divide, *Chronicle of Philanthropy*, 13(6), January 11, 2001. Retrieved from *http://www.philanthropy.com/premium/articles/v13/i06/06000101.htm*

Grobman, G. & Grant, G. (2008). *Fundraising on the internet* (in *The nonprofit handbook*, 5th Edition); Harrisburg, PA: White Hat Communications.

Grobman, G. & Grant, G. (2006). *Fundraising online: Using the internet to raise serious money for your organization.* Harrisburg, PA: White Hat Communications.

Grobman, G. (2001). The nonprofit organization's guide to e-commerce. Harrisburg, PA: White Hat Communications.

Grogan, P. (2013). *Wealth transfer and the future of philanthropy.* Retrieved from *http://www.tbf.org/blog/2013/march/wealth-transfer-and-philanthropy*

Guidestar. (2013). Collect donations through Guidestar. Retrieved from *http://www.guidestar.org/rxa/news/articles/2013/collect-donations-through-guidestar.aspx*

Henry, K. (2008). An expert on philanthropy takes think-tank job. *Chronicle of Philanthropy.* June 12, 2008. Retrieved from *http://philanthropy.com/premium/articles/v20/i17/17005701.htm*

Herwit Associates. (2014). Sarbanes-Oxley and nonprofit organizations. Retrieved from *http://www.hurwitassociates.com/l_sarbanes_oxley.php*

IHRSA. (2014). About the industry. Retrieved from *http://www.ihrsa.org/about-the-industry*

Internal Revenue Service. (2008). Form 990 redesign for tax year 2008 (Filed in 2009). Retrieved from *http://www.irs.gov/pub/irs-tege/990_instructions_overview040608.pdf*

Internal Revenue Service. (2013). IRS update on the proposed new regulation on 501(c)(4) organizations. Retrieved from *http://www.irs.gov/uac/Newsroom/IRS-Update-on-the-Proposed-New-Regulation-on-501%28c%29%284%29-Organizations*

Isidore, C. (2003). U.S. stuck on duct tape: Latest terrorism preparation warning spurs sales, production of American icon—duct tape. February 13, 2003. CNNMoney. Retrieved from *http://money.cnn.com/2003/02/12/news/companies/ducttape/*

Johnston, D. (1999). A larger legacy may await generations X, Y and Z. *The New York Times.* October 20, 1999. Retrieved from *http://www.nytimes.com/1999/10/20/business/a-larger-legacy-may-await-generations-x-y-and-z.html*

Kellogg Foundation. (2003). *Blurred boundaries and muddled motives: A world of shifting social responsibilities.* Battlecreek, MI: Author.

Kirby, J. (1995 Spring). Single parent families in poverty. *Human Development and Family Life Bulletin,* 1(1). Retrieved from *http://www3.uakron.edu/schulze/401/readings/singleparfam.htm*

Knake, R. (2010). *Internet governance in an age of cyber insecurity.* Council on Foreign Relations Press. Retrieved from *http://www.cfr.org/publication/22832/internet_governance_in_an_age_of_cyber_insecurity.html*

Kramer, M. (1999, April). Venture capital and philanthropy: A bad fit. *Chronicle of Philanthropy,* April 22, 1999. p. 72.

Kramer, M. (2003). Members of Congress don't understand what good grant making takes. *Chronicle of Philanthropy.* May 29, 2003. p. 35.

Lawrence, D. (June 2014). The global cost of cybercrime: More than $400 billion per year. *Bloomsburg Business Week* (Technology). Retrieved from *http://www.businessweek.com/articles/2014-06-09/the-global-cost-of-cybercrime-more-than-400-billion-per-year*

Lenkowsky, L. (2006). Charities and politicking: The rules get murkier. *Chronicle of Philanthropy.* March 9, 2006, p. 46.

Light, P. (2000). *Making nonprofits work: A report on the tides of nonprofit management reform.* Washington, DC: Brookings Institute Press.

Lipman, H. (2003). Majority of private foundations pay their trustees, survey finds. *Chronicle of Philanthropy.* 15(23); September 18, 2003. p. 11.

Lipman, H. & Williams, G. (2004a). Charities bestow no-interest loans on their well-paid executives. *Chronicle of Philanthropy,* 16(8), February 5, 2004; page 11.

Lipman, H. & Williams, G. (2004b). Several states are reviewing loans charities made to their officials. *Chronicle of Philanthropy.* 16(10), March 4, 2004, p. 34.

Magat, R. (2004). Stop the looting of charitable assets. *Chronicle of Philanthropy.* 16(13), April 15, 2004; p. 34.

Maskell, J. (1998). *96-809: CRS report to Congress: Lobbying regulations on non-profit organizations.* Washington, DC: Congressional Research Service. Updated May 19, 1998.

Medicare Payment Advisory Commission. (2008). Evaluating medicare's hospice benefit. Retrieved from https://www.yumpu.com/en/document/view/15317914/june-2008-report-to-the-congress-reforming-the-medpac/225

Merrill, J. (2013). Government shutdown reveals the "independent" sector's dependence. Retrieved from *http://www.philanthropydaily.com/government-shutdown-reveals-the-independent-sectors-dependence/*

Morning, M. (2014). Stock market crash history: The Dow's 10 biggest one-day plunges. *http://beforeitsnews.com/economy/2014/02/stock-market-crash-history-the-dows-10-biggest-one-day-plunges-2595042.html*

National Conference of State Legislatures. (July 2013). For-profit colleges and universities. Retrieved from *http://www.ncsl.org/research/education/for-profit-colleges-and-universities.aspx*

NASW. (2010). Home page. Retrieved from *http://www.naswdc.org*

Network for Good. *(2014). Online giving continues to grow for charities across the country.* March 25, 2014. Retrieved from *http://www1.networkforgood.org/online-giving-continues-grow-charities-across-country*

Nonprofit Leadership Alliance. (2014a). Mission. Retrieved from *http://www.nonprofitleadershipalliance.org/aboutus/mission.html#sthash.aLZuzkel.dpbs*

Nonprofit Leadership Alliance. (2014b). Campus map. Retrieved from *http://www.nonprofitleadershipalliance.org/campus/campusmap.html#sthash.kkaLFozj.dpbs*

OMB Watch. (2003). Istook strikes back—Another attack on nonprofit speech. Retrieved from *http://www.foreffectivegov.org/node/1762*

Ortman, J.; Velkoff, V.; & Hogan, H. (May 2014). *An aging nation: The older population in the United States.* Washington, DC: U.S. Census Bureau. Retrieved from *http://www.census.gov/library/publications/2014/demo/p25-1140.html*

Osborne, D. & Gaebler, T. (1992). *Reinventing government: How the entrepreneurial spirit is transforming the public sector.* Reading, MA: Addison-Wesley.

Pennsylvania Department of Health. (2002, August 5). Schweiker Administration announces potassium iodide to be distributed from August 15-21: Citizens, workers and schools within 10 miles of nuclear power plants to receive KI pills. Press release. August 5, 2002. Retrieved from *http://www.dsf.health.state.pa.us/health/cwp/view.asp?A=190&Q=231990*

Philanthropy News Digest. (2006). IRS warns tax-exempt groups to avoid campaigning. July 19, 2006. Retrieved from *http://www.philanthropynewsdigest.org/news/irs-warns-tax-exempt-groups-to-avoid-campaigning*

Picone, G.; Chou, S.; & Sloan, F. (2002). Are for-profit hospital conversions harmful to patients and to Medicare? *Rand Journal of Economics.* 33(3), Autumn 2002. pp. 507-523.

Raymond, N. (2003). Internet users raise over $600,000 in 6 days for Oxfam's humanitarian relief fund for Iraqi people. Press release of March 27, 2003. Retrieved from *http://www.oxfamamerica.org/newsandpublications/press_releases/archive2003/art4544.html*

Reagan, R. (1981). First inaugural address, January 20, 1981. Retrieved from *http://www.bartelby.net/124/pres61.html*

Reaves, J. (2003). Living with terrorism: A how-to guide. *Time* (Online edition). February 12, 2003. Retrieved from *http://www.time.com/time/nation/article/0,8599,422141,00.html*

Riedl, B. (2008). $700 billion bailout? You ain't seen nothin' *San Francisco Chronicle*, p. G2.

Rodgers, W. (1999). The most creative moments in the history of environmental law: The whos. *Washburn Law Journal*. Retrieved from *http://heinonline.org/HOL/LandingPage?handle=hein.journals/wasbur39&div=10&id=&page=*

Saidel, J. (1991). The relationship between state agencies and nonprofit organizations. In *The nature of the nonprofit sector*. Ott, J. Stephen (Ed.); (2001), Boulder, CO: Westview Press, pp. 380-390.

Salamon, L. (1999). *America's nonprofit sector: A primer* (2nd Ed.). Washington, DC: The Foundation Center.

Salmon, J. (2002, November 3). Given to skepticism? With charity scandals in the news and less money to give, donors are asking more questions. *The Washington Post*. H01. November 3, 2002.

Schervish, P. (2009, October). *Wealth and Commonwealth Newsletter. October 2009*. Retrieved from *http://archive.constantcontact.com/fs034/1010966812709/archive/1102818622822.html*

Schumer, C. (2000). Statement of US Senator Charles E. Schumer, "I Love You Virus" Hearing Senate Banking Committee - May 18, 2000, Retrieved from *http://www.schumer.senate.gov/new_website/record.cfm?id=324493&*

Schwinn, E. (2003). Poll finds holiday shoppers hope to help charities. *Chronicle of Philanthropy*. 16(4), November 27, 2003. p. 23.

Silk, T. (2004). Ten emerging principals of governance of nonprofit corporations. *The Exempt Organization Tax Review*. 43(1), pp. 35-39, January 2004.

Stehle, V. (2009, April 9). An important vote to protect charity lobbying rights. *The Chronicle of Philanthropy*. 21(12), April 9, 2009, pp. 38-39.

Stirland, S. (2008). Propelled by internet, Barack Obama wins presidency. *Wired*. Retrieved from *http://www.wired.com/threatlevel/2008/11/propelled-by-in/*

Teaparty.org. (2013). IRS admits targeting teaparty groups. May 10, 2013. Retrieved from *http://www.teaparty.org/irs-apologizes-for-targeting-conservative-tea-party-groups-24020/*

Tierney, T. (March 2005). *The nonprofit sector's leadership deficit.* The Bridgestone Group. Retrieved from *http://www.bridgespangroup.org/Publications-and-Tools/Hiring-Nonprofit-Leaders/Hiring-Strategy/The-Nonprofit-Sectors-Leadership-Deficit.aspx*

Twin, A. (2008). Stocks crushed: Approximately $1.2 trillion in market value is gone after the House rejects the $700 billion bank bailout plan. CNNMoney.com. Retrieved from *http://money.cnn.com/2008/09/29/markets/markets_newyork/index.htm?cnn=yes*

U.S. Census Bureau. (1996). Population projections of the United States by age, sex, race, and Hispanic origin: 1995-2050. Washington, DC: U.S. Department of Commerce, Economics and Statistics Administration, Bureau of the Census.

U.S. Census Bureau. (2010). Income, poverty and health insurance coverage in the United States: 2009. Press release of September 16, 2010. Retrieved from *http://www.census.gov/newsroom/releases/archives/income_wealth/cb10-144.html*

U.S. Census Bureau. (May 2010). The next four decades: The older population in the United States. Retrieved from *http://www.census.gov/prod/2010pubs/p25-1138.pdf*

U.S. Census Bureau. (2011a). 2010 Census shows U.S population is aging. Retrieved from *http://www.census.gov/newsroom/releases/archives/2010_census/cb11-cn147.html*

U.S. Census Bureau. (2011b). Census Bureau releases comprehensive analysis of fast-growing 90-and-older population. Retrieved from *http://www.census.gov/newsroom/releases/archives/aging_population/cb11-194.html*

U.S. Census Bureau. (July 2012). Americans with disabilities: 2010. Retrieved from *http://www.census.gov/people/disability/*

U.S. Census Bureau. (2013a). Families and living arrangements. Table FG5. One-parent unmarried family groups with own children/1 Under 18, by labor force status of the reference person: 2013. Retrieved from *http://www.census.gov/hhes/families/data/cps2013FG.html*

U.S. Census Bureau. (2013b). Income, poverty and health insurance coverage in the United States: 2012. September 17, 2013. Retrieved from *http://www.census.gov/newsroom/releases/archives/income_wealth/cb13-165.html*

U.S. Census Bureau. (2014a). State and county quickfacts, Updated July 8, 2014. Retrieved from *http://quickfacts.census.gov/qfd/states/00000.html*

U.S. House of Representatives. (2003). Making appropriations for agriculture, rural development, food and drug administration and related agencies for the fiscal year ending September 30, 2004, and for other purposes: Conference report to accompany H.R. 2673. November 25, 2003. Retrieved from *http://thomas.loc.gov/cgi-bin/cpquery/T?&report=hr401&dbname=cp108&*

Verton, D. (2003). *Black ice: The invisible threat of cyberterrorism.* Emeryville, CA: McGraw-Hill/Osborne.

Wagner, L. (2002). The "new" donor: Creation or evolution? *International Journal of Nonprofit and Voluntary Sector Marketing.* 7(4), November 2002. pp. 343-352.

Walden, G. (2008). Expansion part of Capella's lesson plan. *Minneapolis-St. Paul Star Tribune.* September 6, 2008. Retrieved from *http://www.startribune.com/business/27932419.html*

Wallace, N. (2004). Online donations surge. *Chronicle of Philanthropy.* 16(17), June 10, 2004; pp. 25-29.

Wallace, N. (2006). Charities make faster connections. *Chronicle of Philanthropy;* 18(17), June 15, 2006. Retrieved from *http://www.philanthropy.com/premium/articles/v18/i17/17001901.htm*

Webster's. (2004). Definition of cyber-terrorism. Retrieved from *http://www.webster-dictionary.org/definition/cyber-terrorism*

Weisbrod, B. (1997). The future of the nonprofit sector: Its entwining with private enterprise and government. *Journal of Policy Analysis and Management,* 18, 541-555.

Wikipedia. (2010). *University of Phoenix.* Author: Retrieved from *http://en.wikipedia.org/wiki/University_of_Phoenix*

Wikipedia. *(2014). University of Phoenix.* Author. Retrieved from *http://en.m. wikipedia.org/wiki/University_of_Phoenix*

Wikipedia. *(2014b). Benefit corporation.* Retrieved from *http://wikipedia.org/wiki/Benefit_corporation*

Wilhelm, I. (2008). New hope or hype? *Chronicle of Philanthropy.* 20(24), October 2, 2008. p. 35-36.

Williams, G. (2003). Advocacy group's online savvy nets more than donations. *Chronicle of Philanthropy.* 15(13), April 17, 2003, p. 23-26.

Wilson, S. & Larson, M. I. (2002). Nonprofit management students: Who are they and why do they enroll? *Nonprofit and Voluntary Sector Quarterly.* 31(2),, pp. 259-270.

Zoll, R. (2012). Political activity by religious groups continues unchallenged as IRS not enforcing rules. *Huffington Post. November 3, 2012.* Retrieved from *http://www.huffingtonpost.com/2012/11/03/political-activity-religious-groups_n_2069128.html*

Chapter 21
The Spirit of the Nonprofit Sector

> **Synopsis:** The spirit of the nonprofit sector developed in the United States with distinct values of individuals banding together to promote the public good. The sector is in danger of losing this spirit, which can be restored if current and future leaders stay true to the sector's roots of altruism and ethical collaborative action.

Introduction

Many readers will be familiar with an inspiring story attributed to anthropologist Loren Eiseley (1907-1977) titled "The Starfish Story." Here is a short version it:

A man walking on the beach encounters another man picking up starfish from the sand and throwing them back into the sea. The first man asks why he is doing this.

"The sun is up and the tide is going out. If I don't throw them back in the water, they'll die," the man replies.

"But there are miles of beach, and thousands of starfish. Do you really think you can make a difference?"

At this, the man picks up another starfish, and throws it back safely into the ocean, and replies, "It made a difference for that one."

The starfish in this story can serve as a metaphor for apparently hopeless, intractable challenges of society. In thousands of cases, individuals take it upon themselves to literally roll up their sleeves and make a difference in some small way, as the man in this story did.

These everyday heroes among us become foster parents to abused and neglected kids. They might take a home-cooked meal to an elderly neighbor. They might teach an inner-city child from a failing school system to read. They may take a blanket to a homeless person they find shivering in the night cold beneath a bridge.

Yet there are thousands who do not receive the help that they need because of limited government resources, or simply because, figuratively, there are simply too many miles of beach and too few individuals interested in saving starfish. One person, regardless of his or her ability and motivation, can only do so much.

There may be hundreds of individuals in that beach neighborhood who share that individual's passion for saving these starfish, literally or figuratively. But it is a challenge to identify them, train them, and coordinate their efforts.

Fortunately, our society has created a culture in which one individual can harness the efforts of tens, hundreds, and in many cases, thousands of like-minded individuals to do good. It is not beyond the realm of possibility that by creating a nonprofit organization, the individual in this story could create the infrastructure that would save EVERY starfish on this beach, and every other beach, every single day. Or effectively deal with any other problem faced by society.

The nonprofit sector has been created as a business form by government for the purpose of minimizing the transaction costs (to use an economic term) of coordinating the efforts of many individuals to accomplish some purpose that is good for society. Yes, it is possible for one person to make a difference, but there are constraints on how much one person can do alone. But one individual can create a nonprofit organization and harness the energy of like-minded individuals. Working together in a coordinated way, often with government subsidies, these teams of individuals have an almost unlimited capacity to make the world better in some way.

This behavior, working together to improve the lives of others (and as a result, all of us) with no expectation of pecuniary reward, captures the spirit of the nonprofit sector: collaboration of many individuals to accomplish an objective that makes things better, and which would be virtually impossible to achieve by any single individual acting alone. The fact that millions of individuals do get paid to operate and manage these organizations does not detract from the basic principle that these organizations are created and governed to make society better in some way rather than to make a profit.

Ask that man on the beach WHY he is saving starfish and he quickly tells you he is trying to save their lives.

Now, it is possible he answers the question posed to him about why he is throwing the starfish back into the sea with:

Because they are costing me business, as my customers renting my beach umbrellas no longer come here because of these &%$#@ starfish!

My point here is that it is possible, in some cases, that some individuals are motivated to do "good" for selfish reasons. And I have no problem with that—I would certainly prefer people to do "good" for selfish reasons rather than "bad" for selfish reasons—and we know all too well that there is a lot of that going on in our society.

Yet, the "spirit of the nonprofit sector" is about doing the *right* thing for the *right* reasons. And what follows in this essay is more about why this is important.

The Case of the Flooding of the Red River

It's March 2010. The Red River is swollen and threatening to crest at 38 feet, well beyond the 30 feet of depth that is its flood stage. The city of Fargo, North Dakota, is threatened. Hundreds of individuals—school children, farmers, college students, and even prison inmates—respond to a clarion call from city officials and cooperating nonprofit organizations, and make a pilgrimage to the riverbank, helping to fill sandbags to save low-lying neighborhoods. Some are motivated by the task of saving their own houses from devastating flooding. Most others are simply helping their neighbors. They are all volunteers. They work hard, long hours. They sweat. They have fun. They have the satisfaction of knowing that they made a difference. According to press reports, they fill more than a million sandbags (Associated Press, 2010a).

A picture found on the Web is highlighted by this caption: *Mary, 8, and Kelly Noah, 10, look for customers at their lemonade stand along Eighth Street in south Fargo. The sisters thought it would be a good idea to raise money for flood relief on their day off from school. They raised $1,000, which was matched by the Impact Foundation for another $1,000 (Inforum, 2010a).*

The above vignette is another metaphor for the spirit of the nonprofit sector. There is a commitment among individuals and organizations to altruism, caring, self-sacrifice, and contributing to the public good. Is it all motivated by pure benevolence? Well, not quite. As previously mentioned, some of the volunteers are trying to save their own homes. The City of Fargo established a program to pay nonprofit organizations to recruit volunteers (Inforum, 2010b). The National Guard troops who participated in the effort were following orders from their commanders. Prison inmates who filled sandbags received some tangible benefit from their warden.

Putting that aside, it was the outpouring of effort by volunteers for the benefit of the community that made the difference between tragedy and success.

Our American culture has a proud history of efforts such as what occurred in Fargo. Whether motivated by secular or nonsecular impulses, altruistic behavior has been institutionalized and is part of the fabric of our culture. Neighbors have always helped neighbors. History records an early example of this in "America" when, in 1621, the Wampanoag Indians helped the Pilgrims survive their first winter (About.com, 2010).

More recent disasters, such as Hurricane Katrina, the World Trade Center collapse, the Boston Marathon bombings, and the BP oil spill, elicited a well-documented response as thousands of volunteers arrived on the scene, ready to roll up their sleeves and save lives and/or enhance the response of government. And every day, there are thousands of individual scenes that are never chronicled in the media of individuals and organizations working to help those in need. Scenes such as a 90-year-old widow, living alone, receiving a delivery of a hot meal from a Meals on Wheels program volunteer. A busy executive taking time after work to coach a Little League team. Or an individual serving on the board of a homeless shelter, and making calls to raise money for the facility so it can expand.

We have always had a healthy skepticism about government intruding in our day-to-day lives. With limited resources, the need for help is so great that government would be unable to take care of all of us even if it wanted to do so. And for every story that finds its way into the media—such as the Red River sandbagging project—hundreds of thousands of individual acts of kindness and community service go unreported and unheralded.

Teenagers shovel the snow of a homebound, elderly neighbor. Volunteers clear the brush and remove litter from the local trail. Adults without children of their own mentor school children in their community.

Some of these acts are quite small in scale and performed and organized spontaneously—or not organized at all. Others are organized as a result of formal programs that may involve thousands of individuals, including professional staff, and be funded by grants and donations. Regardless of their magnitude, these types of activity are not motivated by a desire to make money, but rather to accomplish a mission that has some benefit to those who need it. Usually, there is no expectation of any monetary payment in return, although the psychic payment to those who provide these services can be substantial.

In many respects, community service has been encouraged by government, which provides special benefits to those who create the organizational infrastructure to help individuals participate in these voluntary efforts. In addition to offering limited funding, government exempts such organizations from taxes, offers subsidized postage rates, and limits the liability for those who volunteer. Government also encourages financial support of such organizations by providing a tax deduction for donations made to them. These benefits are available to organizations that are formed to pursue *public* benefit by *private* means.

Capturing Benjamin Franklin's Spirit

Our history is replete with examples of individuals coming together to accomplish something for the public benefit, collaborating to build community, and making sacrifices for the public good. It is one of the factors that make us stronger than our enemies. It is nurtured by the same spirit that brought us together after the September 11 tragedy.

Bringing people together for a common purpose to promote the common good, without pecuniary benefit to those participating in providing the services, without compelling anyone to participate or provide funding for the enterprise, is an aspect that is unique to the nonprofit sector and that is a fundamental aspect of its inherent "spirit."

It is a spirit captured by Benjamin Franklin, a visionary who recognized that government could not, or would not, meet the needs of society, and the market would not be capable of responding to these needs in all cases. Reading about his entrepreneurial instincts, one almost sees a history of the nonprofit sector itself. Franklin is credited with founding one of the first volunteer fire companies, the first hospital, the University of Pennsylvania, and the first public library.

The Commons

Roger Lohmann has written extensively about how to explain the formation and growth of organizations that are consistent with the spirit of the nonprofit sector. His *Theory of the Commons* is described in detail in Chapter 3. For many nonprofit organization entrepreneurs and those who lead them, this model predicts behavior quite well. Creating wealth is not the end goal, as it is for many for-profit businesses. Wealth is a tool that is used to provide resources necessary to accomplish some mission and improve the quality of life for individuals, groups, and communities. Such leaders keep themselves focused on how much they can serve marginalized populations—not on how much net revenue they can accumulate.

These leaders tend to be frugal in their spending of resources for administration, squeezing every last penny they can to serve the need for which their organization was created. They do not spend lavishly, using expense accounts at their annual conferences held at fancy resorts. They do not pay themselves unreasonably high salaries. They have no problem opening up their books to the public, as they have nothing to hide. They feel a real connection to the clients they serve and would not think of exploiting them or those who fund the organization's services. They are genuine—they fit the old stereotype of putting service first. Many have been influenced by a, perhaps old-fashioned, concept of "noblesse oblige," a belief that those who are privileged have a duty to serve those who are not as fortunate.

Recent Abuses of the Spirit of the Nonprofit Sector

In recent years, the reputation of the nonprofit sector has declined. The "Commons" model of nonprofit organization formation and operation has been severely compromised. Scandals involving nonprofit organizations have made the front pages. Some of the most trusted names among our nonprofit sector—including, among others, the Catholic Church, the United Way, the Republican National Committee, the American Red Cross, and the Boys and Girls Clubs—have been linked to allegations of abuse and violation of the public trust.

These cases have appeared on the front pages of our newspapers. But beneath the surface, there is also a less celebrated, but more dangerous trend of many nonprofits not honoring the lofty and altruistic values of their founders.

A landmark court case in Illinois that sent shivers of fear throughout the hospital industry in 2010 revoked the tax exemption of a nonprofit hospital, charged with not providing much community benefit in exchange for its valuable tax exemption. How many nonprofit hospitals truly act in ways that are consonant with their obligation to provide genuine charity to the needy? And how many act to minimize this to the extent they can, dun those who do not pay their bills with threatening notices of court action, and then claim as "charity" any expenses they are unable to recover after such harassment? Such was the case of one large Pennsylvania nonprofit hospital in Erie, Pennsylvania, that lost its local property tax exemption case as a result of such an attitude.

What might motivate a tax-exempt hospital to close down its emergency room in a poor neighborhood and increase its resources in nearby middle- and upper-class neighborhoods?

Another salient example of a disregard of the sector's values is the case of Harvard University's treatment of homeless people on its property.

Harvard is arguably one of the richest nonprofit institutions in America and one of the best known, boasting an endowment of $32.4 billion, as of July 2014. In January 1986, Harvard had a problem. Homeless people were keeping warm during the bitter winter by sleeping on heating vents outside of Leverett House, its largest dormitory for undergraduate upperclassmen. Harvard officials responded by installing $850 metal grates over the vents. The vents remained for five days, dismantled only after a national outcry (Winslow, 1986).

It was only four years earlier that I attended my graduation from Harvard, at which Mother Teresa was one of several Nobel Prize winners to receive an honorary degree. Although not without her critics, Mother Teresa's selfless devotion to the marginalized epitomized the spirit that many feel is unique to the nonprofit sector.

Restoring the Spirit of the Nonprofit Sector

Unquestionably, this spirit has been on the decline, with the apparent and well documented blurring of the sectors (see Chapter 20). When large nonprofits "do the right thing" today, it can be surprising and even newsworthy. One recent example illustrating this is the case of Capital Blue Cross (Pennsylvania), which faced a dilemma concerning how to deal with a situation involving the health insurance of employees of a financially failing for-profit firm. The company failed to pay its insurance premiums without notifying its employees. Scores of employees, facing the loss of their jobs as the company was going bankrupt, found that they were being stuck with bills from health providers that they had assumed were being paid by their employee health insurance policies. Blue Cross had negotiated with their company to try to preserve benefits for the workers. But after five months and no payments, the insurer decided to drop the company. Employees' insurance benefits were dropped retroactively to the date payments were stopped by their company, leaving many employees facing bills of tens of thousands of dollars. After considering the problem, the CEO of the nonprofit recognized that it had an obligation to be fair to the employees. He wrote:

> *Capital BlueCross is a business — but we also are a non-profit organization with a 70-year community mission. And this is one of those instances where mission should prevail. So I have directed that we will reach out to the affected covered employees in the coming days, to develop a plan to address the situation with them* (Wenner, 2009).

What is this "spirit" to which I refer? I would begin by suggesting some values compiled by the Josephson Institute of Ethics (2010) that are consistent with a virtue ethics approach to nonprofit organization management. They are:

1. Trustworthiness: honesty, integrity, promise-keeping, loyalty
2. Respect: autonomy, privacy, dignity, courtesy, tolerance, acceptance
3. Responsibility: accountability, pursuit of excellence
4. Caring: compassion, consideration, giving, sharing, kindness, loving
5. Justice and fairness: procedural fairness, impartiality, consistency, equity, equality, due process
6. Civic virtue and citizenship: law abiding, community service, protection of environment

This is not to suggest that for-profit organizations never operate consistently with these principles, and that is clearly not the case. Yet, we maintain that nonprofit organizations are *obligated* to honor these values as a condition of their formation. For-profit organizations that do not do so are judged by the marketplace. The very nature of nonprofit organizations makes it difficult, if not impossible, for the market to police them, and there is a special trust required of such organizations simply because they operate outside of traditional business market forces, and because government provides special benefits to them. By law, they are not permitted to distribute their earnings to their leadership, but rather are required by law to plow back any net revenue they accrue to the organization for its exempt purposes.

Unlike for-profit organizations, these nonprofits depend on the public trust. This trust is inherently validated by the fact that individuals will volunteer to work for them and gratuitously donate money to further their missions. There is an expectation by those who do so that the nonprofit will not violate their trust, and will not divert any incidental net revenue they earn for private gain.

Unquestionably, the leaders of large nonprofit organizations today are much more sophisticated than their predecessors. They are, for the most part, highly educated, and almost all have advanced degrees and technical training. They focus on outcomes rather than outputs. And they are often as well-paid as their for-profit counterparts.

But this change has not come absent any cost. Many see those they serve as customers rather than as clients. They are often as comfortable speaking about their organization's "bottom line," "return on investment," and "utility maximization" as their for-profit organization counterparts. Many expect to be with an organization only a short time, and then "move up" to another organization that might offer not only more challenge, but a commensurate increase in salary, benefits, and perquisites. And it might not matter much if their next employer is a for-profit or nonprofit organization. They may not be as squeamish about the exigencies of dealing in an environment that provides incentives for exploitation, manipulation, and engaging in fierce, if not destructive, competition. The values of cooperation and serving the needs of the marginalized that their predecessors learned as students of social work may have been deemphasized in their own business administration programs.

Much has been written about the merging of the sectors. More nonprofit staff positions are identical to those in the for-profit sector (e.g., accounting, Web development, and Information technology), and individuals move freely from one sector to another. Nonprofits have formed for-profit subsidiaries and vice-versa. For-profit-nonprofit partnerships (such as Cause-Related Marketing) have raised conflict-of-interest questions. Nonprofits and for-profits find that they are operating virtually identically in some subsectors (e.g., hospitals, nursing homes, day care, health and fitness, higher education), and employees move freely between these subsectors, without any regard to cultural differences that may be inherent in the sectors—differences that I find to be disappearing. As a result, what may have been viewed as a distinct, more public-serving culture of the nonprofit sector in the past has been supplanted by a more universal "business" culture that focuses much more on the instrumental efficiency of the organization rather than its public mission. And perhaps the leaders of these organizations tend to be more self-interested.

I mourn any loss of the spirit that made the nonprofit sector a beacon of hope to all of us in need of help in one way or another. But if I am correct that some of this spirit has been lost, I also maintain some optimism that we can help restore these lost values.

How? I suggest the following:

1. Educate future nonprofit leaders about the values we hold dear: ethical decision-making that honors the tradition of the sector of putting the needs of our communities above our own personal needs.

2. Develop and enforce codes of ethics to spell out acceptable and unacceptable behavior, and provide sanctions against those who violate these standards.

3. Promote continuing education of nonprofit organization professionals to enhance not only technical skills, but ethical values that are consistent with the spirit of the nonprofit sector.

4. Recruit nonprofit leaders who are not only technically good managers, but are also committed to making a difference in our communities, supporting social justice, being change agents, not simply leading the organization to earn a living.

5. Speak out at every opportunity to communicate a moral and spiritual component to social change.

6. Be role models ourselves for the culture we value. This means making our organizations' operations transparent, making decisions in the best interests of our communities rather than our own personal interests, not living lavishly on our expense accounts, and not paying ourselves exorbitant salaries while at the same time paying our staff less than they need to support themselves.

References

About.com. (2010). *Thanksgiving*. Retrieved from *http://americanhistory.about.com/od/holidays/a/thanksgiving.htm*

Associated Press. (2010). *Fargo area at 'major flood' stage.* March 18, 2010. Retrieved from *http://www.msnbc.msn.com/id/35892022/*

Inforum. (2010a). *Flood 2009: A second crest*. Retrieved from *http://www.inforum.com/content/flood-2009-second-crest*

Inforum. (2010b). Fargo Flood Update: City rolls out details for volunteer sandbag effort. Retrieved from *http://www.inforum.com/content/fargo-flood-update-city-rolls-out-details-volunteer-sandbag-effort*

Josephson Institute. (2010). *Six Pillars*. Retrieved from *http://josephsoninstitute.org/MED/MED-2sixpillars.html*

Wenner, D. (2009). Capital BlueCross promises to help laid-off workers with huge medical bills. Harrisburg Patriot-News. October 12, 2009. Retrieved from *http://www.pennlive.com/midstate/index.ssf/2009/10/capital_bluecross_promises_to.html*

Winslow, Thomas *(1986)*. A grating problem. *Harvard Crimson.* June 5, 1986. Retrieved from *http://www.thecrimson.com/article/1986/6/5/a-grating-problem-pin-the-dead/*

Appendix 1
Case 1
Jane's Dilemma—
Hiring the Development Director

"Thank you, and I appreciated our meeting," Jane said, rising to shake Bernie Plotkoff's hand. She would have preferred to avoid this customary gesture at the end of such a meeting, but she knew it would have been rude to do so. "I'll be in touch soon, perhaps next week, about whether you were the successful candidate for this position," she added stiffly, trying to conjure up a smile—which was a struggle, considering the circumstances.

Jane's stomach knotted up, and she began to sweat profusely as she considered her options, none of which were attractive.

For fifteen years, Jane Doesky had devoted herself to making the A. K. Schwarzkin Charitable Foundation the best charity it could be. She was well-paid as the executive director of the organization, and the income was now much more necessary than when she was first hired, because her mother was in a nursing home, and she was making payments of $6,000 each month to the home. Mom showed increasing signs of developing Alzheimer's, and Jane feared that this would necessitate having her moved to a unit that provided services to these patients, with a substantially higher monthly charge.

Jane had sacrificed her personal life, making herself available to the organization 24/7. She had the usual number of crises during her tenure, but had always come through with solutions that were creative. Her colleagues in the general nonprofit community held her in high esteem for her integrity and leadership.

Now, it appeared that not only was her job on the line, but the continued existence of the charity was at risk. It was a perfect storm that had put her in this unenviable situation—a flagging economy, the trust of a friend and colleague that was violated, and the resignation of the organization's dependable, long-time Director of Development and de facto chief financial officer, Myron Cohn, for "personal reasons." Almost everyone knew what those "personal reasons" were by now, as

Note: *The eight cases in Appendices 1-8 are taken from* The Nonprofit Management Casebook: Scenes from the Frontlines, *by Gary M. Grobman and published by White Hat Communications (2010).*

the newspapers had had a field day documenting the financial scandal that had rocked the Jewish charitable community in general and the Schwarzkin charity in particular.

Cohn had fallen hook, line, and sinker for the Madoff Ponzi scheme, investing most of the foundation's assets, lured by a promise of returns that were substantially better than the market. Doesky had trusted Cohn's judgment, providing only cursory oversight over his financial management, recognizing that he had an exemplary track record and almost 20 years more experience than she had. Once it became evident that $30 million in Foundation assets were gone with virtually no chance of any recovery, Myron had submitted his resignation, content to retire to a comfy condo in Florida. Leaving Jane and the Foundation holding the bag. An empty bag.

Jane thought back to her meeting a month before with her board chair, Goldie Sharafsky, who had been livid after hearing about how much the Foundation had lost. She had summoned Jane to her own office, located in a posh, downtown office building adjacent to Rittenhouse Square in Philadelphia. Once there, she had provided Jane with a deftly-delivered ultimatum.

"I'll be frank," Goldie had begun, closing the door for privacy, her tone of voice masking any cordiality that had usually been there whenever Jane was asked, infrequently, to meet in Goldie's office. More often, meetings between the two were held over a casual lunch in one of the trendy cafés along Broad Street. Jane did not expect this meeting to be pleasant, but she felt blindsided by what followed.

"I've exchanged some telephone calls with the Foundation leadership, and we have come to a consensus on how to handle this unpleasant situation with the financial scandal," Goldie began, her words measured. Jane did not take this as a good sign for what was to come.

"Your job is on the line here. Since the Foundation has taken such an unexpected hit from both the scandal and poor fundraising brought on by the tanking of the economy, everyone's job is on the line, including mine as chair. One of our board members, I won't tell you which mumser that was but you could probably guess, even suggested liquidating the Foundation. Others wanted to simply fire you and rebuild. Even your supporters are kvetching."

Jane felt the blood rush to her head. But she said nothing. Maintain some control, she thought.

"I fought to keep you. I can't find any justification for simply giving up," Goldie continued. "So many people depend on our programs. And you have considerable talent that I think can work to our advantage as we try to recover from this debacle. I know Myron let you down, and God knows, I can understand why you let him have free rein over investment policy. But when push comes to shove, you are responsible and accountable for the results of all of the Foundation's employees."

Jane took a deep breath, waiting for the shoe to drop. It did.

"So, here's what we decided. You have two years to rebuild the Foundation's assets to a level that we feel comfortable funding our commitments, and you will be evaluated in a year and must demonstrate that you are making significant progress toward achieving that goal. If you can agree to do that, you can stay; otherwise, we will provide you with two months of severance pay, shake hands, thank you for your service over the years, and launch a search for your successor."

Jane, speechless, shaken, simply nodded her head and left after exchanging the bare minimum of parting pleasantries.

Now back in her office, contemplating what was told to her in confidence by the third candidate she had interviewed that day for the vacant Director of Development position, her anxiety heightened as she considered what he had offered to her.

Bernie Plotkoff was a name well known to her. She was intrigued that he had applied for the vacant position although she granted him an interview more out of curiosity than any realistic expectation that she would actually hire him. He was the current Director of Development for the S.D. Leibman Foundation, the Swartzkin Foundation's principal competitor for charitable donations directed to serving Jewish adolescent runaways and missing children. Both foundations had been established at about the same time, inspired by the disappearance of Chandra Levy in Washington, D.C. during the summer of 2001. At one time, the boards of both foundations had considered merging, but relations between the two organizations had soured during negotiations and both had gone their separate ways. The board chairs of both organizations at that time had once been personal friends, bonded by the shared trauma of separate, but similar, family tragedies involving young family members.

Yet following the breakup of the proposed merger, they were no longer on speaking terms. Although this breakup appeared to be irreconcilable at the time, most board members and staff leadership, including Jane, judged that an eventual merger would be inevitable, particularly when economic times necessitated an end to competition for funds and programs that served essentially the same clients.

Jane had to admit that the Leibman Foundation was the more successful of the two, attributed for the most part to the aggressive fundraising tactics of the development director whom she had just finished interviewing as part of her process to find a successor to Cohn. "Aggressive" was perhaps too polite a word to describe

Bernie's fundraising reputation. The Leibman Foundation raised millions of dollars, including from some folks who contributed to both foundations.

The Leibman Foundation's fundraising tactics were anything but low-key. It was among the first to enclose a check in its direct mailings that recipients could cash regardless of whether they made a contribution, instilling an additional level of guilt to make one. It was one of the few Jewish charities that enclosed a small prayer book or religious article such as a yarmulke (a skull cap), which would make recipients who were religiously observant to be violative of Jewish law if they simply tossed the mail piece into the trash rather than having it undergo a ritual burial.

It was rumored that Leibman's annual development budget included a line-item for the hiring of a private detective, and that Plotkoff utilized the services of shady Internet database businesses that sold information to anyone for a fee—information that most of us would assume would not be available publicly to anyone. This was part of what is called "prospect research," what otherwise was a legitimate technique of fundraisers to learn about the capacity of donors and potential donors. As "refined" by Plotkoff, it was more akin to "spying."

In short, the Leibman Foundation sanctioned whatever worked, kept constant pressure on giving, and held over-the-top lavish fundraisers that attracted giving that only minimally was provided because of the organization's mission. And the grand conductor of the fundraising strategy was Bernie Plotkoff, looked upon with undisguised disdain by many of his colleagues, most of whom were secretly envious of the results he recorded for his employer.

Prior to the interview, Jane had no evidence to think that he did anything overtly illegal, although it would not have come as a surprise to her if he routinely crossed the line of ethical conduct without a second thought. If he did so, she would have attributed it to being a zealot for the cause, and she would not have expected that he violated professional ethics for his own personal gain. Now that she had finished her interview with him and heard his pitch, she had second thoughts about her judgment about both his ethics and his allegiance to following the letter of the law in pursuing his craft.

What Bernie had offered her was communicated quite directly, and he did not make any effort to veil his proposal in euphemistic references to make it appear less distasteful to her. She was shocked by his brazen chutzpah, and she felt even a bit insulted that he would trust her to keep his offer in confidence.

He offered to leave the Leibman Foundation for Cohn's position, giving two week's notice. He would want his current salary that he received from Leibman, plus a 10% raise. He would want an unvouchered expense account of $20,000 annually and a company car. On top of that, he would expect an annual incentive bonus of 2% of the amount he raised. He would guarantee that he could increase the Foundation's fundraising income by 100% in the first year, and make up most of the losses from the Madoff financial scandal by focusing particularly on donors who had the capacity to participate in planned giving.

What gave Jane even more pause was what he told her would be his strategy for achieving these lofty goals, and when he disclosed that, Jane didn't doubt his ability to come through and save her own job as well as keep the foundation viable for many years to come.

Bernie intimated that he had on disk all of the fundraising records of the Leibman Foundation, including all of the prospect research files and history of giving for 10,000 donors, about four times the number of donors that were in the Schwarzkin fundraising database. Hire him, and he would integrate that disk into the fundraising operations of the Schwarzkin Foundation. Even without this database, his contacts alone would result in millions of dollars in additional donations to the Foundation. And with this database and the files that came with it, the Schwarzkin Foundation's future would be cemented, and its major competitor for donations, the Leibman Foundation, would be crippled. Within a year or two, the Leibman Foundation leadership would be begging for a merger, so the integration of the database files and the end to destructive competition between the two organizations would come to an end. So, although his plan might be somewhat on the shady side, all of the money raised would be going to a cause both organizations support, so in the long run, what would be the harm?

As Jane contemplated how difficult it might be to find another job in this economic environment, she considered the pros and cons of Bernie's proposal.

Discussion Questions

1. What are Jane's options, and what are the pros and cons of each option?

2. Should Jane report the offer she received from Bernie to anyone within or outside of her organization?

3. How much should the fact that Jane needs to maintain her income to support her mother's nursing home costs factor into her decision? Discuss any conflict between Jane's ethical responsibility to act in the best interests of the organization and the need to serve her own interests, and how such a conflict should be resolved.

4. How much does the fact that these two organizations are likely to merge sometime in the near future factor into her decision?

5. Discuss the ethics of each of the fundraising strategies used by Bernie Plotkoff.

6. Discuss what is appropriate with respect to prospect research and what are some of the prospect research techniques that might cross the line of acceptability, even if they are effective.

7. Discuss the pros and cons of paying fundraisers based on the amount they raise. Why do almost all organizations that represent fundraisers have ethics codes that consider compensation based on the amount a fundraiser raises to be unethical?

Appendix 2
Case 2
I Choose to Live Foundation—
One Man's Vision to Form a New Charity

John Buck was a man with a mission and a vision, and he wasn't going to let anyone stand in his way until he got what he wanted. Whatever it was. Whether it was finding a wealthy, socially connected spouse; getting his MBA from Columbia; helping his wife raise twin boys; furnishing a small yet tasteful summer home in the Hamptons; or winning his age group in the New York Marathon (actually, the best he could achieve was third, but he resolved to train hard enough to move up in the national Master's road race rankings each year).

Regardless of the goal of the moment, he focused on it with the concentration of a Zen Master and did whatever it took to achieve his objective—often taking no prisoners. At 60, he felt he was in the prime of his life, and he often referred to his wife of 35 years, Stacy, an attorney who specialized in family law, as his "trophy wife," although she was his first and only love.

He conceded to himself that he often ruffled some feathers, but he had minimal patience for those who found objections, usually specious, for his aggressive problem-solving. Whatever he got involved in, he did so in a manner that did not leave very much out of his control, either at work or managing his personal life.

When he was diagnosed with prostate cancer two years earlier, he initially assumed that he was beginning a downward spiral that would end in a slow, painful death. He was taken totally by surprise by the diagnosis. He had had a routine PSA blood test at the age of 55 to diagnose the presence of an antigen that often shows up in those with this cancer. It had been negative, but even with a positive test, many doctors recommended against aggressive responses because prostate cancer tumors are often so slow developing that most men with this cancer will die from other causes. Regardless, he had learned that prostate cancer was the most common form of cancer among men in the U.S. and the second leading cause of cancer death among men, with only lung cancer having a higher rate.

It was not a positive blood test but rather some difficulty urinating that had triggered the diagnosis, which was confirmed after a biopsy.

Upon hearing the diagnosis, John didn't spend a minute wallowing in self-pity. Rather, beating the disease became another challenge, even when his long-time primary physician had suggested that he might consider simply letting the disease take its course. In consultation with an oncologist he knew from his running club, John had some radiation treatments, took hormones, and eventually underwent surgery to remove his prostate. After a six-month absence, he resumed his running workouts.

Inspiring him to not only survive but to thrive was Lance Armstrong, who at the age of 25 overcame testicular cancer that had spread to his lungs and brain and a prognosis of having only a 50% chance of survival to become one of the greatest athletes in modern history. Almost every day, before his workouts, John would visit the Lance Armstrong Foundation Web site at http://www.livestrong.org and create a virtual bond with this icon of the bicycling world who also competed alongside him, somewhere in the crowd, in the New York Marathon.

John networked with other upper middle-class male prostate cancer survivors in Northern New Jersey where he lived and in the Big Apple, where he still worked a modified schedule. Many men he spoke with had survived much longer without the return of cancer, some for as many as ten years. Unlike John, some had gone through the five stages of grief after learning of their diagnosis. Many had suffered bouts of depression. Some had retreated from their friends and families, losing their zest for life. For those with advanced forms of the disease and who were in chronic pain, morphine was one drug of choice. Some turned to an overdependence on other drugs, both prescribed and those that were not, to relieve their physical and psychic pain.

Occasionally, someone in his network died. John's mother had died of breast cancer when she was 60. John remembered that Mom had spiraled into depression, shutting herself off from family and friends, isolating herself in her Manhattan apartment with only a mangy cat for companionship, never venturing out to enjoy what life could offer one even in the clutches of the late stage breast cancer that claimed her life prematurely. The cancer had metastasized to her bones, lungs, and liver. She became emaciated, and her spirit had been ravaged along with her body. John had watched his mother die slowly, receiving daily reports from the nurse whom he had hired to care for her while John managed his hedge funds, earning more in a week than his Mom earned in nearly a lifetime—at least until the Madoff scandal and the economic meltdown of 2008-2009 had encouraged his clients to seek more secure, stable investment options, if they had any assets left to invest.

These men with prostate cancer with whom he networked became his friends and extended family. They would meet in the City to attend Knicks games at Madison Square Garden and have dinner afterwards at trendy, expensive restaurants on the West Side. And they would talk. What they had in common was a resolve not to let cancer claim their spirit and zest for life.

John recognized the therapeutic value of being with others who shared the unique experience of being diagnosed with this killer disease. And he also saw that the stress of this disease accrued not just on the men struck by cancer but on their families.

One of his friends suggested organizing a trip to see the Broadway musical "In the Heights" for nearly a dozen men with advanced stages of prostate cancer in and around John's bedroom community of Harristown, New Jersey, a short 25-minute train ride to Grand Central Station. This might possibly be the last opportunity for independence for some of them before the disease claimed their lives. Most of these men were like John—professional men who would not give a second thought to buying a new suit for $800 if it was both fashionable and functional. But John knew that other men on the invitation list would be making a major financial sacrifice to accept the invitation, and some men were unable to afford the trip at all. Many had lost their livelihoods as a result of their cancer diagnosis, and others were victimized by the economic recession the entire country was sinking into beginning in 2008.

John didn't hesitate in writing a generous check to subsidize the trip for several men whom he knew would not be able to afford to accept this invitation. But this spontaneous philanthropy planted a seed of an idea. Why not start an organization that would be the conduit of charitable contributions for this purpose? At least this way, the funds he was providing out of his own pocket would be tax deductible. And there were hundreds of men who might benefit from programs that would focus on letting those with prostate cancer have some fun and enjoy the precious little time they had left, when most money directed to the issue of prostate cancer seemed to be focused on finding a cure. And unlike the days when his own mother was diagnosed, new drugs and treatments afforded thousands of men and women diagnosed with cancer much better odds for survival, and for longer periods.

John latched on to his idea as if it were a new toy. His wife was smart enough not to discourage him, not that there was anything she could have said that would have convinced him to drop the idea. First, he would begin raising money so he could quit his job as a hedge fund manager (the firm was going under anyway, and employees were talking among themselves about how to negotiate severance packages) and be the full-time director of this new program. Second, he would need to form a board of directors for him to lead. It would have to be a small board, and not have anyone who would interfere with his vision. His wife would be a good choice for Vice-President, he thought, as she was an attorney, and that would come in handy for handling all of the legal affairs of this new organization. Their twin boys, now grown, and one daughter-in-law would also provide some valuable skills and be excellent board members. (He and his wife were not on speaking terms with the other daughter-in-law, after his wife got into an irreconcilable disagreement with her over the color of bridesmaid dresses.)

And perhaps a couple of the men from the network would make good board members, provided they didn't try to run things and would be satisfied with being major donors and finding others to donate. But if they did expect to have more than a cosmetic role, he would be assured of control of at least a majority of votes through his relatives, if anything ever came down to a vote or his influence to direct the activities and substantive programs of the organization was challenged. If that occurred, he would be assured of having enough power to throw anyone off the board who didn't cooperate with his vision.

It has been pointed out by many that board members should be recruited who offer at a minimum, one of the three "W's": wealth, wisdom, or work. In John's mind, the first was a priority, and any of the second or third attributes any of these individuals could bring with them would be gravy.

The ideas for making this dream become a reality were flowing, and he needed to get them down while they were still fresh in his mind.

He took out a pen, found a legal tablet, and started writing down what he would need to do to form his new organization, which he decided to name the "I Choose to Live Foundation."

- Incorporate: New Jersey or NY?
- Recruit board members
- Write bylaws. Gotta keep everything under my control.
- Design a Web site. Reserve a domain name. Should have an area for men to leave their stories about their experiences with diagnosis and treatment and help others with questions. Needs an "Ask the Doctor" page.
- Prepare a fundraising plan. Need to register with anyone to do this? Can raise money at a dinner with a celebrity speaker. Can auction off sports memorabilia online?
- Open a bank account
- Apply for 501(c)(3) tax-exempt status. Does this cost any money??? Can Stacey do this?
- Make sure no one else is using this name. How do I do this?
- Find a celebrity (New York Rangers player?) to be an endorser/sponsor. Maybe a goalie who can help make a "stop" or a goal scorer can help score a goal of helping those with prostate cancer.

Discussion Questions

1. If John came to you for advice on whether to start this organization, what would you tell him?

2. What would you advise John with respect to the governance model of his organization?

3. What problems might you see if he decides to apply on behalf of this organization for 501(c)(3) tax-exempt status with his current vision of organizational governance?

4. Would you expect this organization to still be around after 20 years?

5. If he did decide not to invest his time in starting a new organization focusing on providing entertainment options for men with prostate cancer, what other options might he have for achieving his goal of providing these services?

6. Should John's organization consider providing its services to those with other forms of cancer?

7. What other tasks should be on John's list of things to do when forming his organization?

Appendix 3

Case 3
Museum and Historical Association State Budget Cuts

"It's Kevin on line 2," chirped Betty on Louise Wilson's intercom.

Louise Wilson was the executive director of the State Historical and Museum Association, a four-employee nonprofit organization. Betty was the bookkeeper and administrative assistant who did double duty by answering the telephones. Kevin Peters, calling in from the State Capitol, was the communications and government relations professional. The only other employee of the association, Bill Stevens, was an historian who had museum management experience with a large art museum in Philadelphia.

While Louise spent most of her time keeping her 15-member board happy and working with the consultant fundraiser, Bill provided management and other technical assistance to the 67 museums and historical associations that were dues-paying members. In addition to being the association's registered lobbyist, Kevin also maintained the organization's Web site, produced the monthly newsletter, and issued press releases.

All four employees, along with a small cadre of committed volunteers and an occasional summer intern, participated in planning fundraisers, preparing for board meetings, and sorting the bulk mail for the newsletters. Some services, such as the bulk mail tasks for the newsletter and fundraising, previously had been outsourced. A reflection of the economic times, the budget of the Association had eroded steadily in recent years, as its membership had experienced a hemorrhage of income losses and an increase in expenses. Museum visits not only statewide but nationwide, as well, had suffered a steady decline over several decades, victim to a change in the way children and adults alike spent their leisure time. It was tough enough to compete with movie theaters and television. Adding the lure and addiction of the Internet and video games exacerbated the competition.

Although many museums had a loyal following, it was difficult to keep the Association's membership able to finance fresh exhibits that would encourage return visitors. As membership had dwindled and government subsidies had evaporated, many museums found it necessary to raise their admission fees, which fed into the cycle of declining membership.

During the latest economic turmoil, arts and education related nonprofits had suffered disproportionately from budget cuts from government, as well as cuts in grants from foundation funders. Few museums could boast of any sizeable endowments, and even those that were able to divert endowment funding to cover operational deficits recognized that it was only a temporary measure. All arts organizations and museums were at risk from a plethora of challenging crises. Energy costs had gone through the roof (literally, for those that did not have any weatherization program). This not only fattened the heating and cooling bills of facilities, but also affected the willingness of patrons to get in their cars and travel to a museum when they could stay in their homes and download a pay-on-demand movie through their cable boxes. Costs for security and insurance had skyrocketed, along with the cost of health insurance and other employee benefits. And there was nothing on the horizon that promised any relief.

Louise, herself, was often stressed out from the increasing workload. This was not fair. But it was also not a good time to be seeking another job, particularly in this field, which was clearly declining. She remembered that several years earlier, one of her board members had approached her about joining his firm as a manager in the financial services industry at a starting salary that had dwarfed her own. After a long discussion with her husband, she had decided to rebuff the offer, knowing that her heart was in the work she was doing. Whenever she had received the tuition bills from her son's college, she had thought wistfully about the wisdom of her decision. Ironically, that board member was now unemployed after his firm had gone belly up only months before it might have benefited from federal bailout legislation promoted by an outgoing President Bush and an incoming President Obama.

Kevin waited patiently as Louise braced herself and took the call.

"Good news or bad?" Louise asked, as she picked up the telephone. Most news she had received lately had been bad, as reliable funders had dropped out with hardly a warning. Several large institutional members had indicated to her that they might need to defer this year's dues payments to her and other associations and coalitions that they participated in to avoid laying off even more employees. At one time during the high-flying economic boom of the 1990s, the Association had employed six full-time and a couple of part-time employees. A failing economy and the loss of revenue had necessitated a slow retrenchment of spending by the Association. Two long-time employees, both of whom had been employed since its founding in 1975, had retired and were not replaced. Their duties had been absorbed by other staff.

The residual stress accruing to the organization from this response had its consequences. Louise knew that both Betty and Bill were looking for other jobs. It was not that they were disloyal; Louise conceded that she was requiring them to devote more time to the organization than they could reasonably be expected to sustain for much longer.

"Well, would you rather have the bad news first, or the really bad news?" Kevin responded. Kevin had spent most of the morning and half of the afternoon at the

Capitol Building, listening to the Governor's budget address and obtaining a hard copy of the budget proposal. All of the numbers would be posted online later in the day, but as a state association executive, Louise knew that one of her most critically important tasks was to provide information about developments to her membership as soon as possible. Nothing annoyed her more than one of her members finding out some juicy piece of information about state government from a source other than the Association.

Kevin was good at his job. He would tell her what she needed to know without any equivocation, and he knew that she would not shoot the messenger.

Louise was somewhat prepared for bad news from the Governor, who had a public face as a fiscal conservative, but who had a soft spot in his heart for funding programs that improved the quality of life for his state's citizens, such as the arts, humanities, museums, and programs that improved the health care and education of children. The Governor, an affable, congenial man who made those around him comfortable, had four children and 12 grandchildren, which some said had a great influence on his public policy. Others attributed this warm spot he had for the arts and humanities to the fact that the State's First Lady had been a librarian, and was a sub rosa advocate for programs that were not traditionally embraced by self-proclaimed fiscal conservatives. But having met the Governor a couple of times at ground-breaking ceremonies, Louise judged that he was a sincere supporter of museums and the educational role they play in increasing the social capital of a community.

"I already expect it will be bad," Louise responded, "and the draft Action Alert you prepared for distribution today to the membership about the budget wasn't very optimistic. How much do we need to change it? If I remember, we estimated a 20% cut in the line-item for museums and historical associations."

"Well, I hope you are sitting down," Kevin began his report via cell phone. "The bad news is that the Governor zeroed out our line-item entirely."

"Ouch, what could be the really bad news, then?" she replied as calmly as she could, although she felt the blood rush to her head.

For a moment, she relived the feeling she had felt in February of 2009 when she read about a highly prestigious art museum in Nevada, the Las Vegas Art Museum, simply closing its doors with only a few days of public notice. At the time, many other nationally respected institutions, including the Philadelphia Museum of Art and Atlanta's High Museum of Art, had announced severe layoffs in addition to other budget-cutting measures, but it was the emerging story in Las Vegas that had traumatized those in the "industry." A couple of months before it had summarily closed, the board of the Las Vegas institution had instituted draconian measures intended to save the organization, which was projecting an unacceptable budget deficit. The executive director there had responded by announcing her resignation.

The Las Vegas museum had received only 3% of its budget from government funding, and at the time it had closed, membership had dwindled to only 1,000 individuals. Louise knew full well that many of her members depended on state funds for substantially more than 3% of their income. For a moment, she envisioned "Closed to the Public" signs on the front doors of constituent institutions of the Association. Unthinkable for something like that to happen on her watch!

"The Guv also zeroed out all of the earmarked grants that our members receive, including the $1 million for Harristown," Kevin said. Harristown was the Harristown Art Museum (HAM), the largest and most prestigious art museum in the state, which provided the Association with almost 25% of its annual budget. The current chair of the board of the Association was Dr. Elizabeth Bowman, the crusty executive director of HAM. She would not be happy, and unlike Louise, the "lizard," as Elizabeth was called behind her back, might indeed shoot the messenger who delivered bad tidings.

"The Guv basically said that he will do everything in his power not to raise taxes and to protect every existing service the state funds that directly protects the health, safety, and welfare of the state's citizens. He not only zeroed us out, but he also zeroed out state supplemental funds to libraries, subsidies to parks, the state's athletic programs, and the senior citizen public transportation program. And that might be the really bad news, as the General Assembly will do whatever it takes to find funds to restore the senior transportation program, for the obvious reasons."

"What else can you tell me?" Louise prodded, holding on to her desk for support, and trying not to convey the panic that she increasingly was feeling at the moment.

"Well, I had a minute to chat with Stevens, the House Majority Whip and Williamson, the Senate Minority Leader. Both are sympathetic to restoring some of the money, and both seem to think the Governor cut us to the bone knowing full well that the Legislature would put back some money, so he could present a balanced budget. He probably won't oppose putting all or some of our money back unless it takes something away from some other program he supports more. The problem is that the money has to be found somewhere, and most of the money the legislature had hidden away for purposes such as this were dug up from their hiding places last year when the libraries were the target of budget cuts." He paused a moment. "And, of course, no one is suggesting raising taxes."

Louise considered this for a moment before responding. "I remember that a nephew of the Senate Minority Leader is a curator for Harristown, and is located in the district of the House Majority Leader, who usually protects their interests. How did this happen to Harristown?"

"I don't know for sure, but I think this may be some payback for Williamson leading the veto override fight on the Governor's pet health care reform plan," Kevin responded. "Look, I am still in shock about this myself. I am a bit blindsided by this, and I would have expected that my friends in the Front Office would have given me a heads up." The "Front Office" was the term Kevin and other lobbyists used to describe the Governor's Office.

"The Governor throws stones at the frogs in sport, but the frogs die not in sport but in earnest," Louise mused, paraphrasing Plutarch, more to herself than to Kevin. "So, come back here as soon as you can. I need to talk to the Lizard about what we can tell the board and what we can tell the general membership about this," Louise commanded. "I guess the only good news is that this budget is only a recommendation, and we have four months before the budget deadline to convince our friends in the Legislature that these draconian cuts simply aren't fair. And we have to send out the Action Alert ASAP."

Louise hung up the telephone, closed the door to her office, and took a deep breath. Although none of the funds the state made available in the Museum and Historical Commission line-item came to the Association directly, there was a general agreement among the board and its members that dues to the Association were based in large part on the state funding the Association was able to obtain. For the past several years, the line-item had received a perfunctory 2-3% cost-of-living increase, along with other line-items that did not have high visibility or a politically powerful constituency, such as programs for the aged, basic education, or subsidies for colleges and universities.

In her heart, Louise had feared that the 20% cut in funding might become reality, but the news from Kevin was far worse than even her worst-case scenario. Being zeroed out was unfathomable. She judged that the Association and its allies had enough political influence to restore some of the funds, but was it realistic to think that it was possible to get all of the money restored? Even getting the line-item restored to its funding from the previous year was a de facto cut, as inflation eroded the value of each dollar of revenue.

Louise pulled up a database on her computer that tracked political contributions made to the leadership of the State Legislature and Governor by friends and stakeholders of the Association. Impressive as it was, the current budget situation could very well trump this aspect of the Association's power. At least, it helped Kevin get access to the movers and shakers in the Capitol to make the Association's case one-on-one. But compared to the access provided by the telecommunications, trial lawyer, and the insurance lobbies, the influence of the entire nonprofit sector was minimal. The good news was that many individuals on Louise's list were associated one way or the other with the powerful organizations that really ran state government. Hopefully, they could be convinced to help.

Louise knew that whereas Kevin was good at providing data and convincing arguments, public policy made in the Governor's Mansion and the halls of the Capitol emanated more on the golf course and at $500 per plate fundraisers. Few nonprofit associations or organizations had the resources to invest in this game, and those that did represented the interests of hospitals and institutions of higher learning—certainly not museums and historical societies. Louise took it as a given that Harristown University's state subsidy was safe from the sharp knives of state budget cutters, partly because legislative leaders and the Governor had access to a private sky box for every home game.

It occurred to Louise that the museums would have some natural allies with which to align themselves and marshal a public outcry. She took out a legal pad and started writing changes to the text of the Action Alert that would be e-mailed that afternoon with the bad news. Included in her draft was a pledge that she would do everything in her power to restore the funds, and that every stakeholder needed to pitch in to help with the coordinated advocacy effort that would be required.

As she looked down at her legal pad, she smiled through the tears.

Discussion Questions

1. What arguments might Louise and her allies make that the state needs to support programs other than those that directly protect the health, safety, and welfare of the state's citizens? If Louise wrote an Op-Ed article about it, what arguments might she make?

2. What are some of the advocacy activities the Association might engage in to help the cause?

3. Do you think Louise has the resources to start and build a successful coalition to restore these cuts? Could she afford not to? Discuss who might be natural coalition partners, and who might be better avoided.

4. What is the author referring to when he uses the term "social capital," and why is this considered an important concept in the study of nonprofit management?

5. How much influence do you think personal experience of public officials (such as firsthand contact with relatives who have a disease or a particular disabil-

ity) has on the execution of public policy compared to general ideology? Is it ever inappropriate to exploit the knowledge of that experience? How might that be done in this particular case?

6. What is the role of the board in helping to restore funding to the Association's membership?

7. Is it unethical for public policymakers to take advantage of the private skybox offered by Harristown University at home football games? Why or why not?

Appendix 4
Case 4
The One (Wo)Man Band Running the Kenmore Midget Baseball League

Looking at a street light outside the second story window of the Clubhouse, Sarah determined that it was still snowing lightly. The Borough's maintenance crew had plowed out the parking lot in Kenmore Borough Park in response to her telephone request earlier that day, as she had expected. No one else would have thought to make that call, she mused, and there might have been no place for cars to park otherwise because of the foot of snow that had fallen earlier in the week. Without me, this organization would be only a skeleton of what it is now, she thought.

A couple of cars were still pulling into the parking lot of the Clubhouse, but Sarah prided herself on starting board meetings exactly on time.

With two minutes to go before the digital clock in the Clubhouse hit 7 p.m., Sarah imagined how the scene outside of this window would be different six months hence, the sun still relatively high in the sky and the temperature hovering in the low '90s, perhaps 70 degrees warmer than it was now. She could almost smell the pungent odor of the mustard that would be spread liberally atop the soft pretzels sold from the concession stand housed in the Clubhouse's first floor, the pretzels often stale, soggy, and delicious!

She delighted in the smell of the freshly mowed grass, the baseball diamond manicured with care by her two sons.

Among the sounds were a cacophony of dogs barking, babies crying in their mothers' arms, the chatter of players shouting encouragement to their teammates, and parents and coaches shouting out instructions. And, of course, the occasional "pong" of aluminum striking a ball. "Swing, batter!"

In the scene she conjured up, there were also younger siblings of the players ignoring the action on the field, instead playing tag with each other or catching lightning bugs and grasshoppers, the latter to use as bait to catch sunfish in Kenmore Creek. Midget League, for kids 10-12, was truly an intergenerational activity. Grandparents, and even great-grandparents, would attend games, some making the trip from the parking lot to the temporary stands using walkers.

Her reverie was interrupted by her BlackBerry chiming the tune "Take Me Out to the Ball Game," indicating that it was 7 p.m. and time to start the meeting.

"The board meeting will come to order," announced Sarah Goodling, banging the ceremonial gavel that was presented to her at a board meeting of the Kenmore Midget Baseball League, Inc. two years ago. Two more parents entered the room as she spoke. They quietly took seats around the large folding table and reached in the center of the table for a printed agenda. The gavel had a small plaque on its handle, lauding her for ten seasons of distinguished service as chair of the League. Her re-election this year was again by acclamation; for the past eight years, she had run for the office unopposed. Most board members were parents of players and rotated off the board when their kids aged out of the program and moved up to juniors.

Kenmore Midget Baseball League had operated in Kenmore since shortly after World War II. In the 1960s, the organization had incorporated as a 501(c)(3) tax-exempt nonprofit organization. It formally incorporated for several reasons, but the principal motivation was to respond to the liability exposure members of the organization thought they might have from injuries players and spectators might suffer as a result of being hit by stray balls. An added benefit of this status was that individuals who made donations to the organization could deduct their value on their federal income tax forms.

League expenses consisted chiefly of equipment, field rentals, insurance, paying umpires, maintaining the fields, and painting the Clubhouse. In addition to an annual dinner dance fundraiser, income came from a modest $50/season fee assessed to players in the league (waived if a family could not afford it) and from tax-deductible contributions by team sponsors whose logos adorned the uniforms, ads sold for the program book, and signs put up on the electric scoreboard. Sarah had been particularly proud of the scoreboard, for which she had found funding by requesting an earmark from a friendly state legislator who himself had played Midgets in Kenmore back in the 1970s.

Substantial additional income came from the brisk business generated by the field's concession stand, which had been operated by a local restaurant that was served by Sarah's food distribution business. That relationship was good for the equivalent of two team sponsorships each season. The agreement between the League and the restaurant was that 15% of proceeds would go directly to the League, and as an added bonus, the players playing in the game would receive a free hot dog and lemonade after the final out.

Volunteer parents staffed the concession stand each game, and this was the major activity in which parents engaged that contributed to the League's operations. The concession stand typically had a steady stream of customers whenever there were games. Many of the customers visited the stand without having any connection to the games, attracted to the reasonable prices for slushies, soft pretzels, roasted peanuts, grilled hot dogs, hamburgers, ice cream novelties, and popcorn.

The One (Wo)Man Band Case

It was not unusual for the cash receipts at the end of an evening doubleheader to exceed $700. After each evening, when the concession doors were shuttered, Sarah would personally collect the cash from the register, count it, place it in a cash bag, and make a night deposit at the Kenmore Community Bank, another team sponsor.

Sarah was generally acknowledged as the glue that held all of the pieces together. Those close to the program's operations knew that she was not only the glue, but for the most part, was the pieces, as well. It was common knowledge that Sarah was indispensible to having a successful season. Almost single-handedly, she recruited coaches, arranged the schedule, hired the field maintenance crew (for the past two years now, comprised exclusively of her twin sons, who had once been stars for Kenmore's Allstars), ordered bats and balls, recruited sponsors, and made sure the uniforms were ordered.

She attended to every detail, including proofreading the designs of the uniforms to make sure the names of the sponsors were spelled correctly. The first year she had chaired the League, she had delegated that task, and was embarrassed to find that the Kenmore Indians sported jerseys that season sponsored by "Katy's Jewlers." Katie, the store owner, had expressed her disapproval, but had been mollified by being offered a free ad in the next year's program booklet. Sarah never delegated that task again, nor most others.

During the summer, Sarah was a professional volunteer, devoting much of her day to the League while her husband ran the family business. Each season, those who served on the board could count on Sarah to be a busy worker bee, making sure every task was completed. On the wall of the Clubhouse, in addition to team pictures of players and coaches, was tangible evidence of recognition of her efforts, of which she was justly proud. Among them was a copy of a proclamation of Kenmore Borough Council commending Sarah for her achievements, alongside a resolution passed by the State House recognizing her ten years of leadership as chair of the board.

Sitting in the stands watching the games on a warm summer evening was heaven to Sarah, basking in not only the sun, but the glow of knowing that this was a masterpiece she had created. Each year, she had added to this masterpiece until the facility and program were the envy of not only nearby communities, but of those around the state who visited, seeking advice on how to emulate the success of the Kenmore program. This year, she had arranged for the construction of pro-style dugouts, complete with a water fountain, courtesy of a cousin who ran a construction company. He had given her a good price and had completed the work well before the deadline. Among the accoutrements added in recent years were an electric scoreboard, a clubhouse (where this board meeting was being held) that housed the concession stand, and net-enclosed batting cages.

Although she solicited ideas for these improvements at board meetings, she generally decided on her own which new feature she would add. This was a closely guarded secret. Universally, there was admiration among the board for how she found ways to make the program better each year. A few board members might grumble about what they perceived as heavy-handed tactics, but no one disputed that the results she achieved were well worth the occasional ruffled feathers. Most respected the fact that Sarah did her homework before engaging in a project on behalf of the League, and she was not perceived at all to be a loose cannon risk taker. Admittedly, she was aggressive in building the League, and she acknowledged that there was some validity to the saying "you can't steal second base with one foot on first."

It was a relief for virtually every board member when they got a notice in their e-mail in January that a board meeting was to be scheduled at the Clubhouse located on the grounds of the Kenmore Midget Field. This served as verification that Sarah was again willing to not only serve as board chair, but likely would make all of the arrangements for the coming season. There was anticipation about what new, creative physical improvements would be made to the fields (or, as sometimes occurred, had already been made in the fall before the construction season came to a halt and before the field was ready for seeding and painting).

Sarah, on the other hand, lived for Midget Baseball, even now that her kids were grown. She was in charge and the League was hers to run without much interference from anyone. In previous years, when she first began taking a leadership role, she had delegated many of the tasks to other parents. But she found that it was rare that anyone else could produce the results required to assure that the product each summer was up to the high quality standards that she demanded and that the kids deserved.

Eventually, parents learned to let Sarah do everything herself and stay out of her way. They knew that Sarah's commitment would solve any problem that might come up, and it certainly saved them a lot of aggravation to let her do all of this work behind the scenes, which she apparently reveled in doing. On one level, they felt that they were exploiting her, but if she was willing to do all of this work, what was the harm? It wasn't like they were capitalizing on this by sitting at home eating bon bons. Most parents of players were busy with work, and in the evenings, they did chores, shopping, and helped their kids with their homework. If they were able to squeeze out an hour or two to relax with a shared TV program with their spouse or perhaps one night each week for a movie, they considered themselves lucky.

Being the parents of eleven-year-olds was so much different than it had been for their own parents. Midget League was not the only activity that required their attention. There were music lessons, religious school classes, and any other number of organized activities that required chauffeuring their kids and often waiting until the activity was completed to drive them home.

Almost to a parent, watching their son or daughter play in the Kenmore Midget League was something they looked forward to well before their child reached the eligible age to compete. Because everything about the program was first class, parents from outside Kenmore clamored for the opportunity for their kids to play their Midget baseball in that community. At first, the board had resisted opening up the program to outsiders in nearby communities, but eventually, it embraced doing so. More playing fields were added in Kenmore Park to accommodate the additional demand for teams.

At its peak the previous season, 10 teams of 14 players each were competing in the Kenmore Midget League. It was not unusual for the stands to have crowds exceeding 100 watching the games. Many graduates of the program went on to play high school and college baseball. Although no one had as yet reached the Big Leagues, two former players were playing AA minor league ball and were in a position to be called up to the Bigs in September.

After so many years of doing this work, Sarah could produce results effortlessly compared to having parents do their share and make a mess that she would have the task of cleaning up. Sarah knew which businesses in the community to squeeze for sponsorships, how to avoid scheduling games on religious holidays, which kids needed to be on separate teams, and how to placate the demands of "Little League Dads" who demanded that their teams consist of the best players. Dealing with some of these parents was the toughest part of Sarah's job, and she often had to serve as the sole arbiter when her coaches were unable to deal with the abuse they had to take for not starting a particular player. Or for taking that player out of a game "prematurely" to let a less talented player meet the League's requirement that each player on the team plays at least two innings in the field.

Sarah had even dealt with one mom who had heaped a constant tirade of abuse on the home plate umpire. Sarah had calmly informed that mom out of earshot of curious onlookers that her behavior was unacceptable and a violation of League rules—and that if she continued her behavior, she and her son would not only be banned from participating in any further competition, but that her husband would somehow find out who she was spending time with every Wednesday morning. The mom had backed down without indicating which threat had intimidated her the most.

Sarah had boundless energy when it came to League business, although during the season, everything else was relegated to secondary importance. One of her brood, in high school, had grown up in Kenmore Midgets, and was a promising pitcher, scouted by several major league teams. Another was an All-American college wrestler who also played for State on its baseball team. Sarah knew that without the experience of playing Midget baseball, many of the kids in Kenmore would have turned to drugs or a life of crime, and they might very well have become permanently entangled within the criminal justice system.

She was proud of her accomplishments. Several years earlier, she had even been nominated to receive one of the daily "Point of Light" awards, created in response to a call by President George Herbert Walker Bush in his 1989 inaugural address and spearheaded by the Points of Light Institute.

Although she was not independently wealthy, Sarah and her husband ran a successful local food distribution business, and they were more prosperous than most parents with kids on the teams. When she found out that a kid with some talent lacked a glove or proper cleats, she often reached into her own pocket to provide them. She was delighted when one of these kids started calling her "Mom," and other players started doing this, as well, making her feel proud. In some sense, they were all like her children to her.

In December, Lenny's Family Restaurant, the restaurant that operated the concession stand, had been forced to close because of lease problems. The owner had decided to move the restaurant to Centertown, more than fifty miles away from Kenmore. This development meant that the League would not only have to find two new team sponsors, but also find another operator for the concession stand.

This new problem didn't faze Sarah at all, as she was a problem solver. Sarah judged that she could kill two birds with one stone and turn lemons into lemonade, perhaps literally in this case. If her board had no objection, she would propose to take over the concession stand management, and continue the terms of the previous agreement, running everything through her husband's food distribution business. The revenues she would receive would pay for sponsoring the two teams that the restaurant had sponsored, and more so. She also calculated that doing this would compensate her for some of the countless hours she put in during all of these years of service. And it would solve a big problem, as it could take a lot of effort to find someone else to provide for concessions on short notice.

It would also help stop the constant nagging of her husband, who continually was complaining that Sarah's devotion to the Midget League, including long hours, was having a harmful effect on the family business and their own relationship, as well. Her husband suggested that it was not fair that Sarah did all of this work without any compensation, while others benefited and did virtually nothing. With no kids in the program any more, her dedication and generosity were being taken advantage of, he persistently pointed out.

Considering how much work went into each successful season, most of it done by Sarah single-handedly, it should be a paid position, he contended.

The One (Wo)Man Band Case

After consulting with her husband, she wrote down more details of her concession business plan that would bring some income into the household to compensate her for all of the work she was doing, without having to propose to the League that it hire her to do this work in the future. Obviously, if she decided for any reason not to continue doing this work as a volunteer, it would be difficult, if not impossible, for the program to continue. She made a note in her Blackberry to add this item to the board agenda, thinking that it was appropriate for the board to consider what she planned to do to solve this last-minute problem.

"The next agenda item is replacing the partnership agreement we had with Lenny's Family Restaurant to manage the concession stand. I've talked this over with my husband, and we are willing to take it on with the same terms of 15% of the revenue going to the League. My business will sponsor the two teams, and we will use parent volunteers as before. Things can go on and we won't miss a beat.

"Does anyone object?"

Discussion Questions

1. Was it a problem that the concession stand was operated by a restaurant that had its food distributed to it by the board chair of the League?

2. How different does this situation become if the board chair herself is operating the concession stand?

3. What is the board's responsibility to question this proposal, and what is an appropriate response?

4. What problems might arise when an organization has one major committed volunteer who does all of the work? What might happen to the organization if that person burns out or otherwise becomes unable or unwilling to perform those duties? What leverage does that person have to make sure the board acts as he/she desires?

5. How should anyone in a nonprofit organization with authority to hire workers do so? What are some of the problems with how Sarah handles this process?

6. Would the governance structure of this organization benefit by having committees?

7. The term "midget" has "fallen into disfavor and it is considered offensive by most people of short stature," according to Little People of America. Discuss how you would handle a situation as the chair of the Kenmore Midget League

if a board member offered a motion to change the name of the organization to the "Kenmore Youth Baseball League" and to forbid the use of team names that may have been used in this League for years that might be offensive to some people, such as "Indians," "Redskins," and "Braves."

Appendix 5

Case 5
Cutting the Budget of the Harristown Family Service

The image that kept returning to Sarah Jordan's brain was the scene from *The Wizard of Oz* where water is poured over the wicked witch, who is screaming, "I'm melting, I'm melting!" In this case, the metaphor did not describe Sarah herself but rather the income stream of the Harristown Family Service. At the same time, demand for the organization's services was skyrocketing, fueled by the credit crunch, burgeoning unemployment, and increases in reported child abuse. For the first time in the HFS's history, clients were being turned away for some services, or placed on expanding waiting lists for others.

HFS was 60 years old now, a pillar of the community's social service safety net. Sarah had been at the helm of HFS for 20 years, after serving ten years with the organization as head of the social work department. Although an administrator, she still managed a small social work caseload so she could keep current with the "street level" aspects of her operation. Another reason for this was that she was a "not afraid to roll up your sleeves and get your hands dirty" social worker at heart, continuing to find immense personal satisfaction in working directly with needy clients rather than moving paper around and attending meetings, the two tasks that dominated her daily agenda.

During her tenure, HFS had grown from 10 to 60 employees. Income financing the $5 million annual operating budget came from a balanced mix of fee-for-service payments from clients, private donations, endowment interest, and government and foundation grants. There had been some lean years in the past, but never had the agency experienced a perfect storm of a deteriorating economy that squeezed income and that increased demand for its services from otherwise eligible clients who were unable to afford to pay HFS enough for the agency to recover its costs. These two trends squeezing the organization were exacerbated by simple bad luck and a culture of corporate greed in the general economy.

Now the chickens had come home to roost. Government bailouts had helped the greedy, not the needy, she mused. The banks, insurers, auto manufacturers, and others who had made bad decisions for years were on the short list for help. No one proposed helping the helpers who had played by the rules.

This morning, Sarah had convened a staff meeting with everyone present, from the COO and CFO to the 87-year-old "retired" social worker who answered the telephones. Everyone was there, including Sean Smithson, one of the front-line social workers she would have been quite happy to have come up with some excuse to miss this particular meeting. Sean was the organization's *énfant terrible,* and he could be counted on to provide unwelcome, nonproductive capriciousness in any serious discussion. For years, Sean broke almost every personnel rule, was contemptuous of authority, thumbed his nose at laws and regulations whenever they got in his way, played practical jokes on co-workers that often were over the line, and was a general pain in the butt.

His actions resulted in several near lawsuits filed by clients. Yet, she had to concede, he was the best social worker she had ever had, his risk-taking always in the interest of the organization's clients, even when not particularly good for the organization.

If the TV show *House, M.D.* ever had a spinoff that focused on a social worker rather than a medical doctor, Sean could be the model for the main character. One thing Sarah could count on was that Sean would play class clown and do everything he could to sabotage the tone she intended to set for this brainstorming session. For today's meeting, her tolerance level for levity was as low as it could get, as decisions made to increase income and cut expenses, influenced by input from staff, would determine whether the agency would survive the economic tsunami that threatened to swallow up similar agencies in other communities.

Her memo requiring all staff to attend and participate in this meeting spelled out its purpose—to engage everyone in a group brainstorming session to get input from staff to increase income and cut expenses before she submitted her recommendations to the board at the next meeting in three weeks. The inspiration for including everyone on staff was an experience she had had in graduate school learning about the benefits of large group interventions (LGI).

It was early March, and a light snow was falling. *Perhaps this is the time to announce my retirement,* she thought, imagining herself lounging on a sun-drenched beach in front of a Florida condo with her husband, Harold, and a grandchild or two, worrying about nothing more important than where and when to have lunch later. But then she dismissed this option, recognizing that her leadership was needed to save the organization, not only to protect the livelihoods of the almost three score people in front of her, most of whom were already under economic distress, but the agency itself. She felt an obligation to preserve the health of the organization that played an important role in improving the quality of life for several thousand sick, impoverished, old, and distressed families and individuals, none of whom were ever turned away because of an inability to pay. At least, until a couple of weeks ago. With the economy in a free fall not seen since the Great Depression, this now described almost every client.

Sarah noticed out of the corner of her eye that Sean was amusing himself by flicking spit balls at a social work student who was working at HFS for her field placement, obviously aiming the wads of paper at her chest. She cleared her throat and was about to begin when Sean quipped, "I thought we already decided to paint this room the lavender blue at the last Large Group Intervention meeting."

Sarah pretended to smile, and began her speech. She had rehearsed it several times in front of Harold, but had never felt comfortable. Sarah knew that some of her staff were already preparing updated résumés in expectation that the axe would fall soon.

"As you are aware, there have been rumors about the upcoming board meeting and what actions the board will take to approve a balanced budget for the next fiscal year. The board has directed me to come up with a plan of recommended expense cuts and income enhancements to balance the budget. To this point, no firm decisions have been made, and everything is on the table. The purpose of this meeting is to get some ideas from all of you on how we can achieve what we need to achieve, which, at this point, appears to be a minimum of a 25% retrenchment. This is not good news, and I am not going to sugar-coat what I have to tell you.

"The trends for income are almost universally going south on us and for everyone else who provides social services. Our creditors are hesitant to extend our credit limits because of our shaky cash-flow position, not to mention their own problems with liquidity. Those who owe us money, including several local government agencies and the state, are delaying their reimbursement payments for expenditures we have already incurred on their behalf. We've tried to get a new loan at a rate we could afford, but were unable to do so. Several major donors have reneged on their annual pledges, and you only have to read yesterday's local section of the paper to read why. Our modest endowment, as with virtually every nonprofit organization endowment, has taken a major hit, losing about 40% of its value just in the last year. Many of our clients are either unable to pay upfront for their services or are delaying payment so they can first pay for food, fuel, and medicine."

"How about if we each agree to liberate rolls of toilet paper from public bathrooms, such as movie theaters or at the mall, and bring them here?" Sean offered with a straight face. Sarah simply ignored him.

"Again, everything is on the table. Planned retirements will save us some money if we don't fill replacement positions. We may need to get more aggressive in pursuing some grant opportunities that we avoided in the past because they were not quite consistent with our core mission."

"I had an idea to save money the last time we stayed at a suite at the Marriott for the national conference," Sean said. "If we each took all of our used light bulbs and switched a couple of them for those in the room, and brought them back here, no one would even notice. I guess you can say when I thought of this, the light bulb went on, literally!"

"Sean, this is a serious meeting, and not anything you should make light of," interjected Howie the maintenance man, with a wink. Howie was often Sean's co-conspirator in pulling off some of the more involved practical jokes. Howie was a punster, and in his mind, the more strained the pun, the better. It was once said that "the pun is the lowest form of humor, and poetry is much verse." Even though he was approaching 70 years old, no one could even think of calling Howie "Howard," other than perhaps his mother, who was still alive and living with her cats in Bayonne, N.J.

"Sean, you're not being either helpful or funny," Sarah chided. "Bill, what ideas have you put together for us to think about?"

Bill was the CFO, efficient, a bit nerdy, and the only one in the room who was wearing a suit and tie. Most staff members were wearing their coats, as Sarah two months ago had ordered the thermostat to be turned down to 65 to save on energy costs.

"Well, even if we adopt both of Sean's suggestions, we would still need to close about a million dollars in projected deficit for the current year," he began. "I've considered a few possibilities that would get us closer to where we need to be, but none is without pain. First, we simply have to stop hiring folks to fill the four vacancies that we have been advertising. Second, we can accelerate staff retirements, and offer modest bonuses to those who agree to retire early. We can freeze all training, travel, and conferences—although if we do so, we would lose any potential savings from Sean's suggestions. To avoid layoffs, we can cut hours, like California State government did in 2009, or we might promote job sharing to save on personnel expenses. We can deplete our meager endowment, and perhaps sell off the land we purchased in 2005 for expansion. We could cut salaries and benefits. Lots of organizations already were requiring their employees to pay a higher share of health benefits even before the current economic crisis. We could start using volunteers or non-licensed professionals to handle some of our counseling duties. And, it goes without saying, we need to increase our fees to those who can pay market rates and be more selective about our marketing strategy so that we are not inundated with requests for services that will hemorrhage our resources. Anyway, that is my short list."

"Each of those comes with some costs," interjected Wilma Williams, head of the Social Work Department. Sarah could almost see Wilma's blood pressure rise highlighting the veins in her neck. Sarah worried that her reaction to these trial balloons might trigger a heart event in the heavy-set woman. Wilma, a two-pack-a-day smoker, had been carried away from the room several years earlier after being involved in a heated discussion when HFS was considering making the campus smoke-free. Wilma had threatened to resign on the spot, and then collapsed. She recovered, but Sarah knew that Wilma was not a healthy woman and was on several medications that seemed to affect her vitality that, before that incident, appeared to be almost limitless.

In some respects, Wilma was the glue that kept everything running smoothly, even though she could be abrasive and perhaps too blunt on occasion. "My department is already straining because of the vacancies, and it just isn't fair to my staff or the clients to have caseloads that don't provide the attention required to accomplish what needs to be accomplished. Every one of our social workers is already stretched beyond the breaking point, and we need those four positions filled or we will have more burnout. As for cutting salaries and benefits, that is simply not a viable solution. All of us have bills to pay and families to support. Our staff are highly committed, but it isn't fair to balance our budget on the backs of our employees, who already are making significant financial sacrifices to work here compared to what they could earn in a comparable position in the for-profit sector.

"Yes, it's true that using uncredentialed workers to provide our services would save money. And it would make just as much sense to use a college intern volunteer to be the agency CEO or CFO—it would save money in the short term, but using those without the appropriate education and training to deliver our services or run our agency is penny-wise and pound foolish," she added, clear that she was only just beginning to rant about what she had heard so far.

"And selling off that parcel would have some major negative consequences, as we raised almost a million dollars in some major gifts, making the case that this land would be used for a particular purpose," added Steve Goldman, another social worker who had been with HFS for a decade. "Selling it off would send a wrong signal to these donors and damage our credibility. When the economy improves, we would no longer have this land for our use. In the long term, it would trash our strategic plan, which envisions a major expansion of our campus to accommodate the changing demographics of our community."

Sarah, impressed that anyone on her staff other than herself was familiar with anything in the HFS strategic plan, then asked for other ideas.

"How about being more entrepreneurial, such as by marketing education programs to our middle-class neighborhoods?" offered Kate Johnson, one of the newly-hired social workers who Sarah surmised was quite anxious about whether her job was in jeopardy because of the perception that layoff notices would be meted out based on seniority.

"Excellent suggestion. This is what I am looking for in this meeting," Sarah complimented. "Could you put together a memo for me on this that I could run past the board?"

"We could train our receptionists and other administrative staff to do more hands-on work with clients, and answer our own phones and do our own paperwork, along the lines of reengineering the office to take advantage of technology," offered another social worker. "Whoever answers the phone could pull up information about who is calling, and be empowered to make minor decisions, improving efficiency and avoiding all of the minor interruptions I get when I am meeting with my clients."

"We could explore an effort of reengineering," Sarah said. "Send me a memo outlining how this might work, and which changes might be affordable in the short term."

"We could charge our board members for the lunch and breakfast at the Hilton in three weeks," Sean suggested.

"I don't think so." Sarah responded automatically, although, on further reflection, perhaps this might not be such a bad thing to do.

"Has anyone considered merging with another organization?" offered Steve Hamilton, a staff member who rarely participated in administrative meetings, but was considered to work well with his co-workers and clients. "We could share overhead and perhaps weather the storm."

"Yeah, let's merge with Hooters, and we could get an employee discount for all of us, and add some new services to our therapy department," Sean said. Sarah heard some snickering from the back of the room, but looking at her audience, she saw more annoyance than amusement.

"We could consider a merger down the road, but we are talking more short-term ideas here," Sarah conceded. She turned to Edie Oliver, the Development Director. "Anything you might suggest?"

"Remember back in April when we turned down that six-figure donation from the founder of Ellen Bowman's Boutiques, a couple of months after she was indicted for tax fraud? We might just be desperate enough to see if she still would be willing to make that donation in exchange for naming our building after her. And I'm learning how to conduct on online charitable auction, although even if it is successful, it probably won't make up for the thousands of dollars we won't be getting this year because of poor attendance at our annual tribute dinner."

The suggestion provided fodder for another unwelcome volley from Sean.

"If we are, in principle, willing to sell our good name to the highest bidder, why don't we literally sell our good name and make her an offer to call us the Ellen Bowman Family Service of Harristown for a seven-figure donation? For six figures, we would name our main building after her. And for five figures, we could offer to plaster a decal on the HFS vans that say, "This vehicle sponsored by Ellen, the Felon.""

"And why not have the tribute dinner this year at McDonald's instead of the Hilton, and give everyone a Happy Meal?" Sean said. "We can all collect extra napkins, spoons, forks, and straws for the office lunchroom afterwards. And we could honor Ronald McDonald himself rather than the clown we picked this year."

"Sean," Sarah admonished icily, "That clown is the board chair of this organization, my boss, and at least for the moment, your boss, as well." Everyone laughed, other than Sean, who got the message and shrunk back into his seat, wounded.

Sarah spent the next 15 minutes fielding more suggestions, tried to mask how disheartened she was by the responses, and then brought the meeting to a close.

"Thank you for all of your suggestions," she said, the cue that the meeting was over. "We will reconvene after the board meeting, and I will share what decisions the board makes with respect to these issues."

As people filed out, some looking shell-shocked and some angry or scared, one of the fluorescent lights began to flicker. *Maybe Sean's light bulb idea isn't such a bad suggestion, after all,* she mused.

Discussion Questions

1. Make a list of the serious suggestions made for increasing income and cutting expenses mentioned in this meeting. What are the benefits and limitations of each?

2. Had you been in this meeting, what other suggestions might you have offered?

3. For the most part, Sarah handled Sean's inappropriate comments by simply ignoring him. What message did that send to the others in the meeting? How would you have handled someone like Sean?

4. Was it appropriate to have every staff member in the room to discuss what strategies might be employed to close the budget deficit? What are the costs and benefits of doing this rather than simply having professional staff hammer out the recommendations it will make to the board?

5. When an organization is in crisis, how much information should be shared with all staff members who might be affected by management decisions? Under what conditions might it be considered ethical for organizational leadership not to be completely honest with staff?

6. What are the pros and cons of HFS considering applying for grants that are "not quite consistent with our core mission"?

7. Discuss the costs and benefits of accepting or seeking donations from convicted felons.

Appendix 6
Case 6
Public Relations Dilemma at the Harristown Hospital and Health System

"This is Roemer," answered Steve Roemer, the Vice President for Public Affairs for the Harristown Hospital and Health System (HHHS), in response to his ringing Blackberry. He didn't recognize the number that flashed on his small screen. However, the area code of 404 indicated the call was from the Atlanta area.

It was 8:30 on a Monday evening, and he was in the middle of watching an episode of *House, MD.* The mythical Princeton Plainsboro Teaching Hospital didn't have much in common with HHHS, and he was aware that most medical staff at HHHS found the show ridiculous, particularly the main character's ethics, or lack thereof. Dr. House would have lasted no longer than a day on the staff of any real hospital, they asserted, regardless of whether he could save lives no one else could, all within a 43-minute timeframe plus commercials.

Reflexively, Roemer hit the pause button on the remote and took the call. Probably nothing that was needed of him that would be on the eleven o'clock news, he judged. Most of those calls involving a request for him to do a taped interview occurred during the early afternoon, for transmission back to the studio for editing in time for the six o'clock broadcast.

Roemer was proud of the fact that he made himself available 24/7 and was accessible to reporters working on deadline. While his smartphone might ring occasionally during the middle of the night, those times were rare. A former beat reporter for a South Carolina daily, he enjoyed the excitement of working with the media, particularly when he was sought out by television stations to appear live to comment on a breaking story. Health care was a broad, high-profile topic that would find itself often as a lead story in some context in the *Harristown Morning News,* and the television news, as well.

During the five years Roemer had served as the chief public relations professional of HHHS, he had developed substantial expertise on topics ranging from medical conditions and their treatment to the complexities of hospital finance and accounting. He had visions of returning to reporting, but he was also getting spoiled by the high salary and substantial fringe benefits and privileges of working in a corporate environment with staff and other resources to help him do his job. Whoever said working in the nonprofit sector guaranteed a low salary didn't know what they were talking about.

Occasionally, at the urging of his wife, he would turn off his Blackberry during "family time" and return any calls he received later. The advanced technology of the smartphone kept him connected, but he recognized that there was also a cost to being available day or night to not only reporters, but to his small staff and his superiors at HHHS. Unlike many other nonprofit organizations, this organization did not go to "sleep" after traditional business hours, although the pace may have appreciably diminished. There was a baseline of 8 a.m. to 4:30 p.m. office hours in the administrative floor of HHHS, with meetings, press conferences, production of the weekly newsletters, and preparing flashy briefing books for upcoming board meetings, filled with eye-catching graphics. But after business hours, the hospital remained a beehive of activity, with newsworthy developments periodically occurring in the evening, throughout the night, and on weekends, as well.

Other than perhaps the CEO, Roemer was the public face of the Health System, and that telegenic face had to remain clean-shaven because of the possibility that it would be on the other side of a camera with minimal notice.

It was Roemer's responsibility to keep the public educated and happy, and to have a positive association with the name of HHHS. Although generally no news was good news, Roemer proactively engaged the local media in covering aspects of hospital activities that would put it in a positive light. HHHS was an important pillar in the community—a respected player in the city's economic and social future, and second only to the state university as the largest employer in the city. It had a brand name to protect, and Roemer was its key frontline defender.

Despite its first-rate reputation, HHHS was in a constant competition for patients, who had a choice when deciding which among the three major acute care facilities in Harristown to patronize. (There had once been six hospitals in the community, but a series of mergers had resulted in HHHS absorbing three others in the 1990s.) Increasing market share was a key component of HHHS's strategic plan, and additional funds had been allocated to Roemer's department based on the premise that good public relations could improve that statistic, as well as improve its overall net revenue.

Despite its nonprofit status, improving net revenue was the principal focus of every management decision. The hospital typically charged its patients exorbitant fees for every procedure, as did the other two hospitals in the community. However, few patients paid the regular fee schedule; most charges were reimbursed by negotiated payments from private and government insurance. Even these rates were substantially higher than costs, so that treatment of nonpaying patients could be cross-subsidized. By state law, nonprofit hospitals were permitted to make a profit, but any net revenue over expenses was required to be funneled back for the hospital's charitable purposes. Those charitable purposes, of course, included investing in the most advanced technology, increasing staff salaries, and providing substantial perquisites to those who worked there, including the use of a Skybox at the NFL Stadium at the Sportsplex across town.

Roemer had attended several games seated in this box, enjoying a lavishly catered lunch and actively participating in the advocacy and fundraising carried on there directed at invited guests, such as the State's congressional delegation and potential donors. As a reporter, he had been able to purchase tickets to only a single Atlanta Falcons pre-season game during his five years at the paper, and he had paid for those seats himself.

In addition to his other responsibilities, Roemer was also part of the team of staff who decided which programs and activities would receive financial sponsorship of HHHS, with several million dollars available annually to support concerts, youth sports, museums, the Harristown Marathon, and other events that would help the community and provide more visibility and name recognition for HHHS. He really enjoyed this aspect of the job, using the Health System's money to benefit community groups.

Roemer's face had become familiar to TV viewers as a result of on-camera duties such as explaining the changing medical status of a celebrity admitted to the facility, updating the public about a train derailment that sent scores of injured to the hospital, or decrying a recent government report documenting an increase in the uninsured.

During one week two summers earlier, he had been a constant guest on all three local newscasts in the Harristown media market following a car accident involving the Mayor of Harristown. Mayor Hawkins had suffered a heart attack while at the wheel of his city-provided Honda Accord, careening into a telephone pole. Shortly after the accident, Roemer had appeared live from the scene of the accident, with five microphones thrust into his face, and reported that Mayor Hawkins was in stable condition, but that his Honda Accord was better described now as a Honda Accordion. People still stopped him to this day to express their appreciation for that quip.

In his position, there were a number of other opportunities he had to educate the public. It was not unusual for him to be stopped on the street and recognized as a celebrity himself. He was trusted by reporters, although he certainly provided a spin on his comments that was flattering to his employer. No one would have expected anything else.

Now that he had built up a good reputation as a straight shooter, reporters came to him for both on the record and off the record comments. He liked his job. He liked being a part of the decision-making as part of the management team that ran the hospital, even though that was not a formal part of his job description. Most of the Vice Presidents, along with the President and CEO, had been there only a few years, and he felt that they valued the institutional memory he brought along with his common sense about how the public and other stakeholders might respond to consequences of a decision.

More than a few times, his advice prevented the management team from taking action that might have been a disaster. Today, however, he had been frustrated that the CEO and Vice Presidents failed to recognize the seriousness of their decision with respect to one particular sensitive matter involving a young surgeon, who was fired for attempting to perform an operation while heavily intoxicated. In this case, the doctor had been partying late into the night, but had been on call. When he responded to a page to come in to perform an emergency appendectomy, operating room nurses had complained that he was not in any condition to operate. Fortunately, another surgeon was available to fill in, and the patient had a normal procedure, unaware of the situation that might have put her at serious risk.

This was the second time the doctor had had a problem with alcohol interfering with his duties. The Medical Director had no second thoughts about firing him, and did so. However, the doctor knew that being fired for alcohol abuse would make it virtually impossible for him to be hired at another hospital. So, this doctor threatened to go public with allegations of gross negligence on the part of hospital staff, resulting in the deaths of two patients the previous year, unless the HHHS complied with a series of demands.

Apparently, hospital staff had participated in a cover-up involving a medical error. In that case, two children had been provided with lethal doses of heparin, a commonly used blood thinner, by hospital personnel. A similar medical error had made the national news in 2007 when a child of actor Dennis Quaid had barely survived such an overdose. The error was compounded by a defect in the package labeling, which failed to distinguish adequately between the weak dose administered to children and the standard dose administered to adults, which was 1,000 times more potent. After considering whether or not to disclose the medical error to the children's parents, the hospital staff had decided to simply explain to the families of the victims that the two patients had died from causes unrelated to injecting these kids with a lethal overdose. And it had issued strict verbal instructions to all staff involved in the incident to keep their mouths shut about what happened.

What the surgeon now demanded was that the hospital would have to provide him with a letter of recommendation and agree not to disclose to anyone outside of the hospital management that he had been fired or the reasons why. Second, the hospital would have to provide him with a severance payment of $500,000, which would automatically become $5,000,000, payable at the rate of $500,000 each year, if anyone in the hospital violated the first provision.

The management team had met that afternoon to decide whether or not to approve the agreement.

Roemer was hearing this story for the first time today, and he was uncomfortable. Had he been in charge, he would not have covered anything up. He would have explained the error and let the chips fall where they may. His experience was that many people understood that errors are made by professionals in all fields, although the consequences of errors in the medical field are certainly more serious than, let's say, allowing a ground ball to go through one's legs during a baseball game. But unlike a baseball game where the mistake is seen and understood by everyone in the stands, medical errors often occur without anyone knowing about them other than the staff. And the consequences can be fatal for the patient. There is a huge incentive for the staff to keep mistakes they make from the patients and their families, avoiding a lot of unpleasantness in addition to civil liability that can amount to millions of dollars in any single case.

At an afternoon meeting, where this situation was discussed among a small group of management with the chief counsel present, the team had decided to minimize the hospital's potential exposure and accept the surgeon's offer. Roemer had been the sole dissenter, arguing that the hospital should acknowledge its mistakes, suffer the consequences of being accountable for its mistakes, and not give in to what he perceived was blackmail. The chief counsel had been neutral on the decision, although she did point out that in the event this doctor was hired by another hospital and was involved in a similar incident, the fact that HHHS failed to take appropriate action rather than covering it up could make HHHS potentially liable.

Roemer was moving up the ladder in leadership of the Council of Hospital Public Relations Professionals, in line to become its next chair. The Council had an ethics code, which Roemer took seriously. Among the provisions of this code was an obligation to be accurate and truthful in representing the interests of one's employer to the public, as well as an obligation to serve the public interest. In Roemer's twelve years as information officer, he had never knowingly lied to the media or the public about a professional issue. He knew that this would be severely tested if anyone ever raised the issue of either the medical error cover-up or the agreement HHHS management had just agreed to make with the terminated surgeon.

Although the decision made at the meeting made Roemer uncomfortable, it certainly wasn't the first time that decisions made at the highest levels of HHHS were inconsistent with his personal and professional values. However, he recognized that he was not the boss, and that overall, HHHS, despite some flaws, was operated in a manner to serve the public. And he never lied about anything, although he occasionally would tell a reporter that he was not free to comment on a particular situation.

With the TV paused, Roemer listened to the voice at the other end of the line.

"Hi, this is Steve Barton. I'm with the Associated Press in Atlanta, and I am working on a story for AP about HHHS. I'm calling with a couple questions. We are working on a story involving problems with the blood thinner Heparin, which had some problems relating to contamination, as well as overdosing. One of our sources referred us to your hospital, which apparently ran into a problem with heparin overdoses last year. While researching this, we came across a story of a surgeon from HHHS who was terminated today for attempting to operate on a patient while impaired with alcohol, and found out that there was some relationship between these two incidents, which we are not clear about. Can you clarify some of this for me? I understand that you were at the meeting today at HHHS where this was discussed...."

Discussion Questions

1. How should a public relations professional deal with any conflict between the principles of one's professional ethics code and the exigencies required to represent the interests of one's organization?

2. Is Roemer obligated to talk to the reporter about the meeting? How should he respond?

3. What boundaries should individuals have between their personal lives and professional lives?

4. Is there anything unethical or otherwise inappropriate about HHHS having a Skybox for entertaining VIPs?

5. Was the decision to agree to the terms of the surgeon appropriate? What other options did the management of HHHS have?

6. If a staff member of a nonprofit is fired for misconduct, is it ethical not to take steps to inform any potential future employer of that staff member that the person has engaged in misconduct?

7. Could the hospital management have had any other options other than firing the surgeon?

8. Compare and contrast two very different types of charities that may be headquartered in the same neighborhood, such as a hospital and a food bank.

Appendix 7
Case 7
Reporting Financial Misconduct at Uncommon Agenda

Jack looked at his computer screen and read the e-mail again. And again. He felt a mix of emotions, among them apprehension, anger, disgust, fear, rage, and astonishment knowing that his life was about to change as a result of reading the content of this electronic message that was intended for his best friend rather than himself. He knew immediately that nothing good would come of this, but that it would be difficult to predict what would happen other than that it would definitely be bad.

Jack was the IT Director for Uncommon Agenda, a nonprofit, 501(c)(4) tax-exempt advocacy organization based in Washington, D.C. with field operations in six states. Nonprofit organizations granted tax exempt status under this provision of the Internal Revenue Code are designated as "social welfare" organizations rather than charities. Although 501(c)(3) organizations are permitted by law to lobby, they are prohibited by law from doing so in a "substantial" amount. In contrast, social welfare organizations are permitted to lobby to the extent they desire, and most of these organizations are formed for the primary purpose of lobbying and advocacy.

One major disadvantage of exemption under 501(c)(4), however, is that those who contribute to these organizations are not eligible to deduct contributions to them on their federal income tax returns. However, many such organizations have affiliated 501(c)(3)s that accept tax deductible contributions and then transfer those donations to fund the operations of the (c)(4). Unlike their charitable counterparts, social welfare organizations may engage in partisan political activities and support candidates for office, although there is a substantial excise tax associated with such expenditures. Many 501(c)(4) organizations, such as Uncommon Agenda, do not engage in overt partisan activity, and boast that their good government activities are nonpartisan.

The mission of Uncommon Agenda was to build support for public funding of Congressional campaigns. It worked in coalition with like-minded organizations to advocate for such funding. Although the organization solicited memberships from the public at $25 annually, most of its funding came from several large foundations that shared the vision of the organization to end the rampant abuses of campaign financing by lobbyists and others with a direct interest in legislative decision-making.

Critics charged that special interests skewed public policy toward the privileged, and that the current system of campaign finance ultimately cost the public billions of dollars in wasteful spending of tax dollars and tax expenditures.

Uncommon Agenda was located in a slightly run-down office building on Connecticut Avenue in Northwest Washington, near the zoo. On most business days, the office was a beehive of activity, the phones ringing, meetings being held to plot strategy, fundraising plans being developed, and 20-something staff members who had only recently served as college interns on the Hill contacting Congressional staff to seek support for the latest version of a bipartisan public campaign financing bill.

Oblivious to most of the activity were a couple of support staff who were not directly engaged in the quest to achieve reform of campaign finance laws. One of these was Jack, the IT Director, who had a nondescript office far away from the main entrance. There was no window; his office was in an inside corridor, deep in the bowels of the 7th floor. Jack's office was lined mostly with software rather than books. Stacked high in a corner was a pile of boxes that held an assortment of equipment one might expect to find in the office of the IT head—assorted mice, cables, wireless modems, old keyboards, laptops that were in various stages of disrepair, and tools.

On most days, Jack was not particularly busy. He may have had some staff training to demonstrate to a group of employees how to use the organization's upgraded software, or to orient a new hire about how to use the existing packages that were on the network. He was also responsible for keeping the Web site in working order and sending out bulk electronic newsletters and fundraising e-mail. On occasion, things got really busy. When that happened, such as when the system server went down or if there was a Denial of Service attack on the Web site, he was expected to work through the night when necessary to get things back in order.

But nothing in his five years in this position prepared him for the situation he found himself in today.

It was mid-March, and Washington was experiencing unseasonably hot weather, coaxing the cherry blossoms to bloom a few days earlier than the official start of the Cherry Blossom Festival still two weekends away. In mid-February, a man's heart might turn to thoughts of love. But in mid-March, it turns to college basketball. Even the President interrupted dealing with an economy that was tanking and crises around the planet to fill out his NCAA brackets along with millions of others.

On Friday afternoon, Jack had received a call on the office intercom system from Steve Pearson, the Vice President for Operations, about a problem he was having accessing his e-mail. Steve was a congenial colleague, as well as a personal friend from Jack's grad school days. It was not unusual for Steve to join him and one other colleague, Bill Higgins, who was V.P. for Human Resources at Uncommon Agenda, to hang out together on Friday nights. They usually frequented a couple of clubs in Georgetown and got drunk together. Lately, Steve had been paying the entire tab for the three of them, explaining that he had just come into a windfall when a childless, distant aunt had died and left her nephews some money.

All of them had come to the organization at about the same time, when it was first formed with a seven-figure combined grant from three national private foundations. Steve had joined the staff first and had suggested that Jack consider leaving his job in New York to fill an opening for IT Director.

Jack was not particularly interested in the nonprofit sector in general, or the organization in particular, when he applied for that position. He would have been just as happy working for IBM or Microsoft. What attracted him were the downtown Washington, D.C. location and the likelihood that he would have a comfortable salary and not have the pressure of working in a typical corporate environment. He had interviewed elsewhere, but was attracted to the casual working atmosphere and the likely prospect that he would be in charge of the department. Actually, he would be the only member of the department, without the annoyance of having to supervise others and with no one looking over his shoulder all of the time. The people he saw in the office seemed quite happy with their jobs and were devoted to the organization's mission. This was certainly in contrast to where he had been working at the time, which he referred to as a software sweatshop where he was required to meet a quota of several thousand lines of code each week.

When Steve, one of his roommates while he was a graduate student getting his MBA from Columbia, told him about the position opening up at Uncommon Agenda, Jack had been flattered and had been delighted to consider leaving the Big Apple. He and Steve were buddies, and Steve had covered for him many times with a girlfriend who was insanely jealous of Jack seeing other women during his relationship with her. Steve had been counted on by Jack to tell more than a lie or two to preserve the relationship, and Steve never let him down. Without Steve around at Uncommon Agenda, Jack might well have left for something else.

It had only been minutes earlier that Jack felt that his life was being turned upside down. It had all started when he had heard a buzzer in the office indicating that he was being called on the intercom system. It was Steve. He expected Steve to review the plans they had for cruising Georgetown the following evening in Steve's new BMW, but instead, it was to relay a problem Steve was having with accessing his e-mail.

"I haven't received any e-mail for four hours now, and I know something is wrong," Steve told him. Almost all of the communications between them during office hours were by e-mail, but without access to that mode of communication, Steve resorted to the more primitive intercom system.

"Let me check it out," Jack had said, planning to see if anyone else in the office was also having this problem. Jack himself hadn't noticed any problem accessing his work e-mail, although such e-mails were infrequent except when there was an IT problem. He, like most staff of Uncommon Agenda, kept a separate e-mail account for his personal mail. There was a written policy that every staff member was entitled to an organization e-mail account, and the organization would respect the privacy of e-mail sent and received on work computers. The few restrictions on this use were that the organization's computers could not be used for illegal purposes, to access pornography, or to violate copyright laws. Jack had thought this policy was flawed, since how would he or anyone in the organization determine if anyone was using the office computers inappropriately without first violating the privacy explicitly provided by the policy? In five years as IT Director, this issue had never surfaced.

Jack always encouraged new staff members to avoid using Uncommon Agenda e-mail accounts for their personal e-mail, and only a handful of staff members did not have separate accounts for their personal e-mail. This was not only recommended to maintain privacy, but to save on bandwidth. With the capacity to download not only music clips but even full-length movies, Jack felt the obligation to conserve organizational resources and not overload the capacity of the server.

Jack was not working on anything in particular when Steve called, but he was still annoyed that he would be diverted from watching some of the action in the first round of the NCAA basketball tournament that was being streamed in real time to his cell phone. A number 15 seed was hanging tough against a number two. Ah, the benefits of technology, Jack thought.

From his office, Jack had begun troubleshooting this new glitch, and came across nearly a score of e-mails that were caught in the network's spam filter that appeared to be potentially legitimate e-mails. Clicking on one of several addressed to Steve, it was clear that this particular e-mail to Steve wasn't spam, with a .ch country code top level domain name that he didn't immediately recognize.

Reading the e-mail, he quickly confirmed his suspicions that it was not spam. What it appeared to be was a confirmation of a bank transfer involving a transaction from the Washington Capital Bank and Trust Company to a bank in Switzerland. Reading it more closely, the transfer appeared to Jack to involve a transfer of $8,000 from an account belonging to Uncommon Agenda to a numbered account. Jack was quite certain that Uncommon Agenda didn't use banks in Switzerland, and that the organization certainly wouldn't use a numbered account. Uncommon Agenda publicly and stridently railed against the lack of transparency of the way cash for political campaigns was funneled into the system. In any case, even if the organization had a legitimate reason for getting involved in having a numbered Swiss account, it would be unlikely that Steve would have had the authority to move funds from the organization to such an account. Clearly, the Chief Financial Officer, Carol Henfield, would be the individual from the organization with authority to move funds in this way. Knowing Carol, it was quite unlikely that she would have anything to do with numbered Swiss accounts, even if the money was her own personal funds. This was not consistent with her personality, which was doing absolutely everything by the book. Although liberal in ideology, she was so conservative that he surmised that she never failed to look both ways even when crossing a one-way street.

Jack's policy was to routinely delete the master file of copies of e-mails every month. Curious about this discovery, however, he searched in the database of archived organization e-mails and looked at more e-mails to Steve. For each of the previous four weeks, the number of weeks that old e-mails were still available in the system (other than on the computers of those who received them, unless they were deleted by those individuals), there was a receipt from this bank for $8,000 of funds transferred out of an account in the name of Uncommon Agenda under the total control of Steve, to the numbered account.

Jack was in shock that his long-time friend and colleague appeared to be an embezzler. Could there be some other, innocent, explanation for these transfers? Not likely, but it was possible. Embezzling would explain a few things, such as the new BMW.

But the more pressing concern was what he should do with this information. Steve was his best friend in Washington.

What if there were others in the organization involved in this other than Steve? Would his job be at risk if he reported this to the CEO? He remembered something from a recent staff meeting about Uncommon Agenda being in the process of creating a whistleblower policy. Doing so had been motivated by something that had appeared on the revised 990 annual tax return for tax-exempt nonprofit organizations. This meant that Uncommon Agenda did not currently have such a policy in force. Someone had mentioned at the meeting that there was a federal law on whistleblowing that applied to nonprofits, but that it was quite inadequate to protect anyone except under the most limited of circumstances.

Curious, he Googled "whistleblower" "nonprofit" "federal" and came up with something called the "Sarbanes-Oxley" law enacted in 2002. Yes, that was the name he had heard at the meeting! Finding the full text of the law, he searched on some terms and found the following:

Sec. 1107. RETALIATION AGAINST INFORMANTS.

(a) IN GENERAL- Section 1513 of title 18, United States Code, is amended by adding at the end the following:
(e) Whoever knowingly, with the intent to retaliate, takes any action harmful to any person, including interference with the lawful employment or livelihood of any person, for providing to a law enforcement officer any truthful information relating to the commission or possible commission of any Federal offense, shall be fined under this title or imprisoned not more than 10 years, or both.

He interpreted that to mean that if he reported Steve's e-mail to law enforcement authorities, he would have protection to keep his job. But if he reported this to anyone inside the organization, he would be at risk. *You would think that the organization would rather have misconduct reported internally so they can deal with it, or cover it up better,* he thought.

Jack, still shocked that his buddy appeared to be siphoning off funds from their employer at potentially the rate of $400,000 annually, took out a pad of paper and started writing out some of his options.

The eight options he considered were:

1. Confront Steve. Offer to keep quiet in exchange for a share of the funds.
2. Confront Steve, and simply demand that he stop embezzling, quietly make restitution, or risk being turned in to the authorities.
3. Confront Steve, and convince him to come forward to the organization voluntarily and admit what he was doing, leaving Jack out of this.
4. Take the matter to the organization's CEO and CFO without informing Steve.
5. Take the matter to the law enforcement authorities without informing Steve.
6. Let someone know about this within the organization anonymously.
7. Do nothing.
8. Seek advice from a third party, such as a friend or attorney, before taking any action.

Jack's consideration of how to deal with this quandary was interrupted as he saw Steve stick his head into his office.

"Any progress on getting my e-mail?" Steve asked.

"Not yet," Jack lied. "Anything interesting going on?"

"Well, I might not make it for drinks tonight, or at least until much later. There was a front page *New York Times* article this morning about campaign financing, and I've been getting lots of calls from the press as well as my field office folks."

"I didn't see the *Times* today. What was in it?" Jack asked politely, not sharing that he hadn't read the front page of *The Washington Post* that day, instead focusing on the NCAA pairings on the sports page.

"The article estimated that Obama raised an estimated $300 million for the general election, outspending McCain by about 3-1. This was after he had first pledged to accept public financing, and he eventually reneged on that commitment, becoming the first major party candidate to finance his general election campaign with private contributions. McCain only got $84 million for the general. Anyway, the *Times* story estimated that Obama raised an estimated $750 million during the entire campaign from close to four million contributors. Had he not done so, he might have gotten his butt kicked."

Jack listened, feigning interest, but he couldn't care less about campaign finance, somewhat ironic since that was the *raison d'être* of the organization that employed him. He admitted to himself that he considered the entire issue to be really boring.

But the good news was that he wouldn't have to decide what to do about Steve's "problem" today, and he could simply hang out in his office and watch some of the late first-round tournament games, or just go back to his apartment. And decide what to do.

Discussion Questions

1. How "private" should personal e-mail be if it is sent and received from a non-profit organization's account?

2. What are the pluses and minuses of each of the eight options on Jack's list?

3. What are the limitations of federal whistleblower protection for nonprofit organizations? What might be appropriate in an organization's whistleblower policy?

4. What are some of the objectives of having an organization whistleblower policy?

5. If you are the CEO of this organization and Jack comes to you and spills the beans, what would your response be?

6. What is Jack's legal responsibility, if any, to let someone know about this? What is Jack's ethical responsibility?

7. How important is it to nonprofit organizations that their staff be committed to the organization's mission and comfortable with the culture of the non-

profit sector, in light of the fact that nonprofit organizations more than ever employ staff who could work in business just as easily, such as Webmasters, accountants, IT professionals, and marketers?

Appendix 8
Case 8
The Disruptive Board Member of the Harristown Vet Center

Oliver Hanson was finally coming to the end of his joke, to the relief of everyone in the room.

...and in the morning after Dad goes to work, the milkman will deliver the milk and have his usual "quickie" with Mom....And then, he'll catch the clap, which is just fine with me! He's the @&%$* who ran over my dog!

There was a nervous laugh, a half-hearted groan, and the 13 others sitting around the board room conference table simply remained silent through their discomfort, staring downward, making no eye contact with either the story-teller or the chair. Other than that, there was no outward reaction to the punch line besides the labored chortling of Hanson, whose already ruddy complexion appeared to deepen even more, if that was possible.

Hanson's jokes were unwelcome at any time—they were usually long, off-color, and it was a stretch to consider any of them even moderately amusing. But coming in the middle of a board meeting, these distractions were doubly inappropriate. Other board members had been complaining about Hanson's incessant interruptions, which often came when the board's deliberations were peaking at the most intense moments. Some found him annoying, while others labeled his behavior insufferable. Without warning, he would launch into a soliloquy only marginally related to the topic. Some board members would shrink back in their seats, embarrassed by the content of the material Hanson insisted on sharing, but wondering if perhaps he had forgotten to take a particularly required dose of medication that day.

"Okay, let's return to our next item on the agenda, the spaghetti dinner fund-raiser," Harold Mathers said, reclaiming control of the meeting. "We need to decide whether we want to partner with a company that will put our silent auction online...."

"I want to bring up the issue of whether board members can participate on the Center bowling team," Hanson interrupted. "Every time I bring this up, you keep putting it off, and I think I have the right to be heard on this...."

Mathers, board chair of the Iraq-Afghanistan Veterans Center of Harristown, a.k.a. Vet Center, was becoming less tolerant of humoring Hanson—even though everyone around the table knew that not alienating this boorish, crude man was necessary to maintain the good will of the Hanson Family Foundation.

The organization had begun with a Hanson Foundation startup grant. Now in its eighth year, the Vet Center had created a relatively stable diversification of its income stream, with the Foundation providing only about 10% of its annual revenue. The remainder came from state grants, fee for service payments from veterans who could afford to pay all or part of the costs, contributions from individuals, an annual spaghetti dinner fundraiser and silent auction, a $25,000 earmark provided courtesy of the state's senior U.S. senator out of the Veterans Administration budget, and a smattering of grants from other foundations. Still, 10% was 10%. In the Vet Center's budget, this amounted to $40,000, chump change for the Foundation, which had assets of more than $50 million.

The Vet Center conducted community outreach to offer counseling on employment, family issues, and education to returning combat veterans and family members. It also provided bereavement counseling for families of service members killed on active duty and counseling for veterans who were sexually harassed. Most of the Vet Center's services were offered on a sliding scale fee basis, although many programs were offered free of charge.

The center was staffed by small, mostly volunteer teams of counselors, outreach workers, and other specialists, including drug abuse counselors, advocates, and social workers trained in helping veterans access the full range of government-sponsored programs. A dedicated core staff of six full-time and four part-time professionals and support staff held everything together. Combat veterans in the area knew they could drop in to the Center, no questions asked, and play a round of pool in the recreation area and socialize. If they decided to receive any vocational or mental health services, they could register, but there was no pressure to participate in the formal intake process if they simply wanted a place to hang out.

Following years of military stalemate and only minimal political progress, it appeared that there was no credible exit strategy in America's overseas armed conflicts. It appeared more and more likely that even with the election of a new President who had pledged to bring them home as quickly as possible, the number of veterans returning from overseas combat in that region had increased each year. The capacity of the Vet Center to serve this demand was diminishing, even with a healthy roster of volunteer caseworkers. As was the case in many cash-strapped nonprofit organizations in the area, the staff continually had been asked to do much more with less. The current headquarters was straining beyond its capacity, with some staff forced to have their desks in the hallways with minimal space for the quiet and privacy necessary for the group and individual counseling staff members of the Center provided.

Mathers and other members of the executive committee had been making overtures to the Hanson Family Foundation to provide a one-time grant of $500,000 so the organization could purchase an office building in downtown Harristown near the bus terminal and within a stone's throw of one of the largest Army bases in the country. This would have been a vast improvement over the current situation of renting space that was expensive, inefficient, and had limited parking for staff and clients.

Although Hanson had been an ally for this proposal, albeit with constant prodding from the committee, the family members with control over funding had so far resisted increasing their investment in the organization. Yet, Mathers thought progress had been made toward realizing the dream whereby the Center could relocate to a modern facility that could meet the needs for expansion for several decades into the future. Even with all combat troops exiting from Iraq, the war in Afghanistan was likely to expand, with no likelihood of any negotiated political settlement nor possibility of a military solution, either. Even if the Vet Center board decided against expanding its mission to provide services to those veterans who were not returning combat veterans—as was considered on occasion—it was almost a certainty that the organization would have a steady flow of new clients for many years to come.

For more than a year now, Mathers had debated with other board members on how to deal with this particular board member's deteriorating behavior. It was clear for a long time that Hanson attended every board meeting, but offered nothing constructive with his participation other than being the conduit for his relatives' philanthropy. The board previously had voted two other board members off simply for non-attendance, consistent with a provision in the organization's bylaws. At the last meeting, the board had surprised the current vice president of the board and charter board member with a plaque for recognizing his perfect attendance at each of the 50 board meetings in its history, the only board member with that distinction. Ironically, most board members would have voted in favor of some award for Hanson if he agreed simply *not* to attend any board meetings.

If the predicament had been limited to only Hanson's propensity for telling off-color jokes, the organization might have been able to weather the consequences. Anyone who spent any time around the Center would have been exposed to language that the nuns in the convent across the street would have blushed at.

But his vulgar behavior extended to verbal abuse, as well. Only an hour before, as lunch orders were being distributed, Hanson had bawled out a staff member for the insult of adding a sprinkling of onions on his hoagie sandwich when, Hanson had insisted, he had explicitly asked for no onions. In a gruff, hostile manner that was as much dog bark as human, Hanson had verbally pummeled the offender in front of the board and her executive director. The staff member, a young social work student doing her MSW program field placement who had volunteered to help out at the board meeting on what would otherwise have been a Saturday off, had been in tears. Two board members had tried to intercede, one of them protectively getting between Hanson and the student in case Hanson had any thoughts of physically attacking her. Although it never came to that, Mathers wondered whether the distinct, quick change from abusing the staff member to playfully telling a dirty joke might indicate some form of bipolar disorder.

And his appalling behavior extended beyond the six board meetings he attended each year.

Perhaps twice each month, Hanson would visit the Center and act as if he owned the place. He would order both staff and clients around as if they were his domestic help, and insist that as a board member, he had the right to examine the personal files of clients. When the executive director had calmly informed him that he could not have access to these files, Hanson had threatened to have the executive director fired at the next board meeting. Literally within the next five minutes, he had scolded one of the staff with a healthy dose of expletives mixed in to his ranting for refusing to agree to pick up his dry cleaning. As gently as they could, several staff members suggested he register for services himself so that he could participate in programs designed to help those like himself who were in need of a trained therapist to help him sort through his problems. Of course, he refused, railing against those who might suggest that he needed any kind of professional help.

At times, he seemed like a motor that wouldn't turn off, sharing comments during discussion that only marginally contributed to the board reaching a conclusion, if at all. During the few times that he was knowledgeable enough about an issue being discussed, he acted as if anyone who had a different opinion was either ignorant or plain stupid, and badgered those who refused to endorse his views until they were forced to show the white flag. It was clear to many on the board that his participation was not designed to serve the Vet Center but rather his own need for attention and power and to assuage whatever demons were inside his head.

Mathers might have forgiven the inappropriate outbursts to some reasonable extent. He, himself, had seen his share of bad things in Iraq, having led a platoon of infantrymen as a young second Lieutenant in Falusha, initially being a true believer hoping to rid the world of the evil dictator, Saddam Hussein. That idealism had inexorably melted away, replaced by a desire to do whatever he could to live another day and escape that hell-hole, the IEDs, and the constant sleep deprivation. Awarded the Bronze Star in 2004 for a Second Gulf War operation that he had difficulty discussing with others, he had returned and reentered civilian life a changed person.

Initially, he had experienced some adjustment problems, but he overcame them, unlike many of his buddies who still had neurons in their brains misfiring whenever they heard the mention of names like Nasiriyah, Debecka Pass, and Umm Qasr. Six years after being back in the States, he still flinched whenever he heard a car backfire. He had found and gotten involved with the Vet Center, and eventually was recruited to serve on the Center's board. Within a year, his quiet leadership merited a nomination as the board's fourth chair.

Hanson, also a veteran of the Persian Gulf War, the First Gulf War of 1990-1991, had seen combat more than a decade prior to Mathers. He had been awarded a Purple Heart and was in many ways emblematic of those individuals the Center sought to serve. Like many veterans, Hanson had seen and heard things during his service that he would have liked to forget. No one really knew whether he had received treatment for mental illness, but it was perceived that he had bouts of depression, alcoholism, and drug abuse following his return from overseas. Like thousands of his colleagues, he had experienced a puzzling array of symptoms, including headaches, joint pain, hair loss, memory loss, rashes, and unusual fatigue. The military had dismissed his symptoms as psychosomatic. It was only years later, as those with the symptoms had traded notes about their frustrations in receiving official Pentagon acknowledgement that they had real maladies, that Gulf War Syndrome was named. No cause was ever identified, and treatment remained elusive.

If Hanson was a sufferer of this syndrome, his outward symptoms were relatively mild compared to some of those who were served at the Vet Center. Yet, it was becoming increasingly clear that the board of the Vet Center was dysfunctional as long as Hanson continued to disrupt the board with his ill-timed outbursts, intimidation of other board members, and abuse of staff.

Had he simply been a filthy-mouthed fool, it might not have taken as much courage for Mathers or his predecessors to find a way to rotate him off the board gracefully without putting the Hanson Foundation funds going to the Vet Center at risk. But it wasn't that simple; there was some sympathy and compassion for Hanson's outrageous behavior that some within the organization thought may have been attributable to factors out of his own control, such as a physical chemical imbalance or a brain disturbance, or emotional problems emanating from his wartime experience.

Mathers had always treated Hanson with respect as a fellow combat veteran, and they were on good terms. It was assumed by the other board members that

Mathers, both as someone with a good relationship with Hanson, and in his capacity of serving as chair, had the responsibility to deal with him.

Mathers had dealt successfully with disruptive board members before as chair of another organization. In one such case, he had scheduled a lunch meeting to discuss this, bringing along another member of the board for support.

He had begun by shaking hands warmly, making good eye contact, and calmly informing that board member that he and other members of the board had noticed behavior that might indicate that he was having problems outside of his board service, and that members were concerned about him. In any case, he had told the board member that there were times when he was interrupting too often and not focusing on the agenda. When he did so, the other board members were distressed, and the board was unable to do its job. Was there anything bothering him about the board that elicited the behavior that was of concern to the other members? It was important that every member have a chance to participate, and not feel uneasy about sharing their views. It was important for this board member to tone down the volume and try to listen more to what others had to say.

The board member, in this case, not only didn't become defensive, but apologized, and agreed to end his rudeness at board meetings. The rest of the meeting consisted of Mathers giving the board member some easily accomplishable assignments to keep him busy and reassuring him that he would continue to serve as a valued member of the board.

Instinctively, Mathers assessed that the outcome would be quite different if he employed the same strategy with Hanson, who would likely become defensive and create a scene, no matter how delicately Mathers handled the situation.

Perhaps they should meet in the park for lunch, with Mathers offering to bring some sandwiches and cold beer. He made a mental note that if he did so, he would be sure to not include onions in Hanson's sandwich.

Discussion Questions

1. Who has the responsibility for dealing with disruptive board members?

2. How useful would it be to have a written policy on the roles and responsibilities of board members?

3. How much power do individual board members have when they visit the organization?

4. What is the role of staff in dealing with abusive and demanding board members?

5. Should Hanson simply be thrown off the board? What would be the consequences of doing so?

6. How can a board chair deal with a disruptive board member at a meeting and after a meeting?

7. Discuss the dilemma of dealing with maintaining the fiscal health of the center by protecting the funds it receives from the foundation while maintaining the functionality of the center and its board.

Appendix 9
Arnova Financial Statements

**ASSOCIATION FOR RESEARCH ON NONPROFIT
ORGANIZATIONS AND VOLUNTARY ACTION**

STATEMENTS OF FINANCIAL POSITION
JUNE 30, 2012 AND 2011

ASSETS

	2012	2011
Cash	$ 236,240	$ 192,427
Cash held by others	63,443	14,062
Investments	789,002	757,673
Grants receivable	12,000	337,000
Accounts receivable	71,627	70,226
Prepaid expenses	19,430	11,508
Inventory	5,538	5,665
Equipment and software	24,798	15,828
	$ 1,222,078	$ 1,404,389

LIABILITIES AND NET ASSETS

	2012	2011
Liabilities		
Accounts payable	$ 16,614	$ 33,433
Accrued payroll and benefits	16,544	17,556
Deferred revenue	30,472	35,692
Total liabilities	63,630	86,681
Net assets		
Unrestricted		
Undesignated	493,913	564,971
Board designated	317,992	317,992
	811,905	882,963
Temporarily restricted	327,368	415,570
Permanently restricted	19,175	19,175
Total net assets	1,158,448	1,317,708
	$ 1,222,078	$ 1,404,389

See accompanying notes to financial statements.

ASSOCIATION FOR RESEARCH ON NONPROFIT ORGANIZATIONS AND VOLUNTARY ACTION

STATEMENT OF ACTIVITIES
YEAR ENDED JUNE 30, 2012
(With Comparative Total for the Year Ended June 30, 2011)

	2012				2011
	Unrestricted	Temporarily Restricted	Permanently Restricted	Total	Total
Support and revenue					
Grants	$ -0-	$ 99,000	$ -0-	$ 99,000	$ 455,000
Membership dues	76,640	-0-	-0-	76,640	83,793
Conference revenue and sponsorships	154,935	36,500	-0-	191,435	166,949
Publications	111,215	15,000	-0-	126,215	132,461
Contributions	9,038	1,000	-0-	10,038	16,625
In-kind contributions	-0-	150,250	-0-	150,250	150,250
Interest income on cash	635	-0-	-0-	635	558
Other	913	-0-	-0-	913	1,592
Net assets released from restrictions	390,133	(390,133)	-0-	-0-	-0-
Total support and revenue	743,509	(88,383)	-0-	655,126	1,007,228
Expenses					
Program					
Conference	234,516	-0-	-0-	234,516	246,568
Publications	189,118	-0-	-0-	189,118	189,711
Membership services	121,544	-0-	-0-	121,544	151,433
Scholarships and awards	39,235	-0-	-0-	39,235	40,687
Other programs	19,935	-0-	-0-	19,935	128,125
Total program expenses	604,348	-0-	-0-	604,348	756,524
Management and general	151,599	-0-	-0-	151,599	153,642
Fundraising	12,204	-0-	-0-	12,204	7,307
Total expenses	768,151	-0-	-0-	768,151	917,473
Change in net assets from operations	(24,642)	(88,383)	-0-	(113,025)	89,755
Investment return, net	7,653	181	-0-	7,834	10,926
Change in net assets before employee dishonesty loss	(16,989)	(88,202)	-0-	(105,191)	100,681
Employee dishonesty loss (Note 10)	(54,069)	-0-	-0-	(54,069)	-0-
Change in net assets	(71,058)	(88,202)	-0-	(159,260)	100,681
Net assets, beginning of period	882,963	415,570	19,175	1,317,708	1,217,027
Net assets, end of period	$ 811,905	$ 327,368	$ 19,175	$ 1,158,448	$ 1,317,708

See accompanying notes to financial statements.

**ASSOCIATION FOR RESEARCH ON NONPROFIT
ORGANIZATIONS AND VOLUNTARY ACTION**

STATEMENT OF ACTIVITIES
YEAR ENDED JUNE 30, 2011

	Unrestricted	Temporarily Restricted	Permanently Restricted	Total
Support and revenue				
Grants	$ -0-	$ 455,000	$ -0-	$ 455,000
Membership dues	83,793	-0-	-0-	83,793
Conference revenue and sponsorships	158,449	8,500	-0-	166,949
Publications	116,461	16,000	-0-	132,461
Contributions	14,025	2,600	-0-	16,625
In-kind contributions	-0-	150,250	-0-	150,250
Interest income on cash	558	-0-	-0-	558
Other	1,592	-0-	-0-	1,592
Net assets released from restrictions	477,054	(477,054)	-0-	-0-
Total support and revenue	851,932	155,296	-0-	1,007,228
Expenses				
Program				
Conference	246,568	-0-	-0-	246,568
Publications	189,711	-0-	-0-	189,711
Membership services	151,433	-0-	-0-	151,433
Scholarships and awards	40,687	-0-	-0-	40,687
Other programs	128,125	-0-	-0-	128,125
Total program expenses	756,524	-0-	-0-	756,524
Management and general	153,642	-0-	-0-	153,642
Fundraising	7,307	-0-	-0-	7,307
Total expenses	917,473	-0-	-0-	917,473
Change in net assets from operations	(65,541)	155,296	-0-	89,755
Other income (loss)				
Investment return, net	10,806	120	-0-	10,926
Change in net assets	(54,735)	155,416	-0-	100,681
Net assets, beginning of period	937,698	260,154	19,175	1,217,027
Net assets, end of period	$ 882,963	$ 415,570	$ 19,175	$ 1,317,708

See accompanying notes to financial statements.

ASSOCIATION FOR RESEARCH ON NONPROFIT ORGANIZATIONS AND VOLUNTARY ACTION

STATEMENTS OF CASH FLOWS
YEARS ENDED JUNE 30, 2012 AND 2011

	2012	2011
Operating activities		
Cash received from publications, conference, and membership dues	$ 261,024	$ 252,793
Cash received from contributions and grants	434,038	157,625
Interest and dividends received	12,397	23,076
Royalties received	128,046	114,532
Miscellaneous receipts	913	788
Cash paid to employees and suppliers	(686,991)	(740,230)
Change in cash held by others	(49,381)	22,153
Net cash flows from operating activities	100,046	(169,263)
Investing activities		
Capital expenditures	(19,848)	(15,649)
Proceeds from maturity of investments	387,048	250,865
Purchase of investments	(423,433)	(211,701)
Net cash flows from investing activities	(56,233)	23,515
Net change in cash	43,813	(145,748)
Cash, beginning of period	192,427	338,175
Cash, end of period	$ 236,240	$ 192,427
Reconciliation of change in net assets to net cash flows from operating activities		
Change in net assets	$ (159,260)	$ 100,681
Adjustments to reconcile change in net assets to net cash flows from operating activities:		
Depreciation	9,701	8,300
Portion of loss on defalcation related to equipment and software	1,177	-0-
Unrealized gain on investments	(273)	(479)
Change in accrued interest included in investments	5,329	12,629
Changes in assets and liabilities		
Cash held by others	(49,381)	22,153
Grants receivable	325,000	(314,000)
Accounts receivables	(1,401)	(17,715)
Prepaid expenses	(7,922)	(160)
Inventories	127	133
Accounts payable	(16,819)	25,035
Accrued payroll and benefits	(1,012)	(268)
Deferred member dues	(5,220)	(5,572)
Net cash flows from operating activities	$ 100,046	$ (169,263)
Supplemental disclosure of cash flow information		
Accrued interest included in investments	$ 28,768	$ 34,097

See accompanying notes to financial statements.

Appendix 10
Nonprofit Ethics Scenarios

In my classes, there is often spirited debate about various behaviors, and whether they might be "ethical" or "unethical." I have capsulized some of these behaviors in 120 short vignettes that are included in the book, *Ethics in Nonprofit Organizations: Theory and Practice.* Twenty-five of these scenarios are included in this appendix.

There is not always a consensus about the answer to this question, and many of these situations are purposely ambiguous. I point out to my students that it is often easy to justify a particular behavior, depending on which ethical approach one uses (see Chapter 7). Even more interesting, many behaviors can be justified or condemned, using either of the two major ethical approaches, the deontological approach (based on principles without regard to consequences of any behavior) and the teleological approach (based on the consequences of the behavior).

Complicating one's analysis of whether behavior might be unethical is the difficulty of distinguishing between ethical violations that are trivial, and those that become more worthy of scrutiny because of the matter of scale. For example, no one is likely to be fired summarily for committing the unethical transgression of making a single copy on the organization's copy machine, although most of us would agree that doing this is not ethical. When a nonprofit organization employee puts an advertisement in the paper offering to make copies for the public and collects money for this, and uses the organization's copy machine to make thousands of copies for this purpose, hardly anyone would dispute that this would be unethical (and criminal) behavior. What is problematic is where the line gets drawn between so-called "de minimus" violations that might be appropriately overlooked and those that should be sanctioned to one degree or another. Each year, I pose a discussion question along the lines of this dilemma, and my students are often passionate—and often disagree—about what they feel is worthy of being punished and what might not.

All of the scenarios included in this appendix are fictional, although some are based on actual cases that I have experienced either firsthand or secondhand. Many that have their origins in actual events have been exaggerated beyond recognition. All have been disguised beyond recognition. Almost all of these scenarios, whether they occurred or not, could have plausibly occurred in a nonprofit organization. I believe that a discussion of these scenarios will improve the ability of our future nonprofit leadership to navigate through many common ethical challenges they could face in the future.

1. Patty is working late at the State Association of Veterans Organizations. She hears some light tapping on the windowpane, and looks out the window to determine how

hard it might be raining. Her office overlooks the office building parking lot. She notices that one of her colleagues, Tom, the organization's government affairs officer, is loading boxes of bubble envelopes into his SUV. Immediately, she suspects that Tom, who recently started a home eBay business selling sports cards, has likely taken these from the supply closet for his personal use. Feeling a bit guilty that she may have jumped to a false conclusion, she leaves her office, walks down the long hallway to the supply closet, and confirms that the four boxes of these bubble mailers that were recently placed there by the office manager are no longer there. Patty and Tom have worked together for several years, and they have a good relationship. She decides to simply ignore this, as it is not her job to police the organization and she doesn't want to get anyone in trouble, particularly Tom.

a. Is Patty acting unethically by not reporting Tom's behavior?

2. Bill is the executive director of the State Track and Field Festival, a statewide association that administers an annual Olympic-style track meet. He has served in this position for almost three decades, and is considering retirement in the near future. His youngest son, Bill Jr., was recently laid off from his job at the local meat packing plant. Bill has always dreamed that one of his sons would follow in his footsteps, and he sees an opportunity to turn this vision into a reality. He offers his son a newly created position of assistant executive director, with the intent of teaching him everything he knows so that when he retires, Junior will carry on the organization's mission. Although some members of Bill's board of directors voice some opposition, over the years, Bill has selected many of the board members who serve on the board, and he is able to convince a majority of the board to fund this new position, and authorize him to recruit and hire whomever he wants. Junior is delighted to work for his Dad, although he knows virtually nothing about the duties he will be required to do in the new position, and certainly has no experience in managing a nonprofit organization should his father retire.

a. Is Bill acting ethically in hiring his son for this position?

b. Was Bill acting ethically when he selected board members to serve on his board?

3. Priscilla is the receptionist for the Harristown Area YMCA. She has a lunch meeting scheduled today with a committee consisting of parents from her son's school to plan a fundraising event. She does not have a photocopy machine at home, and decides to make five copies on the YMCA's photocopy machine of a newspaper article from today's paper on how groups might raise funds for various causes to hand out at the meeting.

a. Is Priscilla acting unethically by making these copies?

b. Is your answer different if Priscilla is making one copy? Fifty copies? A thousand copies?

c. What should an organization's policy be with respect to making photocopies on the organization's copier for personal use? What sanctions should there be for violating this policy?

※※※   ※※※※※   ※※※

4. Alisha is the CEO of Shaping Young Minds Day Care Center. One of her employees, Malory, is having personal problems at home, taking care of a chronically sick parent who is keeping her up at night. She suspects that Malory is using amphetamines to stay awake during working hours. Malory has been a valued employee for almost ten years, and has never had any discipline problems. Before now, there has only been circumstantial evidence that Malory has a drug problem. The day care center has a strict policy that staff members may not use illegal drugs, and those that do are subject to being summarily fired. Today, Alisha accidentally notices that Malory fails to return the meds intended for one of the children with ADHD, and slips it into her pocket, and heads for the bathroom. Alisha follows her into the bathroom, and confronts Malory, asking her to empty her pocket. Malory at first refuses, then starts crying, and admits she has taken the Ritalin tablets intended for one of the clients. She begs for her job, explaining that she has been doing this only since her mother has kept her awake at all hours, and she needs the job to pay for her mother's care during the day. She threatens suicide if she is fired. Alisha agrees to look the other way, provided Malory stops stealing the Ritalin.

a. Is Alisha acting unethically by not firing Malory?

b. What other options might be available to Alisha rather than either firing Malory or looking the other way?

※※※   ※※※※※   ※※※

5. Tidwell University's chief development officer, Ted, receives a call from "Wild Bill" Hanford, one of its best known alumni, requesting a meeting to discuss a possible major gift. Hanford was recently released from a federal prison in Allenwood, PA, having served a 3-5 year sentence for insider trading. At the meeting, Mr. Tidwell asks if the university would consider a $30 million donation for the purpose of building a new facility to house Tidwell's business school, with state-of-the-art technology embedded in the building. The only requirement would be the building would have to be named "The William Hanford School of Business." Ted thanks Mr. Hanford for his offer, and replies that it would need to be a decision of the entire board to decide whether to accept such a donation for this purpose. Two months later, the President of Tidwell puts the issue before the board of the institution. The board approves it.

a. Can the board ethically approve this donation?

b. If the donation is approved and provided, should Mr. Hanford be provided with a substantiation letter permitting him to take a full tax deduction for his donation because of the tangible value in having the building named after him?

c. If the donation is not accepted with the strings attached, is there some middle ground the board might pursue to not offend this major donor and generate needed funds to finance its programs and do so ethically?

6. Ariel is the executive director of the Coalition for Women's Survival, a ten-year-old 501(c)(3) nonprofit, tax-exempt organization dedicated to educating young men about the scourge of sexual violence against women. Each year, as part of her job description, she prepares a detailed, balanced budget consisting of income expected and expenses. After much wrangling and give and take compromise, her board of directors approves the budget after making modifications. Once the budget is approved, Ariel perfunctorily files it and ignores it. She feels that the business operations of her organization are too turbulent to be tied to a spending plan that was devised as much as 18 months before spending is required, and that it makes much more sense to see the board-approved budget as a useful guide, but certainly not as a directive. So, she spends as she thinks necessary to achieve the stated mission of the organization, and usually gets close to the income and revenue projects, even though she tends to have little memory of the individual line-items that comprise her annual budgets. So far, no one on the board has caught on to this, and she certainly isn't going to volunteer anything.

a. Is Ariel acting ethically by ignoring her board's approved budget?

b. How much flexibility should an executive director have over line item spending before it is ethical to ask the board to approve changes?

7. Harriet has been the executive director of the Harristown Chamber of Commerce, a 501(c)(6) nonprofit tax-exempt organization, for almost 20 years. She has never married, and the Chamber has become her entire life. It is not unusual for Harriet to be working in the office 12 hours each day, being the first one to arrive in the morning and the one to turn out the lights in the late evenings, which may be filled with meetings and telephone calls. For the last several years, she has gotten in the habit of having the support staff of the Chamber run her personal errands, justifying that her herculean work hours simply leave little or no time to do this herself and that the organization is better served if she devotes the time for those mundane tasks to her professional life. Some of the staff who are asked to do these errands are sympathetic and understanding, and are quite willing to help. But lately, she has noticed that some appear to be resentful. Fortunately, no one so far has given her a flat "I won't do this for you."

a. Is Harriet acting ethically when she asks her staff to run personal errands when she is devoting the time saved by this to the work of the organization?

8. Leslie is part of the political elite of the community, or at least aspires to be. He has landed a plum position on the board of the Kessler Chocolate Company, where

he earns a six-figure honorarium for simply attending four corporate board meetings each year. As a former elected member of the state legislature, he is expected to offer political advice to the corporation which, since all of the board members are long-time personal friends anyway, he would feel comfortable providing for free. As part of his service, he is expected to serve on the board of the corporation's captive charity, for which he is paid an additional high five-figure stipend, and for which he is also expected to serve without making any waves or questioning the leadership. This reminds him of when he was a first-term member of the state legislator, and was expected to vote for whatever the leadership wanted without question, in exchange for financial help getting reelected, the approval of pet projects in his district, and a lifestyle augmented by taxpayer funded perks. At the board meeting of the Kessler Chocolate Foundation, the Chair of the board is suggesting that the salary of the officers of the board be increased from $100,000 to $150,000 annually. Leslie thinks that is perhaps excessive for a position that is typically volunteer, but recognizes that if he plays his cards right, he could become an officer within a few years and never have any money worries again. With the rest of his colleagues on the board, he votes to approve the chair's motion.

a. Is Leslie being ethical by voting on the chair's motion?

b. Is Leslie being ethical by serving on this board?

9. Rose is a professional singer, who organized the Harristown Early Music Consort consisting of herself, a recorder player, and a lute player. For several years, they have performed in coffee houses, schools, and arts festivals, mostly for minimal pay (if any) and being fed. Lately, word of their talent has spread, and they are beginning to receive more offers for their performances, some of which pay quite well. Rose has decided to create a nonprofit organization, mostly to avoid liability exposure, and also for tax reasons. The board of the new organization consists of herself, the recorder player and the lute player. For each performance, she asks the organization hiring the group to make a check out to the "Early Music Consort," which is deposited into the consort's checking account. Then, after paying for any out-of-pocket costs related to the performance, such as travel, food, and insurance, she divides up the remainder equally, writing a check for that amount to each of the three members.

a. Is Rose being ethical?

10. Petunia is the Director of Purchasing for the Citizens for a Saner World, a 501(c)(3) nonprofit tax-exempt organization, dedicated to reducing tensions among the global nuclear powers. The organization has affiliates in 40 states and 30 foreign countries, and all purchasing for the organization must be approved by Petunia. As the senior officer who buys supplies, travel, giveaways with the organization's logo, telephones, and computers, Petunia is courted by manufacturers and distributors, hoping to convince her to steer the multi-million dollar business of the international

organization their way. To entice her, it is not unusual for her to receive thank-yous from suppliers in the form of boxes of cookies, movie tickets, and flowers. But yesterday, she received two open tickets to Hawaii from a company that has been courting her to choose them to handle the organization's travel business. She considers herself a professional, and doesn't expect that receiving these tickets will influence her decision to choose this company over several others who are equally courting her for this business. So, she decides to keep and use the tickets, and sends a thank-you note to the travel company's sales rep.

a. Is Petunia's behavior ethical?

11. The Board of the Harristown Community Hospital and Healthcare System, a 501(c)(3) tax-exempt charity, is considering a proposal being made by its president and CEO, Michael, to increase its net revenue in the wake of likely massive cuts to its Medicare reimbursements. He is proposing that the hospital shut down its emergency room at its location in the inner-city of Harristown, and invest the millions of dollars being saved by doing this to create satellite clinics and walk-in health centers in the surrounding suburbs. Michael and his CFO, Courtney, explain that the emergency room is draining the hospital of its reserves, and that the satellite centers in the suburbs offer a lucrative investment that can make up for the forecasted revenue shortfalls emanating from Medicare cuts. He dismisses the protests from the only African-American on the board joined by only two others who live in the city as not recognizing the realities, and suggests that the emergency health care needs in Harristown can be served by a regional hospital that is located ten miles away in the neighboring community of Indiantown.

a. Is the President and CEO's proposal ethical?

12. Victor is the Vice President of Development for the nonprofit Brochton Medical Center, a 501(c)(3) nonprofit tax-exempt organization. He has a team of assistant vice presidents who help him raise nearly $40 million annually for the Center, and an additional $30 million for its capital campaign. Victor drives his staff hard, but pays them well and entices them to work even harder by sponsoring competitions in which high performers are rewarded, and prizes are offered for extraordinary closes on major gifts. This year, he offers two tickets to the Super Bowl and two airfares and a hotel suite for four days in New Orleans to the Vice President who closes the most total gifts in the calendar year.

a. Is Victor's compensation program ethical?

13. Connie is a therapist at the RFM Counseling Center, a nonprofit, 501(c)(3) tax-exempt organization that provides services to veterans with PTSD. Connie has dreamed about starting her own practice, but is insecure about whether such a private practice would be financially viable, with two kids to support and soon to

be applying to college. Connie decides to test the waters before diving full-in, and retain her full-time position at the Center, and put out her shingle in a private office located just one block away. At first, she discreetly tells her clients at the Center that she has a private practice as well, offering convenient evening hours, and providing a discount. Later, once she realizes that she can make a go of it, she offers her resignation, and sends a welcome letter to each of her former clients, soliciting them to continue where they left off at her new place of employment.

a. Is Connie's behavior ethical?

14. Quad Fundraising Services (QFS) is a for-profit professional fundraising firm that specializes in providing services to small nonprofit charities that have no internal fundraising staff. Quad handles all fundraising duties, using a bank of trained telemarketing staff, and a sophisticated direct mail operation. QFS is expensive, but they promise that the charity will receive at least something for being added to its client list, and the costs are reasonable considering the upfront investment a charity might have to make to purchase mailing lists and train staff, something QFS has already done. Brad, the CEO of the Harristown Environmental Improvement Fund, decides to hire QFS. QFS raises nearly $450,000 from its telephone and direct mail campaign, and, after expenses and a reasonable fee, presents a check to the Fund for $5,200, money that will go a long way considering the meagerness of the Fund's budget. Brad is grateful he had the foresight to find a professional fundraiser to do all of this dirty work so that he could focus on the actual mission of the organization.

a. Is it ethical for Brad to hire Quad Fundraising Services?

15. Josephine is the Communications Director for the Montrose Association of Nonprofit Organizations (MANO), a nonprofit 501(c)(3) tax-exempt organization formed to bring together nonprofits in Montrose to collaborate on advocacy for the sector, and provide joint purchasing and insurance opportunities. Josephine's husband is running for State House, and she is doing everything she can to support his candidacy. She knows that if he is elected, the nonprofit sector will have a strong, active voice in the state legislature. Today, because her husband is conducting fundraising coffees in their home, Josephine is working in her office, using her computer to create flyers, and printing out hundreds of copies to place under the doors of her neighbors seeking support. At eight o'clock, a group of her friends are meeting with her there to pick up these flyers, and stuff thousands of envelopes in the MANO conference room. She remembers to order four pizzas for delivery.

a. Is Josephine's behavior ethical?

b. What alternatives might be available to her if she wishes to completely separate her political life from her professional life in the nonprofit sector?

16. Louisa, the project director for a grant provided to her employer, the Citizens Vote Project, from the Johnson Foundation, is delighted that her work on the grant is just about finished, and everything relating to this grant has appeared to go well. The final deliverable has been delivered. The only task remaining for her to receive the final grant payment installment is for the program evaluation to be completed. The Johnson Foundation has provided a list of peer reviewers who may be selected by the grantee to perform the evaluation. Louisa looks down the list and sees that one of these evaluators happens to be one of her best friends, Jane. She decides to choose Jane as the evaluator of the grant.

a. Is Louisa's behavior ethical?

17. Hallie is the newly elected Chair of the Women's Advocacy Center of Harristown, a 501(c)(4) nonprofit organization established in 1973 that advocates on behalf of the healthcare needs of pregnant teenagers. Hallie is relatively new to the organization and to Harristown, having served on the board for just two years. But the membership has been impressed by her dedication to the mission and her indefatigable efforts to raise funds for the cause. Prior to coming to Harristown, she had served on many other boards in a leadership capacity, and the board had no qualms about electing her chair of this all-volunteer-run organization. Hallie dives into the work of the organization, but learns of a serious problem with the organization's legal status. Apparently, the organization has never filed 990 tax returns for years, and she finds out the IRS had dropped the organization from its Master list of tax-exempt organizations in the 1980s when its communications to the founder of the organization were not responded to, not surprising since the founder had died only a few years after the organization filed its incorporation papers. Hallie knows that the organization has operated quite well for years without knowing of this problem, and would likely continue to fly "under the radar" for many more years, benefitting by the fact that as a c(4), those who make contributions to the organization may not take a deduction for their contributions on their personal income taxes, making it less likely that the IRS will audit them. So, why open a can of worms?

a. Is Hallie's behavior ethical?

18. Bridget is the President and CEO of the Pennsylvania Heart Disease Education Fund, a nonprofit, 501(c)(3) tax-exempt organization. She receives a letter in the mail proposing a partnership between her organization and the manufacturer of a new cereal. The literature provided in the letter describes the cereal as a healthy alternative to a typical eggs, bacon, and whole milk breakfast. Putting that aside, the cereal is high in sugar, salt, and cholesterol, but certainly much lower in calories than

the other breakfast pictured on the box. In exchange for the Fund providing its seal to the manufacturer to use as an endorsement on its packaging, the manufacturer will pay the Fund $10,000 annually. Bridget knows that the $10,000 will go a long way in advancing the mission of the organization, and could save hundreds of lives, even if the cereal might not be the most ideal formulation for someone seeking to improve their heart health. But it is clearly a better alternative than the full breakfast of eggs, bacon, and whole milk it is intended to replace. She agrees to the proposal.

a. Is Bridget acting ethically by providing this approval?

❋❋❋   ❋❋❋❋❋   ❋❋❋

19. Santos is an assistant development officer for the Wild City Foundation, a nonprofit, 501(c)(3) tax-exempt organization. He is recruited by a foundation in a neighboring community that solicits many of his current organization's donors, and agrees to leave Wild City for a higher paycheck and more job responsibility. As he cleans out his desk, he remembers to download the Excel file that has the data about his accounts, recognizing that it might take many months to reconstruct this data from memory, and it would save him hours of needless work. He also has access to the accounts of his colleagues in his office, but he believes taking those might be unethical, even though it certainly would be useful to have this material.

a. Is Santos acting ethically?

❋❋❋   ❋❋❋❋❋   ❋❋❋

20. Geraldine does not have a home computer, and recognizes that the world is changing and email and Internet access has become a necessity. She did set up a Gmail account, but rarely uses it. Instead, she uses the email account provided to her by her employer, the nonprofit 501(c)(3) tax-exempt Wilson Sports Hall of Fame, located at the football stadium at Wilson University, home of the Fightin' Wildcats. Because she does not have her own Internet access, she is forced to do her personal Internet tasks, including responding to email, booking travel, reading movie reviews, shopping for Christmas presents, and so on at the office. To compensate for this, she usually has lunch at her desk. She notices, however, that since she has set up her Facebook account, she is spending much more time on the Internet than she used to, and is having difficulty tearing herself away to do her work for the organization. And since she has discovered Angry Birds, she questions whether she is starting to become addicted to the computer, and thinks about asking for a raise so she could afford to purchase a computer of her own.

a. Is Geraldine's behavior ethical?

❋❋❋   ❋❋❋❋❋   ❋❋❋

21. Matilda is a nurse at the Harristown Home for the Aged, a nonprofit, 501(c)(3) tax-exempt organization. The home has a substantial waiting list, because of

the reputation it has for providing quality care at affordable fees. Her mother has been getting up in years, and recently suffered a fall and broke her hip. Matilda is unwilling to trust the care of her mother to other facilities that might not have as a good a reputation as the facility for which she works. She recognizes that she cannot afford to take months, if not years, off to care for her mother in her home, and pleads with the executive director, Zeno, to bend the rules and admit Matilda's mom as a patient as soon as there is an open bed. Zeno agrees to accommodate Matilda's request.

a. Is Matilda being unethical by making this request?

b. Is Zeno being unethical by agreeing to the request?

c. Would the situation be any different if it was a major donor of the institution who was making the request rather than a staff member?

22. Viola is the executive director of The Best Time of Your Life Retirement Community, a nonprofit, 501(c)(3) tax-exempt assisted living facility, subsidized by one particular faith community, which has a long waiting list for being considered for residency in the modern, luxury facility. An older couple, Peter and Faith, are meeting with Viola, and are disappointed to learn that the average wait for an apartment in the facility to become available is two years. Viola tells them that if the couple is willing to make a $30,000 donation to the institution, this will entitle them to shave as much as a year off the wait, although there is still no guarantee that there will be an opening as others have made that commitment.

a. Is the waiting list avoidance policy of the Retirement Community ethical?

107. Barbara is hired as the new executive director of the Harristown United Way, a nonprofit, 501(c)(3) tax-exempt organization. As is typical in Harristown whenever a new executive director is hired, the salary negotiation includes an understanding that the executive director will be making a $20,000 "leadership gift" to the United Way, serving as an example to other staff (and members of the community, as well), and the amount of salary is at a level to accommodate this expected gift.

a. Is the organization acting ethically when it "requires" this donation?

23. Juan is the international director for Feed the Big Blue Marble Foundation, an American-based nonprofit 501(c)(3) tax-exempt organization that operates in 30 countries with the mission of alleviating hunger in areas devastated by natural disasters, civil wars, and political unrest, making efforts to avoid taking sides in

political disputes. Juan receives a report from his director in Mali, Achmed, that a local village chieftain is blocking the organization's convoy from passing through a road adjacent to his village and reaching residents of a nearby besieged village, and has demanded that the organization pay him the equivalent of $12,000 to let the trucks pass freely. Juan is a realist, and recognizes that this is how business is done in this part of the world. He approves the payment, and arranges to wire the money to a particular unnumbered account in Switzerland.

a. Is Juan's behavior ethical?

24. The National Association of Biology Teachers is a nonprofit, 501(c)(3) tax-exempt organization that represents the interests of 35,000 high school and college biology teachers. Recently, one of its members posted that the endowment of the organization, now nearly $35 million, is invested heavily in a private equity fund that manufactures assault weapons, including the one that was used in the murder of 20 school children in Newtown, CT in December 2012. The executive director insists that the association does not actually own the company, and that the purpose of the investment strategy of the association is to provide the highest, and most stable return possible on its investment. The chairman of the board has taken the opposite position, and advocates that the association should divest itself of any investments in products and services that are not socially responsible, including tobacco companies, gun manufacturing, and companies that are considered to either pollute the environment or engage in unfair labor practices. The board votes to overrule its board chair and continue with the investment.

a. Is the investment policy of the organization ethical?

25. Portia is the Director of Art and Music Therapy for the West Mountain Heights Nursing Home, a 501(c)(3) tax-exempt organization. She is working on her master's degree online, and spends an increasing part of her day doing classwork. Because of the demands of her family and having a second job at the local supermarket, she finds she is unable to do her schoolwork outside of office hours. Occasionally, she has had to hide what she has been doing from her supervisor, the executive director, because she is not sure whether he would sanction her for doing her school assignments during the working day. But, she rationalizes, what she learns in these classes is often related to her work assignments, and helps her do a better job.

a. Is Portia's behavior ethical?

KEYWORD INDEX

A

abuse, general, 142, 191, 211, 353, 384, 433, 443, 445
   child, 126, 127, 146, 290, 323, 369, 379, 384, 417
   drug and alcohol, 313, 428, 442, 445
   in the nonprofit sector, 46, 47, 81, 87, 88, 142, 191, 192, 195, 196, 211, 353, 384
accountability, 15, 19, 28, 31, 37, 57, 68, 69, 70, 76, 89, 92, 98, 121, 125, 130, 134, 136, 137, 140, 141, 144, 147, 154, 192, 193, 195, 197, 202, 203, 230, 290, 296, 312, 313, 334, 353, 354, 360, 367, 368, 373, 385, 391, 429
accountant, 69, 84, 89, 191, 197, 198, 202, 203, 205, 206, 216, 440
accrual basis of accounting, 199, 203, 212
ACORN, 46-47, 52
advertisement, 158, 163, 166, 167, 168, 170, 173, 207, 219, 227, 252, 254, 273, 274, 277, 278, 279, 283-284, 286, 303, 304, 354, 355, 420, 452
affiliate agreements, 282-283, 291
affiliations, 6, 65, 78, 87, 122, 126, 156, 171, 248, 263, 321, 340, 365, 367, 433, 456
aging (general), 215, 296, 303, 349, 377
   of nonprofit management leadership, 349
application service providers, 279, 288
applications (general), 41, 47, 78, 137, 219, 231, 233, 272, 275, 291, 307, 325, 367, 370
   for employer identification number, 78, 233
   for funding and grants, 40, 104, 154-155, 157, 179-186, 296, 325, 351, 355, 426
   for tax-exempt status, 17, 48-49, 53, 72, 76-79, 87, 151, 353, 398, 399
   for jobs, 219-222, 311, 368, 391, 435
Affordable Care Act, 227, 231, 357
ALS Association, 159, 211, 271, 352,
Armstrong, Lance, 126, 149, 170, 177, 396
articles of incorporation, 14, 67, 68, 70-71, 72, 74, 75, 78, 92, 104, 151
articles, op-ed, 167, 254, 406
assets, 13, 16, 18, 19, 24, 25, 28, 34, 47, 49, 67, 71, 74, 119, 135, 188, 194, 195, 197, 198, 199, 200, 201, 202, 205, 210, 211, 213, 226, 232, 233, 360, 363, 364, 365, 390, 391, 396, 442
audits, 69, 84, 89, 101, 104, 186, 191, 196, 197, 202, 204-205, 213, 312, 354, 356, 459
awards, 243, 250, 263, 414

B

balance sheet, 196, 199, 200
benchmarking, 293, 306, 310-312, 318, 320
benefits, staff, 79, 88, 89, 127, 138, 143-144, 151, 185, 206, 216, 217, 222, 223, 225, 227, 228, 229, 231, 233, 237, 385, 386, 402, 420, 421, 425
blogs, 164, 167, 168, 255, 272, 273-274, 276, 289
board development, 97, 103, 106
board meetings, 69, 90, 95, 96, 97, 98, 102, 103, 104, 106, 107-109, 110, 111, 1112, 145, 256, 272, 273, 293, 296, 297, 298, 332, 335, 347, 401, 409, 410, 411, 412, 419, 423, 426, 441, 443, 444, 446
board minutes, 69, 70, 96, 102, 104, 107, 108, 109, 115, 205, 298, 335
board of directors, 6, 9, 10, 14, 15, 21, 27, 28, 30, 37, 60, 67, 68, 69, 70, 71, 73, 88, 89-91, 92, 95, 96, 97, 98-115, 117, 118, 122, 125, 126, 127, 131, 134, 137, 138, 140, 141-142, 143, 144, 145, 147, 148, 152, 156, 157, 158, 170, 175, 179, 186, 188, 191, 192, 197, 201, 202, 203, 206, 208, 209, 210, 211, 213, 219, 223, 226, 229, 235, 247, 248, 249, 252, 253, 254, 256, 262, 276, 293, 294, 295, 296, 297, 298, 299, 300, 301, 304, 305, 306, 312, 316, 320, 321, 322, 323, 324, 332, 333, 335, 341, 347, 353, 355, 360, 367, 370, 382, 390, 391, 397, 398, 401, 402, 403, 404, 405, 407, 410, 411, 412, 413, 414, 415, 416, 418, 419, 422, 423, 424, 426, 441-447, 449, 450, 451, 452, 453, 455, 458
board surveys (see *surveys*)
bookkeeping, 69, 197, 203, 207, 218, 401
Boston Marathon, 346, 347, 382
BPR (see *Business Process Reengineering*)
branding, 134, 164, 169-170, 176, 177, 257, 328, 363, 371, 426
British Petroleum oil spill, 5, 382
budgeting, 6, 10, 69, 70, 88, 92, 101, 104, 105, 120, 126, 134, 135, 143, 151, 164, 168, 172, 173, 185, 186, 191, 193, 194, 195, 201, 206-209, 210, 211, 213, 235, 277, 295, 297, 305, 308, 335, 340, 343, 348, 356, 357, 358, 365, 367, 368, 370, 392, 401-407, 417-424, 442, 451, 454
Bush, President George W., 45, 46, 236, 260, 402
Bush, President George H. W., 45, 50, 414
Business Process Reengineering, 306, 308, 310, 312, 314, 315, 317
bylaws, 68, 70, 73, 93, 95-98, 101, 102, 104, 106, 107, 109, 110, 111, 112, 113, 115, 223, 398, 443

C

campaigns (general), 134, 141, 164, 169, 170, 173, 268
campaigns (fundraising), 40, 84, 141, 142, 145, 166, 271, 453, 454
campaigns (political), 48, 74, 262, 267, 274, 355-356, 376, 433, 434, 436, 438, 439
Carver model, 100, 112, 114, 131, 148
cash, 8, 24, 40, 153, 194, 195, 199, 200, 201, 202, 280, 411, 436, 442
cash basis of accounting, 199, 203, 212
cash flow, 16, 180, 194, 196, 201, 202, 303, 419
cause-related marketing, 172, 175, 177, 363, 370, 371, 373, 386
CFRE, 367, 368
chairperson (of the board), 68, 88, 96, 97, 99, 102, 104, 105, 106, 107, 108, 109, 110, 111, 112, 113, 126, 138, 209, 223, 229, 235, 297, 299, 304, 316, 390, 391, 404, 410, 411, 412, 415, 423, 439, 441, 442, 445, 446, 447, 452, 455, 458
change management, 11, 122, 293, 305-320
charitable solicitation regulation, 31, 43, 81, 87, 93, 137
charity jacking, 145, 148
Charleston Principles, 85-87
churches, 5, 8, 24, 37, 38, 40, 45, 51, 80, 355-356, 384
Citizens United case, 48
coalitions, 249, 255, 337-344, 402, 406, 433, 451
COBRA (Consolidated Budget Reconciliation Act of 1985), 225
code of ethics, 105, 130, 133, 134, 135, 145, 146, 149, 205, 366, 367, 387, 394, 429, 430
collective goods, 56, 57, 61, 64, 65, 192, 368
colleges and universities, 8, 67, 72, 149, 154, 157, 225, 236, 310, 365, 367, 372, 375, 381, 405, 434
committees (board), 69, 90, 96, 97, 98, 99, 100, 101, 102, 103, 104, 105, 106, 107, 108, 112, 113, 133, 152, 156, 218, 226, 229, 294, 298, 299, 300, 301, 302, 304, 305, 311, 343, 354, 366, 415, 443
   advisory committee, 152
   board development committee, (see *board development*)
   executive committee, 98, 106, 112, 443
   personnel committee, 105, 218, 226, 229
compilations, 191, 204, 205
computers, 68, 187, 198, 203, 238, 241, 255, 274, 284, 285, 309, 311, 346, 348, 353, 405, 433, 436, 437
conferences and workshops, 101, 158, 174, 206, 207-208, 210, 247, 248, 251-252, 273, 276, 277, 324, 347, 352, 383, 420, 452, 454, 456
conflict of interest, 90, 91, 113, 137, 141, 229

consultants, 89, 117, 122, 137, 158-159, 185, 226, 294, 297, 298, 299, 300, 301, 303, 308, 401
contract failure, 55, 58, 60
contractors, 58, 197, 217, 218, 235, 244, 345
credit cards, 87, 191, 197, 198, 202, 209, 280, 284, 285, 286, 287, 352
crowd sourcing, 158
customer service (online), 277, 278, 279, 280
Cyber Assistant, 79

D

day care centers, 8, 13, 17, 39, 59, 65, 165, 166, 173, 253, 321, 362, 363, 386, 450
directors' & officers' insurance (see *insurance, directors' and officers'*)
discipline, 98, 105, 135, 215, 218, 222-226, 229, 232, 243, 450
disclosure of information by nonprofits, 48, 71, 87, 88, 91, 131, 136, 137, 138, 142, 143, 147, 153, 160, 192, 200, 201, 205, 230, 260, 261, 284, 354, 428
diversity, 6, 14, 15, 23, 27, 32, 42, 56, 68, 99, 103, 132, 135, 136, 144, 145, 165, 193, 240, 242, 315, 337, 348, 349
dress code, 229
duty of care, 89, 90, 139
duty of loyalty, 89, 90, 328
duty of obedience, 89

E

economy, nonprofit organizations and the, 8, 9, 13, 23, 24, 41, 44, 45, 47, 120, 165, 347, 357, 359, 360, 364, 389, 390, 402, 417, 419, 421, 434
e-mail, 85, 86, 107, 164, 167, 168, 195, 223, 239, 248, 249, 251, 252, 265, 266, 268, 272, 273, 276, 277, 278, 284, 286, 290, 351, 352, 406, 412, 433, 434, 435, 436, 437, 438, 439
employer identification number, 78, 233
endowment fund, 47, 49, 152, 194, 206, 210, 304, 346, 348, 364, 384, 402, 417, 419, 420, 458
ethical dilemmas, 126, 130, 133, 138-139, 145, 311
ethics, 9, 10, 11, 28, 29, 34, 70, 100, 105, 11, 125-149, 169, 170, 191, 192, 193, 195, 196, 197, 205, 211, 232, 269, 290, 311, 366, 367, 368, 372, 379, 385, 387, 392, 393, 394, 407, 424, 425, 429, 430, 439, 452
ethics codes (see *code of ethics*)
evaluation, 57, 58, 59, 63, 98, 100, 105, 121, 136, 137, 139, 140, 172, 173, 186, 193, 194,

196, 211, 224, 228, 294, 296, 303, 305, 306, 312, 313, 317, 333, 361, 366, 391, 455
executive committee (see *committees, executive*)
executive director, 67, 68, 88, 98, 99, 100, 104, 105, 106, 107, 108, 109, 110, 111, 112, 113, 131, 141, 143, 144, 196, 209, 215, 219, 223, 229, 248, 262, 299, 304, 316, 389, 401, 404, 444, 449, 451, 457, 458
exemptions, tax (see *taxes*)
expense reimbursement, 68, 70, 82, 88, 153, 198, 209-210, 228, 331, 383, 387, 392

F

Facebook, 167, 168, 169, 176, 456
family and medical leave, 228, 231
federal tax exempt status (see *tax exemption, federal*)
federal tax returns (see *tax returns*)
fee for service, 32, 210, 442
fees, for applications, 78
FEMA, 348, 373
Financial Accounting Standards Board, 202
financial reports/statements, 19, 69, 85, 102, 104, 196, 198, 201, 202, 203, 204, 205, 354, 446
firing (see *hiring and firing*)
foundations, 6, 8, 16, 17, 18, 19, 21, 32, 33, 36, 39, 40, 41, 42, 52, 67, 76, 81, 126, 127, 133, 138, 144, 154-155, 157, 170, 176, 179, 180, 181, 187, 188, 189, 193, 194, 205, 233, 312, 322, 324, 325, 342, 347, 348, 353, 354, 362, 363, 389, 390, 391, 392, 393, 395, 396, 402, 417, 433, 435, 442, 447, 459
Franklin, Benjamin, 7, 37, 38, 383
free riders, 30, 59
funding applications (see *applications, for funding and grants*)
fund balance, 199, 200, 205
fundraising, 9, 18, 22, 30, 40, 70, 81-86, 100, 101, 103, 104, 105, 113, 126, 127, 133, 134, 135, 136, 137, 138, 142, 145, 151-161, 165, 166, 168, 169, 171, 175, 187, 194, 199, 300, 201, 205, 215, 238, 248, 271, 272, 274, 277, 290, 297, 304, 322, 347, 349, 352, 357, 359, 361, 362, 366, 367, 368, 369, 390, 391, 392, 394, 398, 401, 406, 410, 427, 434, 441, 442, 449, 454

G

generative, 101
gifts, 197, 198, 260
gift shop, 153, 163, 166

governance, board, 15, 27, 45, 73, 95-115, 131, 134, 136, 152, 213, 295, 305, 338, 354, 376, 399, 415
grants (general), 16, 22, 64, 68, 141, 155, 165, 179-190, 192, 194, 196, 199, 201, 203, 204, 208, 247, 295, 296, 361, 382, 420, 424
foundation, 17, 18, 68, 133, 144, 155, 179-190, 233, 295, 312, 322, 325, 402, 417, 435, 442, 455
government, 6, 29, 38, 47, 48, 57, 133, 144, 157, 165, 179-190, 204, 205, 260, 293, 304, 312, 322, 348, 351, 354, 355, 404, 417

H

"halo" effect, 55, 59, 68
Harvard University, 37, 49, 210, 213, 384, 385
health insurance (see *insurance, health*)
hiring and firing, 49, 56, 69, 70, 98, 105, 109, 111, 126, 127, 141, 143, 144, 158, 159, 160, 172, 175, 179, 180, 198, 215, 216-224, 225, 226, 227, 242, 243, 250, 279, 289, 294, 296, 298, 300, 301, 303, 304, 323, 327, 329, 338, 351, 363, 389-394, 396, 411, 415, 420, 428, 429, 430, 434, 448, 449, 450, 452, 454, 457,
history of the nonprofit sector, 35-53, 80-81, 369
hospitals, 5, 6, 7, 8, 10, 13, 17, 21, 22, 25, 28, 36, 37, 39, 46, 47, 56, 64, 65, 67, 72, 151, 164, 165, 167, 231, 253, 294, 304, 305, 307, 321, 323, 324, 328, 350, 357, 363, 383, 384, 386, 406, 425-431, 453

I

ice bucket challenge, 152, 158, 159, 211, 271, 352, 369
IdeaList, 160, 212, 219, 240, 243, 274, 289, 319, 335, 351
income statement, 199
incorporation (general), 23, 60, 62, 67-74, 92, 113, 395-399, 410
incorporators, 70-71, 77, 113
Independent Sector, 8, 10, 13, 31, 44, 50, 51, 136, 146, 147, 268
insurance (general), 88, 89, 166, 199, 207, 208, 223, 228, 327, 330, 333-334, 335, 336, 402, 410, 417, 426, 452, 454
directors' and officers', 89, 330, 331-332, 334, 335
health, 144, 223, 227, 228, 231, 357, 385, 426
unemployment compensation, 40, 76, 334, 427

workers' compensation, 334
intermediate sanctions (see *Internal Revenue Service, intermediate sanctions*)
Internal Revenue Service (general), 8, 10, 13, 14, 18, 19, 20, 22, 23, 24, 25, 27, 28, 48-49, 72, 76, 77, 78, 79, 87, 88, 89, 92, 93, 113, 138, 142, 144, 147, 153, 154, 200, 218, 230, 233, 234, 235, 264, 265, 287, 353, 355, 356, 362, 370, 455
intermediate sanctions, 87, 88, 144, 230
Internet, 9, 72, 82, 87, 123, 146, 157, 187, 197, 219, 229, 241, 251, 256, 271-292, 347, 351, 352, 353, 392, 401, 456
   chat, 172, 255, 272, 273, 288
   domain names, 276, 291, 398, 436
   e-commerce, 277-287, 290, 291, 328
   firewalls, 285
   fundraising, 82-86, 91, 158, 160, 351, 362
   mailing lists, 272, 277, 278, 291
   search engines and directories, 72, 271, 273, 278, 286, 287, 288, 289, 291, 317, 351
inurement, 14, 27, 71, 88
IRS (see *Internal Revenue Service*)

J

Jewish federations, 18, 40, 154, 205

K

Komen Foundation, 127
Kiva, 142

L

large group intervention (LGI), 11, 293, 306, 314-316, 418, 419
liability issues (see *insurance, liability*)
liberal ethics, 129, 131
libraries, 7, 8, 37, 39, 42, 56, 70, 121, 155, 157, 181, 252, 253, 317, 351, 383, 403, 404
line-item budget, 185, 206-207, 208, 211
LinkedIn, 255, 353
Livestrong Foundation, 126, 169, 170, 396
loans, 142, 199, 200, 202, 260, 354, 419
lobbying, 17, 18, 19, 22, 43, 73, 76, 77, 80, 88, 91, 95, 136, 200, 232, 253, 259-269, 303, 304, 342, 343, 354, 355, 401, 405, 433
logo, corporate, 169, 174, 248, 251, 410, 452
long-term planning (see *strategic planning*)

M

Madoff scandal, 47, 126, 191, 390, 393, 396
mailing lists (see *Internet, mailing lists*)
management letter, 196, 197
marketing, 6, 10, 87, 142, 163-178, 217, 218, 274, 275, 277, 278, 281, 282, 287, 289, 303, 304, 305, 357, 363-364, 365, 367, 370, 386, 420, 422, 426, 440, 454
mediating structures, 13, 55, 61-62
members, corporate, 67, 71, 73, 95
Minimum Wage Act, 230, 233, 256, 339, 359
minutes, board (see *board minutes*)
mission statements, 44, 117-123, 296, 298, 301, 302

N

NAACP, 125
name, corporate, 48, 70, 71-72, 74, 81, 84, 126, 166, 170, 248, 251, 253, 291, 305, 353, 398, 416
newsletters, 82, 155, 157, 158, 168, 181, 207, 208, 219, 239, 241, 248, 249, 251, 256, 272, 276, 277, 304, 324, 327, 401, 426, 434
Nonprofit Leadership Alliance, 367
nursing homes, 17, 21, 65, 165, 195, 253, 303, 321, 351, 386, 389, 393, 458

O

Obama, President Barack, 47, 61, 236, 274, 281, 352, 371, 402, 439
officers (corporate), 28, 67, 68, 84, 88, 95, 97, 98, 102, 112, 196, 200, 299, 305, 328, 330, 331, 332, 335, 452
online charity auctions, 158, 288, 291, 351, 398, 423, 441
online shopping malls, 287, 291, 347
outcome-based management, 196, 293, 306, 312-314, 318
outsourcing, 39, 194, 218, 242, 330, 364, 401

P

parliamentary procedure, 95, 96, 110-111
Penn State University, 6, 126, 127
Pension Protection Act, 48
personal fundraising pages, 158
personal relationships, 141, 144, 229, 254, 297
personnel policies, 70, 105, 226-229, 335
planning, 9, 19, 40, 68, 98, 101, 105, 106, 107, 118, 151, 163, 168, 172-175, 176, 179, 183,

191, 193, 194, 195, 206, 208, 215, 216, 219, 223, 247, 251-252, 293-305, 306, 308, 313, 314, 316, 317, 318, 319, 333, 348, 349, 367, 385, 398, 401, 415, 419, 421, 426, 434, 453, 455
planning, strategic (see *strategic planning*)
pluralistic theory, 55, 61
podcasts, 167, 168, 255, 272, 274, 275
political action committees, 17, 19, 263
political activities, 17, 19, 21, 22, 42, 44, 48, 49, 73, 74, 76, 77, 80, 91, 166, 181, 268, 353, 355, 356, 433
political contributions, 88, 166, 260, 262, 263, 267, 405, 436
postage, 7, 55, 60, 68, 87, 159, 185, 187, 200, 206, 207, 208, 382
president (see *chairperson*)
press conferences, 250-251, 256, 262, 263, 426
privacy, 130, 131, 135, 136, 144, 256, 273, 284, 285-286, 291, 328, 385, 436, 443
professionalization, 133, 305, 366, 368
profit (see *surplus*)
program budget, 191, 206, 207, 208
public service announcements (PSAs), 68, 167, 238, 239, 251, 253,
public-serving organizations, 17-18, 20, 387
purposes, corporate, 15, 17, 23, 28, 39, 41, 68, 70, 72, 74, 75, 76, 80, 81, 82, 93, 95, 98, 117, 121, 143, 152, 163, 247, 248, 338, 386, 427

Q

quality, 47, 58, 59, 60, 63, 68, 107, 118, 119, 120, 121, 132, 172, 173, 222, 254, 293, 294, 303, 305, 306-308, 312, 317, 321-326, 363, 368, 412, 457

R

rebranding, 134, 170
Red Cross, 8, 14, 46, 167, 191, 215, 272, 323, 384
restricted funds, 201
risk management, 327, 333, 336

S

salaries, 6, 7, 23, 28, 40, 74, 84, 92, 105, 109, 138, 141, 143, 144, 146, 151, 165, 185, 199, 200, 206, 208, 215, 218, 219, 222, 226, 227, 228, 229, 233, 234, 235, 237, 304, 311, 329, 366, 370, 383, 387, 392, 402, 420, 421, 425, 427, 435, 452, 457
sales, credit card, 211, 212, 279, 280, 284, 285
sales taxes (see *taxes, state sales and use*)

Sarbanes-Oxley, 203, 354, 437
scandal, 46, 47, 49, 82, 126, 127, 170, 176, 191, 192, 203, 212, 213, 215, 259, 260, 305, 325, 354, 357, 360, 384, 390, 393, 396
secretary (of the board), 102, 106, 108, 109
security, general, 56, 63, 207, 279, 284-286, 287, 291, 324, 328, 330, 346, 347, 348, 357, 396, 402
security, Internet, 279, 284-286, 287, 291, 348
September 11th terrorist attack, 5, 46, 73, 236, 323, 345, 346, 347, 348, 357, 383
sick leave, 227, 228, 229
smartphones, 275, 351, 353, 425, 426
social media, 159, 163, 164, 168, 169, 171, 173, 176, 177, 216, 241, 271, 272, 274, 276, 277, 278, 289, 327, 334, 352, 369
social networking, 169, 172, 219, 219, 229, 248, 251, 255, 256, 274, 290, 353
spirit of the nonprofit sector, 164, 379-388
stamps (see *postage*)
Standards for Excellence, 10, 136, 146, 147, 368
"starfish" story, 379-380
Start With Trust Campaign, 134, 147
statement of financial position, 199, 202
stationery, 182, 252
strategic planning, 9, 172, 174, 175, 193, 208, 293-305, 306, 315, 316, 317, 318, 319, 367, 421, 426
substantiation (of donations), 152-154, 450
surplus (net revenue), 6, 14, 15, 16, 27, 138, 143, 163, 167, 170, 171, 172, 194, 200, 208, 210, 252, 383, 386, 426, 453
surveys, 65, 146, 165, 170, 171, 172, 184, 193, 250, 253, 254, 256, 262, 284, 300, 311, 314, 343, 354
SWOT, 164, 174, 175

T

tax exemption (general), 14, 20, 22, 23, 28, 36, 57, 59, 60, 67, 93, 140, 176, 192, 281
federal, 7, 14, 18, 19, 20, 22, 23, 24, 28, 39, 42, 43, 48, 49, 64, 67, 68, 69, 72, 73, 75-81, 87, 91, 92, 99, 182, 193-199, 200, 231, 248, 263, 264, 343, 354, 355-356, 370, 398, 399, 410, 433, 437
local (property), 6, 7, 22, 24, 37, 49, 359, 384
tax returns (990), 8, 20, 22, 24, 25, 28, 31, 69, 70, 76, 87, 138, 154, 165, 203, 234, 264, 433, 437, 455
taxes,
exemption (see *tax exemption*)
federal unemployment (FUTA), 40, 217, 234
federal withholding, 217, 233, 234
state sales and use, 281

state unemployment, 76, 217, 233, 334
　state sales and use, 281
　unrelated business income taxes (UBIT), 76, 80, 199, 200, 234
taxonomies, 24
Taxpayer Bill of Rights II, 27, 87, 89, 142, 230
Tea Party, 48, 52, 359, 371
text messaging, 164, 167, 191, 272, 351
Theory of the Commons, 55, 62, 65, 383
Total Quality Management (TQM), 132, 293, 306, 307, 308, 312, 315, 317, 318
training, 7, 23, 47, 62, 70, 119, 120, 127, 132, 133, 155, 173, 179, 195, 198, 205, 228, 235, 237, 238, 240, 241, 248, 268, 307, 323, 325, 330, 348, 352, 368, 386, 420, 421, 434
trademark, 72
treasurer (of the board), 88, 102, 107, 209, 329
Twitter, 167, 168, 169, 255, 272, 274, 289, 353
typologies, 21, 99, 127, 159, 166
　board, 99-100
　ethics approaches, 127,
　volunteer, 238

U

unemployment compensation (see *insurance, unemployment compensation*)
Unified Registration Statement (URS), 81, 82, 83, 85, 87
United Way, 18, 19, 40, 76, 82, 126, 146, 154, 169, 170, 191, 204, 205, 215, 307, 313, 321, 325, 349, 360, 361, 384, 457
unrelated business income taxes (see *taxes, unrelated business income*)
utilitarianism, 127, 128-129, 145

V

virtual volunteering, 241
virtue ethics, 129-130, 145, 385
vision statements, 117, 118, 119, 121, 122, 123
volunteers, 6, 7, 9, 10, 15, 16, 23, 26, 27, 29, 30, 31, 35, 37, 38, 39, 40, 56, 63, 65, 68, 70, 84, 99, 110, 112, 135, 136, 137, 144, 153, 157, 163, 175, 185, 192, 193, 206, 215, 218, 235-241, 242, 243, 244, 248, 249, 251, 254, 255, 256, 267, 274, 275, 276, 277, 283, 299, 312, 322, 324, 327, 328, 330-331, 335, 340, 349, 350, 351, 352, 353, 367, 381, 382, 383, 386, 401, 410, 411, 415, 420, 421, 442, 444, 452, 455
voting (at board meetings), 73, 88, 97, 100, 102, 105, 106, 108, 109, 112, 141, 305, 398, 443, 452, 458

W

Web sites, 7, 31, 48, 50, 81, 83, 85, 86, 111, 146, 153, 158, 168, 169, 172, 173, 174, 188, 219, 238, 239, 240, 241, 248, 249, 251, 255, 256, 262, 268, 271, 272, 273, 274, 275, 276, 277, 278, 279, 280, 282, 283, 285, 286, 287, 288, 289, 290, 291, 292, 304, 317, 324, 343, 351, 352, 353, 361, 367, 368, 396, 398, 401, 434
wikis, 255, 272, 275
wireless (also see *smartphones*), 275, 275, 434
workers' compensation (see *insurance, workers' compensation*)

Y

YMCA, 170, 238, 363, 449
YouTube, 167, 169, 176, 274

About the Author...

Gary M. Grobman (B.S. Drexel University, M.P.A. Harvard University, Kennedy School of Government, Ph.D., Penn State University) is special projects director for White Hat Communications, a Harrisburg-based publishing and nonprofit consulting organization formed in 1993. The title of Dr. Grobman's doctoral dissertation is *An Analysis of Codes of Ethics of Nonprofit, Tax-Exempt Membership Associations: Does Principal Constituency Make a Difference?* He has taught nonprofit management classes as an adjunct faculty member at Bay Path College, Indiana University of Pennsylvania, Marylhurst University, and Gratz College.

He served as the executive director of the Pennsylvania Jewish Coalition from 1983-1996. Prior to that, he was a senior legislative assistant in Washington for two members of Congress, a news reporter, and a political humor columnist for *Roll Call*. He also served as a lobbyist for public transit agencies. In 1987, he founded the Non-Profit Advocacy Network (NPAN), which consisted of more than 50 statewide associations that represented Pennsylvania charities.

He has served on the board of directors as an officer of the Greater Harrisburg Concert Band, the Harrisburg Area Road Runners Club, and the Citizens Service Project—the statewide 501(c)(3) that was established to promote citizen service in Pennsylvania. He is the author of *The Holocaust—A Guide for Pennsylvania Teachers, The Nonprofit Handbook, Improving Quality and Performance in Your Non-Profit Organization, The Nonprofit Management Casebook, Ethics in Nonprofit Organizations, Just Don't Do It! A Fractured and Irreverent Look at the Ph.D. Culture,* and other books published by White Hat Communications and Wilder Publications (now Fieldstone).

For information about speaking engagements or consulting projects, contact Dr. Grobman at: White Hat Communications, P.O. Box 5390, Harrisburg, PA 17110-0390. Telephone: (717) 238-3787; Fax: (717) 238-2090; E-mail: gary.grobman@paonline.com

Nonprofit Management Titles by Gary M. Grobman

An Introduction to the Nonprofit Sector
A Practical Approach for the 21st Century (Fourth Edition)
by Gary M. Grobman
ISBN: 978-1-929109-44-9
2015, 468 pages including index, 8½ x 11, $44.95 + shipping

AN INTRODUCTION TO THE NONPROFIT SECTOR: A PRACTICAL APPROACH FOR THE 21ST CENTURY is an introductory text on the nonprofit sector and nonprofit organizations. It provides an overview of the history, theory, and scope of the nonprofit sector. It discusses issues facing nonprofits, such as legal and regulatory issues, ethics, quality, fiscal, and liability issues. It also provides practical guidelines for writing mission and vision statements, strategic planning, hiring, firing, lobbying, communicating, using the Internet, and other functions of nonprofit organizations. Each chapter includes a synopsis at the beginning, as well as discussion questions, activities, and bibliographic references at the end. An index is included.

This book is an excellent resource for introducing students to the nonprofit sector and for providing nonprofit managers with the basic information they need to start or run a nonprofit organization.... While well grounded in literature and current information sources, it is clearly written and easy to use as either a classroom text or a ready desk reference.

**Dennis Young, Ph.D., Director of Nonprofit Studies, Georgia State University
Former President, Association of Research on Nonprofit Organizations and Voluntary Action (ARNOVA)**

Table of Contents
Chapter 1-Defining and Describing the Nonprofit Sector
Chapter 2-History of the Nonprofit Sector
Chapter 3-Theory of the Nonprofit Sector
Chapter 4-Legal and Regulatory Issues
Chapter 5-Bylaws and Governance
Chapter 6-Mission and Vision Statements
Chapter 7-Ethics
Chapter 8-Fundraising
Chapter 9-Marketing
Chapter 10-Grant Management
Chapter 11-Financial Management
Chapter 12-Personnel
Chapter 13-Communications and Public Relations
Chapter 14-Lobbying
Chapter 15-The Internet for Nonprofits
Chapter 16-Strategic Planning and Change Management
Chapter 17-Quality Issues
Chapter 18-Liability, Risk Management, and Insurance
Chapter 19-Forming and Running a Coalition
Chapter 20-The Future of the Nonprofit Sector
Chapter 21-The Spirit of the Nonprofit Sector
Appendices
Index
About the Author

The Nonprofit Handbook, 6th Edition
by Gary M. Grobman
ISBN: 978-1-929109-31-9
2011, 421 pages including index, 8½ x 11, $34.95 + shipping

THE NONPROFIT HANDBOOK is the most up-to-date and useful publication for those starting a nonprofit or already operating one. Each easy-to-read chapter includes a synopsis, useful tips, and resources for obtaining more information. The *Handbook* includes information on how to incorporate, obtain tax exemptions, and comply with charitable solicitation laws in all 50 states and the District of Columbia. An index, bibliography, sample bylaws, and state government Web sites of interest are included.

The Nonprofit Handbook is must reading. While it will have value as a reference tool to be consulted when needed, I highly recommend that you read the book cover-to-cover to familiarize yourself with the panoply of issues that face the modern nonprofit in every state of our United States.
**Joe Geiger, former Executive Director
PA Association of Nonprofit Organizations (PANO)**

The Nonprofit Management Casebook: Scenes From the Frontlines
Short stories that teach

by Gary M. Grobman
ISBN: 978-1-929109-23-4, 2010, 172 pages, 5½ x 8½, $16.95 + shipping
Available in e-book format at Smashwords.com

The Nonprofit Management Casebook: Scenes From the Frontlines is unlike any other management casebook available. The 16 "short stories that teach" are designed for maximum educational value, illustrating key management concepts, many unique to the sector. Highlighted are issues relating to fundraising, ethics, governance, personnel management, board-staff relations, and financial management. Each case is set in a different type of organization, among them a long term care facility, a family service, a hospital, a think tank, an institution of higher learning, and an advocacy organization, providing readers with a sense of the diversity of the sector. Each case is followed by a series of discussion questions guaranteed to engage students in spirited discussion.

I really look forward to using these cases in my classes! It's a wonderfully broad collection. Its covers a wide gamut of settings in which nonprofit organizations operate, as well as a wide range of situations, many of which are not dealt with in the extant case literature.
Peter Dobkin Hall, Ph.D., Hauser Center, Harvard University

About the Author: Gary M. Grobman received his Ph.D. in public administration from The Pennsylvania State University in 2002. He received his Master of Public Administration from the Harvard Kennedy School and his B.S. from Drexel University. He has taught graduate courses in nonprofit management at Bay Path College, Indiana University of Pennsylvania, Marylhurst University, and Gratz College. His practice experience includes 13 years as executive director of a statewide nonprofit in Pennsylvania.

White Hat Communications, P.O. Box 5390, Harrisburg, PA 17110-0390 Phone: 717-238-3787 Fax: 717-238-2090

Ethics in Nonprofit Organizations: Theory and Practice

by Gary M. Grobman

ISBN: 978-1-929109-38-8 2014, 154 pages, 8½ x 11, $24.95 + shipping

Ethics in Nonprofit Organizations: Theory and Practice includes chapters on ethical theory and its practical application to common ethical issues in nonprofit organizations. Also included are 10 highly readable case studies with discussion questions, as well as 120 fictional ethical scenarios that illustrate common (and some not so common) ethical challenges and ethical dilemmas that are faced by nonprofit organizations today.

E-Book! THE NEW SOCIAL WORKER® Magazine's Back-to-School Guide for Social Work Students

Linda May Grobman & Karen Zgoda, Editors

E-book, $4.99 at Amazon.com, Smashwords.com, and other e-book stores.

In this Guide is a collection of articles that have appeared in *The New Social Worker®: The Social Work Careers Magazine*. For this volume in the "Best of The New Social Worker" series, we have chosen those articles that we think you will find most relevant as you start the new school term as a social work student. In addition, the editors asked a panel of *The New Social Worker's* writers and other social work experts for their tips for new and returning social work students.

"As a former admissions director...I'm delighted to discover this recently-released publication by Linda Grobman and Karen Zgoda. Contained in this book are the kinds of resources I'd tried to assemble for new social workers becoming acclimated to the scholarship and service of the profession. Needless to say, I'll be sharing this important publication with colleagues and students enrolled in my social work courses."

Jeff T. Steen, LCSW, PhD student, adjunct instructor, New York University

Check out our new Nonprofit Ethics and Nonprofit Management pages.

We have recently added a new resource to our Web site—the Nonprofit Ethics Education Pages and the Nonprofit Management pages. These pages, sponsored by First Nonprofit Foundation, feature the full text of Gary Grobman's new book, *Ethics in Nonprofit Organizations: Theory and Practice,* as well as full text of several of his other nonprofit management books.

Designed to be interactive, these pages can be assigned to students, who will be able to comment and participate in ongoing discussions with others about the materials.

Nonprofit Ethics Education Pages: http://www.socialworker.com/nonprofit/ethics
Nonprofit Management Pages: http://www.socialworker.com/nonprofit/management

White Hat Communications, P.O. Box 5390, Harrisburg, PA 17110-0390 Phone: 717-238-3787 Fax: 717-238-2090

MC, Visa, AMEX, Discover accepted:
Phone: 717-238-3787 • Fax: 717-238-2090
Order Online: shop.whitehatcommunications.com

Visit our Web site:
http://www.socialworker.com

PLEASE SHIP MY ORDER TO:
NAME _____
ADDRESS _____
ADDRESS _____
CITY/STATE/ZIP _____
TELEPHONE NUMBER _____

❏ Enclosed is a check for $_____ made payable to "White Hat Communications."

❏ Please bill to my: ❏ Mastercard   ❏ Visa   ❏ American Express   ❏ Discover

Card # _____
Expiration Date _____   VISA/MC/Discover 3-digit # on back of card _____   AMEX 4-digit # on front of card _____
Name as it appears on card _____
Signature _____
Billing address for credit card (if different from above) _____
Billing City/State/Zip _____

QUANTITY	TITLE	PRICE	AMOUNT DUE
_____	BEGINNINGS, MIDDLES, & ENDS	$19.95	_____
_____	DAYS IN THE LIVES OF GERONTOLOGICAL SOCIAL WORKERS	$19.95	_____
_____	DAYS IN THE LIVES OF SOCIAL WORKERS, 4th Edition	$21.95	_____
_____	MORE DAYS IN THE LIVES OF SOCIAL WORKERS	$16.95	_____
_____	RIDING THE MUTUAL AID BUS & OTHER ADVENTURES IN GROUP WORK	$22.95	_____
_____	FIELD PLACEMENT SURVIVAL GUIDE, 2nd Edition	$22.95	_____
_____	IS IT ETHICAL? 101 SCENARIOS IN EVERYDAY SOCIAL WORK PRACTICE	$14.95	_____
_____	INTRODUCTION TO THE NONPROFIT SECTOR, 4th Edition	$44.95	_____
_____	THE NONPROFIT MANAGEMENT CASEBOOK	$16.95	_____
_____	THE NONPROFIT HANDBOOK, 6th Edition	$34.95	_____
_____	ETHICS IN NONPROFIT ORGANIZATIONS	$24.95	_____
_____	OTHER_____	$_____	_____

Shipping charges: $8.50 first book/$1.50 each additional book in U.S. $8.50 first set of 10 buttons/$1.50 each additional set. $14 first book to Canada, $1.50 each add'l book to Canada. *Please contact us for rates on rush orders or other methods of shipping, as well as rates to addresses outside the U.S. and Canada.*

PA Sales tax: 6% tax on books and back issues for orders from Pennsylvania, unless accompanied by Pennsylvania Department of Revenue sales tax exemption certificate.

SHIPPING $ _____
SUBTOTAL $ _____
PA SALES TAX (if applicable) $ _____
TOTAL DUE $ _____

❏ Please send me more information about: _____

Send order form and payment to:
WHITE HAT COMMUNICATIONS
P.O. Box 5390
Harrisburg, PA 17110-0390

Examination policy: Examination copies of select titles are available for textbook adoption consideration. Some titles are available as e-exam copies. Request examination copies of textbooks on the form in this catalog or on school letterhead, indicating name of course, when it will be taught, and how many students are expected to enroll. We ask that you send us your feedback and decision within 60 days. Sorry, we do not provide complimentary examination copies to addresses outside the U.S.

Federal EIN: 25-1719745

Other nonprofit management titles published by White Hat Communications

The Nonprofit Handbook
The Pennsylvania Nonprofit Handbook
The Nonprofit Management Casebook
Ethics in Nonprofit Organizations
Improving Quality and Performance in Your Non-Profit Organization

Other titles published by White Hat Communications

More Days in the Lives of Social Workers
Days in the Lives of Social Workers, 4th Ed.
Days in the Lives of Gerontological Social Workers
The Social Work Graduate School Applicant's Handbook
The Field Placement Survival Guide
Is it Ethical?
Beginnings, Middles, and Ends
Riding the Mutual Aid Bus and Other Adventures in Group Work

Visit Our Web Sites/Social Networking Sites:

http://www.whitehatcommunications.com
http://www.socialworker.com
http://www.socialworkjobbank.com

http://www.facebook.com/newsocialworker
http://www.twitter.com/newsocialworker

Online Store
http://shop.whitehatcommunications.com